Constitutional innovation: the creation of a Supreme Court for the United Kingdom; domestic, comparative and international reflections

A special issue of

Legal Studies

The Journal of the Society of Legal Scholars (2004)

edited by
Derek Morgan
Cardiff Law School

LexisNexis™ UK

Members of the LexisNexis Group worldwide

United Kingdom	LexisNexis UK, a Division of Reed Elsevier (UK) Ltd, Halsbury House, 35 Chancery Lane, LONDON, WC2A 1EL, and 4 Hill Street, EDINBURGH EH2 3JZ
Argentina	LexisNexis Argentina, BUENOS AIRES
Australia	LexisNexis Butterworths, CHATSWOOD, New South Wales
Austria	LexisNexis Verlag ARD Orac GmbH & Co KG, VIENNA
Canada	LexisNexis Butterworths, MARKHAM, Ontario
Chile	LexisNexis Chile Ltda, SANTIAGO DE CHILE
Czech Republic	Nakladatelství Orac sro, PRAGUE
France	Editions du Juris-Classeur SA, PARIS
Germany	LexisNexis Deutschland GmbH, FRANKFURT, MUNSTER
Hong Kong	LexisNexis Butterworths, HONG KONG
Hungary	HVG-Orac, BUDAPEST
India	LexisNexis Butterworths, NEW DELHI
Ireland	LexisNexis, DUBLIN
Italy	Giuffrè Editore, MILAN
Malaysia	Malayan Law Journal Sdn Bhd, KUALA LUMPUR
New Zealand	LexisNexis Butterworths, WELLINGTON
Poland	Wydawnictwo Prawnicze LexisNexis, WARSAW
Singapore	LexisNexis Butterworths, SINGAPORE
South Africa	LexisNexis Butterworths, DURBAN
Switzerland	Stämpfli Verlag AG, BERNE
USA	LexisNexis, DAYTON, Ohio

Typeset by Doyle & Co, Colchester
Printed in Great Britain by The Bath Press, Bath

Visit LexisNexis UK at www.lexisnexis.co.uk

Contents

Between the fairy tale and the abyss: the creation of a Supreme Court for the United Kingdom?

Derek Morgan
Cardiff Law School

'... at every moment of our lives, we all have one foot in a fairy tale and the other in the abyss ...'[1]

We live in what Brian Simpson reminds us has been called the age of rights.[2] These 'rights' are now often expressed, formally, in some definitive constitutional document. These rights and those documents pose special problems and afford particular opportunities for courts with final appellate authority. Taken together, the essays that are gathered in this special issue of *Legal Studies* constitute an examination of the authority, accountability and independence of the judges of a final appellate court, the Supreme Court proposed for the United Kingdom in Consultation Papers issued by the United Kingdom Government in June 2003. The importance of these issues may be thought to be self-evident in mature democracies, even where those democracies are themselves in flux, even if there is no simple or fixed core, let alone penumbra, to the concepts of authority, accountability and independence themselves. Alternatively, a reason for engagement with the issues can be readily ascertained, as Tracey Stevens and George Williams remind us, from the statement of Lord Porter in *Commonwealth v Bank of NSW*[3] on appeal from the High Court of Australia: 'The problem to be solved [by the final court] will often be not so much legal as political, social or economic. Yet it must be solved by a court of law.'

The intellectual origins of the United Kingdom Supreme Court, were it to come into being, are traced and examined here, particularly in the essays of Robert Stevens, Kate Malleson, Diana Woodhouse, Thomas Legg and Andrew Le Sueur. And, as Richard Cornes shows, many of the concerns about the 'politicisation' of judicial decision making in a transition to a Supreme Court were mirrored in the debate about the establishment of a New Zealand Supreme Court to replace appeals to the Privy Council from that jurisdiction. That Court began its work on 1 January 2004.

The constitutional changes foreshadowed in the Consultation Papers are likely to be a continuing, developing colloquy. If enacted, and at least half of the current judicial members of the House of Lords have indicated their

---

1. Paulo Coelho *Eleven Minutes* (Sydney: HarperCollins, 2003) p 1.
2. A W B Simpson *Human Rights and the End of Empire: Britain and the Genesis of the European Convention* (Oxford: Oxford University Press, 2001) p 9, citing Louis Henkin *The Age of Rights* (New York: Columbia University Press, 1990).
3. *Commonwealth v Bank of NSW* (1949) 79 CLR 497 at 639.

preference for something closer to the maintenance of the status quo, they might well produce a period of unsettlement or disturbance; if the critics, whose voices are well represented here, prevail, nothing. Nevertheless, these essays collectively ask not just what modern judges do and how they do it (and as John Bell proposes, whether they should continue to do *exclusively* the same sorts of things), various of the essays, most notably those by Thomas Legg and Judith Resnik, ask 'who should judges *be*?' And, implicitly, and in places explicitly, they ask what legislators and executives do in those democracies when subjected to an enhanced judicial scrutiny offered by fundamental principles, such as those enunciated in the European Convention on Human Rights. Several contributors remind us, whatever the formalist position, that the reality – as Robert Stevens describes it – is that the European Community Act 1972 and the Human Rights Act 1998 'have imposed a form of fundamental law well known to American and German lawyers'. The place of the United Kingdom in Europe suggests the value of comparison not just within the families of the common law but with continental European cousins too, as here offered by John Bell and Carlo Guarnieri, in their examinations of several Continental European Supreme Courts, and some of their appointments and career development processes.

Reflection on proposed reforms of the House of Lords in its judicial capacity engages with debates about the changing character of the United Kingdom constitution, the growth of a new sense of 'constitutionalism' and, as Brenda Hale (in an essay written before announcement of her judicial elevation to the House of Lords) puts it, the accessibility and accountability of a final court. Several of the essays argue that the proposed reforms of the judicial branch of government are, in fact, part of an evolutionary process towards a constitutionally limited form of government. Diana Woodhouse concludes her paper by alerting to a further diminution of parliamentary sovereignty. Hugh Corder, Tracey Stevens and George Williams, Andrew Le Sueur, Judith Resnik and Jeremy Webber are amongst those to take up this analysis in their contributions. But as Webber and Resnik separately identify, the notion of independence is 'confused and ambiguous' (Webber), an 'artifact of culture as much as of text' subject to new and emergent challenges in an era of judicial managerialism (Resnik).

The Consultation Papers from the Department for Constitutional Affairs have something of the character of Richard III reforms about them: 'deform'd, unfinish'd, sent before [their] time into this breathing world scarce half made up.' Indeed, it is remarkable how many of the contributing authors here sound notes of caution about the underlying reasons for the presently proposed reforms and the possible implications of implementing them, or, at the very least, of implementing them for the reasons stated. But they do not share a common judgment on the approach of the consultation process, some hailing it as 'principled', others as 'pragmatic … constitutional reform by way of incremental change', as John Bell characterises it. Many do, however, share an exasperation with the limited and partial nature of some of the present proposals (Allan Hutchinson castigates them as 'tepid', Brenda Hale ponders whether the present modest proposals justify the consequent upheaval) and a concern that the Papers have not addressed, let alone explored, many of the issues that the establishment of a Supreme Court would entail. Others see in them the glimmerings of a more principled approach to reform than, it is said, has hitherto been the case with the British constitution. Several pick up on those incomplete themes or problems in the current set of proposals, and examine the means and mechanisms that might be necessary or available to reform the nature or base from which judicial appointments are made and the measures necessary for ensuring public confidence and ensuring accountability in the resulting sets of arrangements. But the comparative essays also suggest that there may be dangers ahead as a significant part of these, indeed perhaps any, reform.

Yet most of the papers share an essential optimism about the processes and values of judging in modern liberal, democratic, pluralistic society. Allan Hutchinson introduces a characteristically sceptical note about the nature of modern adjudication, which he offers as an *inherently* political activity, a necessary *and desirable* part of the political process. He advocates recognition, long denied in liberal legal formalism, that what judges do *is* political, not in the partisan sense, which seems universally to be feared, but in a deeply ideological, indeed philosophical, sense. Thus, easily to approbate judges for taking or making political decisions, for overriding the apparent will of elected representatives, is entirely to miss the point; what courts do, Allan Hutchinson argues, is an inescapably political engagement because, without that, a Western liberal democracy would be poorly served by its Supreme Court. Evidently, this brings dangers for that Court; Diana Woodhouse suggests that ministerial displeasure at judicial decisions is likely to increase with the creation of a Supreme Court. This view is confirmed by Tracey Stevens and George Williams in their examination of the High Court of Australia, illustrating not only the importance of independence in the institutional design of a Supreme Court, but also the need to recognise the potential for politicisation of that Court and its judges. Like the Australian High Court more recently, an independent Supreme Court with a clear human rights mandate could be vulnerable to attack by Ministers, Parliamentarians and the media. They offer practical observations on managing this tension. But, how the judiciary can and should fulfil its legitimate responsibilities in a way which as Allan Hutchinson puts it, 'vigorously enforces contested constitutional dictates as a matter of law against the legislative and/or executive branches of government, but which accepts that it is a body of unelected and unrepresentative bureaucrats which has no direct mandate to make political decisions' *is* the key constitutional question for the judiciary.

But it would be a mistake to imagine that the Consultation Papers constitute nothing more than reforms of antiquated parts of the judicial system. As Jeremy Webber and Kate Malleson show, they sit as part of the continuing project of a new sense of constitutionalism – a 'new vision' of the separation of powers, Malleson calls it – which have not come unheralded onto the constitutional stage. Chris Himsworth and Alan Paterson illustrate how this new vision is played out in front of a remarkably different audience in Scotland compared with England and Wales, or even, arguably, Northern Ireland. In Scotland, there are many who are looking for a different play, let alone a new production of an established classic, and the questions that the Consultation Papers do not ask of that jurisdiction represent some of the most fundamental challenges for continued constitutional stability between the south and the 'Northern Kingdom'. And even those that are broached leave many doubts; how will the Court be composed, to what extent will it operate essentially as a Constitutional

Court (a question that also concerns John Bell), and to what extent should the revised Scottish judicial appointments system offer a model for a Court with the larger jurisdiction?

The late Christopher Hill, in his remarkable, elegant book *The Intellectual Origins of the English Revolution*,[4] wrote that those living through a revolution were often unable to understand the experience of it; that it falls, only later, to the intellectual historians of the period, to examine the place and significance of such people, practices, papers and politics. It can hardly be thought that the Consultation Papers that this special issue records and reflects upon stand alone or apart from the more general concerns that affect or effect the modern constitutional settlement. The present proposals for establishing a Supreme Court in the United Kingdom, for making judges more accountable and for changing the nature of judicial appointments processes at least in part to mould a more socially representative judiciary, continue the task of melding human rights aspirations and the common law in the age of statutes, as Guido Calabresi once called our present legal age.[5] That statutes rather than judge-made law is now the paradigm form of law making *entails* a tension between judges, charged with the application of fundamental principles to those laws, and elected members of a Parliament.

Over 30 years ago, the predecessor version of this journal published an address by Lord Reid called 'The Judge as Lawmaker'. In that celebrated essay he wrote:

'There was a time when it was thought almost indecent to suggest that judges make law – they only declare it. Those with a taste for fairy tales seem to have thought that in some Aladdin's cave there is hidden the Common Law in all its splendour and that on a judge's appointment there descends on him knowledge of the magic words Open Sesame. Bad decisions are given when the judge has muddled the pass word and the wrong door opens. But we do not believe in fairy tales any more. So we must accept the fact that for better or worse judges do make law, and tackle the question how do they approach their task and how they should approach it.'[6]

The essays in this volume variously explore the maintenance of the constitutional love affair with the rule of law, the independence of the judiciary and its political neutrality, on the one hand, and the necessary, flirtatious involvement with political engagement on the other. There is, thus, much in these essays of what the modern judicial task properly comprises. Collectively, they review the proposed new constitutional arrangements for walking between the fairy tale and some real or imagined democratic abyss.

This special issue of *Legal Studies* was conceived in the weekend after the Government's announcement of a reform consultation process in June 2003. The papers were gradually commissioned thereafter, sometimes in something like Old Testament fashion: A begat B; B begat C; and so on. The authors have worked against a formidable editorial deadline (in one case of no more

---

4. (Oxford: Clarendon Press, 1965).
5. *A Common Law for the Age of Statutes* (Cambridge, Mass: Harvard University Press, 1982).
6. (1972–73) 12 Journal of the Society of Public Teachers of Law 22.

than two weeks), but with little editorial mandate, to produce papers that, I hoped, would contribute to the debate as much as be a reflection upon it. There are evident omissions: I failed to commission a paper from India, which, as Justice Michael Kirby of the High Court of Australia reminded us in his recently delivered Hamlyn lectures, has one of the most fascinating of Supreme Courts, and I was unable to contact authors whom I should have liked to reflect on recent constitutional changes in the Caribbean. Nonetheless, I am especially grateful to each author who responded to the task, and for the enthusiastic way in which they approached their essays, often putting aside current work to draft their contribution. To the copy editors and typesetters, Juliet and Jonathan Doyle, I owe a special note of appreciation for dealing with this issue of *Legal Studies* with their customary professionalism tempered, on this occasion, with lightning speed. I am delighted to be able to record an appreciation of the work that they do for this journal, and this is an appropriate occasion on which to do it.

Reform in haste and repent at leisure: Iolanthe, the Lord High Executioner and *Brave New World*

Robert Stevens*
Senior Research Fellow, Constitution Unit, University College, London; of Counsel,
Covington & Burling, Washington and London; Barrister, Bencher of Gray's Inn

> 'Turning and turning in the widening gyre
> The falcon cannot hear the falconer;
> Things fall apart; the centre cannot hold;
> More anarchy is loosed upon the world.'

Labour came to power in 1997 with a commitment to constitutional reform
and joined-up government. New Labour has indeed produced significant
constitutional change: devolution to Scotland and Wales, the Human Rights
Act 1998, partial reform of the House of Lords, elected Mayors, a Freedom of
Information Act, an Electoral Commission and more. Joined up it was not.
Nothing better illustrated this than the (arguably) botched Cabinet reshuffle
on 12 June 2003. On that day, Downing Street announced the resignation (or
sacking) of Lord Irvine, the Lord Chancellor since 1997, and the abolition of
his post, and, in its place, the establishment of a Department of Constitutional
Affairs, and, finally, the creation of a Supreme Court.[1]

No doubt this story of the Cabinet intrigue or at least rather dramatic
constitutional change will ultimately be the subject of a range of investigative
journalism – and perhaps even scholarship. The to-ings and fro-ings about the
responsibilities of the new Secretary of State for Constitutional Affairs – Lord
Falconer – had about them the element of Gilbert and Sullivan. For the present
Falconer, who thought the office was dead, had to remain Lord Chancellor,

---

* The themes in this paper were refined while Welling Professor at George Washington
University in this Autumn of 2003, during seminars at the Law School. They also formed
the basis of evidence to the Constitutional Affairs Committee of the House of Commons
in November 2003 and a public lecture to be given at Cardozo Law School in New York
in February 2004. The translation of the hieroglyphics of this technologically challenged
septuagenarian is the work of Manuela Henrique and Sarah Balfour. To them I am most
grateful. For Yeats' immortal lines, I am grateful to my literary adviser, Professor J A G
Griffith.
1. As a former Editor of *The Times* put it: 'Nothing has been worse handled by the Prime
Minister than his judicial reforms. He did not consult the law lords; he did not consult the
Lord Chief Justice; he could not get the past Lord Chancellor's agreement; he did not perform
his constitutional duty to tell the Queen. He mixed up the most important judicial reforms
in a century with a panic reshuffle of his Cabinet. He thought he had abolished the Office
of Lord Chancellor, which he did not have the power to do.' Lord Rees-Mogg 'The supreme
court: isn't there some law against it?' *The Times*, 4 August 2003.

presiding in the Lords and sitting in the Cabinet, although in his capacity of Secretary of State for Constitutional Affairs. He announced, however, he would not sit as a judge in the House of Lords even before legislation is introduced. Indeed, as the Law Lords will move to become the new Supreme Court, they will cease to sit as legislators as well. Many of these changes are now spelled out in a series of consultation papers, the two most relevant for this paper being *Constitutional Reform: a Supreme Court for the United Kingdom*[2] and *Constitutional Reform: A New Way of Appointing Judges*.[3] A third paper was *Constitutional Reform: the future of Queen's Counsel*; a fourth, on the Lord Chancellorship, appeared in October.[4] The papers are surprisingly polished documents, suggesting that their preparation may have been under way before the departure of Lord Irvine, unlikely as that may seem.

A. THE EMERGENCE OF THE CONSTITUTIONAL SETTLEMENT

Separation of powers is an odd concept for a country that has, at least since the time of Sir Robert Walpole, had a system of responsible government. With the Executive sitting in the legislature, English discussions of the separation of powers and judicial independence have a slightly unreal quality. It was always possible, in theory, that England might have had a more realistic separation of powers and therefore a coherent concept of judicial independence. It is arguable that the Act of Settlement 1701 had such a separation in mind, but the machinations of the Court and Whig oligarchy rapidly undid that. In the eighteenth century, the *Letters of Cato*[5] in England pointed out the inherently authoritarian and centralised nature of responsible government, while Thomas Jefferson in Virginia insisted on the inevitably corrupt nature of responsible government;[6] and that was two centuries before Lord Hailsham coined the phrase 'elected dictatorship'. While the new US developed checks and balances, the separation of powers under the Constitution of 1789 meant that there was a meaningful role for the federal courts.

In England, after 1701, the courts remained part of the central political system. The judges in the common law courts were political appointees; the Chief Justices of these courts were expected to support the government and were often given peerages for that very purpose. They also sometimes sat in the Cabinet. The chief judge in the equity courts was the Lord Chancellor, who presided in the House of Lords in its legislative sittings and again sat in the Cabinet. It was not an arrangement likely to develop a system which saw the courts as an independent arm of government. Indeed, with a hereditary upper

---

2.   CP 11/03 (July 2003) ('*Supreme Court*').
3.   CP 10/03 (July 2003) ('*Appointing Judges*').
4.   *Constitutional Reform: reforming the office of the Lord Chancellor* CP 13/03 (2003). The document is not significant for this paper. It is, however, a reminder that the Lord Chancellor's Office is, like the Smithsonian in the US, 'the attic of the nation'. So much of the debris is the strange result of an established church and academic institutions seeking to be embraced by monarchy.
5.   Bernard Bailyn *The Ideological Origins of the American Revolution* (Harvard, 1992) ch 2.
6.   Bernard Bailyn *To Begin the World Anew* (New York, 2003) p 50.

house, a lower house increasingly unrepresentative because of shifts of population, the undemocratic courts down to 1832, the year of the Great Reform Act, were best understood as part of the great Curia Regis, which, at least in reality, whatever the form, had survived from the Middle Ages.

It is true that, in the 20 years after 1760, the courts produced what later generations have seen as liberal decisions – *The North Briton* on freedom of the press, *Entinck v Carrington* on general warrants and *Somersett's Case*, apparently holding slavery illegal in England. They could equally be seen, however, as decisions by the Whig judges during the period when, to simplify, the Whigs were out of favour and power after the accession of George III. With that exception, from 1701 to 1832, the judges were an integral part of the ruling oligarchy, no matter how much Burke[7] and Blackstone[8] might extol the virtues of judicial independence. In so far as there was a liberal tradition abroad, it was the product of the Enlightenment, which Macaulay at least, believed suffused the Whig oligarchy.

As the Reform Act 1832 brought an element of fairness and democracy to the House of Commons and the enfranchised middle classes, the question was what would happen to the courts. It was the beginning of the age of Liberal Reform. There was no suggestion that responsible government should give way to representative government in the American sense, but the English slowly developed their own mythology so they might claim the best of both worlds. The Trevelyan-Northcliffe reforms of the Civil Service produced a highly trained and well-educated Civil Service which, on a day-to-day basis, ran the country. It reported, however, to its political masters – the elected ministers (although until 1911 many ministers were hereditary peers) – who were allegedly responsible for all policy decisions and who fell or rose at the whim of the electorate, reflected in the House of Commons.

With the House of Commons reformed both as to franchise and equality of constituencies, and with the Civil Service based on merit, the issue of what to do with the judiciary remained. For much of the eighteenth century and the early part of the nineteenth, judges operated under the system of spoils. Few King's Bench judges were appointed without having served in the House of Commons and, until the reign of George III, they had to be reappointed on the accession of a new sovereign – and they did not always survive. With the changed political attitudes in the 1820s and 1830s the utilitarians had to be satisfied with reforming the law, procedure and the court structure. All aspects of procedures were extensively reformed; the Masters and their staff modernised; legal and equitable remedies were allowed in a range of courts. More judges were provided for the equity courts; the Judicial Committee of the Privy Council was reformed and for the first time appropriately staffed. Parliament partially reformed the assize system, attempted to codify the criminal law in 1861 and

---

7. 'The independence of the judges ought to supercede all other considerations. The judges are, or ought to be, of a reserved and retired character, and wholly unconnected with the political world': speech by Edmund Burke proposing a plan for reform of civil and other establishments, House of Commons, 11 February 1780. *Parliamentary History*, XXI, p 11ff.

8. Blackstone argued that there had to be judicial independence to protect the judges' law making powers: William Blackstone *Commentaries*, vol 1.

even began to tackle substantive law – as in Lord Campbell's Fatal Accidents Act 1846. Local courts were re-established by the County Courts Act 1846, while the courts of first instance were united and an overall Court of Appeal created by the Judicature Act 1873, by 1882 housed in Street's new Royal Courts of Justice in the Strand. Only the Appellate Jurisdiction Act 1876 marred the symmetry, by re-inserting the House of Lords as the final court of appeal. In short, between 1832 and 1873, there was a transformation of the court structure, procedure and, to some extent, substantive law.

What lay outside the reforms, however, were the judges themselves.[9] While the notion of an independent judiciary had been sanctified by the Act of Settlement 1701, which gave the judges tenure subject to a modified form of impeachment, it had never been clear what was the ambit of that judicial independence. While the US Supreme Court and the Judicial Committee of the Privy Council, with respect to colonial legislation, stuck down statutes, that was clearly not a vehicle open to the English judges, who were the prisoners of parliamentary supremacy emerging from the Glorious Revolution. To a significant extent what had happened in 1701 was that the judges moved from being lions under the throne to being lions under the mace. Chief Justice Mansfield might be applauded for reforming mercantile law, and judges during the repressive period after the Napoleonic wars were appreciated for their tough commitment to draconian criminal law, but they were basically seen as an integral part of the process of government. As we have seen, most of the 12 judges in the three common law courts (King's Bench, Common Pleas and Exchequer) were promoted for political reasons; the two Chief Justices and the Chief Baron were politicians. Yet buttressed by Hale and Blackstone, and mindful of the role they had played on behalf of the parliamentarians against the Stuarts during the Civil War, the judges incanted their belief in the independence of the judiciary. The incantation largely protected the judges from reform. It is true that their salaries were regularised; elsewhere the mystique of judicial independence was enough to frighten off would-be reformers, even if it was unclear what such a concept meant in a system of responsible government.

At some point, however, it was inevitable that a clash would come. The Hatherley Royal Commission on the Judicature, reporting in the late 1860s, floated the idea of a Minister of Justice responsible for legal matters. That at once signalled to the judges that a non-lawyer might be in charge of the legal system and, more importantly, might be in charge of the judges. Lords Selborne and Cairns, the reforming Lord Chancellors in the Gladstone and Disraeli governments, were adept at handling the judges, particularly their concerns with status. In the strange situation of claims of independence of the judiciary in a constitutional setting where two of the three branches of government were merged, the judges took offence at the possibility that their affairs might be handled by a minister who might not be a lawyer. The two Lord Chancellors hit on an ingenious solution: the Lord Chancellor would become de facto the

---

9.   On this see generally Robert Stevens *The Independence of the Judiciary: the View from the Lord Chancellor's Office* (Oxford: Oxford University Press, 1993); Robert Stevens *The English Judges: Their Role in the Changing Constitution* (Oxford: Hart Publishing, 2002).

minister for the judges. Since, by then, the Lord Chancellor was president of the Supreme Court invented by the 1873 Act (the High Court and Court of Appeal) there was a certain logic to the idea.

Thus in 1880, when Gladstone returned to office, Selborne, on the Woolsack, appointed Muir MacKenzie as Principal Secretary and Clerk of the Crown in Chancery. In 1882, Cairns, while still out of office, wrote to Selborne indorsing this development: 'I have come to the conclusion that the new Judicature System has thrown around the Chancellor such a network of departmental business … that … it will not be possible to prevent serious inconvenience to the public business on a change to the Great Seal … without a really efficient Permanent Secretary.' In 1883, Cairns and Selborne jointly approached the Treasury for a permanent establishment, as they put it, 'in fact, a permanent secretary of the Ministry of Justice'. The Treasury agreed that the Lord Chancellor needed a political secretary for political work and, in addition, for that work 'belonging to a permanent Ministry of Justice' which 'will best be performed by a permanent staff … in whose experience each successive Lord Chancellor may rely': hence the emergence of the Lord Chancellor's Office.[10]

B. THE COMPROMISE

The Lord Chancellor's Office remained a small elite group, outside the regular Civil Service, basically supporting the judges, including those in the county courts, although having responsibility for QCs and law reform until 1970. The Home Office looked after criminal law and criminal law reform, and was responsible for appointing recorders, stipendiary magistrates, as well as supervising the police and prisons. Civil courts outside London were largely run locally and such civil legal aid as there was in the hands of the Law Society, except the 'dock brief', the elementary criminal legal aid policed by the Bar. It was not an unreasonable compromise.

The judges were delighted not to be subject to a political minister. Yet fear of some such solution was to grip the judiciary, with some regularity, whenever the words 'Ministry of Justice' were uttered. Haldane's 1918 *Report of the Committee on the Machinery of Government* suggested there should be a Ministry of Justice. The judges suffered another bout of paranoia. This condition was aggravated by the views of Lord Hewart, the undistinguished Lord Chief Justice during the 1920s and 1930s. He was convinced that Sir Claud Schuster, the Permanent Secretary to the Lord Chancellor during these decades, was secretly planning, probably with Lord Sankey, the Lord Chancellor 1929–35, to achieve such a coup. Clearly the independence of the judiciary was threatened.

In 2003 to some judges the same threat re-appeared. It is believed that the idea of a Minister of Justice was thwarted because David Blunkett, the Home Secretary, was not about to give up control of the criminal law. Perhaps, thought some judges, he would have been the first Minister of Justice. The idea of Blunkett, who has been scathing in his criticism of judicial decisions, having

---

10. Stevens (1993), n 9 above, pp 8–9.

any role in dealing with the judges was anathema to the judiciary.[11] Moreover on the radio and in the press Blunkett continued his attacks on the judges in May 2003 both with respect to immigration decisions and with respect to sentencing policy. Lord Irvine appeared powerless to resist;[12] yet the judges saw his office as their Maginot Line.

Yet clearly some judges remain nervous. What if the Secretary of State for Constitutional Affairs, the substitute for the Lord Chancellor, were one day to be a layman. Many leading lawyers and judges are convinced the quality of MPs is on the decline. How could such a layman then protect the judiciary against the combined force of the other two branches of government? It was apparently such concerns that prompted Lord Woolf, the Lord Chief Justice, to postpone his retirement. Who, in this new world, was going to protect the independence of the judiciary?[13] How could a layman anoint judges, even if recommended by an Appointments Commission dominated by lawyers? The legal world was coming apart.

C. THE OFFICE OF LORD CHANCELLOR: THE POLITICAL CEMENT

Lord Woolf was clear that one of the threats facing judicial independence was the fact that 'the Lord Chancellor was a member of the Cabinet and could influence his colleagues in a way which is not open to the Lord Chief Justice'. This is no doubt true, but the change was in historical terms a relatively recent one. A reading of the nineteenth century entries in Lord Campbell's *Lives of the Lord Chancellors* and *Lives of the Chief Justices* leaves little doubt that the Chief Justice of the King's Bench was a formidable political figure ranking beside the Lord Chancellor. (And John Campbell should have known: he had served as Attorney-General of England and Wales, Lord Chancellor of Ireland, Chief Justice of Queens Bench in England and Lord Chancellor of England and Wales.) The Judicature Act 1873 provided that the three common law courts would ultimately be merged; and this was accomplished in 1880. Yet, it was painfully obvious that the new Lord Chief Justice was but a pale shadow of the old Chief Justice of Queen's Bench. No longer was he a naked politician. Selborne and Cairns even had the utilitarian whim that judges should be appointed 'on the merits'.

Who then, after 1873, would protect the judges in a system of responsible government, with much talk about the independence of the judges and precious little understanding of what that entailed? As we saw, what Cairns

---

11. For the first assault by Secretary Blunkett, see 'The Human Rights Act meets Bruiser Blunkett' in Stevens (2002), n 9 above, pp 128–136. For the second assault, see Anthony Bradley 'Judicial Independence Under Assault' [2003] PL 397. And see Michael Zander 'Lord Woolf's criticisms of Mr. Blunkett's Criminal Justice Bill' [2003] NLJ, 8 August and 15 August.
12. This led to the debate in the House of Lords on 21 May 2003. The article which gave most offence had appeared in the *Evening Standard* on 12 May 2003: see David Blunkett 'I won't give in'.
13. 'Top Judge stays to fight politicians' *The Times*, 1 August 2003.

and Selborne ultimately hit on, as it became clear that the Lord Chief Justice no longer had the political clout to be the judges' shop steward, was the Lord Chancellor. The holders of that office had always been politicians and equity judges. As the nineteenth century progressed, they were increasingly seen as head of the judiciary, but with respect to the common law and its judges, they deferred to the Lord Chief Justice. With the establishment of the Lord Chancellor's Office in 1880 all that changed. Thenceforth, it was the Lord Chancellor and his office who were responsible for the appointment of judges and the issue of judicial independence.

It was not long before the incumbents of the office of Chief Justice came to resent the flowing of power to the Lord Chancellor. Sir John Duke, as Gladstone's Solicitor-General (1868–71) and Attorney-General (1871–73) was responsible for pushing the Judicature Act 1873 through the Commons. On the collapse of the Gladstone administration in 1873 he became Chief Justice of Common Pleas, with the title of Lord Coleridge, and then in 1880 when the Chief Justice of Queen's Bench and the Chief Baron of the Exchequer retired, Lord Chief Justice of England.[14] Coleridge, however, felt he had been sold a mess of pottage. A radical who had vigorously supported the end of the House of Lords as the final appeal court, was in favour of merging the two legal professions and codifying English law, who had favoured a Ministry of Justice, as Chief Justice had called for a new Royal Commission on the Courts (denied by Halsbury), he nevertheless found the new powers of the Lord Chancellor impossible. As he retired from the Chief's position in 1894, he wrote: '... if I could have seen, as perhaps I ought, how the Judicature Acts would have worked, I would have resigned sooner than be a party to it ... the enthroning of the Chancellor upon the neck of us ... I find the great traditional influences of the Chief Justice and the deference to him lessened materially, in every way, year by year ...'[15] Political power had moved to the Lord Chancellor, executive power to the officials of the Lord Chancellor's office.

Moreover, while it is always difficult to predict the motives of Lord Hewart, it is clear in reading *The New Despotism* that at least some of his frustrations as Lord Chief Justice, sprang from the realisation that the Lord Chancellor, rather than the Lord Chief Justice, by then controlled the administration and the patronage of the court system. While his attacks on Sir Claud Schuster, Permanent Secretary to the Lord Chancellor, had various motives, one was undoubtedly the feeling that Schuster was making decisions that were rightfully Hewart's.[16] At the same time, it was Hewart who realised that the office of Lord Chancellor was vital to make this system work:

14. The tradition was that the Attorney-General had the right of reverter to the Chief Justiceship. It worked for Hewart in 1922 and the tradition did not finally die until it was denied to Sir Reginald Morningham-Butler, probably because of his personal reputation, in 1958, although he was later consoled with becoming a Lord of Appeal and Lord Chancellor.
15. E H Coleridge *Life and Correspondence of John Duke, Lord Coleridge, Lord Chief Justice of England* 2 vols (London, 1904).
16. 95 HL Official Report (5th series) col 234.

'When I became Attorney General at the beginning of 1919, when the late Lord Birkenhead first became Lord Chancellor, a little scheme was put before him whereby the Lord Chancellor was to cease to exist, all judicial patronage was to be taken from the Home Secretary, and all powers were to be invested in a new person to be called, after the Continental fashion, a Minister of Justice and that scheme had strong backing from some entity, the origin of which I do not know, the legal foundation for which I do not know, the personnel of which I do know, called the Lord Chancellor's Department. The Lord Chancellor was to go, the Home Secretary as the person appointing judicial officers was to go, and we would have a Minister of Justice. Why? It is perfectly obvious why. Because if that were done, it would no longer be necessary to have in this country a lawyer as political head of the judiciary. You might have a layman, a successful merchant, a successful tradesman. And what would follow from that? What would follow would be this – that Minister could be ignorant of the personnel of the Bar; he would not have leaders of the Bar habitually appearing before him in the final Court of Appeal and in the House. When a vacancy occurred he would have to turn to somebody and say: "Who shall I appoint?" And who would that somebody be? The permanent officials of the Lord Chancellor's Department.'

Perhaps in response to this Schuster, the Permanent Secretary, wrote what was perhaps the classic defence of the office of Lord Chancellor. As he prepared for retirement in 1943 he opined:

'The advantages which accrued to the Cabinet from the presence of a colleague who is not only of high judicial reputation but can represent to them the view of the judiciary; to the legislature from the presence in it of one who is both a Judge and a Minister; and to the judiciary from the fact that its President is in close touch with current political affairs, are enormous. In a Democracy, whose legislature may be advancing, or at least moving rapidly, and where the judiciary remains static, there is always present a serious risk of collision between the two elements. Where the Constitution is written and the static condition of the Judiciary is absolute, as in the United States, the danger of such a collision is very great. Even in England, with an unwritten constitution and unwritten common law, unless there is some link or buffer (whichever term may be preferred) between the two elements the situation would be perilous.'[17]

That memorandum became the basis of all later thinking. The independence of the judiciary was protected by the existence of the Lord Chancellor; and further protected by the Lord Chancellor's power to appoint the judges. It was a view that has found favour with the current leaders of the judiciary. In 1998 Lord Woolf, then Master of the Rolls, said:

'As a member of the Cabinet he (the Lord Chancellor) can act as an advocate on behalf of the courts and the justice system. He can explain to his colleagues in the cabinet the proper significance of a decision which they regard as being distasteful in consequence of an application for judicial review. He can, as a member of the government, ensure that the courts are

17.   Memorandum, LCO2/3630, 31 January 1943.

properly resourced. On the other hand, on behalf of the government, he can explain to the judiciary the realities of the political situation and the constraints on the resources which they must inevitably accept.

As long as the Lord Chancellor is punctilious in keeping his separate roles distinct, the separation of powers is not undermined and the justice system benefits immeasurably. The justice system is better served by having the head of the judiciary at the centre of government than it would be by having its interests represented by a Minister of Justice who would lack these other roles.'[18]

The Woolf view was not unique. Lord Bingham, currently the Senior Law Lord and presumably to be the new president of the Supreme Court said of the office in 2001:

'It enables him to act as a guarantor of judges' integrity and independence. Since the Lord Chancellor, unlike other ministers, has no political ambition, he is well placed to argue the judges' case. For that reason, his own independence has never been questioned and he is in a much better position than judges would be to protect – not the judges' interests – but the values of the legal system.'[19]

Lord Irvine's representative in the House of Commons repeated this mantra in 2001:

'The office is unusual in the way that it combines different roles and it is also unusually useful, because through it the judiciary has a representative in the Cabinet and the Cabinet has a representative in the judiciary. As such, we believe the Lord Chancellor is well placed mutually to represent the views of each branch of the constitution to the other.'[20]

To this, Lord Irvine added the thought, in his evidence to the Royal Commission on the House of Lords, that he had:

'no doubt that this dual role has historically proved invaluable in maintaining the independence of the judiciary in England and Wales and we have considerable anxiety that any other arrangement would result, in time, in the encroachment of executive government into the proper sphere of judicial independence essential in a democratic society.'

It was in this context that Lord Woolf, thought by some ministers to be an accommodating member of the judiciary, responded vigorously to the proposed constitutional changes in the summer of 2003. He warned that instead of retiring at 70, he will stay on 'to ensure the independence of this judiciary is protected

---

18. H Woolf 'Judicial Review – the tensions between the executive and the judiciary' (1998) 114 LQR 579.

19. Frances Gibb 'The Supreme Sacrifice' *The Times*, 17 July 2001. Lord Mackay, the last Conservative Lord Chancellor, recently defended the Office, noting, of attacks on the judiciary, 'The fact that the Lord Chancellor is in the Cabinet already has a restraining effect': Frances Gibb 'Closing the silk route is not a "done deal"' *The Times*, Law, 23 September 2003.

20. 475 HC Official Report (6th series) col 155, 4 December 2001.

and the judges' voice heard'.[21] He was clearly irritated: 'it must be a cause for concern that a decision to abolish such a historic office – with its pivotal role in the administration of justice as head of the judiciary – can be taken without any consultation with the judiciary. It does raise questions as to whether our constitution provides the protection it should for constitutional institutions?'[22] One can only assume that Lord Woolf realised that the result of the changes would be to push some of the responsibilities of the Lord Chancellor, as before 1880, on to the Lord Chief Justice, an office which would thus become much more political, although in the twenty-first century might not have the weapons or will to exercise such powers.[23]

D. THE OFFICE OF LORD CHANCELLOR: THE APPOINTMENT OF JUDGES

As Selborne and Cairns were reforming the system of courts between 1867 and 1880, one of the things they assumed was that, with the House of Lords as the final court of appeal gone – at least as they expected – the appointment of judges in the Supreme Court should be based on merit. It was entirely consistent with the thrust of utilitarian reform. The Judicature Acts, however, coincided with the political implications of Irish Home Rule and 'the Strange Death of Liberal England'. The split in the Liberal Party (1885–86) heralded a long period of predominantly Conservative government, first under Salisbury and then under Balfour. With Lord Halsbury being Lord Chancellor for most of the period between 1880 and 1905, it was as if the constitution had been turned back before 1832.

21. Frances Gibb 'Lord Chief Justice warns ministers he is not crying wolf' *The Times*, 2 August 2003. For the continuing concerns, see, for example, Lord Woolf's view that 'we mustn't let the English legal system end up like our railways' *Daily Telegraph*, 9 November 2003; 'The wrath of judges' *Evening Standard*, 7 November 2003; 'Judges warn of threat to judicial independence' *Financial Times*, 7 November 2003.
22. Department of Constitutional Affairs, Speech of Lord Woolf, Mansion House, 9 July 2003.
23. *The Judges' Council Response to the Consultation Papers on Constitutional Reforms* demands that the Lord Chief Justice replace the Lord Chancellor as Head of the Judiciary and be given appropriate powers: p 17. The paper also calls for more control over the courts and guaranteed resources. The Judges' paper would also put the disciplining of judges under the Lord Chief Justice: Part III. This would presumably transfer the power of ultimate accountability currently vested in Parliament by the Act of Settlement. The time is clearly ripe for a modern version spelling out what is meant by dismissal after addresses to both Houses of Parliament.
     Sadly the response of the judiciary bears some of the hallmarks of 1960s complacency. Remarks like 'our judiciary being admired round the world' (p 26) suggest a degree of hubris. The theme continues 'our judiciary also has a record of being entirely free of corruption – a record that not all other jurisdictions can match'. This is true of the High Court, although only fully established in the twentieth century; circuit judges have recently been removed for cheating customs and other offences.

The tone was set by Lord Salisbury:

'It is ... the unwritten law of our party system; and there is no clearer statute in that unwritten law than that the rule that party claims should always weight very heavily in the disposal of the highest legal appointments. In dealing with them you cannot ignore the party system as you do in the choice of a general or archbishop. It would be a breach of the tacit convention in which politicians and lawyers have worked the British constitution together for the last two hundred years. Perhaps it was not an ideal system – some day no doubt the Master of the Rolls will be appointed by a competitive examination in the Law Reports, but it is our system for the present: and we should give our party arrangements a wrench if we threw it aside.'

Salisbury certainly had a robust view of these matters. His view was that 'within certain limits of intelligence, honesty and knowledge of the law, one man would make as good a judge as another, and a Tory mentality was *ipso facto* more trustworthy than a Liberal one'.[24]

Halsbury loved it. While there were a few High Court appointments based on merit, Halsbury filled many of the appointments on the High Court Bench with Conservative back-bench MPs, some with limited success at the Bar. Salisbury already had opined on the Law Lords, arguing that they should be members of the House of Lords ('since practically they have often to make law as judges, they will do it all the better from having also to make it as legislators').[25] Certainly Halsbury was not concerned about inherent conflicts in the role of Lord Chancellor.[26] He packed panels in the House of Lords, especially when hearing cases about trade unions and he happily took a narrow or broad view toward precedent, depending on his particular goal. The House of Lords' Judicial Committee and the Judicial Committee of the Privy Council were seen as important political players.

With the establishment of a Liberal government in late 1905 and the landslide election of 1906, it was clear to the new administration, by then supported by the first Labour MPs, that the Tory attitude towards the

24. R F V Heuston *Lives of the Lord Chancellors, 1885–1940* (Oxford, 1964) p 52; A Roberts *Salisbury: Victorian Giant* (London, 1999) p 684.

25. R Stevens *Law and Politics: The House of Lords as a Judicial Body 1800–1976* (N Carolina, 1978) p 55.

26. [1915] 1 KB 893. When, in 1914, the Court of Appeal, in *Continental Tyre v Daimler*, refused to 'lift the veil' of Continental to show that it was controlled by a German parent, there was considerable discontent. *The Times* took up the issue and judges were active in the correspondence columns. The matters were debated extensively in Parliament. Lord Halsbury, no longer Lord Chancellor, introduced a Bill in the Lords to reverse the decision, or at least to allow the Attorney-General to petition to have such decision overruled. The Bill (Companies of Enemy Character Bill) was supported by Lord Mersey and Lord Wrenbury (who had dissented in the Court of Appeal). The Bill reached the Committee Stage in the Lords, when the Government itself introduced a Bill. At that late point, Daimler decided to appeal to the House of Lords in its judicial capacity. The good Lord Halsbury – then aged 93 – presided, and Lord Mersey sat. The Court of Appeal was overruled, in the eyes of most of the Law Lords because the directors did not have the authority to issue the writ; for Lord Halsbury because they were really Germans: [1916] 2 AC 307. See especially, David Foxton 'Corporate Personality in the Great War' (2002) 118 LQR 428.

appointment of judges could not continue. Nor was it any longer acceptable to have naked political appointments to the judiciary. Under Loreburn and Haldane as Lord Chancellors (1906–15) appointments to the High Court and the Court of Appeal became non-political in the sense that they generally went to the leading members of the practising Bar. (In England assimilated to appointments on 'merit'.) This self-denying ordinance was not extended to the Law Lords in the House of Lords, for as the Attorney-General, Robson, put it: that court was handling 'disputes that are legal in form but political in fact'.[27] Robson himself and Shaw, the Lord Advocate, were made Law Lords to interpret the Trade Disputes Act 1906 in favour of the unions and to weaken administrative law, which might have been used to thwart the Liberal's social legislation. Indeed, political appointments were to remain the norm in appointments as Law Lords until around 1930, when promotion from the Court of Appeal became the norm.[28]

Having said that, of course, one must record the exceptions. The Lord Chancellor still sat regularly as presiding judge in the House of Lords, at least until the Second World War; and periodically thereafter. From 1800 until 1940, with the brief exception of the temporary Lord Trevethin (1921–22), the Attorney-General succeeded to the Chief Justiceship. Even after that, Sir Donald Somerrell (Attorney-General 1936–45) became a Law Lord. There was also the Scottish exception, whereby the Lord Advocate (the Scottish equivalent of the Attorney-General) moved to a senior judicial position in Scotland and then to become a Law Lord, a route followed, in recent decades by Lords Reid, Mackay and Rodger.

Moreover these latter appointments were important. Scottish Law Lords took a broader approach to precedent and were more sensitive to political nuances. After an initial period, in which the transformation of the House of Lords around 1930 led to a generation of thoughtful appeal judges such as Atkin and Wright, the War Years, followed by the Attlee government (1945–51) led to a form of judicial catatonia in the House of Lords and, to some considerable extent, throughout the legal system. It was a period of high formalism where the law-is-the-law-is-the-law was the order of the day. Kilmuir, the Lord Chancellor 1954–62, talked of making service to the House of Commons count in judicial appointments; but it was almost too late to turn the clock back. While in 1960 a quarter of judges had either been MPs or candidates for the House of Commons,[29] appointments became more apolitical rather than less. However, Kilmuir's efforts to make the legal system more relevant to society's problems was to achieve some success.

In the meantime, however, the English legal system had established – with some justification – the myth that it was above politics. Judges were appointed 'on their merits'. Rules decided cases; policy was for Parliament, not for the courts, even in controversial matters. Judges and politicians operated in two different worlds. If there were conflict, it was at the point of the Lord Chancellor – judge, speaker of the Lords and Cabinet Minister. Yet just as civil servants could provide the administration which ran the country without allegedly

27. Heuston, n 24 above, p 151.
28. Stevens, n 25 above, Part II, 'The Rise of the Professionals'.
29. Lord Woolf had toyed with becoming a Tory candidate.

'making policy', the blatantly political figure of the Lord Chancellor could appoint judges without any political fall-out. Foreigners were understandably mystified by such claims.[30] It was the largely unimportant role played by the judges that allowed the mythology to continue.

E. THE CHANGING ENVIRONMENT: FROM THE 1960S TO THE 1990S

The various factors played into one another. By the 1960s the judges were playing a far less important role in society than they had been at the beginning of the century: the formalistic approach to law allowed judges to disclaim creativity or a policy element; the choosing of judges from the leading members of the Bar created the image of meritocratic appointments; and the view of liberal and left-wing academic commentators that judges should apply precedent solely and not be handed responsibilities over any contentious policy areas completed the establishment view that judges were independent. With the growth of central government and the welfare state the relative power of the judges shrank, while their status (and the deference to them) increased. The 1787 warning of George Mason of Virginia to the Constitutional Convention at Philadelphia that 'Appointment by the Executive is a dangerous prerogative' meant that early drafts of the US Constitution had the power of appointing judges either in the Senate or the Senate and House. Only the final draft of Article II of the US Constitution left the power with the President, subject to confirmation by the Senate. In contrast, by 1960 the reduced role of the English judges meant that few questioned the Lord Chancellor's role as the selector of the English judges.[31]

The role of the judges, however, was changing. In 1956, Lord Kilmuir had piloted through competition legislation, submitting registered restrictive agreements to a new court – the Restrictive Practices Court – to be presided over by a High Court judge. The judges were outraged. Those in the Chancery Division, whose work was minimal since they were so personally disagreeable, refused to have anything to do with the new Court. The Queen's Bench judges, with the exception of Mr. Justice Devlin, took a similar view. Needless to say Devlin became the President of the new Court, and he proceeded to explain why the process was a legal and not a political one. During the 1960s too, the judges, of their own volition, began rebuilding administrative law which had largely been demolished by the Liberal Law Lords just before the First World War. Naturally they explained that, in fact, judicial review was merely a restating of what had been good nineteenth-century law. It was, however, to change the face of administrative decision making in Britain. Suddenly, ministers and their

30. To many lawyers, the ideal Lord Chancellor was the second Lord Hailsham, Edward Heath's and Margaret Thatcher's (until 1987) Lord Chancellor. He had been a vigorous politician, had sought the leadership of the party, been a scourge of Labour, yet no one had any doubts that he was 'above politics' once he had become Lord Chancellor.
31. John Griffith in 1970 argued that, rather than being chosen by a political Lord Chancellor, judges should be chosen by the legal profession itself. See now T C Hartley and J A G Griffith, *Government and the Law* (2nd edn, 1981) p 180. Some critics had argued in favour of a Judicial Appointments Commission: Brian Abel-Smith and Robert Stevens *In Search of Justice* (London, 1968) pp 192–196.

civil servants had to live with *The Judge over your Shoulder*, as the resulting Civil Service pamphlet was called.

The Heath Government (1970–74) was to experiment still further with the purposes of the legal system and the role of the judges. The Industrial Relations Court sought to apply the registered agreements approach of the Restrictive Practices Court to trade unions. While its President, Lord Donaldson, and in the House of Lords, Lord Diplock, explained that judges were merely doing what they had always done, namely applying the law laid down by Parliament, trade unions and Labour MPs were not convinced. The courts were being dragged back into policy – or, if you wish, political areas. The Heath years also brought Britain's membership in what is now the European Union. The European Communities Act 1972, drafted by Geoffrey Howe, made clear that EU law was to trump English law and was to permeate the legal system. While that was perhaps not fully clear to the public until the *ex p Equal Opportunities Commission* decision,[32] the British courts might thereafter strike down UK legislation which was inconsistent with EU laws. Laymen could be pardoned for thinking that the UK now had a Supreme Court.[33] Moreover, the EU link accustomed the English judges to think in more continental terms, especially as they appreciated that it was the European Court in Luxembourg that was main the driving force of European integration. At the same time the Human Rights Commission and Court in Strasburg were altering the approach to civil liberties in the UK.

There were administrative changes that emphasised that the old order – with a tiny Lord Chancellor's Office linking the judiciary with the executive and legislature – was changing. The Courts Act 1970 restructured the court system and management of the courts passed to the Lord Chancellor. As criminal legal aid began to be paid at market rates in the late 1960s, the Lord Chancellor's Office, by then renamed Department, was seen as the logical place to monitor the activities of the court officials responsible for determining fees. Gradually control of civil legal aid passed from the Law Society to the Department. The Lord Chancellor's Office, which had been responsible for the judiciary and law reform, was by then seen as a real department, with a significant budget. Even the senior civil servants, originally all lawyers, were slowly incorporated into the administrative grade of the Civil Service and increasingly subject to Civil Service regulations. The Lord Chancellor at last had serious departmental responsibilities and was, for the first time, an important Accounting Officer.

All these matters inevitably had a gradual impact on the appointment of judges and the concept of judicial independence. For Lord Chancellors, appointing judges and protecting them from political fall-out had become but one of their jobs. Lord Hailsham (Lord Chancellor 1970–74 and 1979–87) was perhaps the last Lord Chancellor who was treated with judicial deference and whose ability to operate a 'Chinese Wall' between the political and non-political part of his job was accepted. Yet even he was subjected to harassment over his handling of legal aid. He was sued by the Law Society on behalf of solicitors, while the Bar and the judiciary felt that it was obvious that there

---

32. *R v Secretary of State for Employment, ex p Equal Opportunities Commission* [1995] 1 AC 1 (1994).
33. *The Times* commented that 'Britain may now have, for the first time in its history, a constitutional court': Stevens (2002), n 9 above, p 46.

should be no caps on legal aid; rationing resources was only for health and education.

The traditional deference towards the Lord Chancellor was only clearly seen to have slipped during the Chancellorship of Lord Mackay (1987–97).[34] In so many ways, James Mackay, although he came from the Scottish tradition, was a perfect candidate for Lord Chancellor. He was a moderate Conservative, he seldom spoke in Cabinet meetings, he appointed and promoted judges with great sophistication, and he had served as a Law Lord. Yet the change in the political atmosphere made his life troubled. As part of Mrs Thatcher's efforts to make England more competitive, he presided over the highly controversial Green Papers on the legal profession's restrictive practices. The profession did not welcome such an intrusion. The Bar Council and the Law Society both rejected 'government interference with the independence of the judges and the legal profession'. The High Court judges saw 'a grave breach of the separation of powers' which threatened 'the administration of the law on which our civilisation depends'.

It was in the House of Lords, sitting in its legislative capacity, that the most extreme claims were made – by the Law Lords. Lord Elwyn-Jones, a former Labour Lord Chancellor, saw shades of Hitler and Singapore – where the Lee dynasty was alleged to have tampered with the judges. The Nazi analogy was also picked up by Lord Lane, the retiring Chief Justice, while Lord Hailsham, the former Lord Chancellor, knew that 'the independence of the judiciary depends more upon the independence and integrity of the legal profession than upon any other single factor'; while Lord Donaldson warned that 'to maintain the independence of the judiciary is not enough. We must maintain the independence of the entire judicial process'. (This coded warning that independence of the judiciary embraced the Bar but not solicitors has continued to make reform of the judiciary difficult). The idea that the government should control professional conduct was 'an affront to the constitutional doctrine of the separation of powers'. It was at this point that Lord Donaldson demanded that of Lord Mackay that he 'get your tanks off my lawn'.[35]

The late 1980s were a time when the judges were under a great deal of pressure. The popular press played up a series of cases where there had been a travesty of justice where persons had been wrongly convicted. While the legal profession pointed the finger at the police, the press pointed the finger at the judges. The IRA convictions figured prominently. The release of the 'Guildford Four' and the Birmingham bombers was made more embarrassing by the quotes from Lord Denning and Lord Lane. Lord Lane had also been involved in the Tottenham Riot case where the Court of Appeal felt it had to apologise to the wrongly convicted man. When Lord Lane retired, however, Lord Donaldson and the Chairman of the Bar both blamed the Lord Chancellor and his civil servants for the Chief Justice's mistakes.[36] The Lord Chancellor was by then seen by the profession as primarily a political figure; it was the beginning of the end.

---

34. On both Lords Mackay and Irvine see now Diana Woodhouse *The Office of Lord Chancellor* (Oxford: Hart Publishing, 2001); and Richard Abel *English Lawyers Between Market and the State* (Oxford: Oxford University Press, 2003).

35. Stevens (1993), n 9 above, pp 173–176.

36. Stevens (1993), n 9 above, p 177.

The problems facing the judiciary, however, had only just begun. While the new generation of judges eschewed the political pyrotechnics of the Hailshams, Donaldsons and Ackners, the political spotlight was increasingly focussed on their decisions. When the judges held up a decision on the enforceability of an English statute to defer to the court in Luxembourg to determine constitutional issues and when, it was held that British legislation on part-time employees violated an EU Directive and was therefore unenforceable, there were outcries in the press.[37] It was, however, the ever-expanding remit of judicial review that caused especial excitement. Douglas Hurd, then Foreign Secretary, was not well pleased by judicial intervention in the Pergau Dam affair, questioning, as the judges did, the basis of foreign aid. His reaction was calm, however, compared with that of Michael Howard, the Home Secretary, who was outraged – and combative – in his attacks on the judiciary over sentencing policies and immigration decisions.

The judges were also to find themselves battling the Major administration in a different field. As one would expect in a Parliament that prided itself on its sovereignty, traditionally investigations of contentious issues were undertaken by a Committee of one or both of its Houses. The system worked reasonably well, as the nineteenth-century Blue Books can attest. Then, in the 1880s, in the so-called Pigott forgeries matter, Parliament entrusted to the judges the task of investigating the veracity of the allegations. It was true that the judges appointed were good Unionist judges in whose flesh Parnell – the object of the forgeries – had been a thorn; but an important precedent had been set. As the judges backed away from naked political ambition, Parliament passed the Tribunals of Enquiry Act in 1921, inviting an important new role for the judges. Parliament thereafter left the investigations of many areas to the judges, even if not always under the 1921 Act. By 1945, with the judges announcing they had but a passive role in society, they were used to chair all manner of inquiries, some of them with highly charged policy content. 'Government by Radcliffery', as A P Herbert described the process in honour of Lord Radcliffe – a frequent chair of these commissions – was a remarkable phenomenon.

As the judges, however, beginning in the 1960s were given or seized back jurisdiction over various areas of responsibility, it was unclear what impact this would have on this strange area of judicial responsibility. Mrs Thatcher's 11-year Prime Ministership helped quieten the problem: she believed decisions should be taken either by the Cabinet or, better still, by her and not by Commission or Committee. John Major, however, with a weaker majority and more of a commitment to consensus, was different. He was willing to give the judges their previous traditional role of chairing policy-oriented committees. The Nolan *Report on Standards in Public Life* (1995), appointed to quieten public fears after a series of embarrassing examples of 'Tory sleaze', received qualified government support. The Scott Inquiry of 1993 into the sale of arms to Iraq was, quite frankly, destabilised by government spin. There was at once an outcry that the independence of the judiciary was being questioned.

As already suggested, the concept of judicial independence in a system of responsible government, is difficult to define. For a judiciary which, for much of its history since the Act of Settlement 1701, when its tenure was established,

---

37. Stevens (2002), n 9 above, ch 4.

had been appointed by politicians for political reasons, claims of judicial independence frequently sound hollow. As the twentieth century progressed and judges were appointed increasingly because of professional success rather than political connections, the claim of judicial independence was more part of constitutional rhetoric than constitutional reality. It was a wonderful stick with which to beat MacDonald in the 1930s when he wanted to cut judicial salaries, or in the 1950s to attempt to persuade Churchill to pay their salaries free of tax. (And it was to be trotted out in the early twenty-first century to explain why judges should be exempt from the £1.4m limit on accumulated pension benefits.[38]) Of course it is important that judges be impartial, tenured, reasonably paid and not subject to pressure from government; beyond that the notion of judicial independence has been subject to whatever content its advocates have been interested in pouring into it.

In a parallel development, some reformers, often motivated by an interest in a more socially diverse bench or a more transparent system of appointments, called for a Judicial Appointments Commission,[39] at least to supplement the discretion of the Lord Chancellor. The appointment of judges suddenly took on a life of its own. In most Commonwealth countries, some form of Commission existed, normally because the judges – at least in the final appeal courts – were assumed to have important political functions, and there was an interest in maintaining the pretence of merit, although as the Chief Justice of Canada has recently noted 'merit is in the eye of the beholder'. For the lower courts the concern was often to restrain the political interests of the appointing politicians. Each jurisdiction, however, developed its own solution, depending on the changing role of the courts. In Israel, essentially a British-style common law country in 1948, the Judicial Appointments Committee, having begun as a largely apolitical body became more politicised, ultimately including members of the Knesset, as the Supreme Court, especially after 1992, began developing a system of fundamental laws. Astute observers of the English scene assumed that, as the courts took on more political roles, they too would be a need to pay at least some deference in the democrat ideal. It was not a notion that appealed to the legal profession, let alone the judiciary.

Whereas outsiders were looking for some way to justify what political critics saw as the un-elected and non-responsible (and generally non-representative) nature of a judiciary, increasingly involved in political issues, this too did not necessarily appeal to the legal profession. In 1989, the Bar Council decided that judicial appointments should be taken away from the Lord Chancellor and given to the profession, ideally a committee of judges.[40] In 1991, the Institute for Public Policy Research (IPPR), a generally left-wing think tank, produced a draft Constitution for the UK. It proposed a Supreme Court that could strike down Acts of Parliament. At the same time its underlying belief

---

38. 'Woolf guards judges' pensions' [2003] NLJ, 8 August, at 1222 The Chief Justice claimed subjecting the judges to the rules applicable to non-judges would affect 'recruitment and retention'. The Treasury took the view that 'tax is universal'. See also, 'Judges unite to fight taxman's raid on pensions' *The Times*, 6 September 2003. The excitement will be even greater, one expects, if judges are required – as looks possible – to contribute to their own pensions.

39. Eg JUSTICE *The Judiciary in England and Wales* (1993).

40. General Council of the Bar *Quality of Justice: The Bar's Response* (1989) p 187.

was the traditional English one that judicial decisions were apolitical. The Introduction therefore warned:

> 'As can be seen from the example of the USA, the power to appoint judges to courts with important constitutional powers can become a controversial political issue. If no changes were made to the present system of appointing judges, the temptation to depart from the recent tradition of impartiality in judicial appointments might become impossible to resist.'[41]

The solution was to have a Judicial Services Commission of 15 persons to choose the judges, of whom, five would be judges and two lawyers. That would then, it was assumed, insure 'independent' judges, who could then strike down legislation without being accused of being 'political'. It was all wonderfully English.

The idea of taking the 'political' element out of judicial appointments, by having judges chosen by an apolitical group, took on a life of its own. It had many of the elements of Mussolini's corporatism. The IPPR *Constitution* announced that the first principle of judicial independence was 'freedom from political influence in the appointment of judges'. That was escalating a recent political convention into a constitutional principle. What is 'political' is a concept that has to be unpacked. The five judges on a Judicial Services Commission are not value free. They have social views and political assumptions, even if they have never been politicians. The underlying notion that a court could be given the power to strike down Acts of Parliament, by theoretically value-free standards, and that all would be well if the judges were chosen by a 'non-political' body dominated by judges, to be charitable, was taking political naivety to an advanced degree. Without the opportunity for a politician to be involved, at least in the appointments process, could well make the judges objects of unrestrained political attacks on the un-elected branch of government by those in an elected legislature. Under the IPPR scheme, there would be no political checks on un-elected judges, who held the fate of legislation in their hands. It was not something that was likely to appeal to the House of Commons; but that did not mean it did not appeal to the English legal profession.

A gap was growing between the House of Commons and the judiciary. In 1900 a third of the House had been lawyers and, as we saw, even in 1960, 25 per cent of the judges had been MPs or parliamentary candidates. Membership to in the House of Commons was consistent with a successful practice at the Bar. Things were changing rapidly. As the Bar became more successful, beginning in the late 1960s, there seemed less room for barristers who spent part of their time at the House. In turn, the Commons became increasingly the province of professional politicians. The two worlds became increasingly mutually exclusive. By the 1990s, therefore, there was a generation of judges and senior members of the profession who had limited time for most professional politicians. The demands of the whips and the miserable existence on the back benches tended to favour the party hack rather than the dazzling intellect who might compete with the leaders of Bench and Bar. It was an understandable gulf, but an unfortunate one.

---

41. IPPR *The Constitution of the United Kingdom* (1991).

F. THE COMING OF NEW LABOUR

A sea change came over the English judges in the 1990s. They were more liberal, more intellectual, more given to ideas from the continent and from the Commonwealth and the US. As Chief Justice, Lord Taylor, while not an intellectual, was prepared to do public battle as Michael Howard berated the judges. Lord Bingham, while he supported the concept of the Lord Chancellorship and was an articulate advocate of the need for one person to pick the judges, was also a strong advocate of a Supreme Court and the incorporation of the European Convention of Human Rights. It was a changing world.

The arrival of New Labour in 1997[42] was probably as much a relief for the judiciary as it was to most of the electorate, who provided Tony Blair with a landslide majority. The Major years had not been a happy time for the judiciary and Blair was a barrister with a barrister wife, who had inherited a programme of constitutional reform from John Smith. It was clear that the judges would be required to play a more active role in the constitution, but the assumption was that the new generation of modernising politicians would be understanding of the difficulties the changes might cause. With devolution to Scotland, the judges, illogically this time sitting as the Judicial Committee of the Privy Council, would be required to develop rules for the elementary form of federalism. More pressing for the judges was the incorporation of the European Convention of Human Rights, brought into UK law by the Human Rights Act 1998.

To set the tone of New Labour's approach to the law, Derry Irvine, in whose Chambers both Tony and Cherie Blair had been, was appointed Lord Chancellor. A good lawyer and incredibly hard-working, his legal skills probably outpaced his political antennae. His early years were marred by lack of wisdom in handling the wall papering of his official apartment, the sending of personal invitations in official envelopes and his own unfortunate parallels of himself to Cardinal Wolsey. What was perhaps most interesting, however, was his rather conservative approach to reform of the judiciary and especially towards any change in the office of Lord Chancellor. Before the election New Labour had talked of Judicial Appointments Commissions and a clearer separation of powers. After the election, Irvine pooh-poohed the separation of powers. He confirmed the Mackay policies – begun by Hailsham – of attempting to rein in legal aid, by the contract system in criminal legal aid and by expanding the conditional fee in civil legal aid. His judicial appointments were cautious, indeed less imaginative than James Mackay's (Laws and Sedley still languish in the Court of Appeal). His approach to reform of the House of Lords as a legislative body was equally conservative. Ideally he thought it should remain an exclusively nominated body. He saw no reason to tamper with the dual legislative and judicial roles of the Law Lords. Indeed, he arranged the appointment of a rather tame Royal Commission under Lord Wakeham, a Tory 'fixer', to confirm his views.[43]

---

42. On this period, see Stevens (2002), n 9 above, chs 8 and 9.
43. A fixer, not a lawyer. He was on the Main Board of Enron when it went bankrupt. He was also on the Audit Committee, although he was reported as saying he had never understood the accounts.

On legal matters, he naturally found that there was an expectation that New Labour would establish some form of Judicial Appointments Commission. Irvine was unenthusiastic. The clamour rose. He made various modest changes: advertising and more formal application procedures were established and efforts to recruit women and minorities were made. Still the pressure continued. He then appointed Sir Leonard Peach, a former Commissioner for Public Appointments, to look at the process for appointing judges and QCs. Perhaps to the Lord Chancellor's surprise, Peach recommended a Judicial Appointments Commission, at least to ensure that such appointments were transparent. As the Chair of that Commission, Irvine selected Sir Colin Campbell, Vice-Chancellor of the University of Nottingham. Once again the Lord Chancellor may have been surprised. Campbell proved a most rigorous Commissioner, highly critical of many existing procedures and suggesting active new ways of proceeding.

The Human Rights Act 1998 was also to cause problems to Lord Irvine. While he agreed that New Labour was committed to its implementation, it had been opposed by Lord Mackay because it involved passing political decisions to the judges. As Lord Browne-Wilkinson put it, the Act required the judges to give 'moral answers to moral questions'. Lord Irvine appeared to accept that, but he hoped he had 'warned off' the judges about getting into these dangerous waters, despite the passage of the legislation. In some respects he was successful. Frequently pleaded, it has far less frequently been applied. Yet the psychological change was to judicialise many political issues. For instance in the summer of 2003, in the debate about the funding of universities and the composition of their student bodies, the independent schools threatened to sue under the Human Rights Act 1998 to prevent universities discriminating against students from private schools, while the Chairman of the Bar announced the Bar would sue the government to have top-up fees struck down under the Act, because it prevented the poor coming to the Bar! Meanwhile the Chairman of the Commission on Race Relations announced that his body would be suing because of the inherently discriminatory nature of top-up fees![44]

Derry Irvine had other reasons to worry about the Human Rights Act and related issues. The judges were unhappy about David Blunkett's Criminal Justice Bill, restricting many traditional common law rights in criminal trials, some of which appeared contrary to the letter or spirit of the Human Rights Act. David Blunkett was unhappy with the judges as they threatened his draconian immigration policies. He explained 'elected politicians now seem to come second to judges because of the Human Rights Act'.[45] 'Un-elected' judges were not the flavour of the month.

Irvine also had reason to fear the Human Rights Act with respect to his own office. Soon after he took office, the court in Strasbourg decided the *McGonnell* case,[46] holding that the Bailiff of Guernsey, whose office bore a similarity to

---

44. See Robert Stevens *From University to Uni; the Politics of Higher Education in England* (Politicos, 2004) ch 9.
Of course, the changed attitude went far further than the Human Rights Act 1998. Eg 'End this compensation nightmare, say judges' *Daily Telegraph*, 3 August 2003; 'Judge opens floodgates for patients to charge NHS for surgery abroad' *The Times*, 2 October 2003; 'Judge ends women's rights of motherhood' *The Times*, 2 October 2003.
45. *Daily Mail*, 8 September 2001.
46. *McGonnell v United Kingdom* (2000) 30 EHRR 289.

that of the Lord Chancellor, did not satisfy Article 6 of the European Convention, calling for judges to be independent and impartial. Academics thought the writing might be on the wall for the Lord Chancellor. It was not a view shared by Derry Irvine. He preferred to analogise himself to the Counseil D'Etat or the Swedish Minister of Justice. The academic views, however, permeated to the profession. Irvine was forced to recuse himself in a high-profile criminal case and his role in government slowly changed. The Law Officers increasingly believed that the Office of Lord Chancellor violated the separation of powers; fundamentally it could not survive.

Lord Irvine, however, carried other political baggage. Despite his defence of his office many of the judges felt he had provided scant protection during their battles with Blunkett (nor had Mackay in the disputes with Michael Howard). Yet there were far wider problems. From the beginning of his term of office there was an enemies list. Lord Jenkins, something of a mentor of the Prime Minister, let it be known that Irvine had too much power. Irvine certainly, from the beginning, chaired a range of Cabinet committees and took an active role in Cabinet debates. He was responsible for the Queen's Speech, setting out the party policies, as well as being responsible for constitutional issues such as devolution, human rights and reform of the Lords. It was said that he arranged Lord Richard's dismissal as Leader of the Lords and he engineered a deal for a cadre of hereditary peers to remain in the Lords after reform – a deal done with Lord Cranborne behind the back of William Hague. Lord Irvine was not well liked on the left of the party. There were those who remembered his closeness to Blair, were dubious about his socialism and saw him more as a 'claret-swigging fat cat'.

Irvine also irritated some of the reforming senior judges by making light of their suggestion that there be a Supreme Court, and refusing to consider not sitting as a judge. This irritation bubbled over in a lecture at Oxford by the about-to-retire Law Lord, Lord Steyn, in the spring of 2002.[47] Steyn saw the judiciary 'potentially compromised' by the participation of the Lord Chancellor in judicial matters. The participation of the Law Lords as legislators 'is no longer defensible', said Steyn and 'nowhere outside Britain … is the independence of the judiciary compromised in the eyes of citizens by relegating the status of the highest court to the position of a subordinate part of the legislature'. Steyn implied that it was the ego of Irvine that prevented rational reform. The time for a Supreme Court had come.

The final story has yet to be written. We know, however, that relations with David Blunkett, the Home Secretary, were hurt by Irvine's attempt to take over responsibility for criminal law after the June 2001 General Election. By 2002, the position of the Prime Minster, to whose coattails Irvine was inevitably tied, was weakening. The success of spin during the first Blair administration was beginning to backfire. Blair's unctuous style was beginning to grate; Cherie's lifestyle (and especially her lifestyle guru) had become a source of ridicule. It was Blair's support for George W Bush's and Donald Rumsfeld's war in Iraq that caused immense scepticism, not only in the party, but in the country at large. The pressures meant that Blair had few chips to protect his Lord Chancellor when the reformers among the leadership of the profession –

---

47. Lord Steyn 'The Case for a Supreme Court' (2002) 118 LQR 382.

including allegedly Lords Goldsmith and Falconer – insisted the time had come to tidy up the grosser absurdities of the separation of powers in England, inevitable as some were in a system of responsible government. Irvine is reported to have resisted the changes vigorously; he lost. It was difficult, however, not to sympathise with him. Some of his arguments were undoubtedly right.

G. CONSTITUTIONAL REFORM: A NEW WAY OF APPOINTING JUDGES

The consultative document on judicial appointments is both logical and disappointing. It is logical because it reflects the culmination of all the reports over the years seeking to make the process of appointment more transparent. It recommends a Judicial Appointments Commission. Such a Commission already exists in Northern Ireland and Scotland. Whereas, however, those Commissions have a majority of laymen, the one proposed for England and Wales will have (or the government would like it to have) five judges, five members of the legal profession and five lay persons. The government's preference would be for the Commission not to be an Executive one, but a Recommending Commission, with the final decision being made by the Secretary of State for Constitutional Affairs. If, however, the limited precedent of Scotland is followed, this will mean that the final decision is really that of the Commission. There will also be two related bodies. First of all there will be a Committee to choose the members of the Commission and an Ombudsman, or the continuation of the Commission for Judicial Appointments, to monitor that the appointments system is working fairly.

Apart from receiving the recommendations from the Commission, the Secretary of State for Constitutional Affairs would be responsible for the criteria for appointment to the judiciary; he would also be responsible for protecting the independence of the judiciary and this protection might even be enshrined in statutory form. The government would also remain responsible for the number of judges. Promotions from the High Court to the Court of Appeal (and certain offices) would be handled by a sub-Committee of the Appointments Commission.

It is arguable that the consultative paper represents the culmination of the utilitarian reforms of the nineteenth century. After all, the cult of competition for public appointments was parodied by Gilbert and Sullivan, suggesting that the House of Lords should be open to competitive examination; the new independent selection body effectively achieves that at least for the Lords. Salisbury's sneering observation that one day the Master of the Rolls would be chosen by an examination in the Law Reports may well be at hand. Even Selborne and Cairns, however, would be surprised by the seemingly mechanical basis for judicial appointments.

Of course most of the criticisms have gone to the mechanics of the proposed Commission. The current Commission for Judicial Appointments, through its Chairman, Sir Colin Campbell, called for the new Commission to be dominated by lay persons rather than judges and lawyers. Campbell saw this as vital in implementing one of Lord Falconer's main goals – a more diverse bench.[48]

48. 'People power to pick judges' *The Observer*, 31 August 2003.

The consultative paper calls for such goals, and some diversity could undoubtedly be produced by building on a wider recruitment base – including not only solicitors, but employed lawyers. (The cult of 'independence', which has judicial independence lapping over to the Bar, will discourage such developments.) Already the suggestion for part-time arrangements for women bringing up children has been attacked by a leading woman barrister who sees it as a way the government can manipulate the judiciary.[49] Overall, however, all sections of the legal and lay community claim an interest in a more diverse bench.

There are, of course, other criticisms. Can any Commission, no matter how wisely staffed, ever have the Solomanesque judgment of a good Lord Chancellor – or some appropriate single person. This was put most elegantly and eloquently by Lord Bingham:

> 'I proceed to lay down as a rule that one man of discernment is better fitted to analyse and estimate the peculiar qualities adapted to a particular office than a body of men of equal or perhaps even superior discernment. The role and undivided responsibility of one man will naturally beget a livelier sense of duty and a more exact regard to regulation. He will, on this account, find himself under stronger obligations, and more interested to investigate with care the qualities requisite to the station to be filled, and to prefer with impartiality the persons who may have the fairest pretensions to them.'[50]

Lord Woolf has also pointed out the difficulties of having promotion to higher courts done by Committee. It tends to lead to 'Buggins turn next'. He used the example of India and the selection of the Chief Justice;[51] he could just as easily used promotion to final court of appeal in Connecticut (the quaintly named Supreme Court of Errors and Appeals). It will surely be more difficult for a Commission, no matter how distinguished its membership, to pass over less distinguished judges to make a promotion to the Court of Appeal than it was for a wise Lord Chancellor.

The government has already announced, without any consultation, that the Lord Chancellor is to go. (In the best *Alice in Wonderland* tradition it has been sentence first, trial later.) The argument has moved on. The accepted wisdom among leading judges and lawyers is that the Secretary of State for Constitutional Affairs could not appoint the judges because he might not be a

49. Barbara Hewson, letter, *Financial Times*, 18 July 2003: 'Acknowledge the judiciary's diversity before letting a mums' army loose in the courts'. And see a mock advertisement in *Private Eye*, entitled 'Hey, you! Wanna be a High Court judge?', adding, 'don't be put off by old-fashioned ideas that judges are elderly upper-class men in wigs and pin-stripe suits, that's all changed. The 21st century judge of today is much more likely to be a twenty-something, black, single mother who is having to work part-time because one of the old-fashioned judges sent her husband to goal for selling dope': *Private Eye*, 23 July 2003.
50. JUSTICE *Bulletin*, Autumn 2001, p 9. And for the view that Morris Finer and Peter Pain would not have been judges without Elwyn-Jones as Lord Chancellor, see Sir Michael Kerr *As far as I Remember* (Oxford: Hart Publishing, 2002) p 307.
51. Department of Constitutional Affairs, Lord Woolf 'Speech at the Annual Dinner for HM Judges', 9 July 2003.

lawyer, therefore he would not know the legal profession and that he might pack the courts with government supporters.[52] This is not a totally convincing argument. A wise layman might well prove a more effective protector of judicial independence and a wiser selector of judges than have many Lord Chancellors. Lord Mackay had been at the Scottish Bar, but he was remarkable as a selector of judges. Within the last 100 years, Lord Halsbury packed the High Court bench with Tory supporters, although he was Lord Chancellor and sat regularly. Chamberlains' Lord Chancellor in 1939–40, Caldecote, typified the mediocrity of some 'political hack' Lord Chancellors. An enthusiastic supporter of Munich, Churchill suggested that the Prime Minister had sought to choose someone of inferior abilities to himself as Lord Chancellor, while the young Michael Foot quipped that no more surprising announcement had been made since Caligula appointed his horse as consul. That, of course, did prevent Caldecote being 'promoted' to Lord Chief Justice.[53]

Assuming the Secretary of State had good judgement – something not all Lord Chancellors have had – there is no reason why the Secretary, with an Advisory Committee (not a nominating Committee) should not continue Lord Bingham's goal as the Renaissance appointer of judges. It may well, of course, be too late, partly because the judges have convinced themselves that the Secretary will not have the ability to run political interference for them because he might be a dreaded layman. Worse than that, as a member of the House of Commons, he is likely to be mediocre. The judges may well, however, have attempted to sabotage a system of judicial selection that blended the traditional and the reformist. The preferred solution of the judges is apparently to have an Appointments Committee with the heads of division maintaining a veto; and the decision about new judges would then be conveyed by the Lord Chief Justice directly to the Queen without the interaction either of the Prime Minister or the Secretary of State.[54] Critics will inevitably see this as a self-perpetuating oligarchy; yet Lord Falconer, on the behalf of a government increasingly on the political back foot, has recently suggested that he may be willing to capitulate to the judges' demands.[55] Indeed with the Prime Minister increasingly losing control of his majority in the Commons and of government business in the Lords it was becoming less clear that the constitutional changes would go through in this Parliament.

52. Woolf, n 51 above. And see Frances Gibb 'Top Judge stays to fight politicians' *The Times*, 1 August 2003.

53. Stevens, n 25 above, p 245.

54. Judges memorandum, para 105ff. The alternative model would allow the Secretary of State to reject a nominated candidate if he gave reasons. 'Any greater involvement than that envisaged by the second model would mean that, while the reforms are intended to protect the judiciary, they actually result in the judiciary's role in appointments being substantially reduced and the executive's contribution remaining the same or, on one view, increasing. This latter argument is based on the fact that the involvement of the minister who was Head of the Judiciary will have been replaced by a minister who is not a judge': para 109.

55. 'Power to veto judges could be negotiable, says Falconer' *Financial Times*, 24 November 2003. The Law Lords, are reported on willing 'to make life bloody for this government' in the legislative debates on the abolition of the Lord Chancellor, the appointment of judges and the creation of a Supreme Court. 'Lords behaving badly' *Economist*, 24 November 2003.

If they do go through, the changes would be buttressed by a new statute, section 1 of which would be a 'Guarantee of continued judicial independence', which would mandate that 'those with responsibility for the administration of justice must uphold the continued independence of the judiciary'.[56] Without unpacking the concept of independence of the judiciary, the statute would be largely meaningless. More embarrassingly, it is all faintly reminiscent of another rather infantile outburst of judicial chagrin about independence, when the government sought to reduce judicial salaries during the financial crisis in the 1930s. In response to judicial paranoia, the government introduced the Judiciary (Safeguarding) Bill 1934. The Permanent Secretary to the Lord Chancellor, Schuster, urged the Statutory Draftsman: 'Begin with a recital, which should be as long and pompous as possible, … the independence and all the rest of it … then declare that notwithstanding all this they are affected by the cut.' Schuster thought the whole thing 'extremely silly' and the Bill died[57] – a useful precedent for the current crisis.

The attitudes of leading members of Bench and Bar are, however, worth unpacking. As already suggested, just as the judges over the last 40 years have been busy moving towards the centre of the political stage, the composition of the elected House of Commons has been changing. The intellectual quality of MPs, and hence ministers, has not been maintained. The arrival of a more presidential system of government is likely to insure even weaker MPs and ministers – including of course the Secretary of State for Constitutional Affairs. Compliance will be more important than integrity. It is in this context that the legal establishment is worried about the absence of a legal heavyweight to protect the rather arcane concept of judicial independence. The Secretary of Defence is not expected to be a military person; the Secretary of Health is not expected to be a medical person; judges think that the Secretary of Constitutional Affairs must be a heavyweight lawyer. It may be an arrogant position;[58] it is also an understandable one.

The response of the judges to the Consultation Papers is deeply revealing. The approach to the composition of the Appointments Commission is a reminder that the four senior judges have currently – despite the efforts of James Mackay to weaken this – veto power over judicial appointments. It is therefore natural that the judges should expect a judicial chair and a judicial majority and to give the Secretary of State minimal discretion in rejecting recommended

---

56. Paras 44 and 45.
57. Stevens (1993), n 9 above, pp 61–63.
58. This presumably explains the embarrassing outburst by the Deputy Lord Chief Justice, Lord Justice Judge, at a press conference, who saw the possibility that in the future, dreadful things would happen in the democratic process from which the judges must be protected: 'I am not making a party political point against anybody, but we do have to remember the popularity of the second person in the recent presidential election in France. We do have to remember that Hitler came to power in a democratic country by getting a significant popular vote and then subverting the constitution. There are nasty people out there and there is no guarantee that because we are Great Britain none of them will ever, ever come to power'. Press Conference, Lord Chief Justice and Deputy Lord Chief Justice, 6 November 2003. And see 'Top judge fears legal reform will raise ghosts of Nazis': *Daily Telegraph*, 7 November 2003.

names.[59] Some will see the judges' position as the inherent defence of the status quo. In their memorandum, the judges warned of the dangers 'of becoming so anxious to achieve diversity that sight is lost of the primacy of merit. The justice system will be debased if the very best candidates are not appointed'.[60] Yet 'merit' traditionally means outstanding success at the Bar. The Bar, however, is still organised in a way that discriminates against women with family responsibilities and, at least until recently, it was not easy for minority barristers to find tenancies in the kind of chambers from which members of the higher judiciary are chosen. However, each time the leading judges extol the wonders of the independence of the Bar, allegedly as important as the independence of the judiciary, the potential for appointing solicitors to the bench – a branch of the profession with a high proportion of women and relatively high proportion of minorities – is undermined.

Equally one can understand the view of the Howards and the Blunketts. The current Home Secretary announced that he was 'fed up with having to deal with a situation where parliament debates issues and judges then overturn them'. He also took the view that 'if public policy can always be overridden by individual challenge through the courts, then democracy itself is under threat'.[61] David Blunkett demanded in the *Evening Standard*[62] that judges live in the 'real world',[63] having in mind apparently Mr Justice Popplewell.[64] The latter was an admirable judge, but the world of Charterhouse and Cambridge University, cricket and the Oxford Circuit, is very different from Mr Blunkett's tough inner-city politics in Sheffield: 'There are no newspaper editors, columnists or opinion formers living in my inner-city Sheffield constituency. If I don't speak about the experiences of my constituents and millions like them, they have no voice at all in the public arena.' So too, when the Chief Justice warns that the judges are underpaid at £147,198 pa because the leaders of the profession are earning ten times that,[65] it does seem

59. One of the great ironies is the selective use of Council of Europe documents. The judges had no time for suggestions that the Lord Chancellor violated the Separation of Powers (see Kate Malleson 'Modernizing the constitution: Completing Unfinished Business', this volume). Yet they embraced the European Charter on the Statute of Judges that half the Commission should be composed of judges (para 132). There was no mention of the politician members of the Commission, customary in continental countries nor the recommendations that seem to spell the end of the lay magistracy and perhaps the jury. Nor did it discourage the judges from suggesting that the Lord Chief Justice (and the equivalents in Scotland and Northern Ireland) should be members of an appointed House of Lords! (Paras 158–160.)
60. Para 80.
61. Speech of Lord Lester, 648 HL Official Report (5th series) col 894, 21 May 2003.
62. The article proclaimed: 'I won't give in to the judges … judges now routinely rewrite the effects of a law Parliament has passed.' They use 'ever more ingenious ways of getting what they want … we need a long hard look at the constitutional relationship between Parliament and the judges and be clear how it has changed'. See speech of Lord Rodgers, 648 HL Official Report (5th series) col 875, 21 May 2003.
63. David Blunkett 'I won't give in' *Evening Standard*, 12 May 2003. At least he spared the judges Signor Berlusconi's view of the Italian judges: 'anthropologically divorced from the rest of humanity': 'Forza Berlusconi!' *The Spectator*, 6 September 2003.
64. See Sir Oliver Popplewell *Benchmark : Life, Laughter and the Law* (London, 2003).
65. 'Woolf guards judges' pensions' (2003) NLJ, 8 August 2003, p 1222.

to politicians that the leaders of the legal profession live in a cocooned corporatist other world, when the average person in England earns £34,197 and MPs little more. Too often MPs are sceptical of the judicial claims about their innocence with respect to judicial review. The Conservatives opposed the Human Rights Act because it would pass too much power and inevitably political decisions to the judges. Labour backbenchers unwisely took the assurances from Blair and Irvine that all was well with parliamentary sovereignty. No wonder the mystique of judicial independence is under stress.

As always in the English scene, so much has depended on the strange interpretation of the words 'judicial independence'. The English have been late comers to the separation of powers, but they have all the zeal of converts. In the US, where, since 1789, there have been clear divisions between the judicial, the executive and the legislative, there has also been a realisation that to make the system work there must be a system of 'checks and balances'. The English (or British), having merged the legislative and the executive in the 1720s, were happy to treat the judiciary as a poor cousin, subject to various public and private controls. Suddenly, over the last 30-year period the obsession with the independence of the judiciary has emerged fully formed from the head of Athena and the assumption is that it should be subject to no checks and balances at all. The traditional idea that independence of the judiciary meant that High Court judges had tenure under the Act of Settlement, were entitled to a decent salary, should be impartial with respect to decision-making and free of political pressures in their judicial work, has given way to a far more expansive doctrine.

This is reflected in Lord Falconer's introduction to the consultative paper. He extols independence. 'The appointments system must be, and must be seen to be, independent of Government'; although at the same time 'those responsible for judicial appointments must be accountable to Parliament without it becoming part of the political process'. The idea that this tenuous link with the democratic process will be enough to protect the judges from the claim of being a 'unelected' is dubious. Since Michael Howard and David Blunkett started attacking the judges for being 'unelected', 'undemocratic' and 'elitist', the response of the legal profession has been to suggest that 'our' judges are independent of politics. If what they mean is that judicial decisions are significantly determined by legal rules, that is of course true. If, however, they are taking the Italian concept of corporatism as their model, they are likely to be doomed to failure.

Judges do have their own personal and political views which they take on to the bench with them and help shape their decisions; the law is not a value-free process. In a democratic society, the elected legislature, and those legislators who serve in the executive under the system of responsible government, need to be involved in the selection of the judiciary in more than a tangential way, if only to protect the judiciary from political attack. This will be all the more important now the office of Lord Chancellor is disappearing. The theory behind this was put most persuasively by Richard Posner of the Federal Court of Appeals in the US. He argued that it is the political involvement in the appointments process that protects the tenure of judges during their judicial life.[66] The refusal to address this issue in the UK may well be storing up long-term trouble for the judiciary. It will only add to the Lord Chief Justice's concern 'about the relationship between the different branches of government'.[67]

The mere mention of matters such as the 'democratic deficit' is enough to send shivers and tremors through the English profession and bench. One of the obvious parallels is the US federal bench. The debates at Philadelphia had centred on the legislature making the appointments to the Supreme Court. The ultimate compromise was appointment by the President, with confirmation by the Senate. It is a political tussle; but it has ensured over the last decades representation in the judiciary for women, African-Americans, Hispanics, Jews and Westerners. Superficially this would seem to support Lord Falconer's demand for 'more women, more minority members, and lawyers from a wider range of practice'. The idea of a potential judge being subjected by politicians to the kind of grilling leading members of the Bar inflict on members of the public daily is, however, anathema to Bench and Bar alike.

It is true that it is sometimes suggested. Sir Thomas Legg, the former Permanent Secretary to the Lord Chancellor, suggested that as judges have moved to take a more central stage in various political matters it might be reasonable to require senior judges to be interviewed by an appropriate committee of a reformed House of Lords.[68] Would that have prevented the conflicts between the Lords Chief Justice and Michael Howard and David Blunkett over sentencing, criminal justice reform and the like? Would it have given an element of democratic legitimacy to judges so that successive governments would not have launched attacks on the judges for their decisions in judicial review and civil liberties cases? Lord Kingsland, the Conservative Shadow Lord Chancellor, has twice suggested in the House of Lords that nominated Law Lords should appear before a joint committee of Lords and Commons. William Hague, Conservative Leader 1997–2001, said the House of Commons should have a veto on senior judicial appointments,[69] a position supported by the current Co-Chair of the Conservative Party.[70]

66. And see generally William M Landes and Richard A Posner 'The Independent Judiciary in an Interest-Group Perspective' (1975) 18 J Law and Economics 875.

67. Lord Woolf, 648 HL Official Report (5th series) col 879, 21 May 2003.
One of the lamest parts of the judges' submission is the brief paragraph on 'Democratic Accountability': '... we recognise the need for democratic accountability. This will be provided by the continuing role of the Ombudsman, who will scrutinise the appointments process and publish an annual report. In addition, the Chairperson of the Judicial Appointments Commission should be required to report annually to Parliament. We would also expect the Constitutional Affairs Select Committee regularly to scrutinise the appointments process': para 113.

68. *Daily Telegraph*, 19 January 1998.

69. *The Times*, 25 February 1998.

70. Liam Fox 'Judiciary Needs Greater Scrutiny' *The Times*, 15 April 1999. See also 'If judges are able to make law then they must be subject to review and checks and balances in the same way as other legislators. In the new political climate it is now appropriate to institute greater parliamentary scrutiny of those who are appointed to the higher judicial positions, eg the Lords of Appeal in Ordinary (the law lords) and ... the Lord Chief Justice, the Master of the Rolls, the Vice-Chancellor and the President of the Family Division': Liam Fox 'Holding Our Judges to Account', Politeia, 1999.

Moves in that direction, however, soon ran into the paranoia created by the televised hearings on Robert Bork and Clarence Thomas before the US Senate. While most Judiciary Committee hearings are far more dignified, the die has probably been cast. As Lord Neill, the former Chair of the Committee on Standards in Public Life put it:

> 'This is a disastrous way of appointing the judiciary. We can carry openness to its full length – I believe that openness is one of the great seven principles of public life; I proclaim that – but there must be limits to it. The limit comes when we try to interrogate potential judges.'[71]

Politically, any suggestion that a legislative body might vote on judges was probably killed by the behaviour of Labour MEPs in the European Parliament when they attacked the nomination of Nicholas Bratza as a judge of the European Court of Human Rights on the ground that he had represented the Thatcher government in privatisation matters. The judges will argue that English politicians are too unsophisticated to understand the nuances of judicial activism and restraint.

Indeed, Lord Falconer has moved to cut off any suggestion that Parliament itself might be involved. In the consultative paper, the simplistic assumption is made that any political considerations (as opposed to gender, race and social considerations) are out of the question. Any legislative involvement is, rather naively, thought to be inconsistent with judicial independence. The American Federal System is raised briefly only to be dismissed: 'Due to the pivotal role played by the legislature, appointment arrangements at federal level are not relevant to the issues raised in this consultation and are not discussed further here.'[72] There is greater discussion of the selection of US state judges, with emphasis on how the states now seek to avoid the election of judges. There is no mention of the fact that the system of election was developed in the nineteenth century, during the period of Jacksonian Democracy, because the judges were thought to have taken over too many political tasks and were not sufficiently representative of society at large. That parallel would be too uncomfortable.

One suspects that the die is now cast. Despite the scepticism of the Lord Chief Justice and the Senior Law Lord it is difficult to see how, at the very least, a recommending Appointments Commission, effectively an executive Appointments Commission, can be avoided. It runs the danger of leading to a bland, antiseptic bench, technically competent, but 'safe'. At least the Commission may be forced to produce a panel of names if the trade union pressures of the Judges' Council can be resisted. The concerns of Bingham and Woolf are of course primarily related to the absence of a Renaissance figure from the legal profession to provide leadership.[73] Equally serious, as has already

---

71. 597 HL Official Report (5th series) col 1446, 1 March 1999. See also Sir Sidney Kentridge 'The Highest Court: Selecting the Judges' [2003] 62 CLJ 55.
72. *A New Way of Appointing Judges* (2003) p 75.
73. In a recent debate in the Lords, Lord Lester suggested that the Attorney-General might act as a substitute Lord Chancellor, while Lord Alexander made a plea for the retention of a scaled-down Lord Chancellor. See 652 HL Official Report (5th series) cols 112 and 117 respectively, 8 September 2003. Lord Mackay is also now on record suggesting the Attorney-General as a substitute Lord Chancellor: 'Law Diary' *The Times*, 23 September 2003.

been suggested, is the camouflage required by a judiciary which is de facto, if not de iure, undertaking increasingly political roles in the courts; let alone with respect to other public functions. Under Michael Howard the more aggressive of the judges were talking about remedying the 'democratic deficit' represented by the British system of 'elected dictatorship'. The boot is now on the other foot. It is the judges who run the danger of suffering from the 'democratic deficit'.

The elected representatives need a role in the selection of judges. Perhaps the parties could nominate three members for the Committee choosing the Commission. Failing that, assuming there is to be a Commission, then if not immediately, at least shortly, the House of Commons, as the representatives of the people, will, like the Knesset in Israel, demand representation on the Commission. After all, in France, both the Senate and the National Assembly nominate members of the Conseil Superieur de la Magistrature and in Portugal the seven non-judges on the Conselho Superior da Magistradura are nominated by the legislature. In this country, if the judiciary continues to expand judicial review and if the Human Rights Act becomes ever more popular, the demands for a more political Commission will grow. The irony is that judicial appointments may become more political than they have been under the last 40 years of the Lord Chancellor system.

H. CONSTITUTIONAL REFORM: A SUPREME COURT FOR THE UK

If the consultation paper on the appointment of judges was both radical and naïve, the consultation paper on the Supreme Court was both conservative and cautious. In so many ways, what it was recommending was what the Hatherley Commission recommended in the 1860s and the Judicature Act 1873 provided through an Imperial Court of Appeal. Of course things are now different, but the unsatisfactory solution in the Appellate Jurisdiction Act 1876, of having the House of Lords continue as the final court of appeal will be ended. Critics see a separate final court of appeal as inevitable under Article 6 of the European Convention on Human Rights. Sceptics – and they have included both Lords Irvine and Woolf – see the changes as architectural, of less importance than new court buildings in Manchester. The majority of Law Lords believe the changes are both 'unnecessary' and 'harmful'[74] and with a commendable concern for the public fisc something not always shown where legal aid or judicial salaries are involved, 'they consider that the cost of the change would

---

74. Lords Nicholls, Hoffmann, Hope, Hutton, Millett, Rodger. On the other side were Bingham, Steyn, Saville and Walker. They regarded 'the functional separation of the judiciary at all levels from the legislature and the executive as a cardinal feature of a modern, liberal, democratic state governed by the rule of law.' See House of Lords *The Law Lords' response to the Government's consultation pages on Constitutional Reform: A Supreme Court for the United Kingdom* (2003) p 1. Some Law Lords were becoming increasingly outspoken in their opposition to the proposed constitutional changes. Lord Lloyd referred to the changes as 'constitutional vandalism'. Lord Nicholls noted, of the efforts to emulate other democracies: 'Dull uniformity adds nothing. It is not a virtue.' 'Senior Law Lord attacks Supreme Court move' *Daily Telegraph*, 2 December 2003.

be wholly out of proportion to any benefit'. That does not appear to be the view of Lord Falconer, although with the exception of the severing of the link with the House of Lords as a legislative body, there are precious few other changes – which is a disappointment to critics, although it may well be politically wise for the substitute Lord Chancellor.

The paper rightly announces that the severing of the link with the legislature 'will reflect and enhance the independence of the Judiciary from both the legislature and the executive'.[75] It was after all following the suggestions of the senior Law Lord and the Chairman of the Bar, and reflects the rational side of independence of the judiciary. As the consultation paper continues, however, it gets caught up in the mythological side of judicial independence. After discussing the expansion of judicial responsibilities through devolution (to be transferred from the Judicial Committee to the new Supreme Court), 'the considerable growth of judicial review' and the Human Rights Act, the paper argues that: 'It is essential that our systems do all they can to minimise the danger that judges' decisions could be perceived to be politically motivated.'

While such an approach is no bad goal in the abstract, it is to be achieved by pretending nothing has changed. The reasoning is that of *Alice in Wonderland*. If we say often enough that our judges are apolitical they will be. The UK will be different, unlike the US and Germany which have Supreme Courts:

> 'to protect the written constitution. In our democracy, Parliament is supreme. There is no separate body of constitutional law which takes precedence over other law. The constitution is made up of the whole body of the laws and settled practice and convention, all of which can be amended or repealed by Parliament. Neither membership of the European Union nor devolution nor the Human Rights Act has changed the fundamental position. Such amendment or repeal would certainly be very difficult in practice and Parliament and the executive regard themselves as bound by the obligations they have taken through that legislation, but the principle remains intact.'

The principle may remain intact to formalists, but the reality is that the European Community Act 1972 and the Human Rights Act 1998 have imposed a form of fundamental law well known to American and German lawyers.

The paper continues the concern about how to appoint the new Law Lords – or whatever they will be called. It continues, however, to work on the premise that these are legal appointments of persons who have no political role. At least it manages to overcome one prejudice; while a Recommending Appointments Commission will present 'a limited number of names', this time it will be to the Prime Minister, who will consult the First Ministers in Scotland and Northern Ireland, who will make the decisions. The concern shown in the *Appointing Judges* paper over the fear that a non-lawyer might be involved (ie a layman being Secretary of State for Constitutional Affairs)

---

75. For criticism of the logic of this by a political scientist peer, see Lord Norton, 652 HL Official Report (5th series) col 122, 8 September 2003.

appears to be overcome, noting that the First Minister in Scotland is involved in the appointment of the Lord President of the Court of Session.[76]

What the Paper is clear about is that it is opposed to any suggestion that Parliament might have more confidence in the judiciary if there were confirmation hearings:

> 'The Government sees difficulty in such a procedure. MPs and lay peers would not necessarily be competent to assess the appointees' legal or judicial skills. If the intention was to assess the more general approach to issues of public importance, this would be inconsistent with the move to take the Supreme Court out of the potential political arena. One of the main intentions of the reform is to emphasise and enhance the independence of the Judiciary from both the executive and Parliament. Giving Parliament the right to decide or have a direct influence in who should be the members of the Court would cut right across that objective.'

Superficially, this sounds impressive. It, however, confuses the legitimate aspect of judicial independence – having the judges independent of executive and legislature – and accepts the more naïve side of the alleged value free aspect of judicial independence. If the judging process is value free, apolitical and isolated, why the obsession with changing the composition of the judiciary. *Appointing Judges* complains that 'the current judiciary is overwhelmingly white, male from a narrow social and educational background' so that 'the Government is committed to setting up a system of appointments, to attract suitably qualified candidates both from a wider range of social backgrounds …'[77] South Africa has similarly been broadening the composition of the bench, yet it is a little more realistic about the need for such diverse appointments. As Mr Justice Cameron of the South African Supreme Court put it: 'Judges do not enter public office as ideological virgins. They ascend the Bench with built-in and often strongly held sets of values, preconceptions, opinions and prejudices. They are invariably expressed in the decisions they give, constituting inarticulate premises in the process of judicial reasoning.'[78]

The 'inarticulate premise' argument comes from Mr Justice Holmes of the US Supreme Court more than a hundred years ago. It is a concept, however, that English lawyers have always claimed did not apply in England. Little has changed since Harold Laski wrote to Justice Holmes in March 1932, explaining why he dissented in the Scott-Donaghmore Committee, established in the wake of Hewart's *New Despotism*: 'my fight was the old one against regarding a judge as an automatic slot-machine into whom you put the statute and from whom you get a construction in which there is no articulate major premise.' The reason

---

76. The arrogance of the *Judges' Council Response to the Papers on Constitutional Reform*, n 23 above, knows few bounds. Para 164 seems to suggest that the Supreme Court Appointments Commission should consist only of Supreme Court judges, chaired by the President. Para 165 makes it clear that open applications and hearings would be inappropriate.

77. *Appointing Judges*, n 3 above, p 4.

78. Clare Hogan 'In search of justice fit for a Rainbow Nation' *The Times*, Law, 9 September 2003. And see Edwin Cameron 'Judicial Accountability in South Africa' (1988) 6 South African J Human Rights 251.

England needs a more diverse bench is because there needs to be greater diversity in the 'inarticulate premises'.[79]

While every effort is made to hide this in the discussion papers, the truth occasionally breaks through. The Supreme Court paper does admit that 'the selection of the judge to hear the case may at least in theory affect the outcome', naively adding that: 'It is impossible to tell after the event whether it has done so or not.' (What of Pinochet?[80]) The paper concludes that it is more important to have the Court sit in panels, so the Court can get through more work, than it is worrying about the remote possibility that the composition of the panel might affect the outcome. Then, sounding rather like the Pharisee, the discussion concludes: 'In the United States, appointments to the Supreme Court are more political, and therefore there is a stronger possibility that the composition of the court might affect the outcome. This is not the case in the United Kingdom.'[81]

In short, on most issues, the paper should gladden the heart of Lord Irvine – it is intensely conservative. Obviously the new Supreme Court could not sit in banc (as the US Supreme Court does – 'The reason for this is to prevent the possibility that the composition of the panel will affect the outcome of the case' – something that could not be relevant for apolitical English judges)[82] because of the need to get on with the work. Another important unarticulated reason is that to sit in banc, the orality of English proceedings would have to be curbed. That would deeply offend the Bar and cause outrage among the retired Law Lords who would attack the government for undermining the independence of the Bar. The mythology goes deep!

The same conservatism permeates the search for judges. The agenda requires appointing Supreme Court judges from the lower courts. 'The criteria for selection for members of the Court must be consistent with those for selection to the lower courts. The principles will be that selection must be made from a pool of properly qualified candidates on merit alone. The impartiality of the Judiciary must be maintained, and appointment must be free from improper influence.'[83] Memory is short. Many of the more successful appeal judges have been promoted directly from the Bar – Radcliffe, Reid, Mackay (during his period as a Lord of Appeal), all with experience of politics in the broad or narrow sense. It also ignores the American experience. Currently eight of the nine justices of the US Supreme Court were judges before they were appointed, but as a distinguished academic, and former Solicitor-General put it: 'we have

---

79. M de W Howe (ed) *Holmes-Laski Letters* (London, 1953) p 1368.
80. For a discussion of how the various panels affected the outcome in *Pinochet* see Stevens, n 9 above, pp 107–112. In particular, see the alleged observation of Lord Bingham, then Lord Chief Justice, when he heard the two South African liberals – Hoffmann and Steyn – were to sit: 'Well, that's two votes against.' Stevens, n 9 above, p 110. And see Lord Steyn's later observations about the internment of al Quaeda suspects at Guantanamo.
81. Supreme Court, n 2 above, para 52.
82. *Supreme Court*, n 2 above, para 51.
83. *Supreme Court*, n 2 above, para 47.

never had so many Justices with previous judicial experience, or such an undistinguished Supreme Court.'[84]

The paper, as one would expect of a British document, is concerned with titles for the new Supreme Court judges, who will no longer be members of the legislative House of Lords. It makes sensible suggestions for consultation with authorities in Scotland and Northern Ireland and makes intelligent proposals for filtering cases to the new Court. It – and the Appointments paper – raises one other significant issue. One of the reasons for having as many as 12 judges in the final court of appeal is 'to allow for the continued release of members of the Court to undertake other functions such as the chairing of public enquiries'.[85] Lord Falconer, in his introduction to *Appointing Judges*, explained that judges 'are very often entrusted to chair major inquiries whenever an impartial, independent investigation is required'.[86]

As explained earlier, the regular use of judges as chairs of 'independent' inquiries is relatively recent, with the Tribunals of Enquiry Act 1921 encouraging them and the period of judicial quiescence after 1945 giving legitimacy to the process. In those days, judges were active in pay awards, industrial disputes, colonial misadventures and the like. With a far more activist judiciary over the last 35 years, the system may well be ripe for re-examination, as Lord Bingham has noted.[87] This is especially true as the Parliamentary Committee system has developed. The recent Report on Higher Education by the Select Committee on Education of the House of Commons fulfils what would have been a Royal Commission in former days. The House of Commons Foreign Affairs Committee would be the right place to discuss whether the UK should have gone to war in Iraq. It may be appropriate for Lord Hutton to handle a more factual inquiry, like the circumstances surrounding the death of Dr Kelly, but the demands from Ian Duncan Smith and Charles Kennedy for a judicial inquiry into the causes of war would have been an inappropriate use of the judges now the judiciary has a more central role in political life through its judicial work. Perhaps closer to the line is Lord Saville's Bloody Sunday Inquiry, although that too may be justified as a factual inquiry, although one now predicted to take eight years and cost £200 million. Over the line were the Scott Inquiry on Arms to Iraq which more appropriately belonged to the Foreign Affairs Committee and the Lawrence Inquiry which went far beyond the inquiry

---

84. See, for instance, Lord Lester in a recent debate in the new Supreme Court: 'The quality of independence is well provided by judges drawn from the independent Bar, for the Bar is a profession of self-governing and inner-directed individuals, trained to be robustly independent. But the Bar still lacks diversity and it has no monopoly for providing judges with such qualities. Judges and barristers need to recognise that experience of advocacy is not a necessary condition for a good judge. The qualities needed can be well provided on the basis of wider professional experience beyond the Bar, including solicitors, those who have chaired tribunals or who have been distinguished academics and civil servants.' 652 HL Official Report (5th series) col 113, 8 September 2003.

85. *Supreme Court*, n 2 above, para 31.

86. *Supreme Court*, n 2 above, p 3.

87. See also Lord Morris of Aberavon, discussing the Scarman and MacPherson Inquiries: 'When a judge enters the marketplace of public affairs outside his court and throws coconuts, he is likely to have the coconuts thrown back at him. If one values the standing of the judiciary ... the less they are used the better it will be.' 648 HL Official Report (5th series) col 883, 21 May 2003.

into a tragic death and undistinguished police work to a political analysis of racism and the defects in the police service. The Home Affairs Committee would have been a far better venue. So too the government was right to refuse a judicial inquiry into its handling of the 'Foot and Mouth' crisis. That was a political issue requiring political analysis.

It is ironic that a series of documents that insist that the judiciary and politics live in totally different systems and never the twain shall meet should offer the judges on the sacrificial altar of public inquiries, which inevitably have a greater or lesser political content. Yet there is a theme. To Conservatives, these consultation papers will seem dangerously radical. Yet, in so many ways they are immensely conservative and unimaginative, too often reflecting the completion of Victorian reforms, rather than fulfilling the claims of modernisation, so beloved of New Labour.

A Supreme Court for the United Kingdom?

Brenda Hale
House of Lords

The Government's Consultation Paper[1] does not have a question mark in its title. It does not purport to be a serious discussion of the role of a Supreme Court in a democracy.[2] This is scarcely to be expected of such a document or its respondents, so I propose to respond in its own terms rather than on the loftier plane usually adopted by contributors to this journal. More unexpectedly, the Consultation Paper does not even put forward a serious set of options to consider. At the Law Commission,[3] we always had (at least a metaphorical) question mark in our title because we almost always put forward two options which do not appear in this consultation: the 'do nothing' and the 'let's abolish it' options. Both have a lot to be said for them here.

'DO NOTHING'

'Do nothing' is the product of the 'if it's not (very) broke, don't fix it' mentality. Such pragmatism is usually very attractive to the English (the Scots, having a greater adherence to doctrine and principle, may not agree). What does it really matter if our highest court happens to be a committee of the upper house of our legislature? The upper house no longer interferes in what the Law Lords do and the Law Lords have committed themselves to a self-denying ordinance which means that they decreasingly interfere in what the upper house does.[4] Leaving things as they are avoids the need to resolve some tricky little conundrums. These will seem of small importance to those whose minds are set on higher things but are remarkably important to those of us who work or litigate in the courts.

Prime amongst these is the anomaly that civil appeals to the House of Lords in England and Wales require leave, either from the Court of Appeal or from the House, while most civil appeals in Scotland do not. One of my more notable failures in the House of Lords is the English half of *Pearce v Governing Body of Mayfield Secondary School; MacDonald v Advocate General for Scotland*.[5] My guess is that Ms Pearce would not have been given leave to appeal had her

---

1. Department for Constitutional Affairs *Constitutional Reform: a Supreme Court for the United Kingdom* CP 11/03, July 2003 ('CP').

2. Cf President Aharon Barak 'Foreword: A Judge on Judging: The Role of a Supreme Court in a Democracy' (2002) 116 Harv LR 19 and the numerous sources cited there.

3. Of which I was a member from 1 May 1984 to 31 December 1993.

4. CP, n 1 above, para 34; but the CP makes clear that they are still much in demand for chairing important committees and similar work.

5. [2003] UKHL 34; [2003] ICR 937.

case not raised exactly the same point (whether discrimination against homosexuals falls within the Sex Discrimination Act 1975) as did Mr MacDonald's. Now that they have both lost, and indeed the law may be thought by some to be in a worse state than it was before the House of Lords got their hands on it, getting leave may seem a mixed blessing.

But in principle how can such discrimination against the litigators of England and Wales be justified? The Consultation Paper is in a quandary.[6] Removing it by imposing a leave requirement on the Scots would obviously be controversial with them. Removing it by removing the leave requirement from the English and Welsh would be a disaster. It would run counter to the now almost universal requirement of permission to appeal in civil cases. Judging by the number of unsuccessful applications for leave to appeal to the Lords which are routinely made to the Court of Appeal, it would swamp the court. Above all, it would contradict the basic principle upon which the House has selected cases, at least in recent times. The criterion for granting permission to appeal to the Court of Appeal is either that an appeal has a 'real prospect of success' or that 'there is some other compelling reason' why an appeal should be heard. The criterion for making a second tier appeal is more stringent: the case must raise an important point of principle or practice or there must be some other compelling reason why an appeal should be heard.[7] The House of Lords applies a similar test in granting leave to appeal to them: a real prospect that the Court of Appeal has got it wrong is not enough. As the senior Law Lord put it before he joined them, the House of Lords 'dines a la carte'. The real criterion is whether it is something important that they fancy doing. If it is, they may take the case even if there is no real prospect of success. A good example is *Pretty v Director of Public Prosecutions*,[8] on whether there is a human right to be helped to commit suicide: the appeal had no chance of success but raised issues about which the Law Lords understandably wanted to have their say.

There are other less serious practical questions, like what to call the Supreme Court for England and Wales when its title is usurped by the United Kingdom body,[9] and what to call the Law Lords when they are no longer real Lords, but should not be seen as in any way inferior to the non-Lords in both the English and Scottish systems who use the title.[10] These would all be avoided by doing nothing.

ABOLISH IT

On the other hand, all these problems would also be avoided by the other undiscussed option: abolition without replacement. Devolution issues could remain, along with overseas appeals, in the Judicial Committee of the Privy Council. There is no right of appeal to the House of Lords from the Scottish

6.   CP, n 1 above, paras 53–56.
7.   Access to Justice Act 1999, s 55(1). Only the Court of Appeal can grant such permission.
8.   [2001] UKHL 61; [2002] 1 AC 800.
9.   CP, n 1 above, para 58.
10. CP, n 1 above, para 59.

criminal courts, so removing that (heavily restricted) right in England and Wales and Northern Ireland would remove what might be seen as a discrimination against the Scots. The excuse for this has always been that Scots criminal law is so different from criminal law in the rest of the United Kingdom that it should be left to its own specialist devices uninterfered with by the English, Welsh and Irish. This raises the legal system's equivalent of the West Lothian question: if the Scots can interfere in English criminal law why cannot the English interfere in the Scots'? Whatever the differences in detail, the fundamental principles of criminal liability ought not to be different each side of the border. But the Consultation Paper does not even question this: the only jurisdictional change proposed is to take over the Privy Council's jurisdiction over devolution issues.[11]

The main argument for retaining the House of Lords' jurisdiction over ordinary civil cases is also that there should be uniformity of approach. This is particularly so in the interpretation of the many statutes (such as the Sex Discrimination Act 1975) which apply throughout the United Kingdom, but also in the development of those areas of the common law in which the principles are thought or assumed to be the same (such as the law of negligence).

I am somewhat sceptical of this argument. There are probably all sorts of differences in interpretation, subtle variations in formulations of common law principles, from case to case and court to court all over the country, let alone as between England, Scotland and Northern Ireland. Certainly, there can be subtle differences of approach between the Law Lords from different countries, even if they all concur in the result: the speeches of Lord Hope and Lord Clyde in *MacFarlane v Tayside Health Board*[12] are interesting in their attempts to accommodate the recent developments made by the House of Lords in the English law of negligence within the conceptual framework to which they were accustomed.

The opportunity to correct these rarely arises and then only randomly. Cases only go to court at all, let alone on appeal, if one of the parties wants them to.[13] The way cases are decided depends very largely on how they are formulated by the parties and argued by their lawyers. The search for an appealable point (bearing in mind the number of things an appeal court will not do) means that the dispute which reaches the Court of Appeal, let alone the House of Lords, often bears little resemblance to the one decided by the trial judge months if not years earlier. Few lawyers do much comparative research (they have neither the time nor the resources nor are they invariably thanked for it by any court short of the House of Lords). It is very rare indeed for the Court of Appeal to have Scottish authorities cited to it. But if they are, the Court treats them with great respect and tries to avoid inconsistent results. My suspicion is that English cases are also rarely cited north of the border. If serious anomalies do arise, it is the role of the two Law Commissions to sort them out.[14] Nor are differences necessarily deplored. Nearly ten years of

---

11. CP, n 1 above, paras 19–21.
12. [2000] 2 AC 59; 2000 SC (HL) 1. For a typically trenchant Scottish attack on Lord Steyn's 'person on the underground' test, see Professor J Thomson 'Abandoning the law of delict' (2000) 6 SLT 43–45.
13. Thus, eg, the House of Lords were not able to express their opinions on the difficult issues raised by the case of the conjoined twins (*Re A (children) (conjoined twins)* [2000] 4 All ER 961), surely one of the most important ever to have reached the courts.
14. Law Commissions Act 1965, s 3(1).

statutory co-operation with the Scottish Law Commission did from time to time give the impression that its real role was to preserve the principled purity of Scots law from the onslaughts of the impure English rather than to achieve the harmonisation between the two systems which the Law Commissions Act 1965 envisaged. Now that so much Scots law is devolved to the Scottish Parliament, the case for treating it in the same way as the criminal law is stronger.

The strongest case for uniformity can be made in relation to United Kingdom legislation of constitutional significance, principally the Human Rights Act 1998 and European Union legislation. Hence I shall return to this when putting forward my own option for change.

Before turning to the Government's option, I should acknowledge that the other argument against abolition lies in the manifest deficiencies of the Court of Appeal (at least in its civil division where I sat). We worked under considerable pressure of time (so of course do the Lords, but they can choose how much work to take). The quality of our decisions was heavily dependent on the quality of the arguments before us, and this is very variable (while I assume that it is much less so before the Lords). Above all, the Court sits in approximately 11 constitutions each week. Inevitably members do not always know what the others are doing. The office tries to alert members but they do not always know exactly what points will be raised in any appeal and therefore what may become the *ratio decidendi* of any case. There is a real risk of outright inconsistency, let alone more subtle differences in approach. Yet each of our decisions is binding on the lower courts and, more significantly, upon every other constitution of the Court. Of course, distinguishing the apparently undistinguishable binding decision is the great skill which the common law has given to legal reasoning. But some decisions are bound to defeat them. The Court of Appeal would have to work out a way of resolving mistakes and inconsistencies if there were no House of Lords to do it for them. But this is not impossible: the Court of Appeal already sits in special constitutions (special either in status or in numbers or both) for especially important cases. In many ways this would be a preferable method of sorting out discrepancies than waiting for a case which the parties thought worth taking to the Lords and the Lords wanted to take. Of course the Court may fall into error, but the House of Lords does not seek to correct all the Appeal Court's errors.

There is, therefore, a good case for abolition, just as there was in 1873. The difference between then and now, however, lies in our international commitments, particularly to the European Union and the European Convention on Human Rights. It could well be said that final resolution of the issues they raise should not be left to the final courts in each part of the United Kingdom.

DO A LITTLE SOMETHING

The next option is doing something, but not very much. That is the one to which the Government is committed. There are two good declared reasons for doing something. First, it is undoubtedly anomalous to have our highest appeal court as part of the legislature.[15] The more active and relevant the

---

15 CP, n 1 above, para 2.

House of Lords becomes, the more apparent that will be. Removing the Law Lords also deals with one of the questions raised by the reform of the House of Lords, which is a far more urgent and important constitutional issue than any of those discussed in the July Consultation Papers.[16] Secondly, it is undoubtedly inconvenient to have the Law Lords cluttering up the House of Lords.[17] They do not have the space or the facilities they need and the Lords need the space and facilities they do have.

There is a third reason, which is only touched on in the Consultation Paper[18] and on which the Government is not consulting at all, and that is the need to do something about the Lord Chancellor. Successive holders of the office stoutly defended his triple role as Head of the Judiciary, 'Speaker' of the House of Lords, and member of the Government.[19] There is nothing wrong with Government ministers being members of the legislature. Indeed, under our constitutional 'balance' rather than 'separation' of powers, it is the convention that they must be. The objection is to his also being a Judge and Head of the Judiciary. The main plank in the case for his judicial role was blown apart by Lord Steyn:

> 'The proposition that the Lord Chancellor represents the judiciary in the Cabinet reveals the fragility of the argument. The judiciary does not need a "representative" in the Cabinet. In no other constitutional democracy does the judiciary have a "representative" in the Cabinet. In any event, in respect of all matters discussed in Cabinet, including all aspects of policies in regard to civil and criminal justice, the Lord Chancellor is subject to collective responsibility. He cannot therefore act as a representative of the judiciary.'[20]

If he is no longer a judge, he cannot be top judge (and the Consultation Paper acknowledges this[21]). Quite how one separates out the things he does in that capacity and the things he does as a Minister of the Crown will be hard to fathom: where, for example, do his functions in making court rules and approving practice directions fit? Perhaps the Government will in due course think that some specialist consultation on these issues will be helpful, but that is another story. Back to the Supreme Court: once it is a separately constituted body there would be no case at all for including the Lord Chancellor among its members.

The proposal, then, is for a Supreme Court doing exactly what the Appellate Committee does now, together with the devolution issues handled by the Judicial Committee of the Privy Council at present. So along with the European, human rights and other constitutional type cases, it will continue to hear

---

16. Although the CP, n 1 above, para 37, touches on whether those who have reached the very top of the judging profession should continue to be appointed to the House.

17. CP, n 1 above, para 4.

18. CP, n 1 above, para 3.

19. The Lord Chancellor's speech writers are well qualified to take their line from the former permanent secretary, Sir Claud Shuster, in a 1943 memorandum cited by R Stevens *The Independence of the Judiciary: the View from the Lord Chancellor's Office* (Oxford: Oxford University Press, 1993) p 3; see also R Stevens *The English Judges: Their Role in the Changing Constitution* (Oxford: Hart Publishing, 2002) p 91.

20. Lord Steyn 'The Case for a Supreme Court' (2002) 118 LQR 382.

21. CP, n 1 above, para 61.

ordinary civil and criminal cases, including among the former (but not the latter, because the court below must certify that a criminal case involves a point of law of general public importance) the cases which are important only to the parties and their insurers: for example, the 'big money' shipping and commercial cases which used to dominate its lists.[22] In other words, it will, if it chooses, continue to do the same sort of job that we do.

It will also be done by the same people, and the preferred option for the future seems to be that it will continue to be done by the same sort of people: in other words, by promoting serving judges (and usually serving appellate judges). The Consultation Paper nods in the direction of including other distinguished lawyers but then suggests that the better way to increase professional diversity amongst the judges is by recruiting from more diverse backgrounds lower down the scale.[23] This is a clear indication, not only that the role of the court will remain just as it is now, but also that it is expected that the court will go on performing that role in just the same way that it does now. The case for members of a *first tier*, error-correcting, appeal court having had experience as a trial judge is much stronger than the case for members of a *second tier*, points of important principle-resolving, Supreme Court. They do not need to have the same knowledge of what it is like at the sharp end. By then the issues have been refined into points of seemingly purest principle.

Another related indication that nothing much will change is the discussion of whether the court should continue to sit in panels rather than en banc. Sitting en banc avoids the risk of the composition of the panel affecting the outcome of the case (one only has to think of the *Pinochet* saga[24] to accept that there is a risk). The Consultation Paper suggests that appointments to the United States' Supreme Court are 'more political', and thus there would be a stronger possibility there that the composition of a panel might affect the outcome, but is satisfied that: 'This is not the case in the United Kingdom.'[25] The super-cynical might wonder whether there was an element of chicken and egg here: if the court always sits en banc, a politician wanting to achieve particular outcomes might be more tempted to make political appointments;[26] if the court itself determines who hears what case, there is less to be gained by trying to achieve a political majority.

The Consultation Paper suggests that the method of appointment should be the equivalent of that now being proposed for first judicial appointments:[27] on the recommendation of an appointments commission drawn from each of the three jurisdictions (each of which will by then, it is assumed, have their own judicial appointments board or commission).[28] An interesting passage

22. A good recent example is *Lloyds TSB General Insurance Holdings Ltd v Lloyds Bank Group Insurance Co Ltd* [2003] UKHL 48.
23. CP, n 1 above, para 46.
24. *R v Bow Street Magistrate, ex p Pinochet Ugarte* [2000] 1 AC 61 at 119, 147.
25. CP, n 1 above, para 52.
26. There is an alarming account of the extent to which Senate confirmation hearings have become politicised around the issue of abortion in J Toobin 'Advice and Dissent: The fight over the President's judicial nominations' *The New Yorker*, 26 May 2003, p 42.
27. Department for Constitutional Affairs *Constitutional reform: a new way of appointing judges* CP 10/03, July 2003.
28. CP 10/03, n 27 above, para 43.

rejects the idea (which has some prominent supporters here) of parliamentary confirmation along the lines of the Senate hearings in the United States.[29] But the paper argues that appointments should remain in the hands of a minister accountable to Parliament. What exactly does this mean? So far as I am aware, neither the Prime Minister nor the Lord Chancellor is ever questioned in the House about individual appointments. The Consultation Paper on judicial appointments is careful to refer to ministerial accountability to Parliament 'for the appointments process'.[30] But it is only quite recently that the Lord Chancellor's Department has had ministers in the House of Commons, which is the true source of parliamentary accountability unless and until the House of Lords becomes at least a partially elected body. It is even more recently that its work has become subject to select committee scrutiny in the same way as that of other departments. Yet I think it is important that the process of appointing judges, if not the individual appointments made, is subject to some sort of democratic accountability. Otherwise it will be much more difficult to introduce innovations in criteria and procedures: just as there is a risk that too much political control will lead to too much politics in the appointments made, there is also a risk that too little public and democratic accountability will lead to even greater control by the existing judiciary. What Helena Kennedy called the 'potential for cloning'[31] would be just as strong if not stronger. The new proposals do have the potential for increasing diversity on the Bench at all levels and for that reason I, for one, support them.[32] But I would go further …

ANOTHER WAY?

If we are to have all the upheaval this will entail, is it not worth contemplating doing something a little more radical? President Barak, of the Supreme Court of Israel, says this of the role of a Supreme Court:

> 'The primary concern of the supreme court in a democracy is not to correct individual mistakes in lower court judgments. That is the job of courts of appeal. The supreme court's concern is broader, systemwide corrective action. This corrective action should focus on two main issues: bridging the gap between law and society, and protecting democracy.'[33]

By 'bridging the gap between law and society', he meant developing the law to meet the changing needs of society, in partnership with the legislature. By 'protecting democracy', he meant protecting not only formal democracy but substantive democracy in the shape of fundamental human rights, in particular to dignity and equality for all.

29. CP 10/03, n 27 above, para 45.
30. CP 10/03, n 27 above, para 38.
31. H Kennedy *Eve was Framed: Women and British Justice* (1993) p 267. The Commission for Judicial Appointments also refers to the 'cloning effect' in its *Annual Report* (2003) para 4.31.
32. B Hale 'Equality in the Judiciary: A Tale of Two Continents' 10th Pilgrim Fathers' Lecture, 24 October 2003.
33. Barak, n 2 above, at 28–29.

It should be emphasised that a Supreme Court can undertake some such strategic role without having any greater powers of judicial review of the legislation of the United Kingdom Parliament than is already entailed by the European Communities Act 1972 and the Human Rights Act 1998. Nor is such a role incompatible with continuing to practise our traditional judicial restraint in questioning the merits of administrative decisions.

What it could mean is taking away the ordinary criminal and civil cases, no matter how much money is involved, and leaving them to the domestic courts of each jurisdiction. Only cases of real constitutional importance would go to the Supreme Court. These would include the ground-breaking human rights cases, cases about our relationship with Europe or the rest of the world, including important cases interpreting international treaties or concepts such as sovereign immunity, and devolution cases. They might also include those public law cases which raised points of real significance even if the Human Rights Act 1998 was not invoked: the general approach to tax avoidance schemes or the amenability of Government ministers to sanctions for contempt of court might be examples. The Supreme Court might also take more ordinary cases, in both private and criminal law, but only on the basis that a serious inconsistency had arisen between two or more jurisdictions of the United Kingdom in the interpretation of United Kingdom legislation or the development of the common law on a subject where the law ought to be the same throughout the realm. The criteria would have to be carefully thought through and laid down in an authoritative source. This would probably have to be legislation, whether primary or delegated, because it would be difficult for the Court to do this for itself through a practice direction. But the Court would still choose which cases to take within those criteria. The appeal courts of the three jurisdictions would lose the power to send cases to the Supreme Court.

If that were done, there would be a much stronger case for changing the composition in a radical way. Robert Stevens is a believer in the virtues of judicial restraint, but he has also said of a new Supreme Court:

> 'There would of course be places for former Lords Justices of Appeal from the Court of Appeal. To have it totally staffed in this way, however, would be a disaster. As a distinguished American professor of constitutional law said recently of the Supreme Court of the United States: "we have never had a court with more judicial experience [eight of the nine judges held prior judicial office] and we have never had a worse Supreme Court".'[34]

I am not qualified to judge that issue, but I note that judicial restraint is not incompatible with fearless interpretation and application of the existing law. Stevens points out with obvious approval that none of the nine Justices who decided *Brown v Board of Education*[35] had had previous judicial experience before appointment to the Supreme Court. Whether he would take the same view now that it has become clear that the new court will continue to perform the same role as the old Appellate Committee, I do not know. But it is commonplace elsewhere in the world for members of the Supreme Court,

---

34. Stevens (2002), n 19 above, p 152.
35. 347 US 483 (1955).

whatever its constitutional role, to come from a much wider range of professional backgrounds and experience than our Law Lords do. They may come from the lower judiciary, but also from the Chief Prosecutor's or Attorney-General's Office, or other public service, or the universities, or private practice. The 'poacher turned game-keeper' argument can apply just as much to former Government officers as it can to private practitioners. Members may even come direct from politics, as Robert Stevens controversially suggests they might do here.

If the composition of the court were widened in this way, the outcome might be a change in the style of argument and judgment. Our judgments at all appellate levels rely heavily on reciting the competing ingenious arguments of counsel and often extensive quotation from decided cases. To some extent, courts which are bound by those authorities cannot avoid this. But such judgments can often seem highly technical and opaque to outsiders. It is easy to lose sight of the real reasons for the decision. To an informed and intelligent non-lawyer, the judgments of the European Court of Human Rights are much easier to read and understand than are the judgments of the House of Lords.[36] The same has also been said of the judgments of Supreme Courts elsewhere in the common law world. It is hard for those of us who spend our lives reading (or writing) English judgments to look at them through others' eyes. But if the comment has any force at all, it would be hard to get a judiciary which has learned its trade in the more technical areas of English law to change the way it expresses its reasoning, let alone the style of that reasoning.

If our Supreme Court had a different, more explicitly constitutional, role and in time a rather different sort of membership, might there come a time when the ordinary citizen might read, understand and appreciate its decisions – in other words, when the Court became accessible and accountable to the public in a way we cannot imagine now?

---

36. N Johnson *Reshaping the British Constitution* (forthcoming) ch 11.

Brave New World – The new Supreme Court and judicial appointments

Sir Thomas Legg KCB QC*

PART 1 – THE NEW SUPREME COURT

First and foremost, I welcome the move to establish a new Supreme Court for the United Kingdom, separate from the House of Lords. I have favoured this for years, and I regard the Government's proposals as a real step forward. It is a piece of long-unfinished business nearly achieved by the mighty reformers of 1873–75. Their shades must rejoice to see it at last being tackled. All my other comments hereafter should be seen in that positive context.

Jurisdiction

The jurisdiction of the new Court should, in principle, be universal and uniform across the United Kingdom, and I agree that it should include devolution. I am pretty unimpressed by the consultative paper's limp arguments, as they seem to me,[1] for retaining the present anomalous arrangements for Scottish appeals. But I recognise that this is part of a wider political and constitutional difficulty about Scotland, from which Ministers will have to extract the least irrational answer that they can.

Predictably, but I think regrettably, the paper proposes no change to the non-devolution jurisdiction of the Judicial Committee, stating that the Committee 'does not belong to the UK alone'.[2] I think this is dubious, and I have never fully bought the argument that we are somehow bound to provide an elegant court and very senior judges to determine cases for the benefit of other independent and self-governing nations, just because they want us to.

* This paper is adapted from two lectures delivered at the Cambridge Centre for Public Law 'Judicial Reform Conference; Function, Appointment and Structure', held at the Faculty of Law on 4 October 2003. There, I was speaking in my capacity as a consultant to Clifford Chance, and expressing their provisional opinion on the Department of Constitutional Affairs' consultation papers. I was also speaking from my experience as a former member of the Lord Chancellor's Department, and one who spent the best part of 20 years working on the appointment of judges. As then, I declare both interests. Here, I have accepted the editors' invitation to summarise my contribution to the Cambridge conference in the form of a reflective overview of the issues. I have tried to adhere to their injunction that the paper should be published, as far as possible, in the form the lectures were originally delivered, although their order has been reversed to comply with the focus of the present compilation.

1. Department for Constitutional Affairs *Constitutional reform: a Supreme Court for the United Kingdom* CP 11/03, July 2003 ('CP') paras 26, 27 and 56.
2. CP, n 1 above, para 28.

The historical basis is now very ancient history indeed, and the judge-power requirements of the Judicial Committee impinge seriously on those of Britain's highest court, which must be our main concern. I personally favour a polite declaration of independence. If this is not yet felt to be practical politics, I hope at least that the Judicial Committee – which is very capably managed – will be run so as to minimise calls on the judges of the new Supreme Court.

Appointment of judges

I will deal below with the Government's proposals regarding the appointment of judges in England and Wales. The same general principles should apply to the appointment of judges to the new Supreme Court. But here, of course, we are dealing with a United Kingdom court, and one placed at the summit and confluence of all three separate jurisdictions. A special system for appointment is therefore needed. In my view, the judges of the Supreme Court should be appointed on the advice of the Prime Minister, after consultation with the Ministers most closely concerned, that is to say the Secretary of State for Constitutional Affairs, the First Minister of Scotland, and the First and Deputy Ministers of Northern Ireland. The Prime Minister should act on the advice of a special commission consisting of the chairmen of the three United Kingdom Appointments Commissions. This special commission should be free to consult in turn whomever it thinks fit, save that it should be required in al cases to consult the President of the Supreme Court itself, the Lord Chief Justice of England and Wales, the Lord President of Scotland, and the Lord Chief Justice of Northern Ireland. After these consultations, the special commission should submit to the Prime Minister a list of not less than two and not more than four names, in order of preference. The Prime Minister should be free to recommend any of the listed names to the Queen. He should also be free to reject the whole list and ask for another. However, if he does so, he should be required to state the fact publicly, though without necessarily giving his reasons.

My next point may seem slightly more heretical. Notwithstanding the difficulties mentioned in the paper, I think there is now a strong case for requiring the candidate selected by the Prime Minister to be confirmed by a joint committee of both Houses of Parliament before his or her name is submitted to the Queen. This need not necessarily involve a public hearing, as happens in the Judiciary Committee of the United States Senate.

The fact that MPs and peers are not competent to judge the professional qualities of the candidates is not relevant to this issue. The same will be true of the lay members of the judicial appointments commissions across the United Kingdom. Parliamentary confirmation will not bring the new Court into the political arena any more than it will be anyway, and may help to keep it out. The question is one of transparency and, above all, legitimacy – of which the new Supreme Court will need as much as it can get. It is not just fitting, but, I believe, necessary that both the other two branches of government, that is the legislature as well as the executive, should concur in the appointment of the nation's most senior judges. This is especially so since the legislature is the only branch of government with power to remove a senior judge.

Number of judges

My guess is that, even if the requirements of the Judicial Committee can be slimmed a bit, it will still be preferable to increase the number of judges of the new Court from the existing 12 to about 15, so as to reduce, without altogether avoiding, the need for part-time assistance. Nowadays we have to reckon that, at any one time, at least one or two of our most senior judges will be dealing with inquiries or other extra-curricular duties.

Control of case-load

I think it imperative that the new Court should have full power to determine its own case-load, except in devolution cases. There should be no exceptions to the requirement of leave from the Supreme Court itself, which should apply equally to Scottish civil appeals as to all others from all parts of the United Kingdom. I would like to see the new Court being sparing in granting leave, but I think that should be left to the judicial policy of the Court itself, and not be fettered by Parliament.

In banc or panels

There is much to be said for the United States Supreme Court's practice of sitting always in banc. In practice, however, the new United Kingdom Supreme Court will no doubt continue to sit normally in panels of five judges. But this raises a question which is not discussed in the paper, namely who is to have the important power of deciding the composition of the panels? I see no obvious alternative to entrusting this power to the President of the Court, and this is what the paper probably assumes. Recent history has shown that this may prove a more sensitive and onerous responsibility than in the past.

Relationship with the House of Lords

I fully endorse the Government's proposal to separate completely the new Supreme Court and its judges from the House of Lords, and I think it should be followed through. Accordingly my preference would be for the existing Law Lords to lose the right to sit and vote in the House of Lords while serving on the new Court, as should any future judges of the new Court who happen to be peers. There should, I submit, be no presumption that retired judges of the Supreme Court will be appointed to the House of Lords. I see no objection, however, to occasional appointments, say of a retired President of the Court, provided that they are genuinely exceptional. I am inclined to add that I think it might be best to extend the bar on sitting and voting in the House of Lords to all holders of high judicial office, such as the Lord Chief Justice, the Master of the Rolls and the Lord President. I know and respect the arguments the other way, but it really does seem desirable to take this opportunity to make a clean break between the legislature and the judiciary. After all, that is essentially the principle on which the Government proposes to abolish the office of Lord Chancellor.

Administration

I agree with the paper that the administration of the Court should come within the responsibility of the Department for Constitutional Affairs, whose Permanent Secretary should accordingly be the Accounting Officer for the Court. That will require him to have a special relationship with the President. However, the statute establishing the Court should provide for an office of Registrar of the Court, to be its judicial and administrative manager, under the direction of the President. The Registrar should be legally-qualified, and should hold office, like the judges, during good behaviour – though no doubt with an earlier retiring age.

Accommodation

The accommodation of the new Court has rightly attracted a lot of attention. The Court will be the head and showcase for the whole judiciary of the United Kingdom, and it really matters that it should be worthy of its position. The size and quality of the Court's building, and its equipment and facilities, not just for the judges and their staff, but for litigants, practitioners and spectators, should meet all reasonable needs in the modern age.

Implications for the court structure in England and Wales

The establishment of the new Supreme Court will call for some consequential re-carpentering of the court structure in England and Wales. The new Court will be 'the Supreme Court of the United Kingdom'. This means, as the paper implies, that we must change the title of the existing Supreme Court of Judicature of England and Wales – which of course was only given that title in 1873–75 on the footing, later changed, that it was going to be the true Supreme Court now at last being established. The existing Supreme Court, which comprises the Court of Appeal, the High Court and the Crown Court, would now be better re-named 'the Superior Court of Judicature', or something of the kind. Its existence as a unified court has always been somewhat tenuous. Almost the only purpose of the collective concept has been to make the Lord Chancellor its President. It might usefully now be dropped altogether, and the three constituent courts, together with the county courts and the magistrates' courts, be governed by a single Courts Act.

But, if we take that route, it will I think be important to provide that the Lord Chief Justice, as the Lord Chancellor's presumptive successor, is clearly designated as the head of the judiciary of England and Wales, and the president of all the courts.

PART 2 – APPOINTMENT OF JUDGES

In approaching the appointment of judges in England and Wales, I am not seeking to defend some traditional *ancien regime*. On the contrary, the present arrangements are a relatively modern development. They only emerged in the late 1970s and early 1980s, and they were themselves radical reforms in their day. They were never conceived as finished and set in concrete. The system has been continuously developed and improved ever since it began, not least by the establishment of the present Commission on Judicial Appointments headed by Sir Colin Campbell, and that process is still going on. The reforms now proposed should be seen as part of that evolution.

The Government's consultation paper is based on the political judgment that, although the quality of our judiciary is very high, there is such a deficit of credibility in the way they are selected that public confidence requires new methods which are more transparent and independent. Realistically, I accept that as axiomatic, especially since in any event the concurrently proposed abolition of the office of Lord Chancellor requires major changes in this field in any event.

However, to balance my welcome to further reform in this field, I enter one caution. With judges, we are not talking about ordinary jobs, but about state officials who are for good reasons virtually unsackable, and who yet are armed with, and daily exercise, formidable powers over their fellow citizens. In appointing them, there is little room for experiment and none for political correctness for its own sake. Above and beyond all the issues about qualifications, criteria, procedures and institutions, what really matters is the spirit in which those concerned with this work approach it. It is a task not to be enterprised unadvisedly or lightly.

Merit and process

It is commonly agreed that judges should be appointed on merit. But there are two separate sets of issues about this, which often get run together in discussion. To some extent the consultation paper runs them together. But they are best kept separate.

The first set of issues is about *merit* – what we mean by it, what kind of people we want as judges, and on what principles their claims should be evaluated. The second set of issues is about *process* – finding the right institutions and procedures to apply these principles. The consultation paper says that it is dealing with *process*.[3] As I see it, however, the paper does in fact trench onto at least two important aspects of *merit*. That is not necessarily wrong, but we need to disentangle the issues and get out clearly on the table what those aspects are, and what they may mean for the kind of judges who will be appointed in future. Then the proposals on process can be looked at separately.

Against that background, I would pick out of the paper three points on merit, and then three on process. I should make it clear that I am here confining my remarks to senior appointments, especially to the High Court Bench and above.

Merit

THE NEED TO PRESERVE JUDICIAL QUALITY

My first point is so obvious that it hardly needs dwelling on, especially as the consultation paper explicitly re-affirms it. This is the overriding need to

---

3.   See *Constitutional Reform: a new way of Appointing Judges* CP 10/03, July 2003, paras 28, 30.

preserve, and of course if possible to improve, the professional and personal quality of our judiciary. Although this is a foremost interest of all citizens, I would add one special gloss from the point of view of international commercial firms. The acknowledged excellence of the High Court Bench, especially in the commercial field, is a matter of high importance to the financial and economic interests of the country. The fact that major contracts across the world frequently provide that they shall be governed by the law of England and adjudicated in the English courts brings a huge amount of work to British lawyers, and thereby contributes to the maintenance of London as a pre-eminent global financial centre. The reason this jurisdiction is chosen is because of the reputation of our judges. So this is an area where we need to tread very carefully.

SOCIAL DIVERSIFICATION

My next two points, and my main concern about appointment on merit, arise from the paper's section on *diversity*.[4] While praising the quality of the present judiciary, the paper observes that it is 'overwhelmingly white, male and from a narrow social and educational background'. To counter this, the Government commits itself to 'opening up the system of appointments, both to attract suitably qualified candidates from a wider range of social backgrounds and from a wider range of legal practice'. So here are two separate forms of proposed widening, one *social* and the other *professional*.

'A wider range of *social* backgrounds' pretty clearly means more women and ethnic community judges. This underlying policy aim is perfectly respectable, namely that the public may well have more confidence in their judges if they are more reflective of the make-up of the community at large. The question, of course, is how much priority to give that aim over appointment of the fittest when the two aims come into conflict, as is likely to happen from time to time. The paper again casts this in terms of *process* – it speaks of affording equal opportunities to all suitably qualified candidates, and says that this will require 'fresh approaches and a major re-engineering of the processes of appointment'. However, in substance, and whatever the stated (and I am sure sincere) intention, I think that in practice the paper's words imply a different approach to *merit*.

There is a real tension between diversifying the composition of the judiciary on the one hand and appointing on merit on the other – at least on merit as we have hitherto understood it. This tension cannot be finessed away by redefining merit as somehow including reflectiveness of the community. Selection on merit can have one of at least two quite separate meanings. One of these meanings is what one might again call *maximal* merit. On this approach, there is only one candidate who is fit for appointment, namely the single candidate who is judged to be the best available. This approach leaves no room at the point of decision for supplementary policies about the social and professional make-up of the judiciary. That is the approach which has been adopted up to now. It is sometimes difficult to apply, but it has represented the underlying, and usually achievable, principle.

4.   CP, n 3 above, paras 27–29.

The other approach, which I have called *minimal* merit, is where all candidates who are judged to reach an agreed minimum standard are treated as equally qualified for appointment. The appointing authority is then entitled to select among the qualified candidates in accordance with any relevant supplementary policy, for example, about a need to have a more socially reflective judiciary, which might include more women or ethnic judges. Both of these approaches can genuinely claim to be appointment on merit, but they can lead to very different results.

The concern must be that the policy implied by the Government's consultation paper will generate so much pressure to diversify the composition of the judiciary that it will in practice lead to numerous appointments on a basis of minimal merit. Over time, that would have a substantial effect on the character of our judiciary. That is not in itself necessarily illegitimate or wrong, and its results may be acceptable. Some other countries have taken that route. But it is a policy with implications which need to be carefully considered in advance.

PROFESSIONAL DIVERSIFICATION

Then the other diversification that the paper wants to see is *professional* – in its own terms a 'wider range of legal practice' on the Bench.[5] Earlier, reciting the present system, the paper states that 'the Lord Chancellor has not ... regarded advocacy experience in itself as an essential requirement for legal appointments to judicial office'.[6] That statement is literally correct. All by itself, however, it is misleading. The reality is that hitherto, the great majority of English High Court judges have been selected on the basis that, among other qualifications, they have had long and successful careers as senior advocates. It was only recently that Lord Chancellor Irvine extended this requirement to include lawyers (typically a few solicitors) with senior litigation experience.

That reform was welcome. But this close and long-standing connection with advocacy, and more recently litigation, has given the English judges their characteristic strengths, especially in trial-handling. Their mastery of the adversarial process, learned and lived over years of courtroom warfare, their personal self-reliance and their ability and readiness to give rulings and judgments on the spot, have been a staple asset of our legal system.

Of course it can be maintained that this policy has also given our judges limitations which could be alleviated by an infusion of other kinds of legal experience. Indeed, I have myself argued for that at the appellate level. But I think we should be clear that, to the extent that we move away from eminent experience of advocacy and litigation as the usual criterion for appointment, to that extent we shall be changing the character and skills of the English Bench, especially at the first-instance level which represents the vast majority of the work of the courts. Here again, there is a real choice to be made between significantly different actual outcomes. And here again there is a special point for international commercial lawyers, who regard it as essential that our judges

5. CP, n 3 above, para 27.
6. CP, n 3 above, para 9.

maintain their justified international reputation for trial-handling of major commercial disputes.

Process

ROLE OF THE SECRETARY OF STATE

My starting point on process is that I hold that the appointment of judges is a proper function of the Executive, as in most other English-speaking countries. In our constitution, that means an accountable minister, and not an unaccountable independent commission, however impeccably composed.

Here, it is important to be clearer than the consultation paper is about the distinction between the independence of the judges and the independence of those who appoint them. Attempts to achieve absolute purity on the latter risk being self-defeating. Judicial independence rests on several pillars: law, convention, tradition, and the culture and spirit of the profession from which judges are drawn are more important than the location of the appointing authority. Certainly the appointers should be free of party political motives, as in fact they have been for many years. But the appointment of judges is properly a political act, in the broadest sense of the term, and I believe that it should be done by a political authority. Hence, my preference for a 'Recommending' Commission. Such a Commission should give the Secretary of State for Constitutional Affairs a *real* choice, for which he should take a *real* and accountable responsibility. And for my part I think it should always be the Secretary of State – the opportunity should be taken to eliminate the Prime Minister from all appointments below the new Supreme Court, except perhaps that of the Lord Chief Justice.

In this connection, I agree that the Secretary of State should be given a statutory duty to uphold and safeguard judicial independence against all comers, including of course his Cabinet colleagues.

RULES OF ENGAGEMENT

The detailed rules of engagement between the Commission and the Secretary of State are crucial. There are of course various options. My own suggestion is that the Commission should put forward a list of no fewer than two and not more than four candidates for each post, in order of the Commission's preference if it wishes. The Secretary of State should be free to advise the Queen to appoint any candidate on the list, or to reject the whole list and ask for another. However, if he rejects the whole list, he should be required to state publicly that he has done so. I accept that this might damage the credibility of the candidate ultimately appointed, at least initially, but on balance that seems a price worth paying in the wider public interest. It exercises legitimate pressure on the minister to accept the candidates recommended by the Commission.

Promotions to the High Court and Court of Appeal should be within the Commission's scope, as the Consultation Paper proposes.[7] But I think that in

7.   CP, n 3 above, para 58.

this case the Secretary of State should be required, and not just enabled, to consult the senior judiciary personally before recommending a candidate to The Queen. Of course, many appointments to the High Court, and even a very few to the Court of Appeal, require a choice to be made between appointing someone or promoting someone else. However, I would be content to leave this to the Commission to advise on.

MEMBERSHIP OF THE COMMISSION

In my view, the consultation paper has got the membership of the Commission mostly right. The method proposed for selecting the membership[8] looks reasonable, although I think that the proposal that the chairmanship might be taken by the Permanent Secretary would put him in an over-exposed position. I wonder too if it would not be right for the membership of the appointing group to be approved by Parliament.

I agree that the Commission itself should have about 15 members, and that they should include judges, lawyers and laymen in about equal proportions. On balance, and accepting that there are arguments the other way, I do not myself favour having a lay chairman of the Commission. Notwithstanding the precedent in Scotland, where differences of scale arguably amount to a difference of kind, I consider that it would be preferable for the English Commission to be chaired by the Lord Chief Justice. Of course, the Chief Justice would not be able to give continuous attention to the Commission's work, except as regards issues of principle, difficult cases, and appointments to the High Court and above. Accordingly, another senior judge should be appointed as Deputy Chairman to the Commission expressly to supervise its day-to-day business and to preside when the Lord Chief Justice cannot, as often must be the case, be present.

Judicial discipline

Finally, judicial discipline. This is a difficult and sensitive area, where the protection of the public from inadequate performance or misconduct by judges has to be balanced against the equally vital public interest in judicial independence. In my view, all three branches of government have a proper interest in the resolution of these issues, at least in serious cases. My own submission, therefore, is that the new Appointments Commission should not be involved in this function at all, and nor should the existing Commission for Judicial Appointments.

Instead I suggest that the Secretary of State should continue to receive complaints about judges, and to answer them where it is clear that there are no grounds for intervention, as it is in the majority of cases. However, the disciplinary functions hitherto vested in the Lord Chancellor should be transferred to the Lord Chief Justice, as the new head of the judiciary, acting no doubt in consultation with the Judges' Council. He would therefore deal with serious complaints worthy of investigation, whether transferred to him

8.   CP, n 3 above, paras 122–130.

by the Secretary of State or otherwise, and impose any sanctions where, after investigation, he upholds the complaint.

I would also suggest that, both in investigating and sanctioning judges, the Lord Chief Justice should be required to act in concert with the Secretary of State. This should provide the necessary element of 'outside' involvement to protect the judiciary from any charge of looking after their own.

As a further safeguard, the statutory power to remove a Circuit or District Judge for misconduct or incapacity could suitably be made exercisable only on an order approved by both Houses of Parliament. Such an order would no doubt have to be promoted by the Secretary of State at the instance of the Lord Chief Justice. This would bring the English position broadly into line with that in Scotland, and would afford even better protection for the independence of the judiciary.

Supreme Courts, independence and democratic agency

Jeremy Webber*
Canada Research Chair in Law and Society, Faculty of Law, University of Victoria;
Visiting Professor of Law, University of New South Wales

INTRODUCTION

This paper explores the reasons for the proposed abolition of the Appellate
Committee of the House of Lords and its replacement by a new Supreme Court
of the United Kingdom. It focuses on the principal justification now advanced
for the project, namely the need to institute full judicial independence. It does
so very much in the spirit of the argument recently made by Lord Steyn in
Counsel[1] (although it comes to a very different conclusion from Lord Steyn's):
even if there is a clear commitment to the reform of the United Kingdom's highest
judiciary, the nature of that reform should depend entirely on the reasons for
change. It is necessary to be clear on those reasons and to weigh them carefully.

The gist of my argument is that the invocation of judicial independence by
the principal advocates of the reform is confused and ambiguous – a confusion,
to be fair, that reflects ambiguities in the meaning and justification of judicial
independence generally. Part of my purpose, then, will be to clarify the
considerations underlying that fundamental principle, in order to determine
what constitutional mechanisms it requires. But more importantly, the language
of judicial independence is misleading, for it tends to suggest that the reform
is a simple matter of separating the judges from the legislative process based
on uncontroversial principles of constitutional propriety. In so doing, it masks
a more fundamental issue: the extent to which this reform represents a further
stage in Britain's evolution towards a constitutionally limited form of
government, one subject to full judicial review of democratic decision-making
on the basis of constitutional limitations.[2]

*   My thanks to Kate Malleson for advice early in the preparation of this paper, to
Marcia Barry and Chad Vandermolen for their able research assistance, and to Marcia
Barry for her comments on an earlier draft of this paper.
1.   Johan Steyn 'Creating a Supreme Court' *Counsel*, October 2003, 14–16 (hereinafter
Creating).
2.   Here too, Lord Steyn's 2003 article is refreshing, for he makes clear the connection
between the creation of a Supreme Court and the subjection of the British Parliament to
constitutional limitations (n 1 above, at 14), although he emphasises that the court would
still not be a Supreme Court on the United States model (at 15). In a previous article,
which to be fair focused overwhelmingly on the role of the Lord Chancellor, Lord Steyn
had suggested that he was not placing in question the supremacy of Parliament: Johan
Steyn 'The Case for a Supreme Court' (2002) 118 LQR 382 at 384 (hereinafter *Case*). It
seems clear that he is edging away from that position. For reasons I develop below, that
move is consistent with the underlying premises of his argument.

The government's consultation paper insists that this is not the purpose.[3] That, it seems to me, is disingenuous, although perhaps not intentionally so: it may be that the broader objective lurks within a conception of judicial independence accepted by reformers more or less at face value, without them realising that it is a highly distinctive form of the principle, founded on premises that are fundamentally inconsistent with continued parliamentary supremacy.

The purpose of this paper is to uncover those premises, to show that there are conceptions of judicial independence that are fully consistent with a commitment to parliamentary supremacy (those conceptions have long shaped British constitutionalism; indeed they have some claim to be the first modern conception of judicial independence), and to join the debate on the underlying issue. If the deeper issue plays the role I suggest, it deserves full discussion prior to the adoption of a new Supreme Court. The nature of the reform may be profoundly different depending on the outcome.

WHY A NEW SUPREME COURT?

Over the years, a variety of reasons have been advanced for the creation of a Supreme Court. The reasons have been complicated by their implication in broader projects of constitutional significance: the participation of the United Kingdom in European integration, the adoption of the Human Rights Act 1998,[4] legislative devolution, and the reform of the House of Lords as a legislative body. The following appear to be the principal justifications for the proposal, not simply in the government's consultation paper but more generally.

First, the devolution of legislative authority to Scotland and Wales raised the question of who should police the jurisdiction conferred, who should adjudicate disputes arising between different levels of government. As the highest court in the land, already exercising jurisdiction on disputes arising under the law of each jurisdiction, the Appellate Committee of the House of Lords[5] may have been the most obvious answer, but the balance of representation among its full-time members was not conducive to the role. It was and is a predominantly English court. Out of 12 full-time members (the Lords of Appeal in Ordinary), by convention only two have a background in the law of Scotland and one in the law of Northern Ireland (although it is possible to supplement the bench with other members of the House of Lords who have held high judicial office).[6] In contrast, the Judicial Committee of the Privy

---

3.   Department for Constitutional Affairs *Constitutional Reform: A Supreme Court for the United Kingdom* CP 11/03 (July 2003) p 8 (also p 21): 'There is no proposal to create a Supreme Court on the US model with the power to overturn legislation.' See also Lord Bingham of Cornhill 'A New Supreme Court for the United Kingdom' The Constitution Unit Spring Lecture 2002, 1 May 2002, p 10.
4.   Human Rights Act 1998, c 42 (UK).
5.   Given the potential confusion between the House of Lords in its judicial and legislative capacities, I will follow Le Sueur and Cornes' practice of referring to the Lords in its judicial capacity as the 'Appellate Committee'. See Andrew Le Sueur and Richard Cornes 'The Future of the United Kingdom's Highest Courts' research report, The Constitution Unit of the UCL (2001) p 6.
6.   Le Sueur and Cornes, n 5 above, p 18.

Council has a broader membership, more flexibility in the determination of panels, and a history of constitutional adjudication. Jurisdiction over devolution disputes was therefore conferred upon the Privy Council. The situation nevertheless is odd. It leaves the United Kingdom with two final courts of appeal, with overlapping membership, and a division of jurisdiction that can produce conflicts of interpretation and duplication of proceedings. The creation of a new Supreme Court raises the possibility of uniting their domestic jurisdiction in a single body.[7]

Second, the adoption of the Human Rights Act is often cited as an important reason for reform. In part, this is because the Human Rights Act incorporated the European Convention on Human Rights into the law of the United Kingdom, and that Convention states, in article 6, that everyone is entitled to have their legal rights and obligations determined by an independent tribunal. Given that the Appellate Committee is a committee of the House of Lords, is it independent?[8] More importantly, some believe that the nature of adjudication has changed as a result of the Human Rights Act, with consequences for the structure of the judiciary. At one level, that act imposes new demands for judicial impartiality, for more directly than ever before, it requires the Law Lords to review legislation, potentially impugning the decisions of the very Parliament of which they are members. At a broader level, some see the Human Rights Act as one step in the evolution of the United Kingdom towards (in Lord Steyn's phrase) 'a true constitutional state'. In the view of these reformers (again in Lord Steyn's words): 'A distinctive characteristic of such a state is that it has a wholly separate and independent Supreme Court, which is the ultimate guardian of the fundamental laws of the country.'[9] Or, to make a slightly different but very similar argument, the creation of a Supreme Court is entirely consistent with the implications of the United Kingdom's acceptance of a series of European instruments. On this view, the United Kingdom is already subject, at least in practice, to constitutional limitation. A Supreme Court, with a different constitutional status (and perhaps an adjudicative stance that is less deferential to Parliament) is seen as an important complement to the new order.[10]

That position is the hard centre of a third consideration: an amorphous commitment to modernisation that runs through the debate. Lord Falconer's foreword to the consultation paper speaks of 'the Government's continuing drive to modernise the constitution', and both the paper itself and other advocates of reform invoke similar language.[11] This may be the abbreviated, popularly accessible code for an argument of function or constitutional principle; 'modernisation' may be necessary for efficient and adequately resourced adjudication, for popular legitimacy, and for ensuring that the judiciary is independent and impartial. But one suspects that, sotto voce,

7. Department for Constitutional Affairs, n 3 above, pp 19–20; Le Sueur and Cornes, n 5 above, pp 24–25, 79–80 and 82–85; Lord Bingham, n 3 above, pp 6–7.
8. Department for Constitutional Affairs, n 3 above, p 11.
9. Steyn, *Creating*, n 1 above, at 14.
10. Steyn, *Creating*, n 1 above; Steyn, *Case*, n 2 above, at 385. See also Le Sueur and Cornes, n 5 above, pp 85–87.
11. Department for Constitutional Affairs, n 3 above, pp 4 and 10. See also Steyn, *Creating*, n 1 above, at 14–15.

aesthetic concerns are also playing a role. The British constitution may be quaint, but would it not be better to have a fully rationalised basic law, one that does not have to depend on explanations of history and long practice? More than one advocate of a new Supreme Court has expressed embarrassment at having to argue, in effect, 'do as we say, not as we do', when discussing judicial independence with the post-communist governments of central and eastern Europe.[12] The very name 'Supreme Court' suggests a desire to reduce British exceptionalism.

But each of these reasons has, over time, receded before what is now unambiguously the primary official justification for the reform: the claim that a new Supreme Court is necessary to establish the independence of the highest level of the judiciary from the other branches of the state, particularly the legislature, of which of course the Appellate Committee forms a part.[13] The previous arguments have not disappeared altogether; at times they are recast as supporting arguments for judicial independence.[14] But they have certainly ceded all priority in government statements.

The government's commitment to judicial independence is genuine. A separate consultation paper, released simultaneously, canvasses mechanisms for appointing judges. These are expressly designed to make judges more independent, both in appearance and fact.[15] The very status of the Appellate Committee seems to violate the separation of powers. Nevertheless, the argument is not as straightforward as it may seem. Few suggest that the Law Lords lack independence in the actual performance of their obligations, especially given the constraints they observe. On the contrary, whether out of politeness or conviction, most advocates of reform emphasise that the Law Lords exercise their judicial functions in an entirely appropriate manner.[16] The only examples of impairment cited in the debate tend to be hypothetical. The closest one comes to an actual example is the disqualification of Lord Hoffmann from the Pinochet extradition proceeding on grounds of appearance of bias. But in that case, the grounds did not arise as a result of Lord Hoffmann's membership of the House of Lords and would have been unaffected by the creation of a Supreme Court. Even in the hands of those who make the argument, the example serves merely as a basis from which to extrapolate how legislative action might lead to situations of apparent bias.[17]

---

12. See, for example, Sir Heydon Phillips (Permanent Secretary, Department for Constitutional Affairs), in testimony before UK Parliament, Select Committee on Lord Chancellor's Department, Minutes of Evidence, 30 June 2003 (Q53–56); Steyn, *Creating*, n 1 above, at 14–15.

13. This focus on judicial independence is abundantly clear from the consultation paper, Department for Constitutional Affairs, n 3 above, passim, but especially pp 4 and 10–13. See also Lord Falconer of Thoroton, UK Parliament, Select Committee on Lord Chancellor's Department, Minutes of Evidence, 30 June 2003 (Q21).

14. See Department for Constitutional Affairs, n 3 above, pp 10–12.

15. Department for Constitutional Affairs *Constitutional Reform: A New Way of Appointing Judges* CP 10/03 (July 2003).

16. See, for example, Department for Constitutional Affairs, n 3 above, pp 4 and 12; Lord Bingham, n 3 above, p 5.

17. Clive Soley questioning Lord Irvine of Lairg, UK Parliament, Select Committee on Lord Chancellor's Department, Minutes of Evidence, 2 April 2003 (Q50–51). The decision in the Pinochet case was *Ex p Pinochet Ugarte (No 2)* [1999] 1 All ER 577, HL.

The debate over judicial independence has been conducted, overwhelmingly, in the abstract. The problem is posed as one of potential conflict, especially given the evolution of the Law Lords' role (particularly the growth of human rights litigation or the adjudication of devolution disputes, should the House of Lords take them on).[18] Or it is posed as a matter of perception. That perception is attributed either to the public (although no evidence is cited; one wonders whether there is any such perception, or whether a fictitious public is being conscripted to support a position decided on other grounds) or to the United Kingdom's European partners (especially given the prospect of an adverse ruling under article 6 of the European Convention).[19]

The fact that virtually no one argues that judicial independence has been impaired in fact suggests that the other reasons given above, particularly a commitment to a more constitutionally constrained political order achieved by evolutionary means, remain significant drivers of the campaign for reform. Certainly those reasons continue to play a supporting role. The buttressing of judicial independence may be the chief objective, but it is portrayed as being all the more important given the framework of constitutional reform, as the United Kingdom moves away from a position of unrestrained legislative supremacy towards at least some degree of judicial review, and renounces an omnicompetent legislature in favour of a quasi-federal structure, both as a member of Europe and internally.

WHY JUDICIAL INDEPENDENCE?

What then is judicial independence all about? The precise import of the principle is less than clear. This is true not simply because of imperfections in the British debate. Judicial independence is a surprisingly elusive concept.

To begin, it can never be complete. Judges have to be appointed and, in the worst cases, removed. Courthouses have to be built, officers and secretaries hired, supplies purchased, judges paid. In all these functions, in any modern democracy, elected representatives have some say, and the decisions made have an impact on judges' performance of their functions. Most importantly, the very norms that the judges apply in the act of judging are (in large measure) determined by legislatures, and those legislatures have the right to revise those norms, at least for the future, if they disagree with the judges' interpretations. Judicial independence is not, then, about the strict separation of functions but about the creation of institutional friction, institutional buffers, such as transparent processes of appointment, cumbersome processes for removal, administrative autonomy and an ethic of restraint in the criticism of judges and judgments. In combination, these ensure sufficient room for the judges to exercise their powers without improper pressure.

---

18. Department for Constitutional Affairs, n 3 above, pp 10–12.
19. Department for Constitutional Affairs, n 3 above, p 11; Le Sueur and Cornes, n 5 above, pp 53–56; Lord Bingham, n 3 above, pp 5–6; Steyn, *Case*, n 2 above, at 383–384 ('in the eyes of the public'). I confess not to be the first to make such observations on the 'public' perception in this context. See the comments of Lord Wilberforce, reported in Robin Cooke 'The Law Lords: An Endangered Heritage' (2003) 119 LQR 49 at 58–59.

To a limited degree, then, the independence of the judiciary is comparable to the relationship between the other two branches of the state, the executive and the legislature. In parliamentary systems, the executive is nested entirely within the legislature, so that it is (at least in theory) the creature of the legislature. Indeed, the party system has further reshaped the relationship so that it is now one of intense symbiosis, in which the legislative majority sees its fate as tied to the executive's and the latter consequently wields considerable influence over the former. Nevertheless, it would be a dramatic and obfuscating simplification to treat the two bodies as though they were one, with no material distinction between them. They remain very different in membership, even though one is a subset of the other. Their contrasting procedures (one making decisions behind closed doors, the other in open debate; one allowing decisions to be taken by a minister alone or by a small group of one's own party, the other subjecting all decisions to the fierce criticism of one's opponents) make a profound difference to public scrutiny and accountability – and to the decisions that result. The extensive interpenetration of executive and legislature is not inconsistent with the need to distinguish between them. Indeed, the vast bulk of administrative law is founded precisely on that distinction. Nor would those living within British parliamentary systems generally push the system in the other direction, in order to separate the executive completely from the legislature (although they may well argue for reforms designed to increase parliamentarians' freedom of action). It is the combination of interconnection and autonomy that provides parliamentary systems with their distinctive blend of democratic control and executive efficacy.

Of course, the same analysis does not apply to relations between the judiciary and the other two branches, at least not without substantial modification. The potential for abuse is materially different. The courts – and, at a more ethereal level, the nature of judicial reasoning – are more liable to be overpowered or shunted aside. The institutional safeguards have to be adjusted to the challenge. But the fact remains that a simple commitment to separation is too blunt. It is never fully realised in practice, and in its simplicity it may displace the more fine-grained analysis on which strong institutions are founded. It may be better to conceive the issues in terms of a different though related image, that of the 'mixed constitution', in which the functions are blended harmoniously, not merely separated.

What then are the ends towards which judicial independence is directed? A second reason why the concept has proven so elusive is that there is great ambiguity in those purposes. Ambiguity is not unusual in a fundamental principle. Principles often serve more than one end. Their justifications participate in and are coloured by the broad range of aspirations, objectives and strategies that people attach to the political order. That has certainly been true of judicial independence.

It is common in the American literature, for example, to conceive of judicial independence within a broader theory of the separation of powers, one marked by the existence of 'checks and balances'. As *Federalist No 51* so famously expressed the idea, each organ of the state is seen as a means of keeping the others within bounds.[20] The potential for oppressive government is weakened by building plurality into the very structure of the state. In its simplest and

---

20. Alexander Hamilton et al *The Federalist Papers* (ed Clinton Rossiter) (New York: New American Library, 1961) pp 320–323.

most libertarian conception, little turns on the nature of the functions exercised by each branch. It is the mere ability to exercise countervailing power – the simple capacity to prevent action by the other branches – that is the fundamental objective. In more complex theories, that justification is supplemented by attributing particular institutional roles to the different branches of the state, so that each branch becomes the guardian of a specific aspect of the political order. A modern version of this is Ronald Dworkin's suggestion that the courts are the distinctive defenders of principle, while legislatures are concerned with matters of policy.[21]

The debate in the United Kingdom has been blessedly free of such arguments.[22] One important feature of parliamentary sovereignty is that it presumes the legitimacy of democratic decision-making. It cleaves to the view that the ability to participate in public decisions through democratic means is, in itself, an important dimension of liberty. It does not see the frustration of government activity as being, inherently, a public good. An extreme libertarian defence of the separation of powers, then, has no currency. But secondly, it does not buy into the simplistic view that courts are uniquely the institution of principle. Parliament is the enunciator of all law, responsible as much for the statement of rights and the establishment of means for their protection as for the achievement of other public ends. Indeed, in the context of the United Kingdom, controversies over rights have often been constructed about the parliamentary/executive axis, with the vindication of rights often achieved through legislative oversight. The courts have a role in the protection of rights, especially through the judicial review of administrative action, through their administration of the criminal process, and through their application of specialised human-rights instruments like the Human Rights Act 1998. But there has been a clear understanding that human liberty can be achieved through a range of institutional mechanisms, including parliamentary action and mechanisms internal to the civil service.[23] The grotesquely simplified vision of a principled judiciary controlling an unprincipled democracy – and the exaggerated argument for institutional separation that follows from it – has held little sway.[24]

21. Ronald Dworkin 'The Forum of Principle' in *A Matter of Principle* (Cambridge Mass: Harvard University Press, 1985) p 33.
22. Although see Steyn, *Case*, n 2 above, at 388ff, which, however, focuses on the relationship between the executive and the judiciary, specifically on the office of the Lord Chancellor. At a more theoretical level, T R S Allan has argued for the recognition of inherent, judicially reviewable restrictions, already applicable to legislation at common law – a position that depends very much on the specialisation of roles rejected here: T R S Allan *Constitutional Justice: A Liberal Theory of the Rule of Law* (Oxford: Oxford University Press, 2001).
23. For an overview of several such mechanisms, see Jeremy Webber 'Institutional Dialogue between Courts and Legislatures in the Definition of Fundamental Rights: Lessons from Canada (and elsewhere)' in Wojciech Sadurski (ed) *Constitutional Justice, East and West: Democratic Legitimacy and Constitutional Courts in Post-Communist Europe in a Comparative Perspective* (The Hague: Kluwer Law International, 2002) p 61.
24. For an effective critique of the jaundiced view of legislation prevailing in much legal theory, see Jeremy Waldron *Law and Disagreement* (Oxford: Clarendon Press, 1999), passim, but especially p 21ff.

A better argument for judicial independence, and one that forms a large part of the debate over the House of Lords, is founded on the need for judges to be impartial. Courts adjudicate disputes between the government and private parties. If the courts are closely implicated in government, their ability to judge these disputes fairly may be questioned. Even if the judges are free from partiality in fact, their formal ties to government may generate an appearance of bias.

There is much to be said for this argument, at least at first sight. The Law Lords do sit in judgment of legislation enacted by the body of which they are members, especially under the Human Rights Act. But it is important not to approach the issue of impartiality too broadly. Impartiality has a very specific focus – one that is not simply concerned with institutional relationships writ large. It is focused, above all, on the possibility that a decision may be compromised in a specific case – that the judge's conclusion might deviate from what would otherwise be his or her judgment, because of an interest extraneous to the issue. Because of this focus, the law on bias has held that, in order to result in disqualification, the judge's interest in the matter has to be reasonably definite. General sympathy with a class of person, a set of ideas, or a political position is not sufficient.[25]

The simple fact, then, that a judge has views on an issue of policy does not create a reasonable apprehension of bias. No judge approaches adjudication as an amoral, normatively vacant blank slate. If he or she did (if such a thing can be imagined), such a judge would be utterly incapable of weighing arguments, assessing testimony, and deciding whether a rule was satisfied – in short, of judging. Rather, we expect judges to come with attitudes, although we also expect them to defer to authoritative pronouncements of the law and, when venturing beyond those texts (as all judges must), to expose their presumptions to reconsideration and revision. The issue is not whether judges have opinions – all judges do – but how able they are to test and revise them. Regardless of their own views, we expect judges to focus on the case before them, on the arguments presented in the hearing, and on previous decisions and legislation, allowing that information to react back upon their presuppositions.[26]

Consequently, the law of bias has always required definite indication of extraneous influence or predetermination. Cases of bias tend to fall into one of three categories: 1) where the decision-maker has declared his or her opinion on the specific case in issue – where he or she has literally prejudged the issue on these facts; 2) where the judge has a strong antipathy or a close connection to a party – a connection that goes beyond mere sympathy, so that the judge might be seen to have an extraneous interest in the outcome (for example, the

---

25.   See Jeremy Webber 'The Limits to Judges' Free Speech: A Comment on the Report of the Committee of Investigation into the Conduct of the Honourable Mr. Justice Berger' (1984) 29 McGill LJ 370 at 389–393. See also the useful set of examples in *Locabail (UK) Ltd v Bayfield Properties Ltd* [2000] 1 All ER 65 at 77–78, CA.

26.   See Jeremy Webber 'The Adjudication of Contested Social Values: Implications of Attitudinal Bias for the Appointment of Judges' in *Appointing Judges: Philosophy, Politics and Practice: Papers Prepared for the Ontario Law Reform Commission* (Toronto: OLRC, 1991) p 3.

existence of family relationship, business association, professional partnership, or close friendship between the judge and a party); or 3) where the judge may obtain a direct personal benefit from the outcome. The disqualification of Lord Hoffmann in the Pinochet extradition case met this higher test: Lord Hoffmann was at the time a director of a charity that was closely aligned to Amnesty International and that shared Amnesty's objects; Amnesty itself had become a party to the Pinochet case precisely in order to argue for a particular outcome.[27]

Seen in this light, the steps that the Law Lords have already taken substantially reduce the possibility of bias resulting from membership in the House of Lords. The statement by the Senior Lord of Appeal in Ordinary, Lord Bingham of Cornhill, setting out the principles that the Law Lords intended to follow in their participation in the general business of the House, notes that the Law Lords should not engage in matters 'where there is a strong element of party political controversy', and should 'bear in mind that they might render themselves ineligible to sit judicially if they were to express an opinion on a matter which might later be relevant to an appeal ...'[28] Without these restrictions, an appearance of bias could conceivably result from a Law Lord taking a strong position on a particular piece of legislation, only later to sit in judgment upon it. Under the restrictions that is unlikely to happen, and if it does, the problem can be addressed by the Law Lord recusing himself. Law Lords do continue to exercise a role within the legislative process, especially on matters that are not charged with partisan significance. For the most part, this creates no more appearance of bias than do judges' contributions to law reform commissions and commissions of inquiry, or their comments on the law delivered from the bench or in lectures. I do not know the extent to which Law Lords exercise their right to vote on legislation. If they wanted to exclude all possibility of bias, the renunciation of that right would certainly accomplish that end. But given the constraints that they already observe, that degree of punctiliousness hardly seems necessary to preserve their impartiality.

All that is left, in the great run of cases, is whether simple membership in the House of Lords is sufficient to generate bias in the same way that being an officer of a company might do so in a private dispute. Might the position of the Law Lords, when viewed in this light, be analogous to that of Lord Hoffmann? The arguments have not generally been posed in this form. They have focused instead on the possibility of bias on a specific issue, for good reason. The Parliament of the United Kingdom is not characterised by a unified commitment to a set of objects. It is a deliberative body in which individuals representing a wide range of interests come together to debate matters for society as a whole. It does not make sense, then, to presume bias on the basis of mere membership, but rather to focus on the specific impairment of decision-making.

---

27. *Ex p Pinochet Ugarte (No 2)* [1999] 1 All ER 577, HL, especially at 589, per Lord Browne-Wilkinson. Compare the decision of the Supreme Court of Canada in *Morgentaler v The Queen* (1974: reported as an appendix to Webber, n 25 above, at 405–406), in which de Grandpré J was asked to recuse himself because of his support for the anti-abortion movement prior to his appointment (the case involved the prosecution of a doctor for performing abortions). The unanimous bench (de Grandpré J not participating) ruled that there was no impropriety in de Grandpré J sitting on the appeal.
28. UK Parliament, House of Lords Hansard, col 419, 22 June 2000.

Thus, there is no strong reason based on impartiality for removing Law Lords from the House of Lords. Additional considerations are raised if the Appellate Committee assumes jurisdiction over devolution disputes. But these do not so much concern membership in the House of Lords as they do the balance of representation among judges drawn from England, Scotland, Wales and Northern Ireland. The obvious solution lies in developing ways for increasing national representation on panels deciding devolution issues. This is precisely what the proposals for reform contemplate in a new Supreme Court.[29] A similar expedient might be adopted for the current Appellate Committee.

That deals with impartiality, but is that all there is to independence? Contemporary discussions, not just in the United Kingdom but worldwide, might lead one to think so. They tend to treat independence as though it were simply a means of ensuring fairness in cases to which the government is a party; justifications for independence tend to concentrate overwhelmingly on judicial review on the basis of human-rights guarantees and the division of powers in a federal system. But that is not all there is. Access to an independent tribunal is also valued when adjudication occurs between private parties, and it is valued especially in criminal proceedings, where the possibility of the decision-maker having a personal interest in the outcome would appear to be attenuated at most (at least in the vast run of cases). Like impartiality, judicial independence is concerned with the need to attend to the integrity of the decision-making process, but it is not so much concerned with bias for or against a party as it is with judges maintaining a distinctively judicial approach in their interpretation and application of the law. It is often expressed as a matter of keeping judges independent from 'politics'.[30] But what does that mean?

This language is sometimes identified with a positivistic theory of judging: Judges should stick to the application of the law. They should not become entangled with debates over what the law should be, which are inherently political. And what the law is can be determined in straightforward fashion by interpreting the relevant legislation and case law. Proponents of this view tend to minimise any creative role for the judiciary. They presume that a stark distinction exists between making and applying law. Courts are located resolutely on the 'applying' side, taking norms as they find them. On this view, judicial independence serves to maintain the clarity of the judicial role.

This story is too simple. Even in situations in which clear norms have been established by the legislature, the application of an abstract rule to a concrete case requires an exercise of judgment that inevitably draws upon considerations going beyond the text – and of course, that is all the more true when much of the law is a result of judicial decision. Those broader considerations at least include general conceptions of justice, general theories of the law as a whole, and the judge's understanding of the policy that supports a particular body of regulation. These broader reasons are not substantially different in kind from those on which legislators base their decisions. They may be deployed in different ways, but the pretence that judges exercise no independent discretion and eschew all concern with 'political' judgment means not that such considerations are absent, but that their operation occurs in a manner exempt

---

29.   Department for Constitutional Affairs, n 3 above, pp 20 and 24.
30.   See, for example, Department for Constitutional Affairs, n 3 above, p 11.

from open acknowledgement, evaluation and criticism. The simple positivistic view is an unsafe foundation on which to base major structural reform.

That is not the only way of distinguishing between legislative and judicial roles, however. Even though there is an overlap in the reasons on which judges and legislators must rely, and even though judges step beyond the text of legislation in the very act of applying it, there remain significant differences. Those differences can, I believe, be summarised in two constraints distinctively applicable to judges:

1. Judges are obligated to apply society's norms, not merely their own personal preferences.
2. Judges are required to attend carefully to the facts of the specific case. They should not be so intent on the establishment of a general proposition that they lose sight of the individuals and circumstances before them.

The first of these constraints maintains the positivist's commitment to law as a body of quintessentially social norms. It does not, however, oversimplify the task of determining what those norms are, or deny the judges' creative role in ascertaining and applying them. It is best conceived as a regulatory principle, requiring that judges seek, above all, to apply their best understanding of what society's law is, regardless of their own preferences as to what it should be. It is compatible with a variety of theories as to how those norms should be determined, although it furnishes grounds for supporting some over others. Some theories of natural law (such as those dependent on personal revelation) are so indistinguishable from individual preference that it is hard to argue that they represent truly social norms. In that respect too, this first injunction is like many positivistic theories. It shares the disenchantment. It shares the demand that the law have a manifestly social warrant. It is, finally, fully compatible with the privileging of legislation as a source of law, so that the judge's interpretation of the law should strive for consistency with the text of legislation. The judges' role involves a self-denying ordinance not imposed on legislators: that they should seek to apply society's law, not their own unmediated will.[31]

The second constraint also involves a distinctive ethic. Judges are charged with applying the law to the facts in issue, ensuring that norms are applied in a manner that pays close attention to the circumstances of the case. At one level this means that judges must focus on these individuals and this situation; they must determine what happened here, and not be so concerned with sending a general message that they fail to attend to the facts at hand – a very real danger, as cases of wrongful conviction make clear. More subtly, in their elaboration of the law, judges should be alive to the possibility that this case may pose fresh normative considerations, considerations that may require the refinement of previous interpretations of the law. This structured focus on the particular circumstances – this attempt to do justice to these specific parties – sets judicial proceedings apart from the normal legislative process which, while it may

31. I develop this view further in Jeremy Webber 'The Foundation of the Rule of Law in the Public Justification of Governmental Action', published in Chinese in (2002) 18 Nanjing University LR (Nanjing Daxue Falu Pinlun) 1 (English version available from the author).

consider cases by way of example, is directed overwhelmingly towards the general statement of the law.[32]

These constraints are relevant to adjudication generally. They do not depend on the government being a party to litigation. They are fully applicable to legal systems in which Parliament is sovereign, unconstrained by a written constitution.

There are at least two ways in which these constraints can be imperilled. The most obvious is through direct pressure by the executive or legislature. That does not seem to be in issue in these reforms. The United Kingdom is not exempt from such concerns. In 2001, there was significant reaction against the Home Secretary, David Blunkett's criticism of the courts for their decisions on the human rights of refugees, on the grounds that those criticisms constituted precisely such unfair pressure. The current reform is not, however, meant to deal with such threats. On the contrary, to the extent that they have been raised in the debate, they have been cited solely in relation to the distinctive status of the Lord Chancellor (which differs substantially from that of other Law Lords, given that he is, in addition to being a member of the House of Lords, a member of Cabinet). Some have suggested that the Lord Chancellor's position enables the executive to have undue influence over judicial decision-making.[33] Others have argued that on the contrary, the Lord Chancellor's hybrid position serves the cause of judicial independence, because it gives the judges an influential defender against executive pressure.[34]

In the Supreme Court debate, the most relevant peril is rather of a second kind, in which judges become so engaged in the legislative process that they

---

32. See Webber, n 25 above, at 377–378; Jeremy Webber 'A Modest Defense of Statutory Bills of Rights', paper presented to workshop on 'Protecting Human Rights in Australia: Past, Present and Future', Melbourne, 10–12 December 2003.

33. Steyn, *Case*, n 2 above, at 386–387.

34. See, for example, Cooke, n 19 above, at 66–67; Lord Irvine of Lairg, testimony before UK Parliament, Select Committee on Lord Chancellor's Department, Minutes of Evidence, 2 April 2003 (Q28).

Indeed, the wisdom of having strong means for addressing executive criticism – and the value of having a consistent defender within the ranks of the government itself – has been reinforced by Australian developments. There, the former Commonwealth Attorney-General, Daryl Williams, systematically declined to defend judges, even when a Senator of his own party launched a highly unfair and prejudicial attack on a justice of the High Court. Williams argued that as a politician, he could not be held to the ethical obligations that had traditionally been expected of Attorneys-General. Others took up the task of defending the justice, and the allegation was quickly found to have been based on fabricated evidence. For one discussion of what was an extensive and dismal controversy, see Jeremy Webber 'Missing: a positive political morality' *The Australian Financial Review*, 26 March 2002, p 63.

I am not arguing that judges should be exempt from criticism. Criticism is an important mechanism for public accountability in an office that is otherwise short on such mechanisms (for very good reasons linked to judicial independence). But it is important that criticism from those in legislative or executive positions observes a basic respect for the institution and is founded on a conscientious attempt to understand both the facts of the situation and the difficult responsibilities of judging. A member of the government, who has an acknowledged responsibility to ensure that criticism is fair and that judges are able adequately to defend themselves – or be defended – is crucial.

themselves fail to observe the constraints inherent in their judicial role. The constraints are subtle. They are not susceptible to hard-and-fast determination. They depend entirely on the judges' conscientious observance of an ethic. For that reason they are fragile. It is possible for judges to become so focused on a general objective that they no longer attend to the case. They can be so immersed in a partisan struggle that they have difficulty developing a fair reading of the law as it stands, or separating their own preferences from a sense of society's norms. This, then, is a good reason for preventing judges from becoming entangled in the legislature, even in systems that do not subject legislation to judicial review. The temptation to blur the functions of judge and legislator, even unconsciously – the risk of losing one's sense of judicial detachment, of fidelity to the principles already determined by the legislature, of attention to the parties in their specific situation – would be too great.[35]

Here too, the constraints adopted by the Law Lords already provide significant protection for judicial independence. The Law Lords have undertaken not to engage in matters in which there is a strong element of party political controversy.[36] They do remain members of the House of Lords, but it is a House which for reasons of tradition, structure and criteria of membership stands at one remove from the principal arena of partisan contention. And within that House, the Law Lords stand at yet a further remove, limiting their engagement in ways that minimise the hazard to the exercise of their judicial functions. Indeed there is a respectable argument that given those constraints, the Law Lords' judicial roles are enhanced rather than impaired by their participation in the legislative business of the House. That participation provides the Law Lords with better understanding of the challenges of law-making and of the processes of deliberation and compromise that underlie statutes, helping judges to avoid the simplistic caricatures of the legislative process that are evident in much of the writing on judicial review and, unfortunately, some of the practice.[37]

In short, the constraints that the Law Lords have voluntarily assumed deal effectively, in substance, with both impartiality and judicial independence. The remaining concerns seem highly abstract and formal. Of course, problems of impartiality and substantive independence may still arise in particular cases – they arise even in courts that enjoy full institutional separation – but those can be addressed by the individual judges withdrawing from those cases. In fact, this remedy is more easily available in the Appellate Committee than it is in most supreme courts. Most such courts have a set membership, combined with a strong ethic that each case should be heard by the full bench. In contrast, less than half the full-time membership of the Appellate Committee sits on any given case, and there remain a number of additional judges who may be called upon if necessary. There is therefore much greater scope for avoiding situations of conflict.

It is true that the Appellate Committee's independence and impartiality depends on the Law Lords' own good sense – on their judgment in restricting

35. See Webber, n 25 above, at 383–386.
36. House of Lords Hansard, n 28 above.
37. See Cooke, n 19 above, at 58–60. For criticism of simplistic caricatures, see Waldron, n 24 above.

their activities in the legislative business of the House, on maintaining their relative freedom from party entanglements, and on recusing themselves when their engagements have compromised their ability to judge, in fact or in appearance. The current structure does not provide the peremptory barriers to legislative entanglement that institutional separation would create.[38] There might be some reason to remove the judges from the House in order to erect such barriers, if the presence of the Law Lords offered no substantial benefits (although it is important to realise that barriers could supplement but not replace the role of a strong judicial ethic; in matters like this, structure can never do all the work). In weighing that balance, one would want to assess carefully the contributions made by the Law Lords to the legislative business of the House – a task I leave to others. But one would also want to weigh the symbolic implications of the change, implications that (I believe) speak to the important subtext that runs throughout the present debate.

JUDICIAL INDEPENDENCE AND DEMOCRATIC AGENCY

I noted earlier that the proposals for the creation of a new Supreme Court take place within a broader agenda of constitutional reform. Although the government's proposal is framed as though it were simply about the separation of the top judiciary from the House of Lords, the adoption of the Human Rights Act 1998, devolution and the United Kingdom's obligations in Europe are all cited as reasons for reform. Their impact is refracted through the lens of judicial independence: each of these, it is said, puts added strain on the requirement that the Appellate Committee both be and be seen to be independent.[39] But one suspects that their role is still more significant, given their ubiquity in the debate and given the absence of concern in practice with the Law Lords' independence and impartiality. The consultation paper is quite correct when it emphasises that this reform is part of a project of modernising the United Kingdom's constitution.[40]

But what does modernisation mean? Is it simply a matter of cleaning up the complexities left by several centuries of muddling through, sweeping away the dusty relics, acquiring new and somewhat simpler constitutional furniture? Perhaps that is part of it. The United Kingdom has demonstrated a remarkable propensity for preserving dusty relics. But I suspect it goes further than this, and that the adoption of a Supreme Court is seen – perhaps vaguely, perhaps without the reformers themselves being entirely settled on the final outcome – as consistent with a gradual evolution towards a full system of judicially enforced, constitutional constraints on the United Kingdom's governments and legislatures.

That certainly would be the effect if the current proposals for reform are adopted. The existing structure does emphasise, inherently, the pre-eminence of the legislature. That is true symbolically: the highest court in the land functions as a committee of one of the Houses of Parliament. Moreover, the

38. Lord Falconer of Thoroton, UK Parliament, Select Committee on Lord Chancellor's Department, Minutes of Evidence, 30 June 2003 (Q21).
39. Department for Constitutional Affairs, n 3 above, pp 10–13 and 19–20.
40. Department for Constitutional Affairs, n 3 above, p 10.

very presence of the judges in the House of Lords reinforces the view that Parliament is, unambiguously, the one institution in which the entire realm is brought together to consider the public good.[41] The governing institutions are not divided into separate branches, with the judiciary constructed as a contending power, pitted against the legislature. There is functional specialisation, but that specialisation occurs within a framework that emphasises the overarching priority of Parliament – and, within Parliament, the priority of the democratic element. That emphasis on legislative primacy has a practical dimension as well, in the Law Lords' close knowledge of the legislative process. There are deeper bonds of understanding, deeper bonds of sympathy, than generally exist between legislators and judges in systems that observe a stricter separation.

Now, I suspect that it is precisely this sympathy, precisely this structural reinforcement of legislative primacy, that most concerns the advocates of a new Supreme Court. To them, the very hierarchy inherent in the structure is inconsistent with judicial independence. Note the implicit premise of the argument: the acknowledgement of parliamentary supremacy is itself inconsistent with judicial independence; judicial independence is precisely about the establishment of a judicial power counterposed against the legislative and executive powers. If this is the view, one is already some distance down the road towards full-scale judicial review. And if the reform were adopted on that basis, one would expect that the new Supreme Court would, from its 'fine supreme court building somewhere in the heart of London of major architectural merit' (to which Lord Irvine referred, with some irony, in his last appearance before the Select Committee on the Lord Chancellor's Department),[42] begin to exercise its powers in something approaching that spirit, even in the absence of a formally entrenched constitution. Certainly the judges' symbolic positioning within the United Kingdom's constitutional order would have shifted and the bonds of sympathy attenuated.

As I have shown in this paper, there are other ways to conceive of judicial independence, ways consistent with a robust commitment to the primacy of the democratic elements in the constitution. That conception is fully compatible with the supremacy of Parliament in the constitutional order, although it also recognises that in applying Parliament's laws, it is essential that the judges enjoy independence in order to protect the distinctive character of the judge's role. Independence is valuable not because legislatures are untrustworthy and need to be overruled, or because they are actuated by interest with little regard for principle. It is valuable precisely to ensure the integrity of the judicial process, so that the norms judges apply have a social warrant, that

41. For the historical roots of this conception, see Jeffrey Goldsworthy *The Sovereignty of Parliament: History and Philosophy* (Oxford: Clarendon Press, 1999), especially the summary at pp 229–235.

42. Lord Irvine of Lairg, testimony before UK Parliament, Select Committee on Lord Chancellor's Department, Minutes of Evidence, 2 April 2003 (Q48). Lest this be considered unfair emphasis on what is simply the provision of quarters for the new court, see Steyn, *Creating*, n 1 above, at 15; and Steyn, *Case*, n 2 above, at 396, where he too emphasises the symbolic significance of having 'a dignified building fit for a co-ordinate branch of government' if the new court is to become, as he hopes, the guarantor of a 'true constitutional state'.

they are not merely the personal opinions of the judge made law. Judicial independence is entirely compatible with a constitutional order in which Parliament has the ultimate say as to what that law is.

It may be that the people of the United Kingdom are ready to move away from that vision and towards the frank judicial enforcement of constitutional limitations on government. If so, the debate should be joined on that question now, rather than enacting a reform based on an abstract and misleading invocation of judicial independence, the effects of which may be far-reaching on the balance between judicial and legislative roles.

If that broader debate is joined, one may find that the public is supportive of constitutional reform, wishes to see aspects of the highest judiciary changed, supports judicial review of issues of human rights, but wants to preserve the fundamental supremacy of the people's elected representatives in Parliament. One gets the sense that many constitutionalists see that combination of aspirations as contradictory: if the public truly wanted safeguards for human rights it would support a fully entrenched bill of rights and would create the Supreme Court to enforce it. They concede it may be difficult to achieve such a major change in the United Kingdom, given the venerable commitment to parliamentary sovereignty and Britons' legendary constitutional conservatism. They therefore settle for what they consider to be an imperfect compromise, one that goes as far as one can without attacking parliamentary sovereignty. One gets the Human Rights Act, *faute de mieux*, and perhaps now an almost-Supreme Court, *faute de mieux*.

But need the combination of human-rights protection and parliamentary supremacy be *faute de mieux*? Is it inconsistent to be committed both to human rights (including a significant judicial role in the enforcement of rights) and the continued predominance of democratic decision-making? The genius of common-law constitutionalism has resided in the ability to conciliate a plurality of ends through the judicious blending of different institutional forms, each addressing a particular dimension of good government. Surely that is what has been achieved under the Human Rights Act. One has combined judges' distinctive concern with the individual case – with doing justice to these parties in this situation – with Parliament's fundamental responsibility for maintaining society's normative order, by having courts give their judgment on the human-rights implications in a particular case, while preserving Parliament's right to establish the standards by which the matter is judged and to take remedial action if a violation is found. That is the balance in the Human Rights Act. It is a principled one, not a compromised one.[43] It is consistent with an approach to constitutionalism in which liberties are preserved not by the pretence of ironclad guarantees and impervious institutional roles, but by carefully adjusted institutional processes and relationships. For after all, even societies that have enacted absolute guarantees are dependent upon institutions for those guarantees' preservation and enforcement. The same spirit should be applied to the question of judicial independence.

---

43. I make this argument in the Australian context in Webber (2003), n 32 above. See also Webber, n 23 above.

CONCLUSION

In this paper, my principal concern has been the extent to which the debate over the new Supreme Court has been a shadow debate, purporting to be about the independence of the judiciary, but vitiated by its reliance on a superficial and formalistic conception of judicial independence and by confusion over the true motive for reform: the desire to move the United Kingdom incrementally towards a constitutionally limited political order. The lack of attention to the true motive for reform is the most troubling. Its absence from the debate is not necessarily the product of calculation. I suspect simply that the notion of judicial independence held by many advocates of reform is founded on a conception that the judicial power should be separate from and opposed to the executive and the legislature – a conception that has little room for the continued acknowledgement of parliamentary supremacy. But regardless of the reason, that issue should be more prominent in the debate. The content of and impetus for reform would be very different, depending on the position one took on that issue.

There may still be a strong case for reform, even given a robust commitment to parliamentary supremacy. It may have seemed rather whimsical that I should portray the Law Lords as a bastion of democratic virtue in the United Kingdom's constitution. The House of Lords is hardly the most democratic of institutions, and the Law Lords' full membership-in that body participates in the House's defects: lack of democratic accountability, skewed representation of gender and social origin, and the reinforcement of social distinction inherent in the very appellation Lord. The Law Lords' expertise may be highly valuable in the legislative process, their exposure to legislative debates may improve their adjudication, their presence within Parliament may reinforce the supremacy of that institution, but can their presence be reconciled with the movement for increasingly democratic institutions in Britain, including the reform of the House of Lords itself? The future of the Law Lords may be determined as a by-product of this larger argument over the character of the House of Lords. One can imagine ways in which their continued presence might be justified – as an injection of expertise into the second House of Parliament, a House that is meant to be neither the equal of the House of Commons nor chosen exclusively by democratic vote. But note the focus: here the concern is not with the ability of the judiciary to call the legislature to account, but with the acceptability of having unelected judges as part of a fundamentally democratic legislature. It is about extending democracy, not limiting it. One suspects that some of the opposition to the House of Lords as a judicial body (especially among the Labour faithful) is a function of this broader scepticism towards the House of Lords itself.

There is also good reason to reform the Appellate Committee so that it can handle devolution cases. It is indeed anomalous to have two top courts for the United Kingdom, with the Privy Council's jurisdiction being only the subset of constitutional issues that satisfies the definition of devolution questions. The anomaly has consequences. Others have remarked on the possibility of inconsistent results in each court on the interpretation of the Human Rights Act 1998.[44] The Privy Council's interpretation would be binding, but the

---

44. Department for Constitutional Affairs, n 3 above, p 20; Le Sueur and Cornes, n 5 above, pp 24–25, 79–80 and 82–85.

prospect of having divergent interpretations at the judiciary's dual apex is regrettable. Moreover, the very division of jurisdiction requires sharp distinctions among areas of law that are often closely interrelated, impeding the development of coherence across constitutional law and raising the prospect of multiple proceedings to address the same events. Nor does the division assist public understanding of the structure of the United Kingdom's institutions. Simplicity is only one of the values to which a legal system should aspire, but it does seem odd to generate new complexities for no good reason. Given the extensive overlap in the membership of the Appellate Committee and the Privy Council, and given the flexibility that each has traditionally enjoyed in summoning ad hoc members, surely this challenge can be resolved by creating special rules for the formation of panels in devolution cases.

There are, then, reasons for change quite apart from the progressive constitutionalisation of British politics. But if the motives for change are clarified, and if the aim of restricting parliamentary sovereignty is laid to one side, the reform may take quite a different shape from that now before us. It would, at the very least, weigh the symbolic implications of creating a separate Supreme Court in parallel with the other great institutions of the United Kingdom, and may take pains to guard against those implications. It may refrain from establishing a power entirely separate from and opposed to Parliament, concentrating instead on formalising the constraints under which the Law Lords participate in Parliament – perhaps through an accentuation of their separate status within the House, with them enjoying voice but no vote. If the reform does create a separate high court, that court may be given a different name, one that expresses less wistful longing for judicial review as it is practised in the United States or Canada. The court may incorporate more tolerance for multiple roles, such as the ability to rely on the service, as ad hoc judges, of retired judges who otherwise sit as full members of the House of Lords. And finally, it may have a clearer sense of its constitutional role, one that goes beyond Supreme Court in the making, or Supreme Court manqué.

Developing mechanisms for judicial accountability in the UK

Andrew Le Sueur[*]

Barber Professor of Jurisprudence, The University of Birmingham

The 'accountability revolution' has lead to an expansion in the concept of accountability and the application of accountability practices to an ever-wider range of public authorities. In a mature democracy, those who exercise significant public power ought to hold themselves open to account, and judicial power should not be excluded from this imperative. In the UK, there are three schools of thought about accountability of judges. 'Opponents' argue that the notion of an 'accountable judge' is an oxymoron. 'Re-conceptualists' point out that courts already engage in a number of practices that make them accountable. The 'radical' claim is that new forms of accountability are needed. To understand the debate better, we need to map out types and levels of accountability. First, a distinction may be drawn between the personal accountability of individual judges and the accountability of courts as institutions. Secondly, we may differentiate formal mechanisms for securing accountability and informal, 'non-state' practices, including scrutiny of judgments and judges by the news media and academics. Thirdly, different levels of accountability may be identified, relating to the 'probity', 'performance', 'process' and 'content' of the judicial function. The final part of the paper considers the design of accountability mechanisms for a new UK Supreme Court.

THE ACCOUNTABILITY REVOLUTION

We all know that 'accountability' has become an amorphous concept.[1] Until 20 years ago or so, accountability was understood mainly as a command-and-control relationship. The person called upon to give an account for his actions or omissions was in a subordinate position and was subject to sanction if it was

* I first commented on some of themes in this article in my inaugural lecture 'Making Judges Accountable' at The University of Birmingham on 5 November 2002 and in a paper at a BIICL seminar on 'Accountability and Independence of the Judiciary' on 14 June 2003. Some of the comparative material used in this paper was collected in research trips funded by the ESRC (grant R000222908) and carried out under the auspices of the UCL Constitution Unit, with Richard Cornes. In 2000 I received an award from the British Academy (grant APN30026) for travel in connection with the project.

1. For discussion of this point, see eg R Mulgan '"Accountability": an ever-expanding concept' (2000) 78 PA 555; D Oliver *Constitutional Reform in the United Kingdom* (Oxford: Oxford University Press, 2003) ch 3; A Arnull and D Wincott (eds) *Accountability and Legitimacy in the European Union* (Oxford: Oxford University Press, 2002) ch 1.

determined that an error had occurred. In the UK, the paradigm was the minister answerable to Parliament, whose resignation could be demanded by MPs. Another commonplace use of the accountability concept was the government's accountability to the electorate at a general election. Clearly, a command-and-control relationship is antithetical to judicial independence (as it is practised in the UK). As the political science and constitutional law literature makes clear, however, the terminology of 'accountability' is now used far more broadly, to include, for example, public dialogue without the presence of any relationship of subordination or the possibility of sanction.

Accountability has also expanded in the sense that its *practice* is demanded in relation to more and different public decision-makers than in the past. Shifts in our mindset can take place quite rapidly. In 1986, the exercise of prerogative powers by ministers was made legally accountable.[2] Another illustration of quick shifts in public expectations about accountability is that only a few years ago it would have been unthinkable to speak in terms of the calling the Queen to account – yet now various reporting and scrutiny processes are in place whereby the Royal Household explains its conduct – and still more are demanded.[3] Similarly, with the Security Service (MI5) and the Secret Intelligence Service (MI6).

The expansion of accountability – in the senses of it both becoming a more fluid concept and its application to a wide range of public activity – has met with something of a backlash. Academic commentators have in some contexts identified accountability 'overload', with requirements to account for action deflecting decision-makers from their main tasks. A further set of concerns about accountability was raised in the 2002 BBC Reith Lectures. Onora O'Neill argued that the current accountability revolution was damaging rather than repairing the gap in trust between the public and professional and political decision-makers. She warned:[4]

> 'Plants don't flourish when we pull them up too often to check how their roots are growing: political institutional and professional life may not go well if we constantly uproot them to demonstrate that everything is transparent and trustworthy.'

The lessons to be drawn from these developments and concerns are not (I believe) that improving the accountability of judges is an undesirable project, but rather that any procedures put in place must be appropriate ones. My straightforward thesis is that a mature democracy requires those who exercise significant public power to hold themselves open to account. Judicial power ought not to be excluded from accountability requirements. The challenge is to develop mechanisms of accountability that do not undermine judicial independence. To call for judicial accountability carries no necessary implication of hostility or scepticism about the exercise of judicial power. On

---

2.   In the GCHQ case: *Council of Civil Service Unions v Minister for the Civil Service* [1985] AC 374, HL.
3.   See www.royal.gov.uk, on the cost of Royal travel: 'To improve accountability and transparency, an annual report is published which includes the income and expenditure account.'
4.   'A Question of Trust: Lecture 3 – Called to Account', available at www.bbc.co.uk/radio4/reith2002/3.shtml.

the contrary, in political systems where the legitimacy of public power is increasingly measured according to the nature and extent to which a public authority is accountable, courts themselves have much to gain from engaging in modern accountability practices.

JUDICIAL ACCOUNTABILITY: THE EMERGING DEBATE

Today in the UK and Commonwealth, it is possible to identify three main schools of thought about the concept and practice of judicial accountability (though, in doing so, one inevitably risks caricature and over-simplification). For convenience, these may be referred to respectively as the opponents, the re-conceptualists and the radicals.

The opponents

Judges must be 'independent'. This requirement is found in the constitutional arrangements of all liberal democracies committed to the rule of law, and also in international human rights instruments (including ECHR, Article 6(1)). Its meaning includes that judges should have security of tenure protecting them from dismissal or non-renewal of office for handing down unpopular judgments.[5] The European Court of Human Rights has established criteria for establishing whether a court can be considered independent which include 'the existence of guarantees against outside pressures and the question whether the body presents an appearance of independence'.[6]

In the UK, there are some who regard the notion of an 'accountable judge' as an oxymoron – a court cannot (it is believed) be both independent *and* accountable. The view that guarding the independence of courts rules out innovations in accountability is well represented by Lord Cooke of Thorndon, a senior New Zealand judge who by virtue of his peerage sat until his recent retirement in several important House of Lords appeals. He wrote:[7]

> 'In what sense are they [ie judges] or should they be accountable for their decisions? So far as appellate tiers extend there is accountability within the judicial system; but a fashionable line of argument might suggest that somehow there should be more ... Judicial accountability has to be mainly a matter of self-policing; otherwise, the very purpose of entrusting some decisions to judges is jeopardised. The old question *quis custodiet ipsos custodies* [sic] remains as unanswerable as ever.'

5. Other indicators include eg how the jurisdiction and composition of a court is able to be altered, the length of office of judges, measures against the reduction of salary of judges, arrangements for the allocation of cases to particular judges, and methods of funding a court.
6. The ECtHR case law is too extensive to cite here; see eg *McGonnell v United Kingdom* (2000) 30 EHRR 289.
7. R Cooke 'Empowerment and Accountability: the Quest for Administrative Justice' (1992) 18 Commonwealth Law Bulletin 1326.

The re-conceptualists

A second approach seeks to reconcile the independence of the judiciary with the demands of the accountability revolution by arguing that current practices amount to effective accountability arrangements. Like Moliere's Monsieur Jourdain who talked prose without knowing it, courts have long had accountability practices without explicitly labelling them as such (the re-conceptualists contend). Among the obvious activities that fall into this category are: the fact that most courts sit in public; the common practice of giving reasoned, written judgments; the possibility that judgments are appealable to a higher judicial body; and the scrutiny meted out to judgments (and judges) by a more-or-less well informed news media and scholarly work of academics. The reported comments of Justice Tan Sri Dato' Seri Mohamed Dzaiddin bin Haj Abdullah, Chief Justice of Malaysia, addressing the Commonwealth Lawyers' Association (CLA) 'Judicial Accountability Workshop' in April 2002, capture this stance well:[8]

'He pointed out that judges of all Commonwealth countries were already accountable. They sat in open court. They delivered their reasons which were published. Those reasons were subject to appellate scrutiny as well as to scrutiny in the media and in the community generally. The Chief Justice accepted that with judicial power went the obligation of accountability to the citizens from whom, ultimately, power derived. He reminded participants of the words of Chief Justice Taft of the Supreme Court of the United States, that the scrutiny of intelligent citizens was a valuable support for the work of judges.'

This lead to the conclusion that: 'the CLA should consider appropriate ways to heighten public scrutiny of the work of judges. Such scrutiny should be performed in an intelligent and informed way. The CLA should consider the means of reinforcing examination of the work of the judiciary which would inform citizens about its true character, difficulties and importance.' The re-conceptualists eschew calls radical change and tend to believe that the courts may 'buy into' the accountability discourse by using its vocabulary without any need to make significant changes to current practices.

The radicals

A third, radical, stream in the debate calls for judges to be subject to 'more' and 'new' forms of accountability. The view may be that judicial independence is not to be regarded as an unqualified constitutional principle, but one that ought to be balanced against others, principally that of accountability; alternatively, radicals believe that courts may be subject to accountability mechanisms with no real loss to their independence. Most of the radical focus in the UK has been on new methods of judicial appointment in England and Wales, Scotland and Northern Ireland. Accountability could be improved, it is argued, by greater transparency of the existing system of executive appointment – or, more fundamentally still, by appointments made by an institution

---

8. Available at www.commonwealthlawyers.com.

independent of government and buttressed by a parliamentary confirmation procedure. In 1991, a Law Society of England and Wales publication argued:[9]

'There appears to be a move internationally away from the position that the merit of judicial independence is beyond evaluation or review. *Calls for judicial accountability* have largely been responsible for the rather defensive approach adopted by those supporting judicial independence. *Proponents of accountability* point out that the judiciary is an arm of both government and administration and as such must be subject to checks, balances and review. Those defending the principle of judicial independence argue that political scrutiny of judges thrusts the judiciary into the partisan world of politics and threatens judges' right and duty to act in an impartial and non-partisan manner.'

Since then, the Judicial Appointments Commission has been established in England and Wales, with a role to oversee the executive's appointments process, including power to hear complaints from disappointed candidates for judicial office (and others). Keith Ewing has argued:[10]

'The challenge is now …the development of procedures which help to ensure that the judges as political actors are more fully accountable to the people over whom they govern, in a manner which enhances rather than undermines their independence. It is a tall order.'

Further change, beyond reform of the appointments process, is demanded. Ewing's reform agenda includes the creation of a new Supreme Court for the UK and scrutiny of judges by parliamentary select committees.[11]

'If judges are prepared to publicize their views in this way [by writing articles for law journals], why not directly before a body representing the people in a public forum, such as a Select Committee of the House of Commons? Quite simply, if ministers and civil servants can be called before a Select Committee to account to the representatives of the people for handling the nation's affairs, why should not judges be subject to a similar obligation?'

Ewing argues that such appearances could have several different aims, including providing judges with 'a larger platform and a more substantial forum than could ever be provided by the Law Reviews for the expression of their opinions' and (more importantly, he argues) 'it would provide an opportunity for the public through the elected representatives to engage with a process of law making from which they are currently excluded'. He writes:[12]

'The purpose of this form of scrutiny … is to promote a form of dialogue between people's representatives and appointed judges about major legal

9.   E Skordaki *Judicial Appointments, Research Summary 5* (London: Law Society of England and Wales, 1991) p iv (emphasis added).
10.   'The Unbalanced Constitution' in T Campbell, K Ewing and A Tomkins (eds) *Sceptical Essays in Human Rights* (Oxford: Oxford University Press, 2001) p 117.
11.   K D Ewing 'A Theory of Democratic Adjudication: Towards a Representative, Accountable and Independent Judiciary' (2000) 38 Alberta LR 708 at 725.
12.   Ewing, n 11 above.

developments, to help the governed understand what is happening and why; and to provide an opportunity to the governors to explain and justify. A good example of where this could usefully have been done is in relation to judicial review of administrative action which has developed very quickly without any input from the people's representatives, and without any opportunity for judges to provide a coherent account of the process.'

For the opponents and the re-conceptualists, such a suggestion is a step too far. Certainly, Ewing's proposal begs many interesting questions about the existence and nature of 'dialogue' between state institutions, and the place of the common law within that conversation.[13]

MAPPING OUT TYPES AND LEVELS OF ACCOUNTABILITY

In order to understand in more detail what is at stake in the debate about accountability of judges, we must move beyond mere sloganeering ('More Accountability Now!' or 'Accountability is a treat to independence!'). The judicial function and the accountability imperative are complex phenomena. As a starting point, it is helpful to draw several sets of distinctions to clarify what is meant by 'accountability' in the judicial context. These permutations are overlapping and are obviously not an exhaustive statement of the whole field. In doing so, comparative study, in two senses, provides a fruitful source of inspiration. Several other countries, whose commitment to judicial independence cannot be doubted, have in place mechanisms for achieving some degree of routine accountability for judicial power. Moreover, other state institutions, including 'supreme audit institutions', have adopted practices for accountability from which the UK courts may learn.

Individual and collective accountability

First, a distinction may be drawn between (i) accountability of individual judges and (ii) that of courts as institutions. In relation to other public authorities, it is quite common to differentiate between individual officer-holders and the institutions on which they serve. Different principles and practices of accountability may be apt. Thus, in UK constitutional law and practice, a

---

13. On the growing literature on constitutional 'dialogue' in the UK see eg T Poole 'Review Article: Dogmatic Liberalism? T R S Allan and the Common Law Constitution' (2002) 65 MLR 463; and R Clayton 'Judicial deference and "democratic dialogue": the legitimacy of judicial intervention under the Human Rights Act' [2004] PL 33. The notion of dialogue is most developed in Canada (see eg P W Hogg and A A Bushell 'The *Charter* Dialogue Between Courts and Legislatures (Or Perhaps the *Charter* of Rights Isn't Such a Bad Thing After All)' (1997) 35 Os HLJ 75, and is being adopted in Australia: see L McDonald 'New directions in the Australian Bill of Rights debate' [2004] PL 22. It is notable that some senior UK judges have rejected the notion that their judgments on the Human Rights Act 1998 should be regarded as a part of a dialogue with the UK Parliament: see below.

distinction is drawn between individual ministerial responsibility (the duty on a minister to give an account of the work of his or her department to Parliament and, in extreme situations, resign if mistakes are made or there is personal misconduct) and collective ministerial responsibility (a set of understandings about the workings of the Cabinet and its relationship to Parliament). An analogous dichotomy can be made in relation to the judicial branch of government. Judges are subject to both individual accountability (they each swear and oath of office and are subject to constraints on their individual conduct in public and private life) and are also a member of a state institution – the court in which they sit – which may itself be called upon to account for its work.

Examples of individual (personal) accountability	Examples of institutional (court) accountability
• discipline for personal misconduct (in serious cases resulting in dismissal/an expectation of resignation) • writing individual reasoned judgments in a multi-judge court • explanations of personal views on law and the constitution delivered in public lectures, interviews with the press or scholarly academic publications	• publication of annual reports about the work of a court • consultation over proposed changes to court rules and practice • financial audit requirements • the requirement for a court to sit in public • the existence of rights of appeal to a higher court • for courts of EU members states/Council of Europe, responding to judgments of the ECJ and ECtHR • parliamentary debates on the judicial function (eg *Hansard* HL, Vol 648, col 876, 21 May 2003)

In the UK, we often have only a very weak sense of the court 'as an institution'. This is especially true of the Appellate Committee of the House of Lords, as I seek to demonstrate below.

Formal accountability and scrutiny by civil society

Another distinction that may usefully be made is between (i) formal mechanisms of accountability and (ii) the interaction of elements of civil society such as work of the news media, the legal profession (eg Bar organisations), and academic commentators.

Examples of accountability via formal processes	Examples of accountability via civil society
• publishing written reasons for a court's decisions	• robust and accurate reporting on judgments in the news media
•	• academic commentary on particular judgments and the conduct of courts generally
• xrights of appeal to higher courts against alleged errors	
• publication of annual reports by a court	• public education by the Bar and other legal professional organisations
• scrutiny of individual judicial appointments and the appointments process generally	

Obviously, in a well-developed system for accountability, there is synergy between formal and informal (or 'non-state') systems of scrutiny. The publication of an annual report by a court that receives no attention from the news media or in academic circles is a less effective mechanism of accountability than one that does.

Detailed analysis of the relationships between courts and civil society (especially the news media) – and the impact of these interactions on the ideas of judicial independence and accountability – falls outside the scope of this paper.[14] An illustration of the range and effectiveness of 'informal' accountability can, however, be provided. Of all the world's courts it is the US Supreme Court that is subject to the most intense and wide-ranging forms of non-state accountability. The major US newspapers have dedicated Supreme Court journalists, who are served by a well-resourced Public Information Office and Pressroom.[15] C-SPAN, a public broadcasting service established by US cable television companies, provides regular, detailed and well-informed television programmes and webcasts about the Supreme Court, including the weekly 'America and the Courts' series.[16] Eight times a year, the American Bar Association (Division for Public Education) publishes a bulletin called Preview of United States Supreme Court Cases on cases awaiting hearing by the Supreme Court; it includes expert analysis and comment and is important in stimulating informed public debate about forthcoming cases.[17] Several pressure groups of varying political hues, including 'Citizens for Judicial Accountability', have

---

14. A particularly useful discussion is by Sir Anthony Mason 'The Judiciary, the Community and the Media' (1997) 12 Commonwealth LJ 11 (focusing on the position in the UK and Australia).

15. Eg for the *New York Times*, Linda Greenhouse who began reporting on the Supreme Court in 1978 and who won a Pulitzer in Journalism in 1998. See L Greenhouse 'Telling the Court's Story: Courts as Communicators, Communicating About Courts', The Alexander Meiklejohn Lecture at Brown University, 12 April 2000.

16. See www.c-span.org.

17. For further information, see www.abanet.org/publiced/preview/home.html.

set themselves up to watch over judicial power. Each November, the Harvard Law Review has a 'Supreme Court issue',[18] accompanied by an annual event known as the 'Supreme Court Forum'. The list could go on.

In the UK's current arrangements – especially in relation to the highest courts – it is arguable that there are insufficient *formal* opportunities for interaction between the senior judiciary and Parliament; moreover, there is inadequate systematic *informal* (non-state) scrutiny of courts as institutions (as opposed to particular and controversial judgments).

Content, process, performance and probity accountability

A final set of distinctions differentiates various levels of accountability. To understand the debate about resisting or developing further attempts to make judges accountable, it is necessary to consider the question 'accountability for what?' The work of judges and courts encompasses a variety of tasks. The most obvious is that they decide cases; but they also adopt decision-making processes, have responsibilities to despatch their business with appropriate efficiency and effectiveness; and all of this is to be done in accordance with basic values of probity. The nature and extent of 'independence' and 'accountability' varies in relation to each task.

Examples of content accountability	Examples of process accountability	Performance accountability	Examples of probity accountability
Written, reasoned judgments Contributions of individual judges to law reviews and public speeches	Methods for selecting which cases to hear Selection of panels of judges (in courts which do not sit en banc)	Explanations for time taken to determine cases	Basic financial audit of court's annual expenditure Systems for judges registering or disclosing pecuniary and other interests

PROBITY ACCOUNTABILITY

The least controversial level of accountability relates to 'probity'. In courts that have their own budgets, it encompasses basic financial audit requirements to ensure that funds have been spent in accordance with an approved budget.[19]

In relation to individual judges, probity accountability entails mechanisms intended to guard against corruption or making judgments in one's own cause

18. This includes a 'Supreme Court Foreword' written by a prominent constitutional scholar, the faculty Case Comment, and 24 Case Notes – analyses by third-year students of the most important decisions of the previous Supreme Court Term – and a compilation of Court statistics.

(to the benefit of a judge's own financial or other personal interests). An example in the UK of such an accountability devise is the requirement introduced in March 2002 that the Law Lords (along with other peers) register 'all relevant interests, in order to make clear what are the interests that might reasonably be thought to influence their actions'.[20] Some may mourn the passing of a time in which the honour and integrity of men in public life could be assumed without the formality of such registers; but given their existence, there seems no good reason to exclude members of the judiciary from this requirement of accountability – not least because of the inconvenience that may flow from a failure to disclose an interest may have in a particular case.[21]

PERFORMANCE ACCOUNTABILITY

For most public bodies, the 'accountability revolution' now entails regular public reporting on the extent to which the body has achieved previously announced 'targets'. Accountability here focuses on 'delivery' and 'outcomes'.

Performance accountability is somewhat more intrusive into the sphere of judicial independence than is probity accountability. It requires a court to state publicly its goals in relation to (for instance) the determination of cases without undue delay. A crucial issue is whether a court itself is responsible for determining its targets for 'delivery', or whether they are decided in conjunction with, or imposed by, the executive. Failure to meet targets relating to case management may prompt intervention by the executive branch of government into matters which judges regard as within their sphere alone.[22]

It is not difficult to find examples of courts subject to performance accountability regimes. One such is the Supreme Court of Canada. In April 1997 the House of Commons [of Canada] adopted a pilot scheme aimed at improving reporting by public authorities to Parliament. Public bodies, including the Supreme Court, were required to produce on an annual basis a 'Report on Plans and Priorities' and a 'Departmental Performance Report'.

19. The questions of who sets the budget, and how, are of course a matter of significance in relation to judicial independence and accountability. See discussion, below, on the mechanisms for setting and scrutinising the US Supreme Court's budget.
20. Thus, the Register of Members' Interests (as at 19 May 2003) reveals in relation to Lord Bingham (the Senior Law Lord) that he is a member of several 'public bodies' (High Steward, University of Oxford; Visitor, Balliol, Templeton, Wolfson, St Cross and Linacre Colleges, Oxford; Chairman, Royal Commission on Historical Manuscripts; Chairman, British Institute of International and Comparative Law) and an 'office-holder' in two 'voluntary organisations' (President, Hay Festival; and President, The Seckford Foundation).
21. Eg following Lord Hoffmann's inadvertent oversight of the relevance of his association with Amnesty International in the appeal by Pinochet against an order extraditing him from the UK to Spain (in which Amnesty International intervened): see *R v Bow Street Metropolitan Stipendiary Magistrate, ex p Pinochet Ugarte (No 2)* [2000] 1 AC 119.
22. Eg the exchange of correspondence in 1993 between Mr Justice Woods and the Lord Chancellor about the mounting backlog of cases before the Employment Appeals Tribunal, which led to the retirement of Woods J: see •• HC Official Report (6th series) col 341, 24 March 1994.

'This initiative is intended to fulfil the government's commitments to improve the expenditure management information provided to Parliament. This involves sharpening the focus on results, increasing transparency of information and modernizing its preparation. ... Results-based management emphasizes specifying expected programme results, developing meaningful indicators to demonstrate performance, perfecting the capacity to generate information and reporting on achievements in a balanced manner. Accounting and managing for results involve sustained work across government.'[23]

In its 'Report on Plans and Priorities 1999–2000', the Supreme Court provided an 'Agency overview' setting out (among other things) its 'mandate, roles and responsibilities' and its 'key plans, strategies and expected results' – one of which was 'to ensure the independence of the Court as an institution within the framework of sound public administration'. The report explained the Court's continued work on its website, the modernisation of the Court Rules, and the Court's new Case Management System. An accompanying 'Performance Report' set out information about (among other things) average time lapses between filing and decision on application for leave to appeal, between hearing of appeal and judgment, and between date of leave granted and hearing. There was also comment on the composition of the caseload of the Court and on the accomplishments of the Court. Under the heading 'Scrutiny by the Public' it stated:

'The continuing increase in cases related to human rights and Canadians' increasing interest in high-profile cases have placed the Court more and more in the public eye. Decisions affect the ordinary citizen in numerous significant ways, making it incumbent on the Court to present itself clearly and accurately and to set an example as an effective, efficient and humane organization. To this end, most appeals are now televised, and the Court's decisions are available on the Internet. Also, the Court pursues a policy of assisting litigants, particularly those who are unrepresented by counsel, to fully understand the procedural requirements of presenting a case properly.'

Performance accountability for the US Supreme Court is different: less formal in the sense that there appears to be no formal requirement to state 'targets' imposed upon the Court, but Congress is involved in reviewing the general performance of the Court through an annual meeting between two Justices and the House of Representatives' Committee on Appropriations. The US Constitution stipulates:[24]

'No money shall be drawn from the Treasury but in Consequence of Appropriations made by Law, and a regular Statement and Account of Receipts and Expenditures of all public Monday shall be published from time to time.'

Each financial year, the US Supreme Court prepares a budget request which is forwarded to Congress by the President. Two Justices of the Supreme Court

---

23. 'Foreword', Supreme Court of Canada Performance Report for the period ending 31 March 1999.
24. Article 1, section 9, clause 7.

attend a hearing of the Appropriations Committee. I have been told that this yearly meeting is regarded by both the Court and by Congress as an important opportunity to exchange views about the operation of the Court. For the 2004 financial year budget request, it was the turn of Justices Kennedy and Thomas to attend the committee hearing, which lasted for approximately 90 minutes.[25] Other officials of the Court were in attendance, and were introduced to the committee by Justice Kennedy. In a respectful opening statement, the chairman of the committee spoke of the 'resources necessary for the important mission of the court' in protecting civil liberties, noting that the budget request represented a 14 per cent increase on the previous year. Justice Kennedy responded with a statement praising the Court's 'talented and dedicated staff' and commenting on the 'excellent relations' between staff involved in preparing the budget and the committee's own staff. He explained in some detail why an increase was requested, including the need for a major upgrade to the Court's information technology (IT) hardware. IT had 'made the Court more open to citizens through the website' which had over 70,000 hits a day. Justice Kennedy said that he 'hadn't spoken to the European Court of Human Rights or the European Court of Justice, but I think we're the most open court in the world' in terms of provision of information about dockets (the case lists). In his opening statement, Justice Thomas said he was 'honoured to appear' before the committee, and 'always appreciated' the committee's 'courtesy'. Revealing his own detailed knowledge of IT in the court, he explained changes in software being used in the court's two computer networks. In exchanges that followed, there was discussion of the Court's security measures and contingency plans for times of emergency, and how these had to be balanced with the needs of over a million visitors a year to the Court's building.

Interestingly, Representative José Serrano began his questions by saying that he 'had unease every year': it felt 'somewhat bizarre to have Justices of the Supreme Court to come and talk dollars', but that was the tradition, even though he 'really wanted to talk philosophy'. There was quite detailed discussion about the increasing workload of the federal courts of appeals (mostly relating to immigration); comment on progress being made to increase the racial diversity of the staff of the Court (and the problem that minorities were underrepresented in the pool of applicants for Clerkships); how the Justices set about writing their Opinions, and the impact of IT on research methods;[26] the composition of the Court's case load; the problem of unfilled judicial vacancies in the federal courts – there was laughter when Justice Kennedy tactfully refused to blame the US Senate for the current 'bottleneck' on appointments; and discussion of the practice of the Court in releasing audiotapes of oral arguments.[27]

25. This description is based on my observations of the C-SPAN webcast on 13 April 2003 of the parts of the hearing in the 'America and the Courts' programme. The hearing took place on 9 April 2003.

26. Justice Kennedy said 'When I get into trouble I use a yellow pad'; the more IT-reliant Justice Thomas exclaimed 'I don't *have* a yellow pad!'.

27. Twice in the previous year the Court had released audiotapes on the same day as the oral hearings (in *Bush v Gore* and the *University of Michigan* admissions case). Justice Kennedy explained the reasons for this, and who had made the decision (the Chief Justice 'who is very good about consulting us on these things').

In an age of 'value for money', ensuring performance-based accountability of courts is now widely accepted as appropriate and – subject to broader constitutional arrangements about court funding – offering no *necessary* threat to judicial independence. In the words of the Chief Justice of New South Wales:[28]

'Case management requires information to ensure its effectiveness for the purposes of managing the court's resources in the most efficient manner and minimising delays to the parties. In such respects, the measurement of what a court does is a perfectly legitimate and, indeed, desirable activity. It is also entirely appropriate that information of this character, but not necessarily of the same degree of detail, should be available to the public. Citizens are entitled to know whether the arms of government which they fund through their taxes are spending that money efficiently and effectively. There is no threat to judicial independence if that is done, although some ways of gathering and reporting such information could constitute such a threat. Furthermore, judicial accountability by publication of pertinent information, both about the reporting court and by comparison with other courts may assist courts to improve the efficiency of their own management and their internal planning. Courts are no longer passive recipients of a caseload over which they exercise no influence. They are now expected to plan for the future and do so. In the immortal words of an English footballer: "If you have the courage to look far enough ahead, you too can see the carrot at the end of the tunnel".'

PROCESS ACCOUNTABILITY

Public authorities may be called upon to explain and justify the decision-making processes they adopt in carrying out their task. For top-level appellate courts in common law jurisdictions, this may include the methods used to select which cases to hear in full and (where a court does not sit en banc) how panels of judges are selected. Lack of openness about such matters may lead to criticism, some of it misplaced. This form of 'process accountability' can be regarded as more intrusive than performance accountability in so far as it is concerned not just with whether or not targets have been met, but also with the internal working practices of the court. The congressional Appropriation Committee's hearing in to the US Supreme Court budget, discussed above, included both 'performance' and 'process' scrutiny.[29]

Two illustrations of the call for process accountability may be provided from the UK. First, some academic commentators have called into question whether the arrangements for the grant of leave to appeal to the House of Lords is sufficiently transparent, with calls for reasons to be given when leave is refused or for there to be more detailed criteria as to the characteristics of a 'point of law of general public importance'. In April 2003, the Law Lords announced

28. Hon J J Spigelman 'Judicial Accountability and Performance Indicators', 10 May 2001, available at www.lawlink.nsw.gov.au/sc\sc.nsf/pages/spigelman_canada.
29. Eg the discussion of how judgments are written, who made decisions relating to release of audio tapes (and on what criteria) etc.

that in future reasons would be given.[30] Secondly, the arrangements for the composition of benches of Law Lords (and other eligible judges), particularly in relation to the Privy Council's 'devolution issue' jurisdiction have also been questioned:[31]

> 'The ... problem is that the composition of the Judicial Committee is in any particular case to be decided in theory by the Lord Chancellor and in practice by the senior Law Lord. There are no prescribed criteria in the Bill according to which the senior Law Lord is to choose from among the large pool of members of the Judicial Committee who have held high judicial office, whether in terms of their special expertise in public law, or in terms of the particular legal system of the United Kingdom where they have performed their judicial functions. [...]
>
> There is a very real danger that without prescribed and appropriate standards and criteria, the way in which the senior Law Lord exercises his discretionary powers of appointment, on the Lord Chancellor's behalf, in any particular case may become a matter of political controversy, whether in Edinburgh, Belfast, or London. If that happened it would impair the independence and legitimacy of the judicial process, turning the Judicial Committee into a political football, kicked hard by politicians for their partisan political ends.
>
> Nor is that all. If because of the great workload already imposed upon the Lords of Appeal in Ordinary, the senior Law Lord were driven to choose less senior and experienced judges than the Law Lords there is a real danger that the Judicial Committee would lack the authority of the House of Lords. There is also a danger that decisions of the Judicial Committee might be inconsistent with decisions of the House of Lords, leading to awkward conflicts and a weakening of the authority of the judicial process and a lack of legal certainty.'

In former years, the internal decision-making processes of courts were often regarded as 'out of bounds' to scholarly academic study, journalism and political scrutiny. The pace of the accountability revolution appears to be making this a thing of the past.[32]

CONTENT ACCOUNTABILITY

In many respects, the most contentious area in the debate about accountability of judges relates to what may be called 'content accountability' – what the law

---

30.   These issues are discussed below.

31.   Lord Lester of Herne Hill, speaking in the debate on the Scotland Bill: 593 HL Official Report (5th series) col 1970, 28 October 1998.

32.   Two revelatory books about the clerking system in the US Supreme Court caused shockwaves in the US legal system: Bob Woodward and Scott Armstrong *The Brethren: Inside the Supreme Court* (1978) and more recently Edward Lazarus *In Closed Chambers: The First Eyewitness Account of the Epic Struggles Inside the Supreme Court* (1998). They bear some comparison with the breach of accepted norms in relation to the UK Cabinet that came from the first publication of minister's diaries, notably *The Crossman Diaries*.

is and what legal and constitutional values a court ought to promote in its judgments. This goes to core of the judicial function and it is here that the highest degree of 'independence' is expected. Justice Gleeson of the High Court of Australia put it thus:[33]

> 'Our society attaches importance to accountability on the part of all governmental institutions. People seek ways of evaluating judges at a personal level, and the courts at an institutional level. This is appropriate, so long as the mechanics of evaluation are not permitted to define the objectives of the court. The starting point for any examination of performance is an understanding of the objectives of the person or institution whose performance is under scrutiny ... Just as the public are entitled to expect appropriate accountability of the courts, they [the courts] are also entitled to expect that assessments of judicial performance will be based upon recognition of those principal objectives.'

Justice Gleeson adopted as a summary of objectives those set out in the Statement of Principles of the Independence of the Judiciary made by the Chief Justices of the Asia-Pacific region in Beijing in 1995: to ensure that all persons are able to live securely under the rule of law; to promote, within the proper limits of judicial function, the observance and attainment of human rights; and to administer the law impartially among persons and between persons and the state.

In common law systems, the traditional methods by which judges are held to account for the content of their decisions are by the giving of reasoned judgments and the possibility of appeal to a higher court where a party is dissatisfied with the outcome. The latter method is not, of course, available in relation to courts at the apex of a legal system. That said, a top-level court may have power to overrule statements of law made in its previous decisions; and the judgments of top-level national courts in EU member states and in the Council of Europe may be the subject of subsequent litigation in the European Court of Justice and the European Court of Human Rights.

In recent years, some senior judges in the UK have sought to explain their thinking and approach to the development of the law outside the courtroom, in academic journals and public lectures. As we have seen, radical calls (such as those of Ewing) demand 'content explanation' to be given in other contexts – particularly in evidence to parliamentary select committees.

Summary

I have argued that the notions and practices of judicial accountability are complex phenomena, encompassing a wide range of explanatory, justificatory and scrutiny activities. I have sought to unpick some of the elements of 'accountability' and have suggested that a nuanced approached is helpful in clarifying the nature and subject of the accountability imperative. I have attempted to provide illustrations, from the UK and overseas, of a variety of

---

33. Murray Gleeson 'The State of the Judicature', Speech to the Australian Legal Convention, Canberra, 10 October 1999 (available at www.hcourt.gov.au). See also M Gleeson 'Judicial Accountability' (1995) 2 The Judicial Review 117.

accountability practices. A further complication may now be added. In order to avoid mere sloganeering about accountability, it is important to include an important variable into the inquiry: the nature and status of the court. The methods of calling a magistrates' court (the lowest level of criminal trial court in England and Wales) to account are likely to be different from those appropriate for the Chancery Division of the High Court, and in turn the House of Lords. We must avoid a 'one size fits all' approach. In particular, courts at the apex of legal systems have distinctive roles.[34] I therefore now move on to look at the arrangements that exist, or might be developed, in relation to the UK's highest court.

MODELLING ACCOUNTABILITY FOR A NEW UK SUPREME COURT

In 2003, the UK government unexpectedly announced the abolition of the office of Lord Chancellor and began consultation on a new system for judicial appointments for England and Wales and a new Supreme Court for the UK.[35] In relation to the new court, the Department of Constitutional Affairs' Consultation Paper focused on how to sever the links between the senior judiciary and the legislature.[36] The removal of the Law Lords from the House of Lords will dislocate the institutional and procedural connections between judges and legislature. What are the channels of communication and accountability to be between the new institution and Parliament? Little attention has been given to these issues. They ought not to be an afterthought but need to be an integral part and parcel of the reform package.

For the purposes of discussion, I want to use as a model of accountability three sets of practices that form the staple of diet for some public authorities. The core elements are the:

- routine giving of explanatory justifications for governmental decisions;
- periodic publication of reports giving an overview of achievements and failings of an institution; and
- parliamentary scrutiny through questions, debates and committee inquiries.

No one supposes that this model for accountability is suitable for use lock, stock and barrel in relation to judicial power.[37] On the other hand, these tried-and-tested practices do provide a starting point for developing a set of arrangements that might be put in place for a new Supreme Court in the UK. Moreover, they are already used to some extent to secure judicial accountability in the UK and elsewhere.

---

34. See further A Le Sueur and R Cornes 'What do the Top Courts Do?' (2000) 53 CLP 53.
35. For an early comment, see A Le Sueur 'New Labour's next (surprisingly quick) steps in constitutional reform' [2003] PL 368.
36. *Constitutional reform: a Supreme Court for the United Kingdom* CP 11/03 (July 2003).
37. Traditional mechanisms for *ministerial* accountability are now widely regarded as ineffective. For a recent study, see B Hough 'Ministerial responses to Parliamentary Questions: some recent concerns' [2003] PL 211.

Justification through reason giving

Generally, reason giving is recognised to be an important practice for securing the accountability of public authorities.[38] Most higher courts, of course, give some form of reasoned justification for their judgments. How effective are the Law Lords current reason-giving practices? How might they be enhanced with the creation of a new Supreme Court?

All final judgments of the House of Lords are accompanied by explanations of the reasons in law for their Lordships' conclusions, as we shall see. Until very recently, however, reasons were not routinely given at the prior stage of case selection when Appeal Committees (comprising three Law Lords) determined whether or not to accept a petition for leave for a full hearing.[39] Academics had suggested that reasons should be given,[40] or that more explicit criteria should be published to explain what constitutes a 'point of law of general public importance' (the yardstick used in deciding whether or not to grant leave).[41] In April 2003, the House of Lords altered its practice and will now give brief reasons for refusing leave to appeal. The immediate reason for this change is a belief that this is required by European Community law, but 'so as not to discriminate between petitions which raise a question of Community law and those which do not, the Appeal Committee will briefly indicate their reasons for refusing any petition for leave to appeal'.[42] This development is to be welcomed. The accountability of the court for its task of selecting which cases to hear goes beyond a desire to make the decisions transparent to particular litigants, for it is through its case selection function that a top-level court sets the agenda for the development of the law – and this is a matter of public interest.

Turning now to the giving of reasons for final appeals. Academic scrutiny of judgments often focuses on the plausibility and coherence of the reasons given by judges in a particular case. There have also been studies of the style and content of judgment-writing more broadly.[43] The concern of this paper is

---

38. See A Le Sueur 'Legal Duties to Give Reasons' (1999) 52 CLP 150. I argue there that reason giving (a) enhances the ability of citizens to challenge decisions; (b) it is an exercise in self-regulation as it both 'confines' and 'structures' official discretion; and (c) where reasons state the source of legal authority for a decision, it provides a salutary reminder that the relationship of a public authority with the law is the opposite of that of a private person: every action taken by a public body must be justified by positive law.
39. Civil Practice Direction 4.5.
40. Brice Dickson in B Dickson and P Carmichael (eds) *The House of Lords: its Parliamentary and Judicial Roles* (Oxford: Hart Publishing, 1999) pp 137–147.
41. A Le Sueur 'Panning for Gold: Choosing Cases for the Law Lords' in A Le Sueur (ed) *Building the UK's New Supreme Court: National and Comparative Perspectives* (Oxford: Oxford University Press, forthcoming 2004) ch 12.
42. Thirty-Eighth Report from the Appeal Committee, 3 April 2003, available at www.parliament.uk.
43. See eg R Munday '"All for One and One for All": The Rise to Prominence of the Composite Judgment Within the Civil Division of the Court of Appeal' (2000) 61 CLJ 321; C McCrudden 'A Common Law of Human Rights? Transnational Judicial Conversations on Constitutional Rights' (2000) 20 Oxford JLS 499; D Robertson *Judicial Discretion in the House of Lords* (Oxford: Clarendon Press, 1998).

to assess the effectiveness of reason-giving *practices* as a *method of accountability*. Reasons for final judgments are published promptly on the House of Lords' website and almost all are reported in the various printed law reports. Leaving aside assessment of quality of legal reasoning (admittedly the most important factor, but one that falls outside the scope of this article), a number of criticisms can be made of the Law Lords' reason-giving practices. Arguably, the manner in which judgments are presented for public consumption falls short of modern expectations in terms of ease of understanding.

First, a significant proportion of House of Lords judgments consist of several speeches by the five Law Lords deciding the case in question. Speeches are delivered in order of seniority of the Law Lords, not in any logical order. Dissenting speeches are permitted and separate concurring speeches are commonplace.[44] The multiplicity of statements of law promotes accountability insofar as this makes transparent the different views held by members of the court. The problem is that no attempt is made in any given case to present to the public a synthesis of the various views. High-level legal skills are often required in order to work out the majority view. In relation to reason giving, the House of Lords is therefore strong on *individual* accountability, but has weak practices in relation to *institutional* accountability. Ernst Willheim makes a similar diagnosis in relation to the High Court of Australia:[45]

> 'Frequently … the Court's view is expressed in a multiplicity of judgments. Yet apart from the Court's formal orders, it is only rarely that the Court itself or the members of the Court will indicate or explain the combined effect of multiple judgments. In this respect, the Court has failed to recognise its role as a law-making institution and thus its responsibility to make clear and intelligible statements of the law … There is a strong case for saying that the members of the Court should see themselves has having a collective accountability, as an institution, for the Court's law-making function, and thus be accountable not only for their individual judgments but also for the combined effect of their judgments … The Justices may have given too much weight to their independence from each other. It is one thing to reach independent conclusions; it is another thing to write judgments in isolation.'

Willheim makes clear that it does not follow from this assessment that Justices should cease to write individual judgments. He suggests however (and it is difficult to resist this in relation to the Law Lords) that 'at the highest level there should rarely be occasion for multiple statements of fact'. He also argues that 'in the area of criminal law, there is a special need for certainty. Trial judges need clarity in the legal principles from which they draw their directions to juries'. The force of this last point has recently been recognised by the House of Lords:[46]

---

44. Their Lordships' practices in the *other* top-level court, the Judicial Committee of the Privy Council (where typically they spend half their time), has until relatively recently been different. Until 1966, dissenting judgments were not given (there being a single judgment of the Board) and until more recently still it was unusual for their Lordships to give separate concurring opinions.
45. 'Collective responsibility' in T Blackshield et al (eds) *Oxford Companion to the High Court of Australia* (Sydney: Oxford University Press, 2001) pp 109–110.
46. House of Lords *Annual Report 2001–02*, 16 July 2002, available at www.parliament.uk; the general significance of these annual reports is discussed below.

'32. For the first time, the Law Lords sitting on a particular appeal [*R v Forbes (appellant) (on appeal from the Court of Appeal (Criminal Division))* [2001] 1 AC 473] introduced the practice of issuing a single statement of the law (in the form of a report from the Appellate Committee) rather than individual opinions. It is the Law Lords' intention that this practice should be adopted whenever they make a statement of the law with a single voice.'

This striving towards modernisation and transparency is only slighted dimmed by the Latin words that introduce the report.[47] The single judgment practice adopted in the *Forbes* case does not appear to have been used in any subsequent decisions. In this context, it should be noted that the court from which most criminal appeals to the House of Lords emanates, the Court of Appeal (Criminal Division), gives a single judgment of the (three-judge) court.

If multiple judgments are to be continued to be used in most cases (and there are good reasons why they should be), are there any ways in which they could be better presented in order to aid accountability? The printed copies of speeches in a case, and the website versions, contain no summary or synthesis of the multiple judgments that have normally been delivered. A summary will usually appear in newspapers such as *The Times* within a day or so, but such reports often focus on only one (the 'leading') speech. Publication of in the printed law reports will include a headnote (prepared by employees of the law-reporting organisation) but these follow some weeks after the case was decided.

Practice in other courts provides opportunities for lesson learning. One possibility is that judgments are accompanied by some sort of officially produced 'executive summary', explaining the gist of the court's decision. Nowadays it would be unthinkable for a government department's report not to include a summary to aid the reader in understanding the scope and main points of the publication. Why are court judgments different? There is, perhaps, a natural inclination to think that the words of the judges in their judgments must always 'speak for themselves', and leave the task of synthesis and interpretation to others (including press commentators and academics). But the UK has abandoned this approach in relation to Bills before Parliament;[48] since 1999, they have been accompanied by Explanatory Notes and these may now on occasion be used by the courts when interpreting Acts, without detracting from the prime importance of the words of the legislation itself.[49]

Some courts in other jurisdictions have adopted the practice of giving official summaries of multiple judgments. The US Supreme Court's decisions are accompanied on publication by an officially sanctioned 'prefatory syllabus'

---

47. For curious reasons, we are told, among other dates, that an Appellate Committee was appointed on 'DIE MERCURII 17° NOVEMBRIS 1999' and that proceedings took place on 'DIE LUNAE 27° NOVEMBRIS 2000'. Elsewhere in the English court system, the use of Latin is now discouraged. For comments, see M Berlins 'Language of the Law' *Guardian*, 26 November 2002.

48. Explanatory Notes are available on the Internet at *www.parliament.uk* for Bills and *www.legislation.hmso.gov.uk* for Acts. For the background to their introduction, see C Jenkins QC (First Parliamentary Counsel) 'Helping the Reader of Bills and Acts' (1999) 149 NLJ 798.

49. See Lord Steyn in *Westminster City Council v National Asylum Support Services* [2002] UKHL 38; [2002] 1 WLR 2956 at [2]–[6].

prepared by Court's official Reporter of Decisions, who is an officer of the Court. The beginning of published Opinions states:

> 'NOTE: Where it is feasible, a syllabus (headnote) will be released, as is being done in connection with this case, at the time the opinion is issued. The syllabus constitutes no part of the opinion of the Court but has been prepared by the Reporter of Decisions for the convenience of the reader. See *United States* v. *Detroit Timber & Lumber Co.*, 200 US 321, 337.'[50]

For the new UK Supreme Court, careful thought will need to be given as to the practices of delivering reasons for judgments.

The apparatus of routine accountability: mission statements, business plans, annual reports etc

Routine accountability is premised on making explicit the goals of an organisation (often in the form of 'mission statements'), the setting of specific objectives (through 'business plans' and the like) and the regular public reporting on progress towards 'targets'. Reports may be subject to public scrutiny. These devices are particularly associated with 'performance accountability'.

A HIERARCHY OF DOCUMENTS

The Chief Justice of New South Wales describes the 'new managerialist focus' succinctly:[51]

> 'This new approach commenced with government trading enterprises, often as a step along the road to privatisation, and thereafter extended to other spheres of government activity. The approach involves a hierarchy of required documentation. At the top, at the highest level of generality and abstraction, are documents described variously as strategic plans, corporate plans, charters or mission statements. The level below concerns annual implementation, variously called business plans or performance plans and the like. These plans are required to contain goals, objectives, targets or standards at a level of generality that is implementable, and, preferably, capable of measurement. At the lowest level of the hierarchy is what are frequently called performance indicators which must be measurable, concrete, collectable at reasonable cost and comparable, either between institutions or over time for the one institution. This process must also be capable of evaluation either by the unit of public administration concerned or by third parties, such as an auditor general conducting a performance

---

50. This 1906 case is intended to be a warning to readers. In the passage referred to, Justice Brewer states: 'the headnote is not the work of the court, nor does it state its decision ... It is simply the work of the reporter, gives his understanding of the decision, and is prepared for the convenience of the profession in the examination of the reports.' The headnote in a case referred to was 'a misinterpretation of the scope of the decision'.
51. Hon JJ Speigelman 'Judicial Accountability and Performance Indicators', speech, 10 May 2001: available at www.nsw.gov.au.

audit. Although the nomenclature varies from country to country and from one area of public administration to another, the broad lines of this development appear to be similar in many countries and spheres of discourse. The position is not a static one. The enthusiasm for strategic plans or charters or mission statements appears to have waned somewhat. The presumed benefits from clarification of objectives, do not seem to be attainable when the objectives are stated at a high level of abstraction. Management is, after all, a fashion industry.'

The Supreme Court of Canada can provide an illustration of such a 'hierarchy of required documentation'.[52] Its 'mandate' is 'To advance the cause of justice in hearing and deciding, as final arbiter, legal questions of fundamental importance'. Its 'mission statement': 'As the final court of appeal, the Supreme Court of Canada serves Canadians by leading the development of common and civil law through its decisions on questions of public importance.' In doing this: 'The Court is committed to: the rule of law; independence and impartiality; and accessibility to justice.' The 'strategic objectives' of the Court are: 'To ensure the independence of the Court as an institution within the framework of sound public administration. To improve access to the Court and its services. To process hearings and decisions promptly. To provide the information base that the Court needs to fulfil its mandate.'

This 'great codification of public life' has its critics who, one can assume, will have doubts about the value of accountability in general[53] as well as judicial accountability in particular. There is something banal about reducing the complex and important role of a Supreme Court to a sentence for use on a website. On balance, however, I think the apex of the hierarchy of documents may serve some purpose (one being, indeed, to state the obvious; another being to require a court, through the *process* of formulating a mission statement, to reflect upon its role). In any event, there seem no overriding reasons why courts should be exempt from having to provide them so long as other public authorities are expected to adopt them. A new Supreme Court for the UK, keen to clarify its role, may be well advised to have a mission statement – but proponents of radical judicial accountability will, I fear, inevitably be disappointed with this kind of accountability activity.

ANNUAL REPORTING REQUIREMENTS

Systems of accountability built on a 'hierarchy of documents' usually encompass a reporting mechanism whereby an institution is required to produce an annual report setting out its achievements (or failures); these reports are subject to varying degrees of public scrutiny. In some jurisdictions, the requirement for a court to write an annual report is a legal obligation;[54] in others it is a voluntary activity at the initiative of the court.[55]

52. See its website at www.ss-csc.gc.ca.
53. See Onora O'Neill's comments at n 4 and associated text above.
54. Eg High Court of Australia Act 1979, s 47 'Annual Reports and financial statements'.
55. Eg the Spanish *Tribunal Constiticional.*

A survey of such reports shows that they may serve a variety of accountability functions.[56] Where financial accounts are included, a report may be mainly concerned with ensuring 'probity accountability'.[57] They may also serve the goal of 'performance accountability', as is in the case of the Supreme Court of Canada.[58] Annual reports may also deal with 'process accountability' in so far as they explain the internal working practices of the court. Two brief illustrations can be provided.

In the UK, there is no *legal* obligation for reporting annually on the 'judicial business' of the House of Lords but by convention comment on the Law Lords' work is included in the 'Annual Report of the House of Lords', a yearly publication that since 1991 provides a brief 'review of the year' in the Upper House, followed by a 'detailed report on the administration which supports the work of the House as the second chamber of the United Kingdom Parliament'. The Annual Report is approved by the Finance and Staff Sub-Committee of the House of Lords. It is fair to say that this publication receives almost no public attention. The *Annual Report 2001–02* deals with the Law Lords in just two brief paragraphs and a page of statistics:

'32. The number of Lords of Appeal in Ordinary remained at 12. In 2001, Lord Rodger of Earlsferry succeeded Lord Clyde. Lord Saville of Newdigate continued as chairman of the enquiry into the events of 'Bloody Sunday' and remained largely unavailable to sit judicially in the House.

33. Statistics on appeals and petitions for leave are given in Part II (page 40). Notable appeals included the rejection of Mrs Dianne Pretty's bid to gain immunity from prosecution for her husband to assist her in suicide; a case of fraud in Westminster City Council (*Magill v. Porter*); the extradition appeal by Mr Al-Fawaz, wanted for trial in the United States on terrorist charges relating to activities carried out on behalf of Al-Qaida; and the question whether provision of cooking facilities is an essential requirement for premises to constitute a dwelling under the Housing Act 1988.'

As an account of the work of a major national institution, this a shockingly brief and somewhat puzzling in its content. Some basic statistics about the caseload of the Law Lords are also contained in the annual *Judicial Statistics* publication produced by the Lord Chancellor's Department.

The High Court of Australia report provides an interesting point of contrast. It takes a fairly standard format every year. There is a series of very short biographical sketches of each justice, accompanied by a photograph. A brief 'review of the year' deals with notable events (in 2002, for instance, the retirement of one of the justices, the publication of the *Oxford Companion to the High Court of Australia,* the creation of the post of Public Information Officer and comment on the statistics relating to workload and litigants). Then there are several pages of 'background' relating to the composition, functions and powers of the court followed by more on the 'administration of the court'.

---

56. For an interesting comparative analysis of annual reports by 'supreme audit institutions' (eg the UK National Audit Office), see C Pollitt and H Summa 'Reflexive Watchdogs? How Supreme Audit Institutions Account for Themselves' (1997) 75 PA 313.
57. See above.
58. See above.

There are very brief 'financial statements' and then 30 pages of annexures dealing with, among other things, judicial workload, litigation information, and staffing. The reports do not comment on judgments.

There seems little doubt that a new UK Supreme Court, like many other top-level courts in other jurisdictions and public authorities in the UK, should be subject to an annual reporting requirement. Such a practice would only build upon existing arrangements, not be a significant departure from them. Again, radicals ought not to expect too much from this accountability activity in and of itself.

Debates, questions and scrutiny by a legislature

In terms of accountability, it is those annual reports that are followed-up by parliamentary scrutiny or debate that are likely to be the most effective at securing explanations and justifications for a court's work. If a new UK Supreme Court were to make an annual report to Parliament, ought there to be an opportunity for parliamentarians to scrutinise and debate it? As we have seen, for the US Supreme Court, annual reporting is closely tied into its budget request each year, though the matters discussed with the Justices at the congressional hearing range into broader questions than merely whether specified targets have been met.[59] The annual report of the High Court of Australia may be (and often has been) one of the annual reports of public bodies subject to scrutiny by the Senate Legal and Constitutional Legislation Committee. The 2000–01 Report of the High Court of Australia prompted the Committee to note the rise in the number of litigants in person appearing before Commonwealth of Australia courts and 'encouraged the courts the courts and tribunals to establish an ongoing dialogue amongst themselves and with outside agencies such as the Family Law Council, the Australian Law Reform Commission and the Australian Institute of Judicial Administration, in order to share information in dealing with the issue of unrepresented litigants'. There are therefore templates from other legislatures that may provide a source of inspiration for devising parliamentary scrutiny arrangements for a new UK Supreme Court.[60]

Comments, questions and debates about the work of courts need not confined to responding to annual reporting mechanisms. In some legal systems, the federal US system being one, the legislature is involved in scrutinising and confirming judicial appointments. As we have noted, radical voices in the UK call for more parliamentary involvement in appointments: Ewing argues that 'there is a role for a parliamentary committee in promoting ... [accountability in terms of greater transparency and scrutiny] by confirming judicial appointments (particularly at the highest level)'.[61] Whether or not a

---

59. See above.

60. Whether Parliament would be interested in scrutinising and debating an annual report of a Supreme Court is of course a rather different matter. The House of Commons has taken relatively little interest in systematically debating the work of the Parliamentary Commission for Administration ('the ombudsman') since its creation in 1967, though select committee oversight and support has been rather more encouraging.

61. 'A Theory of Democratic Adjudication: Towards a Representative, Accountable and Independent Judiciary' (2000) 38 Alberta LR 708 at 733.

legislature is involved in the appointments process, it may be involved in scrutinising judgments and courts in other ways. Codes of conduct for legislatures in most jurisdictions are a mix of constraining rules and practices and facilitating procedures in relation to comment, questioning and debate about the judicial branch of government. The goal is to achieve constitutionally appropriate inter-institutional dialogue.

In the UK, there has been a general disinclination to allow MPs and peers to scrutinise the work of courts or the administration of justice in general. The rules of parliamentary procedure discourage rather than facilitate public comment on judges and judgments.[62] *Erskine May*, the official guide to parliamentary conduct, warns MPs that 'reflections on a judge's character or motives' or 'language disrespectful of persons administering justice' are out of order. The rules of sub judice mean that cases in which proceedings are active in UK courts may not be referred to in any motion, debate or question. These are entirely proper constraints, but they should not deter appropriate comment on the exercise of judicial power. However, with the exception of a series of interesting written questions by Lord Lester of Herne Hill, a search of *Hansard* reveals relatively little interest among MPs and peers in questioning or commenting on the work of the senior judiciary – until the House of Lords debate on 21 May 2003, discussed below. Indeed, while the House of Commons established select committees to scrutinise the work of the major government departments in 1979, it was only in February 2003 that one was set up to shadow the work of the Lord Chancellor's Department (the central government department which, in the absence of a department of justice, had responsibility for the courts, judicial appointments and constitutional matters).[63]

There is a case for saying that the current parliamentary rules are too restrictive, the opportunities for routine parliamentary engagement with the top-level courts too few. MPs and peers in the UK should, I believe, be encouraged rather than discouraged from making formal public comment on not just the work of the courts in general but also particular judgments. Again, there is perhaps scope for comparative lesson learning. For example, in the US Senate, senators regularly make statements commenting on recent US Supreme Court decisions. To take one random illustration, in February 2001 Senator Leahy commented on *Garrett v Alabama* in respectful, but critical, terms:

'U.S. SUPREME COURT – (Senate – February 28, 2001)

Mr. LEAHY. Mr. President [a reference to the presiding officer], I have become increasingly concerned about some of the recent actions of the U.S. Supreme Court. As a member of the bar of the Court, as a U.S. Senator, as an

---

62. *Erskine May*, see below.
63. Its terms of reference are similar to the other departmental scrutiny committees: 'to examine the expenditure, policy and administration of the Lord Chancellor's Department and associated public bodies'; it is made plain that this does not extend to 'individual cases' or individual judicial appointments. For a general discussion of parliamentary scrutiny, see G Drewry and D Oliver 'Parliamentary accountability for the administration of justice' in G Drewry and D Oliver (eds) *The Law and Parliament* (London: Butterworths, 1998) ch 3. In September 2003, the Committee was renamed the Constitutional Affairs Committee to reflect the new name (Department for Constitutional Affairs) for the Lord Chancellor's Department.

American, I, of course, respect the decisions of the Supreme Court as being the ultimate decisions of law for our country. As an American, I accept any of its decisions as the ultimate interpretation of our Constitution, whether I agree or disagree. I have probably supported the Supreme Court and our judicial system more than anybody else on this floor.

Having said that, I think we can at least still have in this country a discussion of some of the things the Court has done. Recently, we have seen another assault by the Court on the legislative powers of Congress.

My concern may be more in sadness than in anger over what has happened. It is very easy to give talks about activist Supreme Courts, but it is hard to think of a time, certainly in my lifetime, with a more activist Supreme Court than the current one.

Last week, the Court held that State employees are not protected by the Federal law banning discrimination against the disabled. The case was decided by the same 5-4 majority that brought us ...'

The idea that parliamentarians should be enabled to comment and question judges in the UK is not as alien and dangerous a practice as it might have seemed only relatively recently, as can be evidenced by two recent developments.

First, in March 2001 three senior judges (the Lord Chief Justice, the Master of the Rolls and the Senior Law Lord) accepted an invitation to appear before the Joint Committee on Human Rights, a parliamentary scrutiny committee consisting of peers and MPs, as it was taking evidence on the implementation of the Human Rights Act 1998. The judges were asked about judicial training, their views on the likely impact of the Act on the courts' caseload and developments in human rights law generally, and the practice of the courts on third-party interventions. The judges declined to answer some questions (for example on whether Article 6 of the ECHR called into question the independence of the Law Lords because they are members of the legislature); on this Lord Bingham simply said: 'I am afraid I see this as a question that will become litigious at some point and therefore I would not like to give any answer to the question here and now.'

A second example is the House of Lords debate held on 21 May 2003, following the recent controversy over the Home Secretary David Blunkett's criticisms of a judgment of Mr Justice Andrew Collins, and his broader remarks about the role of judges and judicial review.[64] One source of the concern about the Home Secretary's remarks was the occasions on which he chose to make them: in an article in the *Evening Standard* (a tabloid newspaper in London),[65] in radio interviews[66] and in a speech to a police officers' organisation. In the unprecedented House of Lords debate a couple of weeks later, initiated by Lord Rodgers of Quarry Bank (a Liberal Democrat peer), Lord Windlesham (the

---

64. See A Bradley 'Judicial independence under attack' [2003] PL 397.
65. David Blunkett 'I won't give in to the judges', 12 May 2003.
66. BBC Radio 4, 'World at One'. Mr Blunkett said: 'Frankly, I'm fed up with having to deal with the situation where Parliament debates the issues and the judges overturn them ... I am absolutely clear that we don't accept what Justice Collins has said. We will seek to overturn it' (quoted in 648 HL Official Report (5th series) col 878, 21 May 2003).

Principal of Brasenose College, Oxford and a former government minister) said:[67]

> 'My Lords, I start with a reflection. The remarkable tolerance of the British constitutional practice has been demonstrated by the Home Secretary, an elected Member of one House of Parliament, criticising the Lord Chief Justice on a public platform outside Parliament, and by the noble and Learned Lord, Lord Woolf, as a Member of the other House of Parliament, replaying from within it – and what an effective replay it has been.'

Mr Blunkett's bad tempered and ill-informed outburst is not the first of its kind from a Home Secretary. Several years ago, a not entirely dissimilar spat occurred between the then Home Secretary Michael Howard, aided and abetted by tabloid newspapers, and fuelled by ministerial frustration at what was seen as judicial sabotage of Conservative government policy.[68] Arguably, one reason for these hostilities may be that there are inadequate *formal* channels of communication between the judiciary, the executive and the legislature in the UK.

These two episodes – the appearance before a select committee and a debate sparked by a particular[69] judgment and a minister's response to it – reveal that it is *possible* for appropriate parliamentary dialogue to be established with and about the senior judiciary. The suggestion made in this article is that such interactions ought to be a routine part of the accountability practices for a new UK Supreme Court.

67. See 648 HL Official Report (5th series) col 884, 21 May 2003.
68. A Le Sueur 'The Judicial Review Debate: from Partnership to Friction' (1996) 31 Government and Opposition 8.
69. Since this article was written, several senior members of the judiciary gave oral evidence to the House of Commons Constitutional Affairs Committee in November and December 2003, in its inquiry into the Government's proposals to establish a new Supreme Court and reform judicial appointments in England and Wales, eg Lords Woolf, Bingham and Nicholls on 11 December 2003 (CH 48-iv).

A Supreme Court for the United Kingdom: views from the Northern Kingdom

Chris Himsworth
Edinburgh University

Alan Paterson
Strathclyde University

A. INTRODUCTION

Of the four Consultation Papers produced by the Department for Constitutional Affairs over the summer of 2003, in many ways the most interesting was *Constitutional Reform: A Supreme Court for the United Kingdom*,[1] not just for what it did say, but also for what it did not. For example, respondents were not asked whether the Government should replace the House of Lords with a Supreme Court or not. That was taken as a given. Yet the omission was all the more curious in the light of the fact, as subsequently became clear,[2] that at least half of the current Law Lords do not favour the introduction of a Supreme Court.[3] Similarly, the Paper asks whether the jurisdiction of the Privy Council in devolution cases should be transferred to the new Supreme Court, but not whether the new court should hear Scottish criminal appeals, or indeed whether it should hear any Scottish cases at all.[4] Agenda setting, was, of course, an

1.   Department for Constitutional Affairs, CP11/03 (July 2003) (hereinafter *Supreme Court*). For an important review of the arguments from a Scottish perspective, see J Chalmers 'Scottish Appeals and the Proposed Supreme Court' (2004) 8 Edin LR 4.
2.   See the Law Lords' response to CP 11/03 of 27 October 2003.
3.   These Law Lords were heavily criticised in the press for their conservatism. See especially P Riddell *The Times*, 13 November 2003 and M Kettle *Guardian*, 11 November 2003. Conservatism does weigh heavily in the corridors of the House of Lords. It was only in 2000, 80 years after an independent Ireland struck out on its own, that the Law Reports dropped the reference in the introduction to the annual Appeal Cases to 'Irish' as well as English and Scottish appeals.
4.   This paper does not address the claims for distinctive treatment made on behalf of Northern Ireland and Wales, where the claims are based not on systemic differences but divergence between rules, especially in the light of devolution, language and 'social arguments' deriving from the need to treat the different parts of the United Kingdom equally. In this last respect, perhaps the different regions of England could also stake separate claims, at least to representation on the bench. For articulation of the claims of Northern Ireland and Wales, see the evidence given to the inquiry undertaken by the House of Commons Select Committee for Constitutional Affairs (hereafter Constitutional Affairs Committee) on 2 December 2003. References in this paper to the oral evidence given to that Committee are to the uncorrected transcript on the Committee's website.

important part of modern-day politics, even before the era of spin; however, if the hope was that these issues would not be canvassed by respondents, it has proved a forlorn one.

Even without these attempts to channel responses onto the issues favoured by the Government, the proposal to establish a new Supreme Court for the United Kingdom was likely to provoke a response in Scotland different from that of mainstream opinion south of the border. The several asymmetries of the twenty-first century United Kingdom would ensure that. The Government could present its case for change in England and Wales and even in Northern Ireland as modernised business as usual, although the manner of the presentation of that case on the back of a Cabinet reshuffle could, of course, be criticised. In this respect it joined the proposed abolition of the post of Lord Chancellor – initially thought to be achievable by simple announcement to that effect but then requiring a stop-gap appointment and a consultation process of its own.[5]

But, in Scotland, the Supreme Court proposal has touched greater sensitivities deriving from (1) different perspectives – both between Scotland and England and within Scotland itself – on the political destiny of Scotland; (2) questions about how the present constitutional dispensation under the Scotland Act 1998, and especially the powers of the Scottish Parliament to legislate for the legal system of Scotland, affect the issue of adjudication at the highest levels; and, of much longer standing, (3) questions about the autonomy of the Scottish legal system itself which derives from the Treaty of Union 1707 and which has done much to determine the existing distinctive relationship between courts in Scotland and the House of Lords. Sensitivities in these three broad areas do, of course, overlap and produce a variety of responses which cannot be fully articulated here. The political nationalist in Scotland will, by nature, be resistant to any proposal to strengthen or raise the legitimacy of a UK institution at the cost of Scottish autonomy. Such a nationalist may also suspend his or her scepticism about the current devolved Parliament and assert that the Westminster Parliament's right to legislate for the regulation of final appeals from the Scottish courts is arguably a power which is not reserved to Westminster by the Scotland Act 1998.[6] A proposal for a Member's Bill in the Scottish Parliament which would abolish the right of appeal to the House of Lords in Scottish cases was initiated in September 2003 by an SNP member.[7] Political nationalists may also subordinate their general antipathy to the Treaty of Union to a regard for the autonomy it has the potential to deliver – a position famously taken in the past in the 'EIIR' case[8] and the campaign against the poll tax[9] – and join those 'legal nationalists' for whom the Treaty is fundamental

---

5.   *Constitutional reform: reforming the office of Lord Chancellor* CP 13/03 (2003).
6.   Alternatively, see Lord Hope of Craighead 'Taking the Case to London – Is it all over?' 1998 JR 135. See also Lord Hope's evidence to the Constitutional Affairs Committee on 2 Dec 2003 at QQ 299–300 where he speaks of the need for a 'Sewel motion' in the Scottish Parliament if the reform is to be implemented at Westminster.
7.   See the proposal of 11 September 2003 of Adam Ingram MSP for a Civil Appeals (Scotland) Bill. See also the motion in the Scottish Parliament by Margo MacDonald MSP on 'The Future of the Scottish Legal System' – S2M-179.
8.   *MacCormick v Lord Advocate* 1953 SC 396.
9.   See eg *Pringle, Petitioner* 1991 SLT 330; and *Murray v Rodgers* 1992 SLT 221. See also N Walker and C M G Himsworth 'The Poll Tax and Fundamental Law' 1991 JR 45.

to the autonomy of the legal system. When the Faculty of Advocates registered its opposition to aspects of the Supreme Court proposal on Treaty grounds,[10] it could do so without commitment to any particular *political* future for Scotland but with a view to retaining the capacity of any future court to continue its special relationship with Scotland and, though the argument may appear rather strained, without risk of subordination to the influence of the UK Department for Constitutional Affairs.[11]

On the other hand, those of a more unionist or federalist disposition will have less of a problem with the general idea of a Supreme Court for the United Kingdom and are indeed likely to welcome a strengthening of the institution, at least in its constitutional aspect. The case for a restructuring of the jurisdiction to determine 'devolution issues' under the Scotland Act 1998 (and the parallel provisions in the Government of Wales Act 1998 and the Northern Ireland Act 1998) by its transfer from the Judicial Committee of the Privy Council (JCPC) will not be unattractive and, although the line of division will be different from that resulting from the Treaty of Union, there will be some recognition that not only devolution issues (including, importantly, those raising questions of compatibility with European Community law and Convention rights under the European Convention on Human Rights) but also adjudication within matters reserved to Westminster by the Scotland Act itself might also be best handled at a UK level by the Supreme Court.

Somewhere in the middle are those who may, at least publicly, profess no commitment to one or other of Scotland's particular political futures but who would wish to see a rational outcome to the Supreme Court debate in so far as this affects Scottish interests in particular.

Whilst some issues will have a general UK character, others have a distinctively Scottish aspect, whether for historical Treaty-related reasons or for reasons deriving from the present devolution settlement. Some, as we saw at the outset, were canvassed quite fully in the Consultation Paper but others were not and may be in danger of being glossed over. From these issues we have chosen two principal aspects for consideration in this paper. First, the question of the scope of the Supreme Court's jurisdiction in Scottish matters and the related question of the rules of access (whether by leave or right) and, secondly, the question of the composition of the Court and appointments to its membership.

---

10. See the introduction to the Faculty's formal response to the Supreme Court consultation.

11. See also the robust submission by the Senators of the College of Justice on the requirements of the Treaty in their response to CP 11/03. However, for an alternative assessment of the intentions of those who negotiated the Treaty see A J MacLean 'The House of Lords and Appeals from the High Court of Justiciary 1707–1887' 1985 JR 192; and *Stair Memorial Encyclopaedia* vol 6 'Courts and Competency' paras 810-13. Separately, Lord Hope has expressed fears that English influence over the Court might increase in an undesirable way if it moves out of Parliament to Somerset House in the Strand and thus nearer to the English courts. At the social level, English judges might take to lunching with their English colleagues across the road rather than with Supreme Court judges. See evidence to the Constitutional Affairs Committee of 2 December 2003 at QQ 279–282 and 290. An answer might be to locate the Court in the Lake District?

B. THE SCOTTISH JURISDICTION OF A UNITED KINGDOM SUPREME COURT

Leaving on one side for a moment the question of *access* to a new Supreme Court, there are probably three different broad approaches to what the Scottish business of the court should be.[12] One approach, that adopted by the UK Government in its Consultation Paper, is simply to carry over to the new court the existing Scottish business of the House of Lords, adding only the 'devolution issues' business of the JCPC, assuming that that separate jurisdiction is indeed abolished. This is a minimalist approach of 'no change'. It involves an acknowledgement of the quite different approach to Scottish civil appeals which may at present be taken to the House of Lords and, on the other hand, criminal appeals which, unless a 'devolution issue' is also raised, in which case the JCPC may be the final tribunal, do not leave Scotland and are decided by the High Court of Justiciary in Edinburgh. The 'no change' approach to reform takes the view that this civil/criminal distinction is justified or at least not worth disturbing and that it should be carried forward as the basis of the Supreme Court's jurisdiction. None of the Government's questions in the Consultation Paper sought to invite any further discussion of the Scottish jurisdiction. The paper incorporated a reference to the Scottish Executive's contentment with the 'no change' approach[13] and, assuming the Supreme Court experiment proceeds at all, that is probably the approach that will be adopted.

A second approach, however, takes the present distinction between civil and criminal appeals more seriously; regards it as anomalous; and, given the opportunity provided by the Supreme Court proposals, would insist on resolving the anomaly. Either there is a case for all appeals going to the new Court or there is a case for none going, but the present half-way house is, in principle rather than as a matter of simple pragmatism, unsustainable. On the face of it, a resolution of the anomaly by sending criminal appeals to the Supreme Court seems, on the basis of the historical practice, which is plainly unsupportive,[14] the less rational answer. On the other hand, the actual case presented by the Government against taking such appeals to the Supreme Court appears to have little strength. The Consultation Paper[15] offers in support of the distinctive treatment of criminal appeals the dicta of Lord Hope of Craighead in *R v Manchester Stipendiary Magistrate, ex p Granada Television Ltd*[16] to the effect that the Scottish and English systems of criminal law are 'as distinct from each other as if they were two foreign countries'.[17] There is, however, a bit of 'sexing up' of the dossier here. Lord Hope did indeed use the

---

12. This section draws to an extent on C Himsworth 'A Supreme Court for the United Kingdom' (2003) SCOLAG 178.
13. *Supreme Court*, n 1 above, para 27 (on civil appeals). See also the Executive's response to CP 11/03 of 14 November 2003.
14. For discussion of this history and, in particular, the leading case of *Mackintosh v Lord Advocate* (1876) 3R(HL) 34, see the response of the Senators of the College of Justice to the consultation in relation to para 18. But see also MacLean, n 11 above; and *Stair Memorial Encyclopaedia* vol 6 'Courts and Competency' paras 810–813.
15. *Supreme Court*, n 1 above, para 26.
16. [2001] 1 AC 300.
17. [2001] 1 AC 300 at 304.

'two foreign countries' phrase but one should, with respect, question whether this can be deployed as a reason for not taking Scottish criminal appeals to a UK court. In an English case involving procedures for the enforcement by English courts of a warrant issued in Scotland, Lord Hope clearly felt it necessary to instruct his brethren, as well as a wider public, on the difference between Scotland and England in relationships between the police and the public prosecutor. What Lord Hope was plainly, and by his own example, not saying was that these differences could not be handled by a court of the standing of the present House of Lords or of the proposed Supreme Court. Nor is it only in the matter of procedural differences that the Law Lords can bridge the jurisdictional divide. The Scottish Law Lords frequently participate in English criminal appeals.[18] And some aspects of civil law must be just as 'foreign' or distinct and yet the judges on both sides of the divide – one thinks perhaps more of the speeches of Scottish judges in English cases because they are much more frequent – survive the experience.

Thus it is very difficult to sustain the argument that Scottish criminal appeals should be withheld from the Supreme Court on the grounds of their 'foreignness' and, if this is indeed the sole argument in favour of sustaining a distinction between criminal and civil matters, that case probably fails. If civil appeals continue to go to the Supreme Court, the argument against their being joined by criminal appeals is weak.

Some would respond to this dilemma by withdrawing all Scottish appeals – both criminal and civil – as the alternative route to removing the anomaly. Against this, however, it may be argued that not only do Scottish judges survive the cross-border experience in the House of Lords but their interventions provide the opportunity for serious contributions to the law of both jurisdictions. It would, of course, be completely different if there were evidence in the late twentieth or early twenty-first century of insensitivity by English judges as there was in the nineteenth century.[19] Lord Hope has himself written about the difficulty that Scottish judges have, 'even in today's much more enlightened climate', in resisting the desire among the English or common law members of the Appellate Committee that the law on each side of the Border should be the same.[20] It was indeed in *McFarlane v Tayside Health Board*[21] that Lord Slynn said that it had been accepted that the law of England and Scotland (on whether there should be a liability for a pregnancy leading to an unwanted but healthy child) were the same – 'It would be strange', he said almost provocatively, 'even absurd, if they were not'.[22]

But, if there are still occasional signs of unnecessary pressures towards uniformity, there is also much evidence of the deliberate use of speeches in the House of Lords to explore the current differences between Scottish and English rules and the desirability or not of future convergence. This inevitably arises

---

18. See eg very recently and very prominently, *A-G's Reference (No 2 of 2001)* [2003] UKHL 68.
19. The story is best told in A Dewar Gibb *Law from over the Border* (Edinburgh: W Green, 1950).
20. Lord Hope of Craighead 'Taking the case to London – Is it all over?' 1998 JR 135 at 146.
21. 2000 SC (HL) 1.
22. 2000 SC (HL) 1 at 4.

on those occasions where cases on the same issue are taken in combination from both jurisdictions with a view to ensuring parallel treatment.[23] But there are countless other occasions where cross-referencing between jurisdictions is used to illuminating effect.

Once again, Lord Hope has been a principal exponent. In *R v Bow Street Metropolitan Magistrate, ex p Pinochet Ugarte (No 2)*[24] and even more so in *Porter v Magill*[25] he took the opportunity in English appeals to reconcile the law of Scotland and England on the issue of the test for 'apparent bias' as an aspect of natural justice. In *R (Burkett) v Hammersmith and Fulham London Borough Council*[26] he discussed the issues of 'promptitude' in judicial review by reference to the English three-month time limit and the Scottish concept of mora. In many other cases, Lord Hope has managed to work into his analysis of the relevant English law a comparative reference to the position in Scots law, to point out present similarities or differences. In the English case of *Canada Trust Co v Stolzenberg (No 2)*[27] he was at pains to make clear that a decision on domicile might well produce a situation in which the law of Scotland and England was different in an area where the international obligation under the Lugano Convention invited a common UK response.[28]

The question of which way one should react to the civil/criminal anomaly tends to expose the fault lines in opinion on the Supreme Court project in general as discussed in the Introduction. In particular, however, it exposes a dissensus on the point of a UK top court[29] at all. On the one hand, there are those whose starting point is the (conceptual) package of separate courts, separate sources, separate professions and separate legal education which constitute the 'Scottish legal system'; whose view of the present House of Lords is that, in respect of Scotland, it operates as an institution within the Scottish legal system and applies Scots law as opposed to the law of the other UK jurisdictions; who would probably, therefore, deny a UK role for the court and the existence of anything called 'UK law';[30] and whose judgment on the need for a Supreme Court at all is based on utility and, therefore, on the perceived 'advantages' to the Scottish system.[31] Do 'we' or does the system 'need' a third

---

23. Recent examples include *Morris v KLM Royal Dutch Airlines, King v Bristow Helicopters Ltd* [2002] 2 AC 628.
24. [2000] 1 AC 119.
25. [2002] 2 AC 357.
26. [2002] 3 All ER 97 at 114–117.
27. [2002] AC 1.
28. [2002] AC 1 at 23–36.
29. A Le Sueur and R Cornes 'What do the Top Courts do?' (2000) 53 CLP 53.
30. For a powerful defence of this position, see the response of the Senators of the College of Justice to CP 11/03 in relation to para 18, and especially on the issue of confining the binding authority of decisions of the Appellate Committee to the jurisdiction generating the appeal. One effect of the proposed transfer of JCPC business to the Supreme Court would be to dissolve the existing difference between the authority in Scotland of decisions of the JCPC and the Appellate Committee explored by Lord Hope in *A-G's Reference (No 2 of 2001)* [2003] UKHL 68 at [102]–[108].
31. As Lord Hope has said: 'I have always looked on the House of Lords as a court which serves Scotland in its own jurisdiction. The idea of a UK supreme court is a slightly misleading one from the Scottish point of view.' (Evidence to the Constitutional Affairs Committee, 2 December 2003 at Q 279).

tier of appeal? What is the gain to the system to be derived from an appeal to London? Does Scots law gain from the exposure of decisions to a court external to the immediate system and staffed by judges, a majority of whom, even in Scottish appeals, are not natives of that system? Is it really a 'higher' or better qualified court than those in Edinburgh when it comes to Scots law? Can one, therefore, expect 'better' decisions on appeal? Are appeals to London worth it, both in terms of expense to litigants and in terms of the investment made by the Scottish legal system when it sends at least two of its most senior judges south of the border?[32] Such an approach tends towards a cost-benefit analysis of the pros and cons of appellate mechanisms which may lead to different views of civil and criminal appeals and perhaps to different categories of civil appeal, on which see further below.

The alternative view is not to start from the question of the benefits or otherwise to any particular one of the UK legal systems but to see the proposal for a new court as something which the House of Lords almost succeeds in being, but not quite, at least expressly, which is the fulfilment for the United Kingdom of the general constitutional imperative for a genuine Supreme Court for the state as a whole. This does not necessarily demand a 'constitutional court', and certainly not a court with a general power to disallow Acts of Parliament, but expresses the need for a general right of access, unless there are the most compelling specific arguments to the contrary, to the state's highest court, and especially if that court is to be seen to have a strategic role beyond that of merely correcting errors in the courts below.[33] Such an imperative appears to operate elsewhere, whether the state concerned has a unitary or devolved or federal character. Even countries which accommodate combinations of broadly common law and civilian systems such as the United States and Canada do not deny a form of universal access to their supreme courts, even if, as with Canada and Quebec, this may produce a case for maintaining a majority of judges from a distinctive system to decide appeals from that system.[34] If respect for a general constitutional imperative of this nature is taken as the starting-point, then one is not concerned with advantages and disadvantages to this or that part of the state but with an assumption of the application of a general rule unless a compelling exception can be argued. On this view, therefore, if the Supreme Court of the United Kingdom is to be available to the citizens of England, Wales and Northern Ireland in both civil and criminal appeals, a heavy onus lies on those who would seek a different dispensation for Scottish citizens. This says nothing about the law to be applied in Supreme Court appeals. It certainly does not demand a sudden uniformity of the law in either civil or criminal matters across the United Kingdom. But it does assert that, however much history may have made it acceptable for the House of Lords in the past, asymmetric access to a state's Supreme Court is highly problematic.

Although it is the existing distinction between Scottish civil and criminal appeals which provides the principal framework within which the jurisdiction

---

32. As Lord Hope has also asked, 'What's in it for us?': 1998 JR 135 at 145. See also H L MacQueen 'Scotland and a Supreme Court for the UK?' 2003 SLT (News) 279.
33. For an articulation of that distinction, see Dame Brenda Hale in evidence to the Constitutional Affairs Committee on 18 November 2003 at Q 167.
34. P W Hogg *Constitutional Law of Canada* (Toronto: Carswell, 4th edn, 1997) p 215.

of a future Supreme Court can be debated – is the distinction anomalous; should the anomaly be resolved? – recent constitutional reforms have provided other possibilities and two variants should be briefly mentioned.

The first would be a proposal[35] that the only UK Supreme Court needed, from a Scottish perspective, is, in effect, a constitutional court confined to the determination of those matters currently defined as 'devolution issues' under the Scotland Act 1998 and decided by the JCPC. These include all aspects of the competence of the Scottish Parliament and Executive and extend, therefore, as earlier noted, to questions of compatibility with EC law and Convention rights. Whatever arrangements are made for England and Wales and for Northern Ireland, this would remove any UK-wide jurisdiction in relation to other civil and criminal matters which, for Scotland, would be determined finally at the level of her own Supreme Court. Lost under such a dispensation would be any formal opportunity for the resolution of issues common to all jurisdictions, although there would doubtless be a continuing assumption that, where appropriate, the several courts of final appeal would take due account of each others' decisions. The determination of a single UK line on 'non-constitutional' issues would be lost by the courts, although the power of the Westminster Parliament to reinstate uniformity, or indeed diversity along different lines, would remain.

If, however, there were to be any general acceptance of the desirability of designating a UK Supreme Court jurisdiction along 'constitutional lines', additional difficulties would present themselves, especially in the matter of the adjudication of Convention rights. 'Devolution issues' are currently confined to the competences of the Scottish Parliament and Executive but would not a 'constitutional' jurisdiction have to accommodate also Convention rights issues wherever they arose, ie where it is the activities of other Scottish public authorities which come under scrutiny? And, of course, the capacity for a Convention rights issue to be raised in almost any case involving a public authority might leave few cases not vulnerable to the jurisdiction of the Supreme Court. The net is cast even wider to the extent that, by involving the doctrine of horizontal effect, human rights issues can be seen to permeate the outer reaches of private law where, on the face if it, no 'public authority' might seem to be involved.[36] Quite quickly a 'constitutional' jurisdiction might subsume, in the name of human rights, practically all categories of appeal, making any distinction on these lines elusive.[37]

---

35. One canvassed by Stephen Tierney, an Edinburgh University Law School colleague, at a seminar on the Supreme Court held at the University on 29 September 2003.

36. See eg H MacQueen and D Brodie 'Private Rights, Private Law, and the Private Domain' in A Boyle et al (eds) *Human Rights and Scots Law* (Oxford: Hart Publishing, 2002).

37. From a quite different perspective it may be questioned whether there is indeed any strong argument in favour of maintaining uniformity across human rights adjudication. See C Himsworth 'The Hamebringing: Devolving Rights Seriously' in Boyle et al (eds), n 36 above. There should at least be room for human rights adjudication which is sensitive to the different rules and procedures of different legal systems. For discussion of the differing impact of delay in criminal cases, see Lord Hope in evidence to the Constitutional Affairs Committee on 2 December 2003 at Q 304. And see now *A-G's Reference (No 2 of 2001)* [2003] UKHL 68.

A rather different redrawing of the categories of UK Supreme Court jurisdiction would be to allocate to the Court the 'devolution issues', as currently proposed by the Government but then to rely on the Scotland Act's distinction between 'reserved' and 'devolved' matters[38] not only to grant to the Supreme Court the jurisdiction to determine the competence of the Scottish Parliament or Executive but also to define the Court's general jurisdiction by the same test, ie the Court's jurisdiction would be confined to the determination only of 'reserved matters' whilst issues in the devolved domain would be decided finally in Scotland.[39] At first sight, this approach would appear to have attractions. There would be a certain symmetry between the judicial and the legislative arrangements for Scotland. These attractions may, however, be quickly exposed as superficial. Such a symmetry would not be one acknowledged in the rest of Scotland's judicial system. Down to their lowest levels, the courts of Scotland have a mixed jurisdiction of devolved and reserved matters which would presumably continue. There is no general recognition of any separation of devolved law with devolved courts and, on the other hand, reserved law and reserved courts.[40] And, in any event, if a strict symmetry is to be found between the legislative and judicial arrangements, the retained power of the Westminster Parliament to legislate on *any* aspect of Scottish affairs[41] would presumably have to be reflected in a power of the UK Supreme Court to determine any matter as well? Such considerations quite apart, the task of dividing cases into the devolved and reserved would present immense practical difficulties and it would be difficult to imagine that, if such division were sought, the role of the Supreme Court could become any more than that of a court of reference for the dispensing of preliminary rulings to the Scottish courts.

A leave filter for Supreme Court business?

The Government's Consultation Paper posed two questions about the control of access to the proposed Supreme Court in the form of a leave filter. In relation to appeals from England and Wales, the question was whether, rather than permitting some appeals to reach the Court, as they can at present reach the Appellate Committee, by leave of the lower court, to impose a uniform need for the leave of the Supreme Court itself. In relation to Scottish appeals, the main question was whether they should be brought in line with whatever rule was adopted for England and Wales. That would involve a significant change from current practice which permits most Scottish appeals to proceed (according to a practice attributable to the Claim of Right 1689) as of right,[42] although subject to the need for certification by two counsel[43] that the point at issue is one justifying an appeal.

---

38. 'Devolved matters' is not a term used in the Act.
39. Hector MacQueen distinguishes 'single market law' from the rest for this purpose. See 2003 SLT (News) 279.
40. See A Le Sueur [2003] PL 368.
41. Scotland Act 1998, s 28(7).
42. For exceptions, see *Stair Memorial Encyclopaedia* vol 6, para 829.
43. Normally, but not necessarily, counsel in the case.

Thus the question of whether a new court would demand a new uniformity of approach again dominates. As the Consultation Paper noted, it could be argued that 'an unjustified anomaly' would be permitted if citizens in different parts of the United Kingdom had different rights of access to its highest court – although presumably no greater an anomaly than that of denying some citizens a right of access in criminal matters altogether which is something the Government was willing to tolerate in its own proposals? On the other hand, there was no evidence, it was said, that change was needed; and there were strong arguments for leaving the position unchanged.[44] None of the strong arguments was spelled out[45] and it seems unlikely that a principled justification for the existing Scottish rules would be forthcoming. What *has* been argued is that, if it were to be recognised, in the light of earlier arguments, that Scottish appeals to the Supreme Court deserve exceptional treatment, this could be achieved by exceptional access rules. They, rather than the rules on jurisdiction itself, could be used to protect the special position of Scots law. James Chalmers has suggested that a filter applicable to Scotland only could exclude any appeal which, whatever its subject-matter, did not raise a 'UK-wide' issue, ie a point of law both of general public importance *and* common to another UK jurisdiction as well as Scotland.[46] As a form of compromise if a wider general exclusion of Scottish appeals were rejected, this would have attractions to those who seek such a narrowing of the Court's powers in relation to Scotland. But, unless it were balanced by a similar filtering out of 'England-only' appeals, it would represent a compromise too far for those who seek a genuine top court for the whole of the state – too much of a concession to the cherry-picking approach to Supreme Court design.

C. COMPOSITION OF THE COURT AND SELECTION OF JUDGES

Inevitably, the jurisdiction of the new Supreme Court has implications for its composition and even the method by which its members are selected. The more closely it resembles an 'ordinary' final court of appeal with a broad jurisdiction (including Scottish criminal appeals), the more its composition should reflect that caseload, much as it currently does, eg by allocating at least two places for judges from Scotland (one of whom would need expertise in criminal matters), Northern Ireland, the Chancery and Family Divisions as well as the Queen's Bench, not to mention someone with commercial expertise. Such an allocation would not satisfy those critics in Scotland who object to Scottish appeals to the House of Lords being determined by a majority of non-Scottish-trained Law Lords. However, solutions such as suggesting that the non-Scottish judges should practise 'judicial deference' to their Scottish colleagues (potentially producing the anomaly of an appeal from a court of three in the Inner House to a final appeal court with only two Scots sitting) or of rotating part-time Scottish

---

44. *Supreme Court*, n 1 above, para 56.
45. The Faculty of Advocates did subsequently argue in their submission that, without further consideration, no change should be made.
46. See Chalmers, n 1 above.

judges into the Supreme Court to hear Scottish cases (likely to fall foul of Art 6 of the ECHR) seem equally unpalatable.[47] Perhaps because of this, the main Scottish responses to the Paper[48] all call for the possibility of three Scottish judges being available in the new Court, even if that means expanding the Court to 15 members. The Faculty of Advocates, in fact, insists that both Scotland and Northern Ireland should be represented by at least three judges with relevant experience of their respective jurisdictions. This is unlikely to appeal to the Treasury, the Government or the English judiciary, particularly in relation to Northern Ireland.[49] Interestingly, neither the existing Law Lords, nor the Bar Council in their responses favoured a statutory entitlement of even two Scots on the Court, preferring a convention of two, which could be flexibly interpreted, *either way*. The question of the comparative number of judges from the UK jurisdictions involves considerations of balance. Indeed, in the discussion of appointments to the Court of Appeal in *'A New Way of Appointing Judges'* the Government refers expressly to the 'overall public interest in a balanced and high quality group of judges'.[50] This seems eminently sensible. The need for balance on the Supreme Court is indeed a paramount one, but it must be an open question as to whether that balance should be restricted merely to these jurisdictional considerations, as opposed to gender and ethnicity, or even, at least in the ideal world, to the social and policy views of the judiciary. The case for enhancing the gender and ethnicity balance on the Supreme Court rests not simply on equal opportunities considerations or even that they will make a difference but also on democratic legitimacy grounds.[51] While there are many who believe in the 'trickle-up' theory, namely, that current imbalances on this front will be overcome in the course of time, other observers are less sanguine that the problem will be resolved in the near or even medium-term future. These include Dame Brenda Hale, the only woman to have made it so far to the House of Lords.[52] Even the Judges' Council faced with the

---

47. See D Carr 'Scotland and the Supreme Court' 2003 SCOLAG 206; and H L MacQueen 'Scotland and a Supreme Court for the UK?' 2003 SLT (News) 279.
48. From the Senators of the College of Justice (p 7), the Faculty of Advocates (Qn 3), the Law Society (p 5) and the Scottish Executive (p 3). The last, however, would accept a statutory entitlement to two Scottish-trained judges provided the door was left open for more Scottish members or reserves.
49. Where the law is closer to English law than is the position in Scotland.
50. Department for Constitutional Affairs *Constitutional Reform: A New Way of Appointing Judges* CP10/03 (July 2003) para 58, p 30 (hereinafter *Appointing Judges*). The Senators of the College of Justice in Scotland also make the point that appointments to the Supreme Court will need to bear in mind 'the balance of membership required by the Court' in their response to the Supreme Court Consultation Paper at p 8.
51. See eg Dame Brenda Hale 'Equality and the Judiciary' [2001] PL 489; Dame Brenda Hale 'Equality in the Judiciary', 10th Pilgrim Fathers' Lecture, October 2003; the Rt Hon Beverley McLachlin CJ 'Promoting Gender Equality in the Judiciary', seminar to the Association of Women Barristers, House of Commons, 2 July 2003; and Kate Malleson *The New Judiciary* (Aldershot: Dartmouth Plg, 1999).
52. 'Most serious outside observers know that this will not happen': quoted in Frances Gibb 'Choice of judges fails democratic legitimacy' *The Times*, 4 April 2001. The Commission for Racial Equality in its evidence before the Constitutional Affairs Committee on 18 November 2003 opposed waiting for the 'trickle up effect'.

handful of female judges in the High Court and above in England and Wales, has said:[53]

'One criticism that can be made of the existing situation is that the senior judiciary lacks diversity. The criticism is accepted, and the negative impact of this shortcoming is readily acknowledged. By increasing the diversity of our judiciary, while continuing to appoint the best candidates, we will help to generate public confidence in the justice system.'

Other than passing the thorny problem of resolving the diversity imbalance in the higher courts to the proposed judicial appointments commission, the Council made no suggestions as to how it might be resolved. The Council, like many before them, makes it clear that diversity cannot be pursued at the expense of merit. This seems unexceptionable except to the critics such as the Chief Justice of Canada, Beverley McLachlin, who argue that the traditional concept of 'judicial merit' is not as objective or as immutable as is often implied. In her view:

'Human beings have a tendency to see merit only in those who exhibit the same qualities that they possess ... Senior lawyers are no exception. So when they look for merit, they tend to look for someone like themselves.'[54]

McLachlin commends the approach to 'merit' taken by Canadian federal authorities in the last 15 years, which has transformed the representation of minority candidates on the Canadian federal courts. Their approach appears to have been to re-interpret the concept of 'merit' in merit selection, and to focus more on the legal requirements for appointment and the potential of the candidate to do the job rather than to apply traditional, unwritten concepts of 'merit', eg the view that the only acceptable candidates for appointment to the higher courts are successful silks generally with at least ten years' standing. This was not seen by the reformers as positive discrimination (although some have classed it as affirmative action) so much as a recognition that traditional concepts of 'merit' indirectly discriminate against minority candidates as well as going far beyond the statutory criteria for appointment to the higher judiciary. As a result of the Canadian federal policy the proportion of female, federal judges there rose from 3% in 1980 to 26% in 2003.[55]

The controversial suggestion that the Supreme Court might ideally contain a balance in the social and policy views of its members, flows from a recognition that in the Supreme Court the judiciary will be engaged in policymaking and lawmaking, as they currently are in the House of Lords. The day is long gone when Law Lords could credibly deny that lawmaking is part of their role. As Lord Reid of Drem observed in relation to judicial lawmaking

---

53. *Judges' Council response to the Consultation papers on Constitutional Reform* (November 2003) para 72, p 16. In November 2003 only six of 106 High Court judges were women and two out of 38 Lord Justices of Appeal.
54. The Rt Hon Beverley McLachlin, Chief Justice of Canada 'Promoting Gender Equality in the Judiciary', seminar to the Association of Women Barristers, House of Commons, 2 July 2003.
55. The up-to-date figure for female judges in England and Wales in 2003 was 14.9%.

over 30 years ago, 'We do not believe in fairy tales any more'.[56] Moreover, the more the Supreme Court resembles a Constitutional Court with a substantial EU, human rights or judicial review jurisdiction[57] or even a 'devolution issues' court, the more the work of the Court will focus on areas where the scope for judicial discretion and policymaking is substantial. Some scholars have even argued that the judicial freedom of manoeuvre in these fields is such that it has created a democratic deficit, leading to a call for greater accountability in the judiciary on the basis that they are wielders of official power in a democracy.[58] One way to increase accountability without necessarily interfering with judicial independence is to reform the judicial appointment procedures for the senior judiciary. This is a matter of considerable sensitivity and an area where consensus is unlikely to be achieved. The response of Mr Blunkett to defeats for the Government in judicial review cases in the past year[59] has understandably provoked some of the senior judiciary in England to speak out against the possibility of political interference in the selection of judges.[60] Despite support in such contrasting broadsheets as the *Guardian* and the *Daily Telegraph* for a more accountable judicial appointment system[61] in an era where the role of the senior judiciary has become more politicised, to pursue issues

56. 'The Judge as Law Maker' (1972) (XII) Journal of the Society of Public Teachers of Law 22. Cited with approval by Justice Michael Kirby of the Australian High Court in his Hamlyn Lectures on *Judicial Activism* (delivered on 19 and 20 November 2003 at Exeter University Law School); by Lord Hoffmann in 'The Role of the Appellate Judge in England', address to the Franco-British Lawyers' Society, Glasgow, 20 September 2003; and by Lord Browne-Wilkinson in *Kleinwort Benson Ltd v Lincoln CC* [1998] 3 WLR 1095 at 1100, adding 'In truth judges make and change the law.' Interestingly, the Law Lords in their response to the *Supreme Court* Consultation Paper, n 2 above, observe (para 30, p 11) that the qualities required of a Law Lord include 'the capacity to formulate legal policy at a high level'.
57.   The entry to Europe and primacy of EU law has led to the judges de facto being in a position to comment on the constitutionality of British statutes. Again, the devolution settlement gives the judiciary the power to challenge legislation of the Scottish Parliament on the grounds that it contravenes the terms of the Scotland Act 1998.
58.   See R Stevens 'A Loss of Innocence?: Judicial Independence and the Separation of Powers' (1999) 19 OJLS 365 at 399; and R Stevens *The English Judges* (Oxford: Hart Publishing, 2002) Curiously, the Judges' Council in responding to the Lord Chancellor's four Consultation Papers, identify exactly these areas of law as having changed the judges' role with a consequent need for judicial independence (n 53 above, para 31, p 7), although there is no reference to the changes having any implications for accountability.
59.   See also his speech to the Police Federation in Blackpool in May 2003: 'I just like judges that live in the same real world as the rest of us. I just want judges that help us and help you to do the job.'
60.   See the remarks of Lord Woolf and Lord Justice Judge at a press conference held by the judges to express disquiet at the proposed reforms. The latter underlined his concerns at possible threats to judicial independence from extremists by referring to the rise of Hitler under the Weimar republic and to the strength of the National Front in the recent French presidential election. Whilst tactically risky, it is unclear that this approach significantly hampered the judges' subsequent discussions with the Government. 'Top judge fears legal reform will raise ghost of Nazis' *The Times*, 7 November 2003, p 4.
61.   See Stevens (1999), n 58 above, at 398.

of balance and judicial activism amongst the new Supreme Court[62] with respect to judicial policymaking may simply prove impossible in the current climate of mistrust between the English senior judiciary and the executive. Suggestions that a Supreme Court Appointments Commission should follow the US or South Africa in allowing public hearings[63] in which the candidate's views on matters of legal policymaking might be explored, are likely to prove far too controversial in today's climate and perceived as an open threat to judicial independence.[64] Even in a private interview conducted by an Appointments Commission such questions are likely to be thought unseemly. But it is unclear that to assert that, at least in abstract theory, there would be merit in a membership of the new Court which was balanced in its outlook, is politically unthinkable. Part of the difficulty, therefore, lies in the method of judicial appointment which is adopted in respect of the Supreme Court.[65] Here, as with so many issues touching on the judiciary, the challenge is to find an appropriate balance between judicial independence and accountability.[66] In the context of judicial appointment this tension manifests itself as a division of power between the executive and the judiciary, each acting in the name of the public interest. The Consultation Paper's first option for appointment to the Supreme Court is simply to preserve what is effectively the status quo. On this approach

62. During the three hearings of the *Pinochet* case in the House of Lords the *Daily Telegraph* on the 18 January 1999 ranked the Law Lords on a conservative-liberal continuum of judicial attitudes. On judicial activism generally, see Malleson, n 51 above, ch 2.

63. See eg Stevens (1999), n 58 above, at 399. As Stevens shows, Sir Thomas Legg – former Permanent Secretary to the LCD – and leading Conservative MPs have called for confirmation hearings for senior judicial appointments in England and Wales: at 400. In practice, public challenges to potential federal judges in the US Senate are much rarer that the popular memory suggests. Only four of 168 Bush nominees for federal judicial appointments have been rejected in the Senate: *New York Times*, 10 November 2003. Moreover, the public hearings in South Africa eschew ideological interrogations.

64. The Consultation Paper, having raised the possibility of confirmation hearings, immediately rejects them since it would bring politics into the appointments process and undermine the independence of the judiciary: *Appointing Judges*, n 50 above, para 45, p 33. As the Law Lords observe in their response to the Paper (n 2 above, para 16, p 6): 'The process of appointment [to the Supreme Court] should be wholly apolitical and should not in any way infringe the independence of the judges.' Interestingly, the Bar Council seems also to have rejected confirmation hearings for the reason that they would encourage unimaginative appointments from the minister. See their evidence to the Constitutional Affairs Committee, 18 November 2003 at QQ 137–138.

65. Part of the problem also turns on whether the Supreme Court is going to sit en banc or in panels. Robert Stevens has been particularly scathing as to the damage caused to the public perception of the authority of the House of Lords in the *Pinochet* hearings by the differing compositions of the panels in each hearing. See Stevens (1999), n 58 above. The *Supreme Court* Consultation Paper whilst acknowledging the problem that the composition of the panel may affect the outcome of the case is unwilling to accept that there is any particular problem with respect to the Supreme Court on this issue: n 1 above, paras 50–52, pp 36–37. Few of the responses favoured the new Court sitting en banc since they regarded this as either impractical in resource terms or opening the door to politicisation of the Court.

66. See A Paterson, T St J N Bates and M Poustie *The Legal System of Scotland* (Edinburgh: W Green, 4th edn, 1999) ch 8.

appointment would be by the Queen on the advice of her ministers (the Prime Minister after consultation with the First Minister in Scotland and the First and Deputy First Minister in Northern Ireland). Each minister in turn would have consulted with the senior members of the judiciary in each jurisdiction. As can be seen, this approach, although sometimes portrayed as appointment by the executive, actually involves a partnership with the senior judiciary. The merit of such an approach is that it would preserve political accountability *through politicians*. Interestingly, with the exception of the Senators of the College of Justice in Scotland,[67] this is not a solution that appealed to many of the major respondents to the Paper. For some, the objection was the involvement of Government ministers;[68] for others it was a preference for a nominating commission composed largely of existing members of the Supreme Court;[69] for the majority the problem was that the status quo was sufficiently unpalatable in terms of transparency, independence, credibility and legitimacy as to have undermined public confidence in the process and led the Government to propose the introduction of a Judicial Appointments Commission in the parallel Consultation Paper, *Constitutional Reform: A New Way of Appointing Judges*.[70] Not surprising, therefore, that the second option put forward by the Government in the Supreme Court paper is a special Appointments Commission. Here the Government's instincts are likely to be sound. All the policy and human rights arguments for a greater separation of powers in the appointing process, in order to preserve judicial independence, apply even more strongly to appointments to a Supreme Court than to lower court posts. Again, the need for the process to command public confidence surely requires a more transparent and practically accountable approach than that which pertains at present.[71] Faced with a choice between a Commission that would advise the Queen directly on appointments or one that would recommend one or two names to a

67. Their view was that an Appointments Commission would lack the necessary expertise to assess the comparative merits of senior judges or the balance of membership required by the Court (p 8). The tenor of the submission suggests that for these posts the status quo is, in their view, rightly dominated by the senior judiciary.
68. Eg the response of the Law Society of Scotland on p 4.
69. A position favoured by the existing Law Lords (p 9), the Judges'Council (p 29) and some in the Faculty of Advocates (Qn 11). Here the power in the process has shifted largely into the hands of the judiciary.
70. *Appointing Judges*, n 50 above.
71. This may not be simple to achieve. Under the current system, in theory the Lord Chancellor could have been held to account in the Upper Chamber for his judicial appointments. However, as Lord Mackay of Clashfern honestly admitted, this form of theoretical accountability was never exercised in practice (see Malleson, n 51 above, p 88). If there is to be a Judicial Appointments Commission it must issue an Annual Report and be prepared to defend it before a parliamentary select committee each year. The current Lord Chancellor, Lord Falconer of Thoroton, indicated in his evidence to the House of Commons Committee on the Lord Chancellor's Department on Monday 30 June 2003 at QQ 66–67 that in order to prevent totally unacceptable individuals being appointed: 'One of the issues we need to accommodate in the Appointments Commission is accountability to Parliament for the judges … [whom they nominate].'

minister[72] who would then advise the Queen, the Government opts for the latter, although no reasons for its choice are given. Judged by the dissensus on this issue amongst respondents, this is clearly a very contentious issue. The essence of the debate appears to be how much residual power to leave with the executive, how much with the judiciary (whether indirectly through consultation, or directly through membership of the special Appointments Commission) and how much to other stakeholders who appear on the Appointments Commission. The Government's approach leaves a delicate balance of power between the various stakeholders whilst retaining a non-trivial role for the executive. Ironically, the very fact that appointing a judge to the Supreme Court is inevitably a more 'political' act than appointing a circuit judge,[73] has led some respondents to argue for excluding the executive altogether and others to argue for a residual area of leeway for the executive.[74] The Government toyed with allowing the proposed Appointments Commissions in each constituent jurisdiction of the UK to nominate members from their own jurisdiction, to the Supreme Court. However, they reject this option because:[75] 'The Court will sit as a single UK court and it is important that it is seen to be a collegiate body.' This seems to be a tacit admission of the need for balance and taking a holistic view in the appointments to the Court, a position which we have argued for earlier. Accordingly, the Government's proposal that there be a separate, composite Supreme Court Appointments Commission made up of members of each of the judicial appointments commissions in England and Wales, Scotland and Northern Ireland appears a

72. The Prime Minister after consultation with the First Minister in Scotland and the First and Deputy First Minister in Northern Ireland. The Scottish Judicial Appointments Board has operated along similar lines in its first year. None of its 44 nominations was queried by the Executive. However, the experience of the Ontario Judicial Appointments Advisory Committee, which offers a wider degree of discretion to ministers, may not have not been entirely satisfactory in this regard – since it is thought by some to have encouraged party politics to come into judicial appointments. Significantly, the majority of the existing Law Lords favour the Commission recommending only one name to the Secretary of Sate for Constitutional Affairs in order that the process be 'wholly apolitical' (see para 24 of the Law Lords' response, n 64 above). The Bar Council prefers one name to be offered to the Prime Minister, with the possibility, in extreme cases of rejection on cause shown (see para 35, p 10).
73. Because in the former court, whatever its jurisdiction, the judiciary will inevitably (for the reasons discussed above) be more engaged in policymaking and lawmaking than their counterparts in the lower courts.
74. As the Bar Council pertinently notes in its response to the Supreme Court Paper, para 27, p 8: 'it is important to recognise that the executive does have a legitimate interest in the composition of the Court … it is important to avoid a situation where the judiciary can be portrayed by a hostile executive as an un-elected body responsible to no-one should there ever be genuine constitutional conflict.' For a similar argument see comments of Ross Cranston MP, former Solicitor General, during the proceedings of the Constitutional Affairs Committee on the 18 November 2003 at Q 143.
75. *Supreme Court*, n 1 above, para 38, p 28.

reasonable one,[76] providing an appropriate balance between lay, legal and judicial members can be struck on the composite Commission.

What would be an appropriate balance? Here we reach another contentious area associated with the reform. The Consultation Paper on the Supreme Court is silent on this issue, but that on *A new way of Appointing Judges* indicates that the success of an independent Appointments Commission depends on the balance of its membership. This, they believe, will prevent any one section from dominating the Commission or 'the vested interests of the groups from which [the Commission's] members are drawn' from so dominating the Commission.[77] The Law Lords, the Judges' Council and the Bar Council consider that in the case of the Supreme Court what is needed is a smallish, ad hoc Commission dominated (numerically) by existing members of the Supreme Court (including the President and Vice-President).[78] Although this would shift some power away from the Government towards the public (represented by the lay members), it would allocate the great bulk of the power of appointment to the senior judiciary and the members of the Supreme Court in particular. Judged by their responses, the Law Lords and the Judges' Council consider this to be an appropriate balance to the Commission because (1) they perceive the candidates for selection as coming overwhelmingly from the appeal courts below and (2) only the Supreme Court members would have the knowledge and expertise to assess the comparative merits of judges from these appeal courts or the balance of membership required by the Court. There must be a risk that disinterested observers (not to mention the Government) are likely to view this as a bid for judicial supremacy.[79] Certainly, it is unlikely to be well received by the school of thought which views judicial dominance of judicial appointment procedures as democratically suspect and a hindrance to greater diversity on the bench. As the newest Law Lord, Lady Hale has observed: 'Depending on the composition of the Commission, the [new] process might be even more under the control of the existing judiciary [than the old]. What Helena Kennedy[80] has called the 'potential for cloning' could be just as

---

76. *Supreme Court*, n 1 above, para 43, p 31. This approach was acceptable to many respondents including the Commissioners for Judicial Appointments, the English and Scottish Law Societies and (in part) the Bar Council. However, the Faculty of Advocates (for slightly convoluted reasons relating to the Act of Union) is opposed to the Commission's members being drawn from the English, Scottish and Northern Irish Appointments Commissions. The Law Lords and the Judges' Council by implication also rejected the composite model (n 2 above, para 26, p 9 and n 53 above, para 164, p 29 respectively).

77. *Appointing Judges*, n 50 above, para 120, p 56. The Government's preferred balance for the JAC, as set out in the Consultation Paper, is five judges, five lawyers and five laypersons. (para 121, p 57).

78. *Appointing Judges*, n 50 above, para 26, p 9 and para 164, p 29 respectively. The Faculty of Advocates has some sympathy with the similar option of the Court appointing its own members but accept that if there is to be a Commission it should have a significant lay membership.

79. In fairness, it should be noted that Lord Mackay of Clashfern has indicated that while he was Lord Chancellor he 'always convened a meeting of all the Law Lords as well as the Lord Chief Justice and the Master of the Rolls in deciding who to nominate to the Prime Minister for appointments in the House of Lords'. See his evidence to the Constitutional Affairs Committee on 16 September 2003 at QQ 18–19.

80. *Eve was Framed: Women and British Justice* (London: Chatto and Windus, 1992) p 267.

strong.'[81] Similarly, the former Permanent Secretary to the Lord Chancellor, Sir Thomas Legg, has indicated that one reason that he has been a long-time opponent of a Judicial Appointments Commission[82] was that it would be likely that the senior judiciary would inevitably have a heavy and often predominating influence on such a Commission. As he noted: 'it is no reflection on our judges to say that this would be undesirable. No branch of government should be effectively self-perpetuating.'[83] As for diversity, the proposals of the Law Lords and the Judges' Council, coupled with their rejection of open applications,[84] would seem to offer little to overcome the 'potential for cloning' and to re-enforce traditional, white, male conceptions of 'merit' in judicial appointments. Certainly the Law Lords' confidence that 'there is no risk of inadvertent oversight' of any appointable candidate[85] – despite the absence of open application is unlikely to reassure female advocates of 15 years standing that their claims will be fully considered by an Appointments Commission almost none of whom will have any familiarity with the Scottish Bar. It is submitted that it would be advantageous if the balance on the Commission is not such as to allow the judicial members to swamp the views of the remainder. If the method of operation for the Commission is, as some appear to envisage, to rely on the personal knowledge of the judicial members, it is difficult to see how this tendency can be prevented – even with knowledgeable laypersons on the Commission.[86] If, however, the emphasis is on objective knowledge equally available to all members on the Commission,[87] this risk will be reduced, particularly if the Commission were to follow the model of the Scottish Judicial Appointments Board of 50% lay and 50% judges and practitioners, with a lay Chair.[88] On the assumption that enhanced diversity is a goal for the new Commission, relaxing the requirement that candidates have either two years experience of high judicial office or 15 years

81. Dame Brenda Hale 'Equality in the Judiciary', 10th Pilgrim Fathers' Lecture, October 2003, p 17. She repeated these sentiments in her response to the Consultation Papers.
82. He was referring to a Commission for the lower courts, but his argument would apply equally to a Supreme Court Commission.
83. 'Judges for the New Century' [2001] PL 62 at 73. Similarly, Sir Geoffrey Palmer (formerly Attorney-General, Justice Minister and Prime Minister of New Zealand) has remarked: 'If judges are on the Commission they will exert great weight on the opinion of the lay members. The tendency to turn the judiciary into a self-perpetuating oligarchy ought to be restricted.' See 'Judicial Selection and Accountability' in B D Gray and R B McClintock (eds) *Courts and Policy: Checking the Balance* (Wellington: Brookers, 1995) pp 81–82. See also Professor Robert Stevens' evidence to the Constitutional Affairs Committee on 11 November 2003 at Q 87: 'It is government by the judiciary and most societies think that is not necessarily a good thing, so you need some checks and balances ...'
84. Above n 2, para 27, p 10 and n 53 above, para 165, p 30 respectively.
85. Above n 2, para 27, p 10.
86. Interestingly, the Law Lords are of the opinion that one or both of the two lay members which they recommend for the Commission might be legal academics, n 2 above, para 26, p 9.
87. This is the approach currently favoured by the Scottish Judicial Appointments Board.
88. Much of the success of the Scottish Board in establishing its independence and legitimacy can be attributed to having a strong lay chair, Sir Neil McIntosh, who commands the respect of the Board, the Scottish Executive and the wider legal community.

standing with a professional qualification, would also seem to have merit. This might increase the chances of distinguished academics being appointed to the Court.[89] Similarly, for equal opportunity and transparency reasons there would seem to a strong case for allowing the appointments process to include open applications.

D. CONCLUSION

At the time of publication the Government seems thirled to its proposals to establish a Supreme Court for the United Kingdom and a Bill to this effect was contained in the Queen's Speech in November 2003. Whatever the shape of the proposals which eventually emerge, it is probably fair to say that the disquiet on both sides of the border as to the method by which they have been arrived at, and the way the consultation process was launched, will not speedily be forgotten. Because of the sensitivities involved, the apparent clumsiness of the initial announcement about the Supreme Court, and the resulting slightness of the Consultation Paper in many aspects has resulted in some disillusionment with the process of reform and, therefore, with the prospects for a well-founded outcome. Perhaps above all, there was surprise and disappointment that, in a matter so closely affecting Scottish interests, there was apparently little prior consultation with the Scottish Executive (although its members provided early statements of welcome),[90] or with the Scottish Law Lords,[91] or the Lord President and the other Senators of the College of Justice who responded so robustly after the event. The Supreme Court announcement and Consultation Paper preceded the Government's launch of its 'big conversation with the nation' in November 2003. But the nation, and especially the Scottish nation, was well aware of the more traditional means already available for assisting the conduct of public debate on one of the biggest constitutional issues of our time. If not a 'conversation', why not at least a Royal Commission? The political reform of the House of Lords attracted a Commission. Why not judicial reform too? Why was early provision not made for a debate in the Scottish Parliament? As our brief canter through some of the issues has, we hope, indicated, there would be plenty to talk about. The Government's preferred strategy has,

---

89. A possibility considered in the Consultation Paper (at para 46) and supported by a number of respondents, including the Society of Legal Scholars, the Bar Council and the Law Societies of England and Wales and of Scotland. Perhaps because the proposal was seen as watering down the requirement of expertise as a court practitioner, it was rejected by the Faculty of Advocates, the Law Lords, the Judges' Council and the Senators of the College of Justice.

90. On 14 July 2003, the First Minister's Official Spokeswoman reported that the First Minister and the Lord Advocate had been involved in the consultation since the announcement that a Supreme Court would be set up, and clearly felt that they had influenced the Consultation Paper in a way that ensured that Scottish interests would be met. The First Minister issued a news release on behalf of himself and the Lord Advocate on the same day.

91. As Lord Hope has explained, he first learned about the Supreme Court proposal when watching the news at Heathrow. See evidence to the Constitutional Affairs Committee on 2 Dec 2003 at Q 288.

however, been to keep the agenda narrow and to curtail thought and discussion. And perhaps, as a strategy to achieve minimal change – change of name and change of premises – it will work. The irritations and concerns that the proposal has caused can be assuaged. However, by creating the conditions in which the biggest questions can be bypassed, they remain unanswered. A selective and partially reasoned consultation has produced a selective and partially reasoned response. Respondents, quite understandably, have avoided a full articulation of arguments which they feared would simply be regarded as irrelevant and therefore ignored. Jurisdictional questions such as the case for and against including Scottish criminal appeals and the continuing impact, if any, of the Treaty of Union and the Claim of Right have gone unexplored. In consequence, the country remains ignorant of what it would mean to create a genuinely new Supreme Court for the United Kingdom in the twenty-first century.

POSTSCRIPT

In the period since the completion of this essay, there have been a number of developments (though still short of a draft Bill to implement the Government's proposals) contributing to the debate and affecting, in particular, the Scottish dimension of the Supreme Court initiative. Four deserve mention:

1. The House of Commons Constitutional Affairs Committee has continued to take evidence. On 6 January 2004 it heard further from the Lord Chancellor who, as well as revealing the Government's difficulties with finding accommodation for the Court, informed the Committee (at QQ 560–568) that, in his opinion, the earlier misgivings expressed by senior members of the Scottish judiciary had been discussed with them and 'adequately dealt with'. In particular, Supreme Court decisions affecting one part of the UK would not be binding in another.

2. The Department for Constitutional Affairs published on its website a document summarising the responses to the consultation on the Supreme Court and on 24 January 2004 the Lord Chancellor made a statement to the House of Lords (col 12) on this and the other Departmental consultations.

3. On 21 January 2004 the Lord Advocate, in a widely reported speech to the Law Society of Scotland, also sought to allay fears. He responded, in particular, to the claims made that the Supreme Court proposals were incompatible with the Treaty of Union.

4. It has been announced that on 29 January 2004, the day following the drafting of this Postscript, there is, at last, to be a debate on the Supreme Court in the Scottish Parliament.

Modernising the constitution: completing the unfinished business

K E Malleson
London School of Economics

Constitutional reform in the UK is usually pragmatic and piecemeal.[1] Occasionally, however, comprehensive changes are proposed which are primarily driven by principle. The current proposals for constitutional change are a rare example of this type of reform. The abolition of the office of Lord Chancellor, the creation of a new Supreme Court and a Judicial Appointments Commission make up a package of measures intended to 'redraw the relationship between the judiciary and the other branches of government' and put it on a 'modern footing' by introducing a much clearer separation of powers between them.[2] Modernisation is the common theme running through these reforms. They are essentially forward looking; anticipating future threats to judicial independence, rather than reacting to instances of current abuse. They arise out of a new sense of constitutionalism which has developed in the UK in recent years which has prompted a greater willingness to question existing institutional arrangements.[3]

The changes both build upon and are necessitated by devolution and the Human Rights Act 1998 which formed the core of the first phase of constitutional reform introduced by the Labour administration in 1997. The indirect and long-term effect of both changes on the constitution was arguably greater than their immediate political or legal impact. The exercise of national power in post-devolution UK continues to be as much influenced by European and global developments from above and local politics below as by the new division of powers within the UK itself. Similarly, the introduction of a domestic rights-based legal order has produced a change of emphasis rather than a fundamental re-ordering of the legal system and the substantive law. Yet both reforms have become the trigger for the release of concerns which have been building up over many years about the weaknesses in the current arrangements which shape the relationship between the branches of government.[4]

---

1.   R Brazier 'The machinery of British Constitutional reform' (1990) 41 NILQ 227.
2.   Department for Constitutional Affairs *Constitutional reform: a Supreme Court for the United Kingdom* CP11/03 (July 2003) para 1.
3.   Department for Constitutional Affairs, n 2 above, para 5.4.3. Lord Bingham quoted in the consultation paper, said that the aim was to ensure that the Supreme Court is so structured as to 'command the confidence of the country in the changed world in which we live'.
4.   The *Economist* noted that 'by embarking upon an ambitious programme of reform the government has encouraged scrutiny of the murkier corners of the constitution ...': 'Judging the Judges' *Economist*, 23 Jan 1999.

THE BACKGROUND TO THE REFORMS

The office of the Lord Chancellor, the judicial appointments process and the Appellate Committee of the House of Lords have been the subject of academic criticism for many years. As early as 1873 an attempt was made to strip the House of Lords of its judicial function. Although the Appellate Committee was reinstated three years later, criticism about the constitutional appropriateness of placing the top appellate court in the legislature have been voiced periodically ever since. Similarly, concerns about the office of Lord Chancellor have been raised from time to time throughout the last century and no textbook on constitutional law would be complete without rehearsing the arguments against the Lord Chancellor's multiple constitutional roles.[5] Likewise, the history of criticism of the judicial appointments process can be traced back at least 30 years. The first serious proposals for reform of the system were put forward by JUSTICE in 1972. Its recommendation for the creation of an independent appointments body to select the judges was, at the time, controversial and was not supported by JUSTICE's governing council.[6]

During the 1980s, although support for change gained momentum, the prospect of securing Government backing for significant reform in these areas was low, since the economic radicalism of the Thatcher and Major Conservative administrations was not matched by equal enthusiasm for constitutional change. Moreover, tensions which arose between the Government and the senior judges in the late 1980s and early 1990s reduced the likelihood of a co-operative programme of modernisation which might impact upon the judiciary.[7] Nevertheless, although constitutional reform was off the Government's agenda, the limitations of the existing arrangements continued to attract the attention of academics, practitioners and opposition political parties. By the early 1990s it was clear that these concerns were being taken seriously by the newly revitalised Labour Party which was formulating a programme of modernisation in which space would be made for constitutional change. As the prospect of a Labour Government became more likely in the mid-1990s, reformers began to address the question of what form those changes should take. The landslide victory of New Labour in 1997 and the high-profile political role of the new Lord Chancellor and champion of the changes, Derry Irvine, ensured that constitutional reform would be an early candidate for parliamentary time.

The Labour party's 1997 manifesto commitments to Scottish and Welsh devolution and the incorporation of the European Convention on Human Rights meant that the Human Rights Act 1998 and the devolution legislation would form the bedrock of the constitutional reforms. It was less clear what other constitutional changes would be included. Although reform of the judicial

---

5.   See D Woodhouse *The Office of Lord Chancellor* (Oxford: Hart Publishing, 2001).
6.   JUSTICE *The Judiciary* (1972). By 1992, however, when JUSTICE carried out a second review of the judiciary it noted that it was hard to see what the fuss has been about since many of those more radical arguments for reform made 20 years earlier were widely accepted as uncontroversial by the early 1990s having been regularly debated in the intervening years.
7.   See J Rozenberg *Trial of Strength* (London: Richard Cohen Books, 1997).

appointments process had been supported in 1995 in a Labour Party paper on the justice system it was not adopted in the manifesto.[8] Nevertheless in 1997 it seemed likely that reform in this area might be included in the first round of change. The new Government commissioned comparative research on the use of commissions in Europe and North America and announced that it was to consult on the possibility of establishing an independent appointments commission.[9] However, this plan was shelved by Lord Irvine a year later on the grounds that the Lord Chancellor's Department already had a full workload implementing devolution and the Human Rights Act 1998 and could not undertake any further structural change. While support for a commission amongst lawyers and some senior judges continued to grow, Lord Irvine's enthusiasm waned.

The case for including the creation of a Supreme Court in the first tranche of reforms was, if anything, even stronger than for a judicial appointments commission, since the top courts were to play an important role in devolution and the Human Rights Act 1998:

'It is something of a paradox that while being given important roles in the schemes to incorporate the European Convention on Human Rights into domestic law and in the devolution settlement, the Appellate Committee and the Judicial Committee have, as institutions, been so little affected by the forces of modernisation. They are instruments not subjects, of change, new wine has been put into old bottles.'[10]

In addition, the establishment of the Royal Commission on Reform of the House of Lords chaired by Lord Wakeham provided an opportunity for rethinking the continuing presence of the Law Lords in the legislature.[11] A number of those who gave evidence to the Wakeham Commission, including JUSTICE, called for the removal of the Law Lords to a new Supreme Court. Support for this proposal was bolstered by the active intervention of some influential members of the House of Lords. Lords Lester and Goodhart, for example, put forward an amendment to the Scotland Bill in 1998 which proposed the creation of a Supreme Court. Critically, some Law Lords, most notably Lord Bingham and Lord Steyn, began to argue in favour of the creation of a new top court removed from the House of Lords.

The build up of pressure for reform in the judicial appointments process and the Appellate Committee of the House of Lords inevitably drew in the role of the Lord Chancellor as the constitutional lynch pin in both institutions. The objections to his many constitutional hats, which had become something of a mantra amongst many academics, were increasingly shared by judges, practitioners and politicians. In 1998, for example, 50 backbench MPs tabled a motion calling for the Lord Chancellor to be replaced by an elected Minister

8.   The Labour Party *Access to Justice* (1995) p 13.
9.   K Malleson and C Thomas *Judicial Appointments Commissioners: The European and North American Experience and the Possible Implications for the UK* Lord Chancellor's Department Research Series No 6/97 December 1997 pp 50–73.
10.   A Le Sueur and R Cornes *The Future of the United Kingdom's Highest Courts* (London: The Constitution Unit, 2001) para 5.2.1.
11.   See *A House for the Future* (Cm 4534, 2000).

of Justice directly accountable to the House of Commons and by 2001 an increasingly broad spectrum of opinion had come to believe that the Lord Chancellorship could not continue in its present form.[12]

By the time of the 2001 election, therefore, many commentators believed that it was only a matter of time before reform in all three areas would be placed on the political agenda. The remaining questions seemed only to be what form that change would take and precisely when it would come about. One person, however, remained to be convinced of the need for change of any kind. Lord Irvine, who had piloted the first phase of reform so effectively in the teeth of some significant opposition, became increasingly intransigent in his defence of the existing constitutional system. His belief in the value of the office of Lord Chancellor in its fullest form prevented him from contemplated changes to the Appellate Committee or the judicial appointments process. His pivotal role in both meant that change in either would have been likely fatally to undermine the interlocking functions on which the justification for the office as a constitutional buffer and protector of judicial independence was founded. In the immediate period after 1998, however, there was general, if reluctant, acceptance of his argument for rejecting change on the grounds that that the existing reforms needed to 'bed down'. Within the Government, his high standing with the Prime Minister and his key role in chairing the Cabinet committee on constitutional reform and a number of related sub-committees meant that his personal view on the necessity or otherwise of reform in these three areas carried considerable weight.

This uneasy consensus did not last. As the Human Rights Act 1998 and devolution settled in with surprisingly few teething problems the arguments against reform overload became less persuasive and the opposition to Lord Irvine's position grew stronger. It is possible that Lord Irvine did not fully understand the constitutional implications of the changes he had championed.[13] There is nothing in his response to the growing pressure for reform which suggests that he appreciated that the Human Rights Act 1998 and devolution would both highlight and compound the deficiencies of the existing arrangements and accelerate the need for a second stage of reforms, a key part of which would be the demise of his own office.[14] He did, however, recognise that some response was required to the increasing public calls for change. In May 2003 Lord Irvine wrote to the Chairman of the Lord Chancellor's Department select Committee to inform the committee that he was issuing a consultation paper on judicial appointment. Yet his reservations about the proposals were clear in his oral evidence to the Committee a month earlier in which he noted his own concerns about handing the power to appoint the judges to a quango and restated his firm opposition to the abolition of the office of Lord Chancellor or the creation of a new Supreme Court.[15]

---

12. R Stevens *The English Judges: Their Role in the Changing Constitution* (Oxford: Hart Publishing, 2002) p 124.
13. Stevens, n 12 above, p 104.
14. Le Sueur and Cornes accurately predicted that the changes would speed the need for reform of the top courts: n 12 above, para 5.4.1. Woodhouse similarly anticipated the same effect in relation to the office of Lord Chancellor: n 5 above, p 631.
15. Lord Chancellor's Department Select Committee, minutes of evidence, 2 April 2003.

Having made clear that while he remained on the woolsack significant institutional change in this area was not an option, Lord Irvine's retirement or removal as Lord Chancellor and the introduction of the second phase of constitutional reform became inexorably linked.[16] The detailed political manoeuvrings which took place in the spring of 2003 between Tony Blair, the Home Secretary David Blunkett and Lord Irvine are, as yet, known to only a few insiders. But what is clear is that Lord Irvine's political star began to fall. The turf war between the Home Office and the Lord Chancellor's Department which had been going on through the 1990s and which, to date, had largely been won by Lord Irvine began to turn in favour of the Home Office.[17] By June 2003 the balance of powers had shifted and Lord Irvine's authority with Tony Blair had waned while David Blunkett's had risen. 'Young Blair' as Irvine was fond of jokingly referring to his protégé, had grown up. Although Lord Irvine had planned to retire at the end of 2003, Blair was persuaded that he had to go sooner. On 12 June the Prime Minister replaced his one-time mentor with his former flat-mate Lord Falconer, who as Secretary of State in the newly named Department for Constitutional Affairs was asked to join the Cabinet as the last ever Lord Chancellor. His task would be to abolish that office, create a judicial appointments commission and set up a new Supreme Court.

The outcome of this shift in political fortunes was that after years of extensive debate about the advantages and disadvantages of constitutional change in these three areas, the reforms were announced when least expected. A Thursday afternoon Cabinet reshuffle became the trigger for a comprehensive reshaping of the constitution. The lack of warning or consultation inevitably provoked criticism and suspicion as to the Government's motives and there is little doubt that the presentation of the changes could have been better handled.[18] Lord Falconer's claim that the absence of briefing and consultations gave momentum to the changes had the ring of a post-hoc justification. But while the timing of the announcements left the impression that the changes were poorly thought out, the consultation papers on the new Supreme Court and the judicial appointments commission published a month later provided a carefully drafted framework for change. Although the details of the reforms were still left to be hammered out, the consultation papers clearly demonstrated that the Government was fully aware of the serious constitutional significance of the changes it was proposing. A new vision of the separation of powers and judicial independence was being set out.

16. Le Sueur and Cornes, n 12 above, para 5.3.1. See also 'Irvine "fought against Blair's legal reforms"' *Independent on Sunday*, 15 June 2003.
17. Under Lord Irvine the Lord Chancellor's Department had expanded dramatically. In 2003 Blunkett successfully resisted any further transfer of functions which would have continued the effective creation of a continental-style ministry of justice.
18. The Scottish First Minister, for example, publicly expressed his anger at not having been consulted about changes. See also Lord Alexander 'Is this a ruthless grab for power?' *The Times*, 1 July 2003.

TRADITIONAL VIEW OF SEPARATION OF POWERS AND JUDICIAL INDEPENDENCE

In 1991 Lord Mackay, then Lord Chancellor, declared that:

> 'Our constitution, unlike that of, for example, the United States, is not built on the principle that the legislative, the executive and the judicial powers should be separate and equal.'[19]

Five years later, shortly before replacing Lord Mackay as Lord Chancellor, Lord Irvine stated during a parliamentary debate on the constitutional role of the judiciary that: 'it is time to return to first principles. The British Constitution, largely unwritten, is firmly based on the separation of powers.'[20] The explanation for these two apparently polar opposite views is not that either Lord Mackay or Lord Irvine had misread their constitutional law textbooks, but rather that they were working from two different definitions of the separation of powers, one formal the other pragmatic. In a strictly formal sense, Lord Mackay is clearly right. Compared with most other systems the UK has, at best, a very lose appreciation of the separation of powers, more accurately described as balanced rather than separated. But in practical terms, As Lord Irvine indicated, the UK system through its laws, conventions, practices and cultural values has very effectively protected the judiciary from improper encroachment by the other branches.

The legitimacy of the institutional arrangements governing the judiciary's relationship with the other branches of government has traditionally been measured by its effectiveness in securing judicial independence rather than their conformity to a constitutional ideal model. The standard defence of the office of Lord Chancellor being that he acted as a buffer between the executive and the judiciary and an advocate on behalf of the judges and the justice system by ensuring that it was properly resourced and protected while at the same time explaining to the judiciary the political and economic realities within which the executive must work.[21] Likewise, the judicial appointments process, it was claimed, worked because by convention the Lord Chancellor appointed judges on a non-partisan basis. Furthermore, by sitting as a judge in the House of Lords, the Lord Chancellor could form a view of the abilities of the senior advocates as potential candidates for judicial office and as a member of the judiciary he could be trusted to discipline errant judges and supervise the judiciary without encroaching on its independence. Similarly, the blatant breach of any formal model of separation of powers committed by having the Law Lords in the legislature was justified as working in practice because their self-imposed restraint in parliamentary debate limited their participation to those areas where their expertise could be most useful, while also giving the judges valuable insights into the legislative and policy-making processes which improve their judicial function.

---

19. Lord Mackay 'The Chancellor in the 1990s' (1991) Current Legal Problems 258.
20. Hansard, HL Official Report (5th series) col 1254, 5 June 1996.
21. Lord Woolf 'Judicial Review: The Tensions between the Executive and the Judiciary' (1998) 114 LQR 114.

FACTORS FOR CHANGE

These essentially pragmatic arguments have, to date, trumped objections based on principle. Indeed, the British legal establishment has often expressed a degree of pride in the eccentricities of a system which breaks all the formal constitutional rules but has a high reputation in terms of outcomes. As Lord Steyn has noted, sceptical questions about the shape of the unwritten constitution have been neutralised by the argument that 'it works'.[22] His arguments for change, on the other hand, have been firmly based on principle:

> 'The practice of the Lord Chancellor and his predecessor sitting in the Appellate Committee is not consistent with even the weakest principle of the separation of powers or the most tolerant interpretation of the constitutional principles of judicial independence.'[23]

Lord Irvine has dismissed these, and similar concerns on the grounds that: '... we are a nation of pragmatists, not theorists, and we go, quite frankly, for what works.'[24] Underlying the current reforms is an acceptance of the accuracy of the pragmatists' claims for the practical effectiveness of the system to date. The consultation papers make clear that the proposals for change are not intended to be taken as a reflection on the standards of the existing practices. In justifying the decision to set up a Supreme Court, Lord Falconer stressed that he was confident that the current members of the House of Lords had never been influenced in court by their views expressed in legislative debate and had decided the cases before them on the basis of the law alone. His rationale for change was the 'fundamental problem of principle' that judges should not be both legislating and sitting as the highest Court of Appeal.[25] Likewise the Government has been keen to emphasise that there is no suggestion that judicial independence has been undermined in the current judicial appointments process. This approach is generally shared by those proposing reform outside the Government. JUSTICE, one of the most long-term supporters of reform, has explained that existing arrangements have 'served the country well'.

The current changes, therefore, are not a challenge to the claim that the present system has worked, but rather a challenge to the argument that: 'if it ain't broke don't fix it.' The principal rationale for change is that the current system undermines the legitimacy of the judiciary and leaves the system exposed to future threats to judicial independence. The consultation paper on the judicial appointments process emphasised the risk of a perception that the system is open to political motivation. It highlighted the danger that the exclusive control of the selection of the judges by a Government minister may reasonably give rise to suspicion that judicial independence might be compromised. The reform programme is underpinned by an awareness that these concerns undermine confidence in the appointments system and so the legitimacy of the judiciary as a whole. Similarly, the consultation paper on the Supreme Court stressed that the fact that the highest court is located in the

---

22. 'The case for a Supreme Court' (2002) 118 LQR at 384.
23. Steyn, above n 22, at 388.
24. Evidence to the Lord Chancellor's Department select committee, 2 April 2003, qu 28.
25. Lord Chancellor's Department Select Committee, minutes of evidence, 30 June 2003.

legislature gives rise to questions as to whether there is: 'sufficient transparency of independence from the executive and the legislature to give people the assurance to which they are entitled about the independence of the judiciary.'[26] The changes therefore represent a shift in the relative value placed on pragmatism and principle. The source of this re-conceptualisation lies in a number of political and legal developments, linked directly or indirectly to the first wave of constitutional reforms.

The changing role of Lord Chancellor

A key factor responsible for undermining acceptance of the traditional constitutional arrangements governing the relationship between the judicial and other branches of government is the shift in emphasis of the role of the Lord Chancellor from the judicial to the executive. One reason for the widespread tolerance for the fluid boundaries of the Office of Lord Chancellor was that successive occupants of the woolsack had traditionally chosen to prioritise their judicial functions. In contrast, Lord Irvine and his predecessor, Lord Mackay both saw their role as located firmly within the Government.[27] Although not a party political activist, Lord Mackay faced down the opposition of the judicial and the legal profession to apply the Conservative Government's free market economic reforms to the legal system by introducing changes designed to tackle restrictive practices in the provision of legal services, cut costs and increase efficiency. Lord Irvine's political agenda was, if anything, even wider than Lord Mackay's while being combined with a more explicit party political dimension. A key member of Tony Blair's administration, he occupied a place at the heart of the Government. The combined effect of the Mackay and Irvine years, therefore, was that the office of Lord Chancellor was transformed from that of senior judges exercising a subsidiary executive function to that of Cabinet minister wearing an occasional judicial hat.[28]

One pragmatic effect of this shift in function was to undermine the argument that the Lord Chancellor's multiple constitutional roles allowed him to make a significant contribution to the judicial work of the House of Lords and to identify potential future candidates for judicial office. As Lord Irvine himself acknowledged, his increasing executive role left him less time for sitting. Having participated in only a handful of cases in the last few years of his time in office, it was difficult for supporters of the office of Lord Chancellor to dispute the claim that its removal would have little practical effect in this respect.[29]

At the same time his more executive-orientated role undermined confidence in the belief that the Lord Chancellor was best placed to protect the independence of the judges. Evidence for this loss of confidence can be seen in the Lord Chancellor's response to the attack by the Home Secretary, David Blunkett, on the decision of Mr Justice Collins regarding the application by the Government of its immigration and asylum legislation.[30] Blunkett's

26. Above n 24, para 2.
27. Woodhouse, n 5 above, p 624; R Stevens *The English Judges, their Role in the Changing Constitution* (Oxford: Hart Publishing, 2002) p 101.
28. D Woodhouse 'The Office of Lord Chancellor' [1998] PL 619.
29. Steyn, above n 22, at pp 387–388.
30. 'Judges Attack Blunkett on Asylum Rules', *Independent*, 11 June 2003.

comments were not dissimilar to those made by the Conservative Home Secretary Michael Howard in the 1980s in response to an equivalent setback in the courts. In both case, the respective Lord Chancellors chose to defend the judges largely behind the scenes rather than in public. However, in the intervening decade which separated the two incidents of conflict increasing numbers of judges, lawyers and academics had lost confidence that the Lord Chancellor could be relied upon to take a firm stance in support of the judges. Lord Steyn was not alone in believing that the time had come to leave the job of defending the independence of the judiciary to the judges themselves.

Changing role of the judiciary

The impact of the transformation of the office of Lord Chancellor over the last two decades has been matched by an equally important shift in the role of the judges. From carrying out a relatively narrow and legalistic function it has, through the development of judicial review, carved out a role for itself in scrutinising the legality of official decision-making. Despite lacking any power to strike down legislation outside the EU law context, the judges have regularly and sometimes controversially, held that the Government's action has been unlawful. The provisions of the Human Rights Act 1998 built on and expanded the functions of the senior judiciary in patrolling the constitutional boundaries and upholding fundamental rights.[31] The Act was inevitably, and correctly, seen by many as representing a shift in power to the judiciary. But without the prior development of administrative law its effect on the judicial function would have been very limited. It is the combined effect of the courts' powers of judicial review and the provisions of the Human Rights Act 1998 which have drawn the judiciary into areas of social, political and economic life which were previously outside its scope. Government policy in the areas of foreign aid and development, health care rationing, immigration and anti-terrorism measures are just some of the issues which have been scrutinised by the judges, and sometimes found wanting.

Opinion is sharply divided as to whether this process of judicialisation represents a legitimate sphere of activity for a judiciary within an advanced liberal democracy or a threat to the authority of elected representatives. But one area of agreement amongst both supporters and critics of this development is that the expansion of the role of the judiciary has long-term constitutional implications. JUSTICE, for example, has argued that as the work of the judges increasingly interacts with political and legislative decision-making, it has become necessary for a 'clearer and deeper' separation of the functions and powers of the judiciary from the other branches of government.[32] The need for reform of the judicial appointments process has been consistently linked to the changing role of the judiciary. As Conor Gearty has noted: 'Anxieties about the selection of judges increase – and rightly increase – in proportion to the

31. See K Malleson *The New Judiciary* (Aldershot: Ashgate Press, 1999).
32. See S Sedley, Foreword to Malleson n 31 above and C Geary 'The Judicialisation of Democracy', paper delivered to the Administrative Bar Association, 7 July 1996.
32. *The judicial function of the House of Lords* written evidence to the Royal Commission on the Reform of the House of Lords (1998) para 21.

amount of direct political power a society invites them to wield on its behalf.'[33] In 2003 the report of the Bar Council working party on judicial appointment and Silk, chaired by Sir Iain Glidewell, cited the changing role of the judiciary as a rationale for reform of the judicial appointments process. The report concluded that the increasing amount of time spent by 'modern' High Court judges adjudicating on the actions of ministers and other public bodies gave rise to the need for clear constitutional safeguards from the risk, or even the appearance of risk, that their independence might be threatened by the executive. For this reason, the report concluded that: '... it has become politically unacceptable for High Court judges to be appointed, in effect, by a member of the Government of the day.'[34]

Equally, a key argument for the removal of the Law Lords from the legislature is the fact that more politically sensitive cases have come before the House of Lords so increasing the likelihood of the Law Lords being called upon to sit in judgment in cases which involve the interpretation of legislation in relation to which they have expressed a view as legislators. In 2000, in response to concerns about this possibility, Lord Bingham issued a statement clarifying the circumstances in which the Law Lords would not participate in debate in the Lords. Lord Falconer, however, highlighted the difficulty of determining the dividing line between what is acceptable and unacceptable in the post-Human Rights Act 1998 era:

> 'The two things they said they would not normally speak on were things involving strong party political dispute or things that they might come to have to decide themselves in court sitting as a judge. Now, since June 2000 one can see a large number of areas where they have spoken where it is very difficult to know precisely where the line should be drawn.'[35]

A number of the Law Lords have concurred with this view.[36] Most have dealt with the increasing difficultly of identifying controversial subject matter, by participating very rarely, if at all. Yet even the most minimal of participation can be problematic, as Robert Stevens has noted:

> 'In 2000 no serving English Law Lord participated in a legislative debate. In 2001 only Lord Scott spoke on the issue of hunting. He is a master of foxhounds. Some would not regard that as a non-contentious issue.'[37]

If, as many of the Law Lords now believe, the only safe course of conduct is a complete self-ordained purdah, the effect is to undermine one of the key pragmatic arguments in favour of keeping the judges in the legislature, that they could contribute their expertise to the law-making process. Lord Cooke, in his recent defence of the status quo, sought to argue that the presence of the

---

33. Gearty, 1996, p 3.
34. *Report of the Bar Council working party on judicial appointments and silk* (3 March 2003) Summary of recommendations, chapter 10.
35. Lord Chancellor's Department Select Committee, minutes of evidence, 15 July 2003.
36. Lord Saville commented that the dividing line between what was political and not politically controversial in determining whether he could speak in the Lords or not was 'very difficult to draw and clearly getting more and more difficult to draw': speech to the City Centre for International Trade and Arbitration (January 1999) quoted in Stevens p 111.
37. Stevens, n 12 above, p 121.

Law Lords enhanced the quality of legislation while at the same time suggesting that it did not breach the separation of powers because they so rarely exercised their right to participate. It is not easy to see how these two arguments can be married.[38]

The right to a hearing before an independent and impartial tribunal

The increased awareness of the need for the Law Lords to avoid bias or the perception of bias in future litigation has been driven partly by the more politicised subject matter coming before the courts but also by a stricter interpretation and application of the impartiality principle. The requirement that judges are independent and impartial has always been a founding principle of any system based on the rule of law. But the interpretation of its requirements in practice has changed as a result of the entrenchment in article 6(1) of the European Convention on Human Rights. In recent years the European Court of Human Rights has refined and clarified what constitutes an independent and impartial tribunal. In 1997 in *Findlay v United Kingdom* the Court held that the test for bias was not limited to proof of actual bias but included the appearance of bias in the eyes of a reasonable onlooker.[53] The establishment of this more stringent definition of independence inevitably increased the likelihood that the Law Lords might, in the future, be held to be in breach of article 6(1).

The Appellate Committee of the House of Lords was not, of course, the only aspect of the UK system which ran the risk of falling foul of the perception of bias limb of the *Findlay* judgment. Applying the rules in *Findlay*, the Lord Chancellor was clearly vulnerable to a challenge.[38] These fears were strengthened in 2000 when the Court in *McGonnell* drove another nail into the coffin of the office of Lord Chancellor by concluding that the overlapping judicial and executive roles of the Bailiff of Guernsey were 'incompatible with the requisite appearance of independence and impartiality for a judge to have legislative and executive functions as substantial as these in the present case'.[39] Although the Court stressed that this decision was on the particular facts of the case, there was little doubt that this finding has serious implications for the office of Lord Chancellor.[40]

With the implementation of the Human Rights Act 1998 in 2000, it could only be a matter of time before a decision of the Lords in which the Lord Chancellor has participated would be challenged in the domestic courts as a breach of article 6(1). The increasing frequency with which counsel became willing to challenge the decision of the Lord Chancellor to sit was evidence of the growing awareness of this weakness.[41] When senior judges appearing before a session of the Joint Committee on Human Rights in 2001 It was not surprising that they refused to express a view on the conformity of Lord Chancellor's judicial role with article 6 on the grounds that they considered that it would be a question which they would be likely to be required to resolve as judges when

38. See Le Sueur and Cornes, n 10 above, para 14.4.1.
39. *McGonnell v United Kingdom* (2000) 30 EHRR.
40. See Le Sueur and Cornes, n 10 above, p 54.
41. See Woodhouse, n 5 above, p 127.

it came before the courts.[42] The precedent for a successful challenge in the UK courts was clear. Moreover, in the immediate period after the Human Rights Act 1998 came into force it became apparent that the UK courts were following Strasbourg's example and applying a strict interpretation of the requirements of article 6(1). One of the first cases which was successfully challenged under the Human Rights Act 1998 concerned the tenure of part-time Sheriffs in Scotland. Their dependence on the executive for their continued employment was held by the Scottish courts in *Starrs* to be a breach of article 6(1) and led to changes in the tenure arrangements of part-time judges both in Scotland and in England and Wales, where a similar challenge to the position of Recorders was anticipated.[43] The consequence of a finding that the Lord Chancellor sitting as a judge breached article 6(1) would be serious. But equally serious might be a finding it did not. Lord Steyn, amongst others, questioned what message would be 'sent across Europe' if the Court allowed an exception for the Lord Chancellor in Britain to the principle of separation of functions.[44]

The UK's changing relationship with the rest of Europe

Lord Steyn was not alone in expressing concern about the impact of the UK's constitution on relations with its European colleagues. By the turn of the century, their tolerance for the eccentricities of the British constitutional arrangements was wearing thin. In 2003 the Council of Europe produced a highly critical report on the role of the Lord Chancellor and the Law Lords. The principal author of the report, Erik Jurgens appeared before the Lord Chancellor's Department select committee to answer questions about its findings.[45] One of the reasons which he gave for objecting to the constitutional arrangements in the UK was the corrosive effect it had as a model for the newer democracies in Europe:

'Every day in my Council of Europe work I am I confrontation with new democracies from central and Eastern Europe. When I tell them they should not do certain things they say "what about the British?" They have these [judges] appointed members of Parliament in the Upper House. They have a Lord Chancellor ... all the things I tell them they should not have.'[46]

Hayden Phillips, the Permanent Secretary of the Department for Constitutional Affairs responded to this concern with the argument that Britain does not seek to act as a model for any other system:

'When we have been dealing with the Council of Europe and this debating point has been raised with us before, we have always said when we go around to other countries, particularly newly emerging democracies in Central Europe, "Don't do as we do. What you need is something quite different."

---

42. See Le Sueur and Cornes, n 10 above, para 5.4.3.
43. *Starrs v Ruxton* 2000 SLT 42.
44. See Steyn, n 22 above, at p 127.
45. Lord Chancellor's Department Select Committee, minutes of evidence, 27 March 2003. Erik Jurgens is the Rapporteur of the Committee on Legal Affairs and Human Rights of the Parliamentary Assembly, Council of Europe.
46. Above, n 45, para 1.

We have been absolutely clear about that under Lord Falconer's predecessor and before so that we were not going around trying to preach to people that what we had was right.'[47]

This 'do as we say not as we do' approach does not, however, sit comfortably in a twenty-first-century European political culture. Moreover, most judges, lawyers and politicians do, increasingly, wish to be seen as a model of good practice. Many share Lord Falconer's hope that the new Supreme Court will be 'a real flagship for the British legal system which would improve its standing both domestically and abroad'.[48] At a time when senior judges are keen to participate more actively in lending assistance to the development of judicial systems abroad, particularly in central and eastern Europe, condemnation of the UK system by the Council of Europe is highly damaging.

SOME UNFINISHED BUSINESS

The construction of a clearer separation of powers between the judiciary and the other branches of government will consolidate the reform process begun in 1997. At the same time it raises a number of new dilemmas. The most pressing being the question of how to ensure that the removal of the Lord Chancellor does not create a vacuum in the relationship between the judiciary and the executive. The proposal for imposing a statutory obligation on the new Secretary of State for Constitutional Affairs to protect judicial independence may be a welcome recognition of the importance of reaffirming the principle of judicial independence but it cannot of itself ensure that judges are protected from improper pressure in their decision-making on a day-to-day basis. It is unlikely, in practice, that the Secretary of State can be relied upon to provide this protection. She or he will be a mid-career politician, possibly not a lawyer, inevitably looking for promotion to one of the higher-ranking departments. Some occupants may be first rate, others may be more mediocre. Either way, it is unrealistic to expect that a passing politician, in post until the next Cabinet reshuffle, will be able to defend the judiciary against attacks by more senior Cabinet colleagues in the same way as Lord Chancellors have done in the past. The position of the Lord Chancellor at the top of the career hierarchy might have encouraged some to hang on to their place on the woolsack longer than they should have done, but it had the advantage that the occupant had nothing to gain by pandering to government in any attack on the judiciary.

The proposals by Lord Woolf and others for the retention of some form of rump Lord Chancellor are almost certain to be rejected as confusing and unworkable. But the rationale for such a proposal is understandable given the legitimate concern about how judicial independence is to be protected in the new order. Nor are these fears purely theoretical. The increasingly willingness of ministers publicly to criticise the decision-making of individual judges has grown in parallel with their increasingly politicised decision-making. In 2003,

---

47. Lord Chancellor's Department Select Committee, minutes of evidence, 30 June 2003, qu 55.
48. Above, n 47, qu 36.

Lord Irvine told the Lord Chancellor's Department select committee that in his six years as Lord Chancellor it has been necessary to argue in Cabinet in support of judicial independence on 'many, many occasions'.[49] Since it is unlikely that future ministers will heed Lord Irvine's advice that members of the executive should neither boo when defeated nor cheer when upheld, the instances in which the Cabinet may need to be reminded of the importance of judicial independence are unlikely to reduce.[50] When the booing and cheering reaches the point of threatening to inhibit the judges from deciding a case according to their understanding of the law alone, it must be clear who will speak up in defence of judicial independence.

Under the new arrangements, the answer is that the judges must learn to defend themselves. The newly revived Judges' Council will be a key tool in their ability to do this effectively. Beefed up by the inclusion of members of the Supreme Court,[51] the Council, together with the Lord Chief Justice, the President of the Supreme Court and the heads of division, must find a way to speak with a common judicial voice on matters which touch on judicial independence and the quality of the justice system. At the same time, formal and informal mechanisms must be established for regular exchange between the Government and the judiciary. One particular area in which the judges will need to learn to take a more active initiate is the defence of the courts' budgets. It is unlikely that the Government will ever accept Lord Browne-Wilkinson's argument that judicial independence requires that the budget should be controlled by the judiciary from funds voted by Parliament.[52] Instead the trend has been to remove the ring-fencing of funds which have in the past partially insulated the judges and courts from some of the more severe cuts in public funding. In the future, without the Lord Chancellor in Cabinet to set out the requirements of the courts, the judiciary will need to argue its case for funding in competition with health, education, defence and other big-spending departments.[53]

Finally, the relationship between the judiciary and the legislature will need to be rethought in the light of the changing constitutional order. There is very little likelihood that the Government will agree to any direct or indirect input to the judicial appointments process by Parliament. Neither the inclusion of MPs as members of the Commission nor the creation of any form of parliamentary confirmation hearings is currently on the agenda. The result is that electoral accountability will be maintained through the indirect and relatively restricted involvement of the Secretary of State for Constitutional

---

49. Lord Chancellor's Department Select Committee, minutes of evidence, 2 April 2003, qu 29.
50. Above, n 49.
51. See Lord Woolf's comments on the resuscitation of the Judges' Council from being a 'semi-moribund institution': see *Current Challenges in Judging* 5th Worldwide Common Law Judiciary Conference, Sydney, Australia, 10 April 2003: http://www.lcd.gov.uk/judicial/speeches/lcj100403.htm.
52. N Browne-Wilkinson 'The Independence of the Judiciary in the 1980s' [1988] PL 44.
53. An example being that the Supreme Court consultation paper proposes that funding of the top courts should be transferred from the Lords and Privy Council to the Department for Constitutional Affairs which would 'bid for and provide resources': Department for Constitutional Affairs, n 2 above, paras 63–66.

Affairs in the selection process. The new Department for Constitutional Affairs select committee goes some way to connect the judiciary to Parliament and it is encouraging that senior judges have been willing to appear before it. However, if the trajectory of judicial power continues on its current course, these limited forms of accountability are likely to provoke increasing disquiet and the pressure for more direct and institutional engagement between Parliament and the judiciary is likely to grow.

CONCLUSION

As the boundaries between law and politics have blurred over the last 30 years, the need for a clearer delineation between the judiciary and the other branches of government has become more pressing. The traditional pragmatism which has underpinned the British constitution is being tempered by a new willingness to shape constitutional and institutional arrangements so as to conform to principles which are designed to protect judicial independence and enhance the legitimacy of the judicial system. The current changes are not, however, exclusively principle-driven. The failure of the judicial appointments process to diversify the composition of the judiciary and the lack of space and resources for the Law Lords in Westminster are examples of more practical and immediate problems which the reforms seek to address. But important as these goals may be, they would not, alone, have been sufficient to bring about the scope of constitutional change currently proposed. Robert Stevens concluded his recent review of the role of the judges and courts in the constitution by noting that the new millennium had began with a backlog of unfinished business which needed to be resolved.[54] The current reforms are an attempt to do just this. These changes have long-term implications of real constitutional significance. They represent a new vision of the future of the British constitution and may, in time, come to be seen as the most significant changes of the 1997 and 2001 Labour administrations.

---

54. R Stevens 'Government and the Judiciary' in V Bogdanor (ed) *The British Constitution in the Twentieth Century* (Oxford: Oxford University Press, 2003).

The constitutional and political implications of a United Kingdom Supreme Court

Diana Woodhouse
Professor of Law, Oxford Brookes University

The constitutional and political implications of a United Kingdom Supreme Court are far-reaching. This paper suggests that its establishment represents an increase in judicial independence, both in terms of the individual judge and institutionally. In so doing, it draws attention to the continued infringement of judicial independence, most notably through the use of senior judges to chair inquiries, and to the need for judicial independence to be safeguarded by the judges themselves. It argues that, somewhat paradoxically, the independence of the Court may increase the extent to which it is perceived as a political player and used for political purposes. It also argues that the requirement for greater transparency in the appointment of judges and the processes and decisions of the Court needs to be matched by the improved accountability of the Court and the Secretary of State for Constitutional Affairs. The paper ends by speculating on the longer-term constitutional implications of a Supreme Court, suggesting that it could result in the further diminution of parliamentary sovereignty, a more even distribution of power between the constitutional actors and the development of the United Kingdom into a constitutional democracy.

INTRODUCTION: THE RATIONALE FOR A SUPREME COURT

The establishment of a free-standing United Kingdom Supreme Court has far-reaching constitutional and political implications, particularly when viewed in conjunction with the accompanying reforms, namely the abolition of the office of Lord Chancellor and the creation of a Judicial Appointments Commission. In terms of constitutional theory, it represents greater adherence to the separation of powers and the requirements of judicial independence. It is also a recognition of the increasing constitutional importance of the judiciary and a manifestation of the ongoing shift in the balance of power, away from politicians towards the judges, which has implications for all the constitutional institutions.

The government's rationale for a Supreme Court is to 'put the relationship between the executive, the legislature and the judiciary on a modern footing, which takes account of people's expectations about the independence and transparency of the judicial system'.[1] Independence and transparency are

---

1. Department for Constitutional Affairs *Constitutional Reform: A Supreme Court for the United Kingdom* (July 2003).

essential characteristics if public confidence in the judiciary is to be maintained. Moreover, they are interrelated, for while, as Stevens notes, 'it is acceptable, if not entirely accurate, to say that England has independence of the judiciary',[2] at least in the sense of the individual judge, the era of trust in, and deference to, public institutions is long gone. Transparency in process, procedure and substance is therefore essential to demonstrate the judicial independence claimed.

The establishment of a Supreme Court, as with the other reforms, is also a response to the requirement imposed by the European Convention on Human Rights, through the Human Rights Act 1998, which emphasises the need for judges not only to be independent, but to be seen as such. Appearances and perceptions matter, legally and for public confidence, and the position of the Law Lords in the Upper House of Parliament not only infringes the notion of the separation of powers but also undermines judicial independence and impartiality. It is no longer acceptable to portray this position as a harmless, indeed beneficial, quirk of our constitutional arrangements or to argue that conventional understandings about the judges' role in the legislature ensure that judicial independence is unaffected. This may be the case. But even Lord Bingham's assurance that 'the Lords of Appeal in Ordinary do not think it appropriate to engage in matters where there is a strong element of party political controversy', and 'bear in mind that they might render themselves ineligible to sit judicially if they were to express an opinion on a matter which might later be relevant to an appeal to the House',[3] is unlikely to satisfy the appearance of impartiality and independence required of Article 6 of the European Convention. This has been recognised by Lord Bingham, himself, who is on record as saying there could be a challenge on this basis.[4]

Moreover, even if the existence of conventional understandings and practices were sufficient to satisfy the European Convention on Human Rights requirement, complying with it increasingly limits the ability of the Law Lords to contribute to the work of the House of Lords. In the three years since Lord Bingham's statement, only three Law Lords had spoken in the House which, as the Consultation Paper notes, 'reduc[es] the value to both [the Law Lords] and the House of their membership'.[5] This is a pragmatic rather than a constitutional point but one that is supported by Lord Bingham, who notes: 'a habit of reticence makes for good judges, it makes for poor legislators and debaters, and serves to weaken the justification for including the Law Lords among the members of the House.'[6]

2.   R Stevens *The English Judges, Their Role in the Changing Constitution* (Oxford: Hart Publishing, 2002) p 79.
3.   Lord Bingham, HL Official Report (5th series) col 419, 22 June 2000.
4.   Joint Committee on Human Rights *Minutes of Evidence* (2000–01) HC 66, Q 103.
5.   Department for Constitutional Affairs, n 1 above, para 1.3.
6.   Constitution Unit Spring Lecture, UCL, 1 May 2002.

JUDICIAL INDEPENDENCE AND THE SEPARATION OF POWERS

The need to satisfy public and legal expectations, regarding judicial independence, therefore provides the rationale for the Supreme Court. However, in so doing, it raises the question of what is meant by judicial independence for whilst the concept is portrayed, and accepted, as a fundamental constitutional principle, it is seldom defined and is subject to the vagaries of interpretation and usage. It has two interrelated strands: independence from the political arm of government and impartiality, the latter being, in part, reliant on the existence of the former but not necessarily ensured by it. Thereafter, the term is variously used to describe the independence of the individual judge or the independence of the judiciary collectively.

In the first sense – the independence of the individual judge – if security of tenure, fiscal independence and freedom from executive interference are the hallmarks of independence,[7] the establishment of the Supreme Court confirms and enhances this independence. Like their Law Lord predecessors, members of the Supreme Court will hold office 'during good behaviour',[8] subject to an address of both Houses of Parliament, until they reach the age of retirement which, since 1995, has been 70.[9] Moreover, while the relevant statutes suggest that a breach of 'good behaviour' is itself sufficient for dismissal, it seems likely that, today, the address procedure would be followed in any case of dismissal.[10] Given that this has not been used since 1830,[11] the tenure of senior judges rates highly on any scale of security. Their fiscal independence will similarly continue, in so much as the executive is unable to reduce judicial salaries without an Act of Parliament and salaries are paid out of Consolidated Funds and thus not subject to a vote from Parliament.[12]

The principle that a judge should have complete discretion in his or her own court to decide a case in accordance with the law and without interference, which was seen by Lord Mackay as 'the essence of judicial independence',[13] is also as applicable to the new court as it is to any other. Indeed, the physical separation of the judges from the House of Lords will make their independence more apparent than it has previously been, removing the danger that those unfamiliar with the workings of the House might perceive judicial decisions

7.   Stevens, n 2 above, p 79.
8.   Supreme Court Act 1981, s 11(3) and Appellate Jurisdiction Act, s 6, as amended.
9.   Judicial Pensions and Retirement Act 1993.
10.   S H Bailey and M J Gunn *Smith and Bailey on the Modern Legal System* (London: Sweet & Maxwell, 1991) p 221.
11.   Sir Jonah Barrington, a judge of the High Court of Admiralty in Ireland, was removed for embezzling money paid into the court.
12.   Although the executive cannot reduce judicial salaries, a refusal to raise them in line with inflation or with the salaries of top civil servants or those practising at the Bar may be tantamount to a reduction. In 1992 John Major's government refused to implement the advice of the Committee on Top Salaries, established in 1971 to make recommendations on judicial pay awards, and gave judges a four per cent increase instead of the twenty per cent recommended.
13.   Lord Mackay, HL Official Report (5th series) col 1308, 5 June 1996.

to have been influenced, even made, by politicians.[14] The fact that the Supreme Court Justices (if that is what they are to be called) will no longer have the right to sit in the legislative chamber, will also enhance the appearance of independence and prevent misunderstandings about judicial involvement in the legislative process.

The removal of this right will, of course, have implications for those judges affected and for the House of Lords and to prevent a complete loss of the judicial contribution to the business of the House, there are proposals that members of the Supreme Court should be appointed to it upon retirement.[15] Whether this happens depends, in part, upon any future reform. Assuming that the House of Lords still contains an appointed element, Lord Goddard, in a debate on the issue, took the view that 'retired Justices of the Supreme Court should be eligible for, though not necessarily entitled to, appointment ...'[16] However, a situation whereby some are offered a seat in the House and others are not could be seen as exerting pressure on those members of the court who are nearing retirement. A few controversial decisions in which the court finds for the government or its agencies, followed, shortly afterwards, by the appointment of one or more retiring members of the panel to the House of Lords, would not only undermine the impartial reputation of the court, but also damage the reputation of the Commission that makes appointments to the House of Lords. The important point constitutionally is, therefore, the adoption of an all-or-none appointment principle. Following from this, and equally important, if retired members of the Supreme Court are appointed to the House of Lords, they should not, as is currently the case, still be called upon to sit, otherwise the separation of judicial and legislative personnel, brought about by the establishment of the Supreme Court, will be flawed and could be open to legal challenge. The same applies to retired Law Lords, currently in the House of Lords, and to the former Lord Chancellor, Lord Irvine, who, in return for his pension,[17] is by convention expected to sit, as required, until he retires.[18] Despite Lord Irvine's claim, shortly before he relinquished office, that 'the judges have been very careful to say ... that in their judgment ... the Lord Chancellor would still be President of the new Supreme Court',[19] it would be particularly inappropriate for him to sit in any capacity for fear of undermining the court's independence. If the court is to gain public confidence as an independent institution, a clean break with the practices which have blurred the constitutional boundaries is essential.

14. For instance, in the *Pinochet* case, some overseas observers thought that because of her position in the House of Lords, Baroness Thatcher was involved in the decision (*R v Bow Street Metropolitan Stipendiary Magistrate, ex p Pinochet Ugarte* [1998] 4 All ER 897, HL; *(No 2)* [1999] 1 All ER 577, HL; *(No 3)* [1999] 2 All ER 97, HL).

15. Department for Constitutional Affairs, n 1 above, para 36.

16. Lord Goddard, HL Official Report (5th series) col 636, 14 July 2003.

17. Lord Chancellor's Pension Act 1832.

18. This, as with all judges, is at 70. The pension of the Lord Chancellor was not originally tied to continued judicial service but in 1965, in a debate over its increase, an amendment was proposed to make it dependent on his being available 'to participate in the legal work of the House of Lords.' (Mr R T Paget MP, HC Official Report (6th series) cols 2069–2074, 22 July 1965). The amendment was rejected on the understanding that by convention an ex-Lord Chancellor who draws a pension is under an obligation to sit judicially.

19. Select Committee on the Lord Chancellor's Department (2002–03) HC 61, Q 48.

Thus only those who are appointed as Supreme Court judges should sit and they should do so only during their period of tenure. (This issue is pursued below under Transparency and Accountability).

The enhancement of the independence of individual judges, brought about by the creation of the new court, is clearly important. However, the establishment of the court will also increase the extent to which there is, and is seen to be, collective or institutional judicial independence. Currently, 'the independence of the judiciary [is] potentially compromised in the eyes of citizens by relegating the status of the highest court to the position of a subordinate part of the legislature'.[20] The physical separation of senior judges from the House of Lords ends this position. Moreover, given that 'in England ... the status of the judges has become the core of the discussion of the independence of the judiciary',[21] the increase in their status, through the Court's institutional separateness, will impact upon perceptions of judicial independence. Related to this is the abolition of the office of Lord Chancellor, whose multi-functional position as head of the judiciary, member of the Cabinet and Speaker in the House of Lords did little to support the notion of a judiciary institutionally and functionally separate and independent from the other arms of government.

Yet the separation of the highest court and its institutional independence is not absolute. The Supreme Court will not have budgetary and administrative independence. The Consultation Paper makes it clear that the Secretary of State for Constitutional Affairs will assume statutory responsibility for the Supreme Court, bidding for, and providing, resources for it as he or she does for the rest of the court system.[22] Moreover, the Department for Constitutional Affairs will provide the administrative staff and central services, including financial, IT, premises management and human resources, 'the relatively small size of the Court and its administrative requirements mak[ing] separate administrative arrangements uneconomic'.[23] The Department will also ensure that, in line with all courts, the Supreme Court accords with the requirements of efficiency, economy and value for money. Thus, unlike some Supreme Courts, the United Kingdom court will not be an autonomous body in charge of its own affairs, regulating its budget and appointing and overseeing its own administrative staff. In this regard, judicial independence in its institutional sense is still limited, and the United Kingdom tradition, whereby concentration is upon the independence of individual judges, rather than the collectivity, is retained.

Whether, in the future, there will be pressure from the Supreme Court and courts in general for further independence remains to be seen. The response from the Judges' Council to the government's Consultation Paper, in which it argues that adequate funding for the courts, protected by statute, is essential for judicial independence, suggests that there will.[24] One thing is sure; there can be no going back on the separation of the Appellate Committee from the

---

20. Lord Steyn 'The Case for a Supreme Court' The Neill Lecture, All Souls College, Oxford, 1 March 2002.

21. R Stevens *The Independence of the Judiciary: the View from the Lord Chancellor's Office* (Oxford: Clarendon Press, 1993) p 183.

22. Department for Constitutional Affairs, n 1 above, para 64.

23. Department for Constitutional Affairs, n 1 above, para 65.

24. *The Times*, 7 November 2003.

House of Lords. As Lord Denning, in an often-quoted phrase, said of the colonies gaining their independence, 'freedom once given cannot be taken away'.[25] The only direction in which the Supreme Court can move, as with the former colonies, is forward. This could eventually mean full institutional independence, which would have implications for all the branches of government.

SAFEGUARDING JUDICIAL INDEPENDENCE

Despite the limitations of the reform, the ending of the dual judicial/legislative role, the physical separation from the House of Lords and the abolition of the role of Lord Chancellor clearly signal the independence of the new court and a greater adherence to the separation of powers. In so doing, they inevitably draw attention to other areas where independence and separation are undermined and infringed, in particular to the constitutional appropriateness of the most senior judges continuing to chair inquiries into matters of public concern, set up by the government. From a government's point of view, appointing judges to chair such inquiries gives an aura of independence and impartiality to the proceedings and can remove the political heat from a situation. However, their use blurs the boundary between judicial and executive functions and there is a danger that, with terms of reference decided by ministers, the process will be seen as political and the judges perceived as instruments of the executive, particularly if their reports fail to satisfy those who are aggrieved. This has implications for the reputation of individual judges and, more widely, for judicial independence. Northern Ireland presents the most obvious example of this, where, during the period 1969–79, a succession of senior judges, including Lords Scarman, Widgery, Parker, Diplock and Gardiner, undertook inquiries and produced reports, all of which were 'unacceptable' 'to different segments in Ulster'[26] and 'threw doubt on the impartiality and independence of the British judiciary'.[27] Lord Saville's inquiry is similarly unlikely to satisfy all concerned.

It is therefore not surprising that in other jurisdictions the use of judges for such purposes is considered unconstitutional. In the United States, which operates under a stronger model of the separation of powers, the Supreme Court has stated: 'The legitimacy of the Judicial Branch ultimately depends upon a reputation for impartiality and non-partisanship.'[28] It continued: 'That reputation may not be borrowed by the political Branches to cloak their work in the neutral colors of judicial action.'[29] The Australian High Court, similarly mindful of the need to safeguard judicial independence, has recently supported this view.[30] In Britain, it is common practice to borrow the judicial reputation,

25. Lord Denning in *Blackburn v A-G* [1971] 1 WLR 1037 at 1040.
26. Stevens, n 2 above, p 43.
27. Stevens, n 2 above, p 43.
28. *Mistretta v United States* 488 US 362 at 407 (1989).
29. *Mistretta v United States* 488 US 362 at 407 (1989).
30. See A Le Sueur and R Cornes *The Future of the United Kingdom's Highest Courts* (London: The Constitution Unit, UCL, 2001) para 16.3.2.

although should the judicial finding result in a report critical of ministers and officials, the government is quick to claim a lack of 'neutral colors', as Sir Richard Scott found when his report on the Matrix Churchill affair resulted in accusations that he was anti-government and lacking in understanding of how Whitehall worked.[31] This may be equally damaging to the reputation of the judiciary, for while the public may applaud the finding of a report which blames the government, accusations of partisanship are likely to undermine public confidence. It may also be affected detrimentally if the matter investigated by an inquiry becomes subject to litigation or the inquiry judge to judicial review.[32] A finding of error or unfairness against any judge, but particularly one from the final court of appeal, is hardly likely to generate confidence in the judiciary.

Members of the Supreme Court should therefore guard their independence and separation by no longer accepting invitations to chair such inquiries. This break with the practice of the last 80 or so years would require the government to find alternative chairs, of which there are plenty within the ranks of retired civil servants, senior practitioners and academics, but would be an appropriate reflection of the fact that, at the beginning of the twenty-first century, the nature of judicial responsibilities and the requirements of judicial office have changed. Senior judges now have a constitutional, and, hence, political, role in the courts which makes it inappropriate for them to take part in any activity that blurs the boundaries between judicial and executive responsibilities.

This constitutional role has become increasingly apparent in the last ten years or so and one of its other effects has been to make members of the judiciary subject to attack by politicians, unhappy with their decisions. The convention which prohibits Member of Parliament from criticising individual judicial decisions within the House, other than in a debate on a substantive motion, provides some protection, but this does not prevent politicians from making their feelings known, through the media and in speeches at party conferences or elsewhere. Both Conservative and Labour ministers have sought to undermine judicial decisions in such a way. In recent times Michael Howard, Home Secretary in John Major's government, and David Blunkett, Home Secretary under Tony Blair, have been particular culprits and the Prime Minister has himself spoken of 'judicial interference' in the sensitive area of asylum seekers.[33]

The articulation by ministers of their displeasure at judicial decisions will not end with the creation of a Supreme Court. Indeed, there is good reason to think it will increase. The court's continued function as the final court of appeal for high-profile judicial review and human rights cases, together with its new role in determining devolution issues, suggests that there will be more than a degree of friction between the government and the court. This is healthy and, in most cases, rather than ministerial attacks on the courts and individual judges undermining judicial independence, they provide evidence of its existence.

---

31. *Report of the Inquiry into the Export of Defence Equipment and Dual-use Goods to Iraq and related Prosecutions* (Chairman, Sir Richard Scott) (1995–96) HC 115.
32. *See* B Hadfield '*R v. Lord Saville of Newdigate, ex p anonymous soldiers*: What is the Purpose of a Tribunal of Inquiry?' [1999] PL 663.
33. Labour Party Conference, 1 October 2003.

However, a concerted campaign may upset 'an equilibrium in Britain's subtle uncodified constitution',[34] sap public confidence and threaten the legitimacy of the judiciary. To minimise the prospect of such a situation arising, it is essential for the court to be open and clear in its decision-making and to employ mechanisms which make its decisions accessible and understandable to the public and the media (see below). This is particularly important when a decision undermines a key plank of government policy, or when a decision of a lower court, which has been publicly criticised by ministers, is overturned. The former leaves the court open to accusations that it is interfering with the democratic process; the latter that it is succumbing to government pressure.

A related issue, which has concerned senior judges, is who should assume the role of defending judicial independence against attacks, both from within and outside government. This has traditionally been the role of Lord Chancellors and one which, according to Lord Woolf, they have fulfilled admirably,[35] but their tendency to operate behind the scenes, for which there are, no doubt, good reasons, means this has seldom been evident to the public. Lord Irvine explained to the select committee on the Lord Chancellor's Department; 'sometimes you can be more influential by speaking strongly in private than you can be by making a great hoo-ha in public.'[36] However, the approach lacks transparency, something that the new reforms are seeking to improve, and at a time when public relations and spin are all important, it would seem to put judges at a disadvantage. If judicial independence is under attack, it needs to be publicly defended but – and here we find another reason for the behind-the-scenes approach – it would be contrary to the collegiality and unity required by the convention of collective responsibility for one government minister publicly to chastise another. As Lord Steyn noted of the position of the Lord Chancellor, this means he 'is unable to discharge the task of protecting judicial independence'.[37]

The government's proposal, whereby defending judicial independence becomes the responsibility of the Secretary of State for Constitutional Affairs, perpetuates this weakness. It also fails to recognise the illogicality of a Cabinet minister being charged with such a responsibility or to take account of the changes in the way in which government is conducted which make ideas of defending or representing the judges in Cabinet outdated and impractical. The notion of Cabinet as a forum for discussion and collective decision-making, in which there are opportunities for the responsible minister to represent the views of the judiciary and defend its independence, is far from the reality. Few decisions are endorsed by the full Cabinet, far less made by it.

It cannot, in any case, be assumed that the judges and the Secretary of State will take the same view of what constitutes judicial independence and thus what needs defending. This was evident during the late 1980s and early 1990s when senior judges and their retired colleagues opposed Lord Mackay's plans

34. A Le Sueur 'The Judicial Review Debate; from Partnership to Friction' (1996) 31 Government and Opposition 8 at 9.
35. See Lord Woolf's Mansion House Speech, 9 July 2003.
36. Lord Chancellor's Department Select Committee *Minutes of Evidence* (2003) HC 611-i, Q 29.
37. Lord Steyn, n 20 above.

to reform the legal profession, legal aid and the civil court system on the often spurious grounds that they were an interference with judicial independence.[38] For Lord Mackay, and, indeed, Lord Irvine, judicial independence was confined to 'the judge trying the case [being] free to decide it according to his judgment and in the light of the existing law'.[39] This included some involvement in the listing of cases but it did not extend, as some judges argued it should, to the judiciary being 'allowed a significant role in the administration of the courts'.[40] The root of the problem was that Lord Mackay, as a member of the Cabinet, was giving effect to the government's programme of improving efficiency and, in so doing, was, in the view of some judges, putting his executive responsibilities above his responsibility for protecting judicial independence or, perhaps more accurately, looking after judicial interests. It seems likely that this will become a more common basis for contention when the defender of judicial independence is a minister, like any other, rather than a member of the Cabinet who also has judicial status.

The issue of why the judges should need representing is also not addressed by those who advocate that a Cabinet minister should retain this role. As far as Lord Steyn is concerned, not only is representation unnecessary, but any conversation between the judges and the executive should be conducted in the public domain, not through a government minister who is subject to the requirements of collective responsibility.[41] Making the defence of judicial independence a responsibility of the Secretary of State for Constitutional Affairs would therefore seem unsatisfactory and fraught with difficulties. It also perpetuates the secrecy surrounding judicial/executive relations, retains the institutional link between judges and government and confirms judicial reliance upon a member of the executive, hardly a feature of an independent judiciary. It would seem more appropriate for any concerns about judicial independence to be articulated by the judges themselves, most appropriately through the Lord Chief Justice, who assumes the role of head of the judiciary, or through a reformed, representative Judges' Council. This transfer of responsibility could be given added weight if, as the Judges' Council suggests, the functions of judges and the executive, as they relate to the justice system, were set out in legislation which might also impose a general duty on ministers to uphold judicial independence. This would rectify the 'constitutional deficit' which, Lord Woolf claims,[42] will be caused by the abolition of the office of Lord Chancellor. Others would argue that such a deficit exists despite, or because, of the office, but, either way, legislation of this nature would provide a constitutional framework for judicial/executive relations and mark the beginnings of a written constitution. It would also bring to the fore the issue of

---

38. See, eg, Sir Nicholas Browne-Wilkinson 'The Independence of the Judiciary in the 1980s' [1988] PL 44; Sir Francis Purchas 'What is happening to Judicial Independence?' (1994a) 144 NLJ 6665 at 1306–1310 and 'The Constitution in the Market Place' (1994b) 143 NLJ 6624 at 1604–1609.
39. Lord Mackay, HL Official Report (5th series) col 1308, 5 June 1996.
40. Purchas (1994b), n 38 above.
41. Lord Steyn 'The Weakest and Least Dangerous Department of Government' [1997] PL 84 at 90.
42. *The Times*, 7 November 2003.

entrenchment, for it would be a constitutional nonsense for a statute, enacted to protect the independence of the judiciary, to be subject to repeal at the whim of the government in office.

As far as the Supreme Court is concerned, it may be that it will find ways of protecting its independence. It would be inappropriate for it to defend individual decisions, but through greater transparency, press briefings and written statements, it could at least ensure that reasons, given in layman's terms, for particularly controversial or complex decisions are in the public domain. In addition, while needing to be careful not to appear to use the mantle of judicial independence to protect vested interests, there may be a case for the court issuing statements of concern, if it believes a particular government policy is threatening the administration of justice and judicial independence. This would further increase the court's institutional independence and counter any perception there might be that the senior judges are part of, or dependent upon, government.

POLITICISATION

While the establishment of a Supreme Court will confirm the independence of the individual judge in his or her own court and increase independence in the institutional or collective sense, it will not neutralise or depolitise the judges. The Consultation Paper notes: 'the considerable growth in judicial review in recent years has inevitably brought the judges more into the political eye.' It continues: 'It is essential that our systems do all that they can to minimise the danger that judges' decisions could be perceived to be politically motivated.'[43] It is unclear whether 'politically motivated' is used in its narrow sense to mean 'party politically motivated' or, as the language suggests, in its wider sense. If the latter, there may be an expectation that the creation of a free-standing Supreme Court will, in some way, project senior judges into a vacuum in which they will make their decisions in isolation from, and without regard to, the political context and their own ideology. This will not happen. Indeed, there is the possibility that greater institutional independence may actually increase the extent to which senior judges are seen as political actors.

First, the status of the new court is likely to increase media exposure of opinions expressed by senior judges, through conference papers, interviews, journal articles and addresses to the profession. Their views on issues, such as sentencing and the reform of the legal system, are not value free, but confirm that judges, like everyone else, are political beings who operate in a political world. Secondly, the increased jurisdiction of the court and its more obvious constitutional role will affect the type and extent of media coverage the court receives. Controversial or sensitive decisions are likely to be scrutinised, with the political leanings and philosophical or moral positions of the various judges being subject to examination. This has already become a feature of press reporting of some cases. It was particularly notable in the *Pinochet* case,[44] where

---

43. Department for Constitutional Affairs, n 1 above, para 1.2.
44. *R v Bow Street Metropolitan Stipendiary Magistrate, ex p Pinochet Ugarte* [1998] 4 All ER 897, HL; *(No 2)* [1999] 1 All ER 577, HL, *(No 3)* [1999] 2 All ER 97, HL.

both the *Telegraph* and *The Times* sought to position the members of the panel along a scale, ranging from 'liberal' to 'conservative'. *The Times* also provided brief pen portraits of the judges, in which Lord Browne-Wilkinson was described as 'humane, liberal and charming', Lord Hope as 'quiet [with a] meticulous style and middle of the road politics', Lord Hutton as the 'most right-leaning of the panel', Lord Saville as 'friendly, affable and sporty', Lord Millett as 'the highest ranking Freemason in the judiciary', Lord Phillips as 'liberal' and Lord Goff as 'known for intelligence and moderation'.[45]

Such reporting also featured in the case of the conjoined twins, Mary and Jodie, heard in 2000 by the Court of Appeal. In this instance, the media paid particular attention to the religious background of the three judges, as the beliefs of the parents, who were devout Roman Catholics, were central to the case. Thus it was reported that Lord Justice Ward, once voted 'the most human face of the judiciary', was a former pupil of the Christian Brothers College in Pretoria, South Africa, which 'offers holistic education based on Christian traditions'; Lord Justice Brooke was 'a deeply compassionate man' who 'hails from a family with strong Anglican traditions'; and Lord Justice Walker was educated at a Roman Catholic School and 'seen as intellectually rigorous'.[46] The number of children each judge had was also reported, including the fact that one had twin daughters. Reporting of this nature, which because of the type of cases brought under the Human Rights Act 1998 is likely to become more common, humanises the judges but also adds to the impression that members of the senior judiciary are part of politics rather than divorced from them. A high-profile devolution case could further add to this impression.

Thirdly, evidence from elsewhere suggests that institutional separation could result in the Supreme Court becoming a political institution in its own right, in the sense of being subject to increased use and lobbying by pressure and interest groups, many of which believe they are more likely to achieve their ends through the court than through elected representatives.[47] In this way, the court is likely to be perceived as being more political than the current Appellate Committee of the House of Lords. Indeed, on occasions, it may seem to be in competition with the executive and the legislature. Much depends on how it reacts to those who seek to influence its thinking, but any idea that the establishment of a separate Supreme Court will in some way remove judges from the political arena is misplaced.

Similarly, to imply that the physical separation of the final court of appeal will in some way reduce, or limit, the relationship between law and politics is to misunderstand the nature of judicial decisions. This relationship may be more apparent during times of judicial activism, but a decision not to intervene is just as political as its counterpart and as likely to have political consequences. Jurisprudence cannot be considered in isolation or divorced from politics. This is evident from the way in which senior judges in the 1990s responded to the

---

45. *The Times*, 25 March 1999.
46. *The Times*, 22 September 2000.
47. See D Robertson 'The House of Lords as a Political and Constitutional Court: Lessons from the Pinochet case' in D Woodhouse (ed) *The Pinochet case: a Legal and Constitutional Analysis* (Oxford: Hart Publishing, 2000); C Harlow 'Public Law and Popular Justice' (2002) 65 MLR 1.

political situation and the policies of the Conservative government, using the concepts of fairness, reasonableness, legitimate expectations and fundamental human rights to protect the individual from an abuse of power.[48] It is also evident in the way in which senior judges have reacted to the Human Rights Act 1998, according 'a very considerable margin of appreciation to political and official decision makers'[49] in order to 'help to allay the fears of those who see incorporation as an objectionable judicial usurpation of democratic authority'.[50] This apparent retreat from their former activist position is a clear recognition by senior judges of the impact on the other arms of government of their increased power under the Human Rights Act 1998, and whilst some commentators are impatient with this policy of judicial restraint, there is no doubting its political astuteness. A new Supreme Court may similarly downplay its increase in status and jurisdiction in its early days. What will happen in the longer term will depend on a number of factors. There will, no doubt, be periods of activism and restraint, as there have been in the House of Lords and in other Supreme Courts. However, as elsewhere, whether or not the court is activist or restrained is a political, not a legal, decision and while jurisprudence may not reflect the party political leaning of the judges concerned, although some would argue that it does, it is political in the broader sense and impacts on the political process and on government policies.[51]

APPOINTMENTS

There are clearly implications for senior judges if, as many believe should be the case, the appointment of members of the Supreme Court comes within the remit of a new Supreme Court Judicial Appointments Commission. Any influence they, as Law Lords, have had over appointments is likely to diminish with the demise of the office of Lord Chancellor and the replacement of the traditional process, whereby he makes recommendations to the Prime Minister who then advises the Queen. While judges will be represented on an Appointments Commission, which may have an obligation to consult with the Supreme Court to determine its particular needs, the judicial voice will be unlikely to carry as much weight as it did when the recommendations were made by 'one-of-them', albeit one who was also a government minister. The process for appointing the most senior judges has, for some time, been seen as constitutionally inappropriate by bodies, such as JUSTICE, particularly with regard to the involvement of the Prime Minister and the secrecy surrounding the process (see Transparency and accountability below). It becomes even more

---

48. Eg J Laws 'Is the High Court the Guardian of Fundamental Rights' [1993] PL 59; 'Law and Democracy' [1995] PL 80; 'The Constitution: Morals and Rights' [1996] PL 622. See also S Sedley 'Human Rights: A Twenty-First Century Agenda' [1995] PL 386.
49. Lord Bingham 'Incorporation of the ECHR: the Opportunity and the Challenge' [1998] 2 Jersey LR 257 at 269–270.
50. Lord Bingham, n 49 above.
51. See J A G Griffith *The Politics of the Judiciary* (London: Fontana Press, 4th edn, 1991).

inappropriate given the status of the Supreme Court as the highest court of the United Kingdom for constitutional matters as well as civil and criminal appeals.

The replacement of the Lord Chancellor by an independent Commission with a strong lay element should help to strengthen the notion of judicial independence, particularly if the Prime Minister is no longer involved in the process and the choice given to the minister with responsibility for advising the Queen on appointments is strictly limited. This will minimise the concern that, given the Supreme Court's increased involvement in politically sensitive cases, the government could be tempted to manipulate the composition of the court for political ends. A Judicial Appointments Commission should also provide reassurance that the judiciary is not a self-perpetuating oligarchy, particularly if, as the Consultation Paper indicates, one of its aims is to build a judiciary which is much more representative than at present.[52] This does not mean abandoning the basic principle that appointments should be made on merit. It does mean a reconsideration of what constitutes 'merit' and a move away from the assumption that it is necessarily demonstrated by a successful practice at the Bar.[53]

If the creation of a Supreme Court is part of a modernising process, the composition of the court must reflect modern practices and public expectations. There are ways of achieving a better balance. If there are to be quotas for Scottish and Northern Ireland membership of the court, possibly two from Scotland and one from Northern Ireland, there could also be quotas for women and ethnic minorities. This would not be contrary to the merit principle but, as with geographical representation, simply a restriction of the pool of those from whom appointments can be made. It is extremely unlikely that such a system will be adopted, at least in the short to medium term. Nevertheless, over time, the Supreme Court should have quite a different appearance from the current Appellate Committee of the House of Lords. Appearances matters and it is essential that the composition of the court moves away from the stereotype of the white, middle-class, elderly, male barrister. A start has already been made with the appointment of Dame Brenda Hale and needs to be built upon to create a court which is more representative. This will increase public support for, and trust in, the court and, ultimately, could have implications for the balance of power and, hence, for the other branches of government.

The jurisdiction of the Supreme Court also requires some thought to be given to the skills required of its members. They will not only need to consider arguments and evaluate evidence of what, under the Human Rights Act 1998, 'is necessary in a democratic society' but also, under devolution legislation, to deal with legal disputes about the location, and extent, of power. These will be hotly contested, particularly if the political party in office in the United Kingdom is different from that holding power in the devolved Parliament or Assembly. As Le Sueur and Cornes note: 'In such cases, the exercise of legal judgment, and the manner in which it is explained, requires political astuteness that is different in character from that needed in adjudication in most ordinary

---

52. Department for Constitutional Affairs, Consultation Paper *Constitutional Reform: A New Way of Appointing Judges* (July 2003).
53. See Dame Brenda Hale 'Equality and the Judiciary; why should we want more women judges?' [2001] PL 489.

civil and criminal cases ... The criterion of professional merit may need to be broadened to encompass these attributes.'[54] It will also need to be considered carefully, given the formalisation of Scottish and Northern Ireland representation in the court and the possibility of judicial experience in Wales being a factor that the Commission will need to take into account.[55] The argument against actual representation for Wales is that, unlike Scotland and Northern Ireland, it is not a separate jurisdiction. However, if the court is to maintain the confidence of all parts of the United Kingdom in its handling of devolution cases, it is essential for it not to be perceived as a predominately English court which, intentionally or otherwise, favours Westminster over Stormont, Hollyrood or Cardiff. This argument could have far-reaching implications if power is devolved to regional assemblies in England. Should there be a requirement that, in making appointments to the Supreme Court, judicial experience in the various regions is a consideration? Logic suggestions that there should.

TRANSPARENCY AND ACCOUNTABILITY

The need for judicial independence, which underpins the government reforms, goes hand-in-hand with a requirement for transparency,[56] the importance of which, given the focus on appearances and perception, increases. Thus it is essential for the process by which members of the Supreme Court are appointed to be open and transparent. Transparency in the workings of the court is also important, both in demonstrating its independence and dispelling the mystique that all too often surrounds judges and the law. Understanding what is happening, and why, aids public understanding and confidence in the judiciary. A Supreme Court, housed in its own building with more space, will be able to follow the example of other Supreme Courts and, in addition to dispensing justice, fulfil the role of educator and facilitator. Whether it does so, and how far it goes, remains to be seen and, to an extent, depends upon the premises, its resources, and the imagination and will of those concerned. It would, however, bolster its legitimacy if it became a public building in all senses of the word, encouraging members of the public to visit, both in person and through imaginatively designed websites.

However the interests of, and need for, transparency, require more. They extend to the need for a Register of Interests for Supreme Court and other judges. The Law Lords are currently required to comply with the Register of Interests of the House of Lords but this requirement will end when they transfer to the Supreme Court and cease to be members of the legislature. The Supreme Court will have to consider how to replace this requirement. It may opt for the lowest level of disclosure, a register of pecuniary interests, but this would be to miss the opportunity to demonstrate its commitment to openness and transparency by adopting a register which included charitable positions, club memberships etc. This has already been recommended for judges in Northern Ireland, where

54. Le Sueur and Cornes, n 30 above, para 12.3.4.
55. Department for Constitutional Affairs, n 1 above, para 48.
56. Department for Constitutional Affairs, n 1 above para 1.1.

the divided community is seen as requiring special measures. Such a register would seem appropriate for all judges in the United Kingdom, and particularly for members of the Supreme Court where there is a public interest in as full a disclosure as possible. More broadly, the establishment of a separate and new institution may act as a trigger for a judicial Code of Conduct, the development of which is long overdue.

The interests of transparency also require a reconsideration of the way in which the highest court conducts its business. The Appellate Committee uses panels of five or, exceptionally, seven judges, the selection of which is far from transparent. The Lord Chancellor is responsible for determining who hears which case and although, in practice, he delegates the task to the senior law, he retains the right to exercise his choice. The result is, as Lord Steyn noted, that: 'nobody will in practice know when the power has been exercised directly or indirectly. Not much legal certainty and transparency there.'[57] The transfer of the power to the President of the Supreme Court, together with the abolition of the office of Lord Chancellor, removes the possibility of involvement by a government minister and will therefore make the situation less contentious. However, the lack of certainty and transparency remains and is exacerbated by the fact that selection is not confined to the 12 Law Lords but extends to a panel of occasional judges who can be called upon to sit when there are insufficient Law Lords available or when particular expertise is required. Thus the choice, in theory, is five from a possible 27.[58] These arrangements, which allow flexibility in the determination of panels, may facilitate the work of the current Appellate Committee of the House of Lords and the Judicial Committee of the Privy Council but, as Le Sueur and Cornes note, they 'undermine the protections offered by fixed, non-renewable terms of office for judges'.[59] They may also result in speculation that the President of the court has been partial in whom he has selected, giving preference to conservative or liberal colleagues, depending on the outcome he favours in a particular case.

Even if the panel of occasional judges were abolished, under current arrangements the President of the court would still be required to exercise choice and this may result in problems in politically or morally sensitive cases. Lord Hoffmann is on record as saying that had the composition of a previous court been slightly different, the law would have been set 'on a different course'.[60] This possibility and the fact that a panel is not known in advance may result in media speculation as to who will be chosen and, subsequently, if the decision is controversial, in speculation about what the outcome might have been had different members of the Supreme Court been sitting. The *Pinochet* case[61] provided an example of what can happen, leading Stevens to comment: 'Those who might not be ready to endorse a Constitutional or even

57. Lord Steyn, n 20 above.
58. Le Sueur and Cornes, n 30 above, para 3.2.2.
59. Le Sueur and Cornes, n 30 above, para 3.2.2.
60. Lord Hoffmann in *White v Chief Constable of South Yorkshire* [1998] 3 WLR 1509 at 1549.
61. *R v Bow Street Metropolitan Stipendiary Magistrate, ex p Pinochet Ugarte* [1998] 4 All ER 897, HL; *(No 2)* [1999] 1 All ER 577, HL; *(No 3)* [1999] 2 All ER 97, HL.

a Supreme Court could not fail to be embarrassed by the lottery which surrounded [the case].'[62] *Pinochet* was, of course, exceptional, but given the constitutional jurisdiction of the Supreme Court, there are likely to be other cases, concerning human rights or, possibly, devolution issues, where the composition of the panel is all important for the outcome. There may not be many, but it only takes the odd one or two, where who sits seems to be crucial to the decision, for the credibility of the court to be undermined. Transparency in the determination of panels would thus seem imperative and requires an end to selection. It does not matter that, in practice, the need for expertise and availability limits the choice, the court should either sit en banc, or have two panels (perhaps seven apiece), one of which determines all civil cases and the other, criminal and public law cases, with the option of the panels sitting together in cross-over cases.[63] These models are not without problems, but if independence and transparency are the key objectives, they are infinitely preferable to the current panel system and, if not adopted when the court is established, may need to be considered before long.

The needs of transparency also extend to judicial decisions and, it is hoped, will result in changes to the way in which judgments are presented. The Supreme Court could adopt a model whereby concurring and dissenting judgments are co-ordinated, rather than continuing to give five (even seven) separate opinions which, on occasions, are repetitious of the facts and law, and baffle many lawyers, never mind lay persons.[64] Alternatively, or in addition, they could decide that, to aid public understanding, judgments should be accompanied by a brief explanation of the case and the court's decision, written in plain English. They could also appoint a press liaison or communications officer and provide journalists with facilities to read the judgments and write their reports. Such developments would have resource implications but are important in terms of transparency and public understanding of what the court does.

Developments which aid transparency are also important for accountability. These concepts are closely related but should not be confused. Transparency does not, necessarily, ensure accountability. It may make it easier to hold those concerned to account, but if there are no mechanisms to extract this accountability, then much of the advantage is lost. How much it helps accountability also depends on the extent to which it permeates the structure and the culture of an organisation. The tendency in government has been to increase the transparency of managerial and financial operations. This has made it easier to extract managerial accountability but has not necessarily improved the accountability of policy makers and political actors who are largely protected from the move towards greater openness, and will remain so under the Freedom of Information Act 2000. As far as judges are concerned, there is no mention of accountability in the Consultation Paper and the accountability of the Appellate Committee of the House of Lords has not been in the frontline of discussion. This could change when the Supreme Court is established because

---

62. Stevens, n 2 above, p 111.
63. See Le Sueur and Cornes, n 30 above, para 3.4.2, for the range of possibilities.
64. See D Robertson 'The House of Lords as a Political and Constitutional Court: Lessons from the Pinochet Case' in D Woodhouse (ed) *The Pinochet Case: a Legal and Constitutional Analysis* (Oxford: Hart Publishing, 2000).

of its increased jurisdiction, greater institutional autonomy and the inevitable comparisons that will be made with Supreme Courts elsewhere. The Supreme Court may therefore have to consider how it can fulfil the accountability required.

There are various types of accountability. Using models of political accountability, these can be defined as explanatory, amendatory and sacrificial, and they require that decisions and actions are accounted for and explained, action is taken to make amends for mistakes and to ensure they are not repeated, and, ultimately, in cases of serious error, the office holder tenders his or her resignation.[65] As far as judges are concerned, some accountability mechanisms are already in place, in that judgments include explanations for the decision, albeit not always very clear ones,[66] hence the importance of the transparency suggestions above, the implementation of which would be a recognition by the court that it owes accountability not just to the parties to the case and their lawyers but to a wider constituency. Explanatory accountability also operates through interviews given to the media and contributions to journals and conferences. These provide accountability to the broader legal community and may be used to explain the reasons for certain trends in judicial decisions. Where amendatory accountability is concerned, the right of appeal, linked with the ability of the highest court, exceptionally, to overrule one of its own decisions or, less dramatically, to limit its effect, provides one mechanism. Another is provided by the Criminal Cases Review Commission, which can take amendatory action when it considers there may have been a miscarriage of justice, referring cases back to the Court of Appeal. Process errors can also be rectified. The decision of the House of Lords to set aside the first *Pinochet* decision and rehear the case with a differently constituted panel was an example of the court taking corrective action or making amends for a procedural wrong. However, the requirement of sacrificial accountability is less easily satisfied. It exists in the form of the address from both Houses of Parliament, but is probably of little practical use and may need to be reconsidered to provide a more appropriate balance between judicial independence and accountability.

There may, in addition, be other developments in the area of accountability. The courts have traditionally been protected from parliamentary scrutiny but, as noted by Drewry and Oliver, writing before the proposal for a Supreme Court, 'the continuing reforms of the administration of justice, combined with the increasing political impact of judicial decisions and the higher political profile of the judiciary, have combined to challenge the continued sustainability of practices and conventions that have traditionally shielded the courts from parliamentary scrutiny'.[67] A Supreme Court, perceived to be more autonomous than the Appellate Committee of the House of Lords, may challenge these even

---

65. See D Woodhouse *Ministers and Parliament: Accountability in Theory and Practice* (Oxford: Clarendon Press, 1994).

66. For a discussion of the effectiveness of reason-giving practices as a method of accountability see the paper, entitled 'Developing Mechanisms for Routine Judicial Accountability in the UK', given by A Le Sueur at the BICL Conference on Accountability and Independence of the Judiciary, 14 June 2003.

67. G Drewry and D Oliver 'Parliamentary accountability for the administration of justice' in G Drewry and D Oliver (eds) *The Law and Parliament* (London: Butterworths, 1998) p 35.

further and result in pressure for it to be accountable to the legislature. There are two possibilities for such accountability. First, prior to, or upon, appointment, new members of the court could be asked to attend parliamentary confirmation hearings. Concern that judges will be subjected to the type of hearings that Robert Bork and Clarence Thomas underwent in the United States senate is unfounded,[68] as is the belief that such hearings would undermine independence. They need not do so. They would, however, provide important information on the ideological beliefs of the most senior judges, and this is something about which it is reasonable for the public to know. Moreover, by providing a link between the judges and elected representatives, the hearings would increase the democratic legitimacy of senior appointments and, hence, of the Supreme Court.

The second possibility is that members of the Supreme Court could be expected to give evidence to select committees of the House of Commons or to joint parliamentary committees. Appearing before select committees is not a new experience for senior members of the judiciary. Most recently, Lord Woolf and Sir Richard Scott, at that time Master of the Rolls and Vice-Chancellor, respectively, appeared before the Committee on Public Administration in 1999 to give evidence on the draft Freedom of Information Bill,[69] while in 2001 Lords Bingham, Woolf and Phillips appeared before the Joint Committee on Human Rights to answer questions on the working of the Human Rights Act 1998.[70] These were ad hoc appearances to give opinions on particular issues but an expectation could develop that representatives of the Supreme Court, most obviously the President and Vice-President, would attend on an annual basis before the Committee on Constitutional Affairs to give an account of the court's activities over the last year. Clearly any arrangements by which judges are accountable to Parliament have constitutional implications. They would not, however, impinge upon the dignity of the court or judicial independence, any more than they have on the office of Lord Chancellor, since Lords Mackay and Irvine accepted the obligation to account to the Home Affairs Committee and, subsequently, the Select Committee on the Lord Chancellor's Department (now the Constitutional Affairs Committee).

Coupled with attendance before a select committee, the court could be required to produce an annual report which would provide the basis for the committee hearing. Such a report could be modelled on that produced by the Australian High Court which gives an account of its activities, budget and an analysis of case trends.[71] It could also include information, such as the throughput of cases, which would provide a measure of the court's efficiency, and, additionally, raise matters of judicial concern which relate to the administration of justice. A report along these lines, upon which the President and the Vice-President could be questioned, would do much to open up the

68. See K Malleson *The Use of Judicial Appointments Commissions: a Review of the US and Canadian models* (LCD, Research Paper no 6, 1997).
69. Select Committee for Public Administration *Minutes of Evidence* (1999) HC570-ix, pp 165–175.
70. Joint Committee on Human Rights, n 4 above.
71. See Le Sueur and Cornes, n 30 above, para 3.4.2, for examples of models from Canada, the United States and Spain.

workings of the Supreme Court and to dispel the aura of mystery which surrounds the most senior judges. Moreover, it would provide the accountability which, with its increased institutional independence, is essential for the legitimacy of the court.

The need to improve accountability to Parliament for judicial and legal affairs is not confined to the Supreme Court but extends to the Lord Chancellor's replacement, the Secretary of State for Constitutional Affairs. The accountability of government departments to Parliament operates through the minister, or Secretary of State, who, with rare exceptions, sits in the House of Commons and is accountable to it. One of the weaknesses of the current system has been that responsibility for judicial appointments and the running of the courts has been overseen by an appointed minister, the Lord Chancellor, who has sat in the House of Lords. This has traditionally been justified on the grounds that judicial independence requires him or her to be protected from the rough and tumble of party politics. This is a spurious claim which has had the effect of limiting accountability. Moreover, since Lords Mackay and Irvine, as Lord Chancellors, appointed junior ministers to speak on their behalf in the Commons, it has lost any credibility it might have had, for why should junior members of the government be exposed and a Cabinet minister sheltered? Junior ministers are, in any case, unable to take departmental, as opposed to personal, responsibility and thus do not satisfy the requirements of accountability. It is therefore important that the Secretary of State for Constitutional Affairs, who replaces the Lord Chancellor, is an elected politician who sits in the House of Commons and is accountable to it for the operation of the court system, including the Supreme Court, and for judicial appointments. This will enable him or her to be questioned by other representatives and, once again, reinforces the link between the appointment of judges and the electorate, legitimising the appointments process and the court itself.

Accountability is not, as is often portrayed, a threat to judicial independence but something to be balanced against it. There may be occasions when its needs are tempered by the requirements of judicial independence. Conversely, judicial independence, at times, may need to defer to accountability to ensure public confidence and support. There is, therefore, nothing contradictory in the claim that an increase in judicial independence should be matched by an increase in accountability. This has implications for any future development of the Supreme Court, for the more independent it becomes, the more it may be required to account for its activities and decisions.

WIDER CONSTITUTIONAL IMPLICATIONS

The establishment of a Supreme Court has obvious implications for the judiciary and its relationship with the other arms of government. Less obvious are the wider constitutional implications of such a development which may, ultimately, affect the basis on which our constitution operates. There has been a steady shift in the balance of power – away from politicians, towards judges – since the expansion of judicial review in the 1990s. It received a boost with the incorporation of the European Convention on Human Rights and will receive a further impetus with the establishment of an institutionally separate court with a wider constitutional jurisdiction. This continued shift in power from politicians to judges will no doubt be exercised discreetly and diplomatic by the new court. Nevertheless, its separateness and independence will make the transfer more apparent and this may put a strain upon judicial/executive and judicial/legislative relations, particular given the corresponding decline of parliamentary sovereignty.[72]

The courts, in constitutional theory, are limited by parliamentary sovereignty but, in practice, this limitation has been significantly reduced by membership of the European Union, the incorporation of the European Convention on Human Rights and the determination of some judges to protect fundamental constitutional rights.[73] This trend is likely to continue, even to the extent that a United Kingdom Supreme Court, seeking to be more like its counterparts elsewhere, may, at some point in the future, claim an inherent power to strike down legislation or, at least, to render ineffective any Act of Parliament which it views as 'unconstitutional'. This may seem an extreme scenario but the embrace of comparative law by senior judges has, according to Lord Steyn, already 'come of age'[74] and the new court's constitutional role may result in comparisons with the jurisdictions of other Supreme Courts and a move, consciously or otherwise, towards a matching, and hence increased, jurisdiction for the United Kingdom Court.

The outcome could be the further diminution of parliamentary sovereignty and the development of the United Kingdom into a constitutional democracy. Such a development is, according to some, already underway. Lord Steyn notes, of the incorporation of the European Convention on Human Rights, that it:

> 'has generally accelerated the constitutionalisation of our public law. A culture of justification now prevails. The renaissance in constitutionalism in democracies such as Australia, Canada, India, New Zealand and South Africa has not by-passed the United Kingdom. As citizens we may now ask the executive to justify, on public interest grounds, inroads on the rule of law, judicial independence and the separation of powers.'[75]

The increased constitutional role of the Supreme Court is likely to advance this development. Moreover, it is one that may find political support away from Westminster where the concept of parliamentary sovereignty means that the position of the devolved institutions is constitutionally unprotected. Indeed, in the long term, it is possible to see parliamentary sovereignty being replaced as the defining principle of the constitution by a more robust version of the separation of powers and a system of checks and balances which recognises the devolved institutions, as well as the Supreme Court, as having a checking function on central government. Much will depend on how the Supreme Court handles devolution issues, concerned with the allocation and exercise of power, and, should the occasion arise, how it deals with legislation from Westminster that seeks to abolish the devolved institutions. Some years down the road might it, in a demonstration of constitutionalism, follow the will of the people rather than the dictates of parliamentary sovereignty?

72. See M Elliot 'Parliamentary Sovereignty and the New Constitutional Order: Legislative Freedom, Political Reality and Convention' (2002) 22 LS 3 at 340.
73. Above n 48.
74. Lord Steyn 'Democracy through Law' [2002] 6 EHRLR 725 at 735.
75. Lord Steyn, n 20 above.

Such a scenario may seem a step (or several steps) too far. In any case, the developments outlined above are not necessarily dependent on the establishment of a Supreme Court. They may have happened if the current configuration of the Appellate Committee of the House of Lords and Privy Council had remained in place. These courts, or more accurately some of their members, have, after all, provided the jurisprudential foundation on which the Supreme Court can build.[76] Yet the lack of a United Kingdom constitutional jurisdiction and the absence of institutional independence suggest that this would have been unlikely. What actually happens in future will depend on how the Supreme Court develops. This in turn depends on its membership and the way in which it operates. It may be that the Supreme Court, concerned about criticisms that it lacks democratic legitimacy, will chose to work within the traditional constitutional boundaries and restraints. Alternatively, it may seek a more even distribution of power between the constitutional actors. If it does, it will need to operate in a climate of openness, transparency and accountability to generate public confidence and support.

The establishment of a Supreme Court has other implications which raise a number of questions. First, will its establishment have an effect on the constitutional structure of the United Kingdom? Will it act as a uniting factor? Will it encourage the notion that the United Kingdom is moving towards becoming a federal state? These are not incompatible for one of the hallmarks of a federal system is a court with an overarching constitutional jurisdiction. Secondly, will it result in changes to the appellate arrangements in Scotland which bring it in line with the rest of the United Kingdom? Thirdly, will the removal of the Law Lords from the legislative Chamber of the House of Lords have any implications for the future reform of that Chamber? In particular, does the removal of one particular group undermine the case for another group, namely the bishops, to remain within the legislature, as of right?

CONCLUSION

Much of the above discussion is speculative. It is, however, possible to conclude that the separation of the judicial and legislative functions of the House of Lords accords, more than has previously been the case, with the institutional requirements of the separation of powers, increases judicial independence and raises the profile and status of the highest court. This has political and constitutional implications not only for the judges but for the other arms of government. As far as the judges are concerned, the Supreme Court is likely to be seen as more overtly political than the Appellate Committee of the House of Lords. Of course, much depends on how it develops, both institutionally and jurisprudentially, but its constitutional jurisdiction, its physical separation from the legislature and its greater independence from the executive, rather than insulating it from politics, are likely to increase its involvement in the political process. Its increased power is also likely to result in calls for greater accountability, with implications for the members of the Supreme Court, both individually and collectively. As far as the United Kingdom's constitutional

---

76. Above n 49.

arrangements are concerned, there are implications, in the longer term, for the relationship and balance of power between the three arms of government and between the devolved institutions and Westminster. The establishment of a Supreme Court could hasten the move towards the United Kingdom becoming a constitutional democracy, a move that some believe is already in its fledgling stage. This would challenge the very basis of the constitution.

Reflections on continental European Supreme Courts

John Bell
Cambridge University

The Government's Consultation Paper Constitutional Reform: A Supreme Court for the United Kingdom *(July 2003) is interesting in that it is written as an argument for a technical 'fix'. The argument essentially is that we need to separate the Appellate Committee from the political House of Lords and abolish the Lord Chancellor. The discussion then focuses on how this can be done with the minimum change to the jurisdiction and composition of the existing courts. There is no attempt at strategic thinking. It is constitutional reform by way of incremental change. What I want to do here is to use some continental European experiences to suggest a number of strategic questions which either do not appear in the Consultation Paper from the Department of Constitutional Affairs or which are handled too rapidly, but which are important for the future functioning of a Supreme Court. There are only a limited number of lessons which can be learnt from any comparative survey. In this inquiry, as in many, the contrasts between legal systems only raise questions, rather than offering solutions. It is an agenda-setting exercise.*

It may be thought that continental Europe is not an appropriate comparator for a common law system. After all, we do not have an early career judiciary, merely an entry in middle age, after professional experience. This may be an issue in some aspects of the work of a Supreme Court, but it is not a major one. We are also more selective in the cases which come before the higher courts. As will be seen, this is a more serious issue. One Supreme Court in France, the Cour de cassation, decided 20,613 civil and 9,581 criminal cases in 2001,[1] whilst the House of Lords decided 85 cases and four points of law in the same year.[2] Clearly the two are just not performing the same role. The contrast points out that we have a particular idea of a Supreme Court and where it fits within judicial institutions. But this idea needs to be made more explicit if one is to understand the particular function which a Supreme Court is to play. Contrast with other systems may help to highlight and make explicit some of the assumptions on which we are working in the UK, and which are not articulated in the Consultation Paper.

My questions for consideration are:

1. Why have *a single* Supreme Court?
2. How should the Supreme Court act as authoritative interpreter of the law?
3. Is the Supreme Court a constitutional court?

---

1. Ministry of Justice *Annuaire statistique de la Justice* (2003) pp 23 and 137.
2. Lord Chancellor's Department *Judicial Statistics Annual Report 2001* (2002) table 1.4.

4. Should the Supreme Court give advisory opinions?
5. How does the Supreme Court relate institutionally to law reform?
6. What is the place of the Supreme Court within the judiciary?

1. WHY DO YOU NEED A SINGLE SUPREME COURT?

Common lawyers commonly think in terms of a single, national Supreme Court. The idea of a neat and hierarchically integrated court system might seem to mirror a hierarchically integrated legal system. A doctrine of binding precedent encourages this perception. But most European systems have a more complex structure. The complexity arises from two challenges that have to be met by a legal system: the specialist character of law and the particular requirements of different regions.

In the modern legal world, it is common for lawyers to become specialists and for legal issues to be raised in court in ways that require specialist understanding. Many continental European countries meet this challenge by specialisation among judges. Within an appeal court or Supreme Court, there will be members or panels with specialist knowledge of particular branches of law to whom cases will be referred. The specialisation is reflected either in the creation of specialist courts, even at the highest levels, or by distinct divisions within broadly based Supreme Courts.

In many countries, there is a separation between general courts of civil and criminal jurisdiction and the administrative courts. In this, there are at least two traditions in Western Europe. We are familiar with the French tradition of a clear separation between the civil and criminal courts leading up to the Cour de cassation and the administrative courts leading up to the Conseil d'Etat.[3] Whilst the Cour de cassation was deciding some 30,764 cases, the Conseil d'Etat decided a further 12,480. There is also, in the field of public accounts, a hierarchy of lower courts, the chambres régionales des comptes, leading up to the Cour des comptes. The principle is that the ordinary courts should not interfere with the administration, but, at the same time, distinct and often more exacting standards are applied to administrative action than would apply to private persons. Whatever the original political justification for this rather rigid distinction, the current situation enables expertise in understanding the administration to be brought to bear, and for expertise in the different branches of civil and criminal law to be gathered as well.

Such a distinction exists also in countries where administrative courts are more recent. In Sweden, separate administrative courts have grown out of internal administrative review. Sweden has two hierarchies of courts. Courts of general jurisdiction covering civil and criminal law (allamäna rätt) and special courts deal with administrative law (förvaltningsrätt). There has been a gradual process whereby administrative decisions have been subjected to the courts.[4] Originally, independent review was an integral part of the

---

3. L N Brown and J Bell *French Administrative Law* (London, 5th edn, 1998) ch 6.
4. S Jägerskiöld in S Strömholm (ed) *An Introduction to Swedish Law* (Stockholm, 1981) pp 75, 85–86; also M Bodgan (ed) *Swedish Law in the New Millennium* (Stockholm, 2000) pp 95–98.

administration. In addition, the existence of the Ombudsman provided an alternative line of redress. The tradition was thus not of judicial review by courts, but of independent redress within the administrative structures. From 1909, appeal from the local governor lay to the Regeringsrätt,[5] but this did not cover control over the actions of administrative boards and ministries. Both reforms to the Constitution and decisions of the European Court of Human Rights on the right under art 6(1) of the European Convention on Human Rights to a determination of the civil rights and obligations by an independent and impartial tribunal,[6] led to a hierarchy of administrative courts being created in the 1970s and 1980s, more clearly separated from the administration, but also from the ordinary courts. The three-tier hierarchy is now headed by the Regeringsrätt. In 2001, the civil and criminal Supreme Court (Högsta Domstol) dealt with 4,691 cases whilst the Regeringsrätt dealt with 7,753 cases.

The German court system is more integrated, in part because there is a uniform pattern of federalism. The main courts are found at the Land level. There is a pattern of distinct courts on general (civil and criminal), administrative, tax, social and labour matters.[7] There is a Land level of courts in these areas, often at both first instance and appellate level. Each branch of courts at a Land level has a Federal Court as a body to which appeals can be made on points of law. To avoid conflicts of case law, which are in practice rare, a *Gemeinsamer Senat* was created in 1968 composed of the Presidents of each Federal Court.[8] This has a greater unifying role than the Tribunal des Conflits in France, which merely determines who has the jurisdiction to decide on particular areas, not to unify approaches. The caseload remains substantial. In 2001, the Bundesgerichtshof decided 5,386 civil cases and 3,164 criminal cases, and the Bundesverwaltungsgericht decided 2,481 cases.

Although Spain has a unitary court system, there are separate divisions within the courts, even at the level of the Tribunal Supremo, for dealing with administrative matters, and judges need to have passed a test in their specialism to work in this area.[9] In 2001, the Tribunal Supremo decided 28,497 cases, of which 4,617 were civil, 6,047 were criminal, 13,076 were administrative and 4,414 were social.[10]

Few in the common law would argue for a distinct hierarchy of courts in specialist areas. It exists, of course, in relation to the administrative tribunal systems, where very large numbers of cases are handled. But these filter out the need for large numbers of cases to be submitted to the professional judges. The key issue is how the need for expertise, which other systems experience, should be met. Of course, one could take the view that a senior member of the judiciary should be able to master any topic which requires the interpretation of legal,

5.   Originally appeal lay to the King-in-Council (statsråd). See generally, Jägerskiöld, n 4 above, p 102.
6.   *Sporrong and Lönnroth v Sweden* (1982) 5 EHRR 35; and *Pudas v Sweden* (1988) 10 EHRR 380.
7.   See generally, N Foster and S Sule *German Legal System and Laws* (Oxford: Oxford University Press, 3rd edn, 2002) pp 66–76.
8.   Foster and Sule, n 7 above, p 75.
9.   E Merino-Blanco *The Spanish Legal System* (London, 1996) pp 78–94.
10.   Supreme Court statistics, available at www.poderjudicial.es/tribunalsupremo.

as opposed to factual issues. But this is increasingly diff
modern complex legal system.

Importantly, the UK selects out all but a few cases f
In many ways, the workload of the House of Lords cannor
that of continental Supreme Courts, because it is so small. It is to
with the German *Gemeinsame Senat* or the *Assemblée plénière* in
Supreme Courts. These deal with the big issues, either because of the
importance, or because there is conflict in the views of different courts or
sections of the Supreme Court. These cases come to these bodies having been
given a preliminary review by another court or section of the court. There will
be an expert reporting judge who drafts a judgment on which the others will
comment in the light of submissions (which are typically brief and written).
The senior judges are given a very focused agenda and act as a review committee
for proposals coming from experts. This is a different way of working compared
with the House of Lords, eg based on paper and for one hearing day a month.
It enables the expert to lead the process, and for other colleagues to play a role
as a sounding board, without having to pretend to have expertise in the
particular field. The idea of a single judgment reflects both a desire to be clear
on the rule of law laid down, and also on the extent to which the different
members of the court can claim expertise.

Any serious discussion of the role of a Supreme Court ought to consider
how the need for expertise can be managed, either in institutional terms or in
terms of methods of working. Even if we do not want to go down the road of
specialist courts or specialist divisions within the Supreme Court, it would still
make sense for us to consider how a Supreme Court best operates in deciding
sophisticated and often very specialist issues in a way which combines
specialist knowledge and generalist legal common sense. The issue of
specialism affects both staffing and procedure. Do we need a larger range of
expertise within the members of the court? How are the non-experts expected
to behave? Is the reporter judge system adopted in many continental courts a
useful approach which recognises the special expertise of particular judges
should be reflected in their role in preparing a deliberation, and the different
role from the other judges? Is the idea that each member of the Supreme Court
should write his or her own judgment appropriate where the case is specialist,
and is meant to give a clear statement of the law?[11]

The Spanish system also suggests another pattern of distinction - between
regional and national Supreme Courts. The Spanish court system is a national
system, but with strong regional and local organisation. Courts are organised
at one of four levels: municipality, province, Autonomous Community and
nation. Not every part of the country is covered by an Autonomous Community,
so there is diversity of hierarchy across the country. There is no template statute
of autonomy, but each area has its own statute, which will regulate the respective
competences of the Supreme Courts in the Autonomous Community and the
nation. As in legislative matters, the Spaniards have a pattern of asymmetric
devolution.

---

11. Cf R Munday 'All for One and One for All: The Rise to Prominence of the Composite
Judgment within the Civil Division of the Court of Appeal' [2002] CLJ 321.

At the level of the Autonomous Communities, the Supreme Court dealing with issues of law (*recursos de casación*) is the Tribunal Superior de Justicia. It has jurisdiction over questions of general civil law, local (*foral*) law, and the modern special law of the relevant Autonomous Community. The court sits in three divisions, civil and criminal, administrative and social. In administrative law, it is the first instance court to deal with the legality of decisions of the Autonomous Community and local elections.

Appeal on typically points of law lies from the Tribunales Superiores de Justicia and from the Audiencia Nacional to the Tribunal Supremo, which sits in five divisions: civil, criminal, administrative, social and military. The Tribunal Supremo has limited jurisdiction in relation to regional laws in civil and administrative matters. It makes decisions only where there is no established case law of the regional Tribunal Superior de Justicia. This has the important consequence that the Supreme Court does not have uniform jurisdiction over the whole country, and its jurisdiction is seen as a matter for the constitution of the region, the Autonomous Community.[12] This would seem a possible way to deal with the relationship with regional laws within the UK, which do not form part of a uniform system of law (unlike eg in Germany).

2. HOW SHOULD THE SUPREME COURT ACT AS AUTHORITATIVE INTERPRETER OF THE LAW?

The principal role of a Supreme Court is to give authoritative rulings on the law. It may be that a system does not have a system of binding precedent, but the Supreme Court does have strong authority.[13] In his work on Supreme Courts, André Tunc noted that the House of Lords is practically the only appellate national Supreme Court in Europe,[14] in that it has jurisdiction to re-decide the merits of the case, as well as the law. The *summa divisio* was, in his view, between appellate courts which were selective and courts of cassation, having an open jurisdiction to quash errors of law by lower courts. Most European Supreme Courts merely quash decisions of lower courts for errors of law, and remit the case for further consideration. Now, the reality is that the House of Lords only makes rulings on the law and does not examine facts. It is remote from the witnesses and it does not have the full case-file with which other courts are supplied. An opportunity to restate formally its role might have been helpful. There are also questions about how this role as authoritative interpreter of the law should be exercised, eg by being a court of cassation, rather than a court of appeal, and by providing preliminary rulings.

In most European countries, the need for a national Supreme Court to provide definitive rulings is accentuated by the regional character of courts of appeal. For example, the French adhere to the principle of the *right to an appeal* (*double degré de juridiction*), which entitles the litigant to a hearing at first instance and then on appeal. This right of appeal on law and fact means that

12. Art 61 LOPJ.
13. See D N MacCormick and R S Summers *Interpreting Precedents* (Aldershot: Dartmouth, 1997) ch 13.
14. A Tunc 'Les cours suprêmes: synthèse' (1978) 30 Revue internationale de droit comparé 5 at 12.

there is no leave required for an appeal. The right to complain that the court of appeal has committed an error of law is similarly unlimited because of the application of the principle of legality. The Supreme Court has the function of deciding on questions of law. There are restrictions on access to the Conseil d'Etat and the Cour de cassation, the national courts at the pinnacle of the public and private law systems, but their functions are primarily to review the legal basis of decisions reached by lower courts, rather than to act as a third level of appeal on the merits. The principal role of other Supreme Courts is to quash, rather than to re-decide, cases where the law has been applied wrongly by the lower court. German and Spanish Supreme Courts stand in a similar relationship to their appeal courts. A third level of court has a distinct contribution if it is able to make rulings on matters of public interest. It may be able to decide some cases without referring the matter back to the lower court for decision, but this is not a principal function.[15] Where there are regional courts of appeal, the national role of the court becomes important. As a final court for Scotland, Northern Ireland and England and Wales, the House of Lords has a similarly national role in relation to regional legal orders. A focus on quashing lower court decisions for error of law might also mark appropriate deference to these different jurisdictions.

In the extensive survey of Supreme Courts in 1978,[16] the issue of controlling the case-load figured significantly in the individual national reports.[17] The principle of legality, respect for the law, has led many systems to allow a wide range of cases to be presented to the Supreme Court. The court then has to develop fast-track procedures for rejecting unmeritorious cases. This will usually by a decision in relation to the appeal, but taken by a smaller formation of the court, or even by its president. A properly lodged request for review requires a judicial decision. In Sweden, criminal cases have to be raised by the ombudsman, the State Prosecutor or the equivalent of the Attorney-General. Such a filter on who can make an appeal is rare. The idea of a leave stage, where a person has to request a court to exercise discretion to allow him or her to bring an appeal is very much a common law approach.[18] Continental lawyers take a view that access to justice requires a decision on the merits of the appeal, however perfunctory, rather than a refusal to listen to it. In considering a Supreme Court, it would make sense to consider clarifying these issues of access. If jurisdiction were sensibly limited to points of law of public importance, then a certification by the lower court or a summary decision of a panel of the House of Lords on this preliminary jurisdictional point would be more in line with European understandings of the right to access to justice than a judicial discretion which is not backed by a requirement to give a reasoned decision.

15. On *cassation sans renvoi*, see J Bell, S Boyron and S Whittaker *Principles of French Law* (Oxford, 1998) pp 47–48.
16. Tunc, n 14 above.
17. On more recent figures, see p 156 above.
18. Tunc, n 14 above, at 17.
19. *Final Report of the Committee on Supreme Court Practice and Procedure* (Cmd 8878, 1953) section IX; C Chakrabarti, J Stephens and C Gallagher 'Whose Cost the Public Interest?' [2003] PL 697.

If the Supreme Court should be limited to deciding points of law of public importance or significant difficulty, then this has implications for funding which the Evershed Committee pointed out in 1953.[19] It suggested that there should be public funding for points of law of public importance. The combination of limiting review, and a role in quashing decisions for grounds of law, provides a special place for a Supreme Court in a system.

In a second place, the court may be asked by a lower court to give a preliminary ruling on a point of law in the course of proceedings. This is rejected in paragraph 24 of the Consultation Paper, but without substantial argument. We are familiar with the reference procedure in the European Court of Justice. This has been adopted by the French.[20] German and Spanish courts do have this procedure whereby the ordinary courts can refer constitutional issues to the constitutional court. While this may introduce some delay in deciding a case, it can be cost effective. Of course, the common law procedure already has interlocutory procedures which can raise preliminary points of law and 'leapfrogging' from the High Court to the House of Lords, where Court of Appeal precedents are clear. Preliminary rulings might be a more effective way of securing decisions on points of law of significance. As in European matters, the lower court can always decide to carry on and try the case, where it is not convinced that a preliminary ruling is necessary. In such a case, the matter would come to the Supreme Court in the usual process of appeals. But preliminary rulings do seem to meet a particular need in a cost-effective way for some cases.

3. IS THE SUPREME COURT A CONSTITUTIONAL COURT?

(1) Is the Constitutional Judiciary distinct?

In addition to Supreme Courts on civil, criminal and administrative matters, many European systems have constitutional courts. Indeed, Favoreu and Philip argue that the 'European model' developed since the 1920s is that there should be a distinct constitutional court.[21] The German pattern and that of Spain, which is modelled on the former, is to have a distinct constitutional court, which is composed of judges chosen by a distinct mechanism from those of the Supreme Courts and whose prior background is often distinct from that of ordinary judges. Both countries have four categories of constitutional review. These actions are divided into (a) actions for constitutional review, usually raised by politicians (*recurso de inconstitucionalidad, abstraktes Normenkontrolle*), (b) questions of constitutionality referred by the courts (*cuestión de inconstitucionalidad, konkretes Normenkontrolle*) and (c) conflicts of competence raised by the Autonomous Communities in Spain or between constitutional organs. Finally, there is (d) the *recurso de amparo* or *Verfassungsbeschwerde,* a distinctive feature of these systems designed to provide a final resort to individuals for the protection of fundamental liberties

---

20. See Bell, Boyron and Whittaker, n 15 above, p 47.
21. L Favoreu *Les cours constitutionnelles* (Paris: Presses universitaires de France, 3rd edn, 1996) pp 5–6.

Table 1 Distribution of types of constitutional cases

Type of decision	Spain 1999	Germany 1992–2000
Abstract actions for constitutional review (*recursos*; *abstrakte Normenkontrolle*)	23 (0.40%)	20 (0.048%)
Concrete questions of constitutionality (*cuestiones*; *konkrete Normenkontrolle*)	33 (0.58%)	192 (0.46%)
Conflicts of competence (*conflictos*):	13 (0.23%)	23 (0.056%)
– Number of state and region disputes among the above three categories	30 (0.54%)	7 (0.017%)
Individual applications (*amparos; Verfassungsbeschwerde*)	5,582 (98.77%)	41,096 (99.4%)
Total	5,651	41,331

infringed by any organ of government, especially the judiciary. The numerical importance of the different types of cases may be summed up in this way:

Abstract norm control involves a reference is made by politicians. Under the Scotland Act 1998, such a reference can also be made by law officers. The decision need not be confined to the issues raised by those with power to refer the law (usually politicians). The Germans and Spaniards, as well as the Swedes, allow concrete review, ie review in the course of a specific legal dispute, which will arise in the ordinary courts. The case can be referred for a ruling by the constitutional court during the course of specific litigation. Again, this is a procedure within the UK's own devolution legislation. But it will be noted that the individual petition provides the biggest case-load. The Swedish and UK approach is to see these more as ombudsman-type issues, or as matters to be raised in the ordinary courts, rather than to be referred to a special constitutional court. This has some advantages, since the decisions most frequently subjected to individual petition in Germany and Spain are decisions of the ordinary courts.

The French *Conseil constitutionnel*, by contrast, only has jurisdiction over abstract review. It is not, formally, a court but a 'council' and emerged by the transformation of a parliamentary committee into an independent constitutional authority. It is not integrated into the rest of the court system at all, though its rulings bind all public authorities (including courts) and, more generally, its rulings are followed.

22. It is worthwhile noting that the new Finnish Constitution (2000) for the first time introduces a system of judicial review of legislation (albeit only following the Swedish model where judges only can strike down laws that they find 'manifestly' unconstitutional) as a supplement to the prevailing (and presumably quite effective) 'pre-view' control system in the hands of the standing committee on constitutional affairs in the Finnish Parliament.

Not all European countries follow this model. One might identify the UK with countries like Denmark, Iceland, The Netherlands, Norway, Sweden – and, since 2000, even Finland.[22] These countries have limited constitutional review and they are handled by the ordinary courts. The countries are not federal and have strong traditions of parliamentary sovereignty. Whilst some countries do have judicial review of legislation, this is frequently limited to where the incompatibility is 'manifest'.[23] As a result the constitutional case-load is not significant and distinct enough to warrant a separate court.

Where there is a separation between a constitutional court and the ordinary courts, there are distinct procedures for appointment and the qualifications for office as a constitutional judge differ from those of ordinary judges.

Against this background, there would seem to be issues about how a Supreme Court relates to constitutional matters. If you take the decision that a court is going to be able to annul legislation for incompatibility with the Constitution, then the European experience is predominantly in two stages. First, you create a distinct constitutional court. In Spain and Germany, the court is a body distinct from the Supreme Court. It is connected to the ordinary courts in that they may make references to it or the ordinary courts are frequently the subjects of an individual petition of unconstitutionality. In France, the constitutional court was not originally set up as a 'court', and so it was not integrated into the judicial hierarchy. Indeed, there is no formal way in which the ordinary courts can refer issues for the Conseil's consideration. On the whole, this is less satisfactory as a way of dealing with constitutional matters. All three systems permit abstract review of laws; indeed this is the only review which the French do allow. Under this system, as permitted under the Scotland Act 1998, the constitutionality of a bill can be examined before it is signed by the head of state.[24] The decision is taken, therefore, in the heat of the political process, rather than at a calmer moment after the legislation has been in force for a period of time. Secondly, you have a specific appointments process and criteria. A distinct constitutional jurisdiction focuses attention on the way the judges are engaged in the interface between law and politics. Where the jurisdiction is over abstract review, then the decision on constitutionality is taken in the heat of a political debate, usually at the instigation of politicians who have been unable to enough political support to prevent the bill from passing. As a result, the criteria for appointment involve a combination of legal and political experience, and, commonly, a mixture of judicial and non-judicial experience.

With the devolution legislation, the UK has introduced both abstract and concrete review of legislation in Scotland and Northern Ireland. Although this preserves the sovereignty of the Westminster Parliament, it raises many of the political issues which lead other European countries to create a separate constitutional court.

If one recognises a major constitutional role to a body, then there are strong arguments for choosing an appointment process which is distinct from that

23. On Norway, see R Slagstad in E Smith *Constitutional Justice under Old Constitutions* (The Hague: Kluwer, 1995) p 81; also C Smith 'Judicial Review of Parliamentary Legislation: Norway as a European Pioneer' [2000] PL 595. On Sweden see J Nergelius in Bogdan, n 4 above, ch 3.
24. Or, in Germany, soon thereafter.

which assesses a judge's suitability for high-level civil or criminal work. The Consultation Paper really does not think through the interaction between workload and appointment procedures.

The question for the UK is the extent to which the constitutional functions of the Privy Council under devolution legislation, and the role of the House of Lords in human rights cases, constitute a sufficient basis to constitute a separate court. The Consultation Paper, in para 23, rejects the transfer of functions of the Judicial Committee of the Privy Council beyond devolution issues (and, of course, human rights issues) on the ground that a 'a Constitutional Court ... would be a departure from the UK's constitutional traditions'. Yet the competence now attributed to the Supreme Court is recognised elsewhere as constitutional. The appeal to 'tradition' is an indication of the lack of thought which has gone into the Consultation Paper.

A more principled defence of the position would be the difficulty of separating constitutional and other issues. We are all familiar with the fact that the European Convention on Human Rights operates pervasively. Human rights issues can arise in any branch of law, both substantive and procedural. Even in countries that have a constitutional court, this has led ordinary judges to annul national legislation, despite the fact that they do not have competence in constitutional matters.[25] In many countries, the superior status of a treaty prevails over a national law, even though it may be compatible with the national constitution. The special status of the Human Rights Act 1998 in the UK moves incompletely in the same direction. All courts will be dealing with fundamental rights questions and these are, surely, major constitutional questions. It may be that the Kelsenian model of a separate constitutional court has major problems in the face of the priority to be given to the European Convention, EU law and international treaties. The extent to which breach of rights complaints go to ordinary courts, rather than constitutional courts, provides an argument for not creating a distinct constitutional court. The entanglement between devolution and human rights issues[26] illustrates a similar point. It is becoming difficult to treat domestic constitutional law as a discrete set of issues. But, if this analysis is right, then all Supreme Courts will end up playing important constitutional roles. As a result, many of the concerns about the character of appointments appropriate to a constitutional court may come to be extended to a Supreme Court. Clearly abstract review places the decision of a court in the spotlight at a moment of intense political controversy. The ability to change the political agenda, either by annulling legislation or declaring it incompatible with a higher norm (the constitution or some treaty creating fundamental rights), is also a matter of significance.

25. For example, see CE 28 July 2000, *Tête*, AJDA 2000, 854; CE Ass, 11 July 2001, *Préaud*, AJDA 2001, 841.
26. *Brown v Stott (Procurator Fiscal of Dunfermline)* [2001] 2 All ER 97.

4. SHOULD THE SUPREME COURT GIVE ADVISORY OPINIONS?

Not all Supreme Court courts give advisory opinions, but some do. The request for advice may come as part of a non-juridical hearing. In France, the Conseil d'Etat might be asked for an opinion by the Government. For example, it gave a very important ruling on allowing Muslim girl students to wear the headscarf in school.[27] In the case of the German Constitutional Court or the European Court of Justice, the matter comes in the more conventional form of a case in open court. Such a practice of advisory opinions is less common in other countries, and pre-empts the solution to specific issues. There is a concern that a court might appear to pre-judge issues by dealing with them in abstract, rather than in concrete situations. But the advantage which Germany obtained from a ruling on the deployment of German troops, or the French from the ruling on headscarves is substantial. The European Court of Justice has specific competence in this regard, and has given some significant rulings. Combined with the jurisdiction to deal with legislation in abstract, such a practice enables issues to be considered in advance of the law being applied. Of course, this is not totally alien to practice within the common law at the moment. The procedure for obtaining declaratory rulings on controversial points can serve effectively to offer advisory opinions. The *Royal College of Nursing* case on new practices of abortion enabled the House of Lords to develop principles to guide the handling of cases in the future.[28] The facts of the individual case serve as a context for reflection, and an opportunity to lay down a rule. But this is not far removed from the sort of situation in which an advisory opinion is sought.

5. THE SUPREME COURT AS THINK TANK

A Supreme Court has both a breadth of experience and an exposure to some of the more difficult issues of law within the legal system. It sees concrete situations which pose legal difficulties, and this can be a valuable perspective from which to review what needs to be reformed in the law. A Supreme Court can be involved at any of three stages. The Supreme Court can offer suggestions for reform, identifying topics which it sees as ripe for change, but perhaps which lie beyond its ability to handle effectively on a case-by-case basis. It is also well placed to comment on ideas for reform generated by government. It can then scrutinise the technical quality of the bills which are presented to Parliament. These three roles can be seen operating in Sweden. Commissions for law reform are frequently chaired by a judge of one Supreme Court and have a more junior judge as secretary. The recommendations of the commission

---

27. See Brown and Bell, n 3 above, pp 64–67; N Questiaux 'Administration and the Rule of Law: The Preventive Role of the French Conseil d'Etat' [1995] PL 247 and 'Do the Opinions expressed by the Conseil d'Etat in its capacity as legal advisor to the Government influence policy?' (2000) 49 ICLQ 672.
28. *Royal College of Nursing v DHSS* [1981] AC 800.
29. K-G Algotsson 'Lagrådet, rättstaten och demokratin' in T Håstad and L Lewin *Politik och Juridik. Grundlagen inför 2000* (Stockholm, 2000) p 37.

are then sent out to all the courts for comments (*remissen*). The final proposals are then examined by the Lagråd, which is a constitutional body charged with reviewing laws before they are submitted to Parliament. Lagrådet is composed of judges from the Supreme Courts.[29] The Supreme Court, acting individually or collectively, makes a major contribution to law reform by suggesting and thinking through ideas. Other Supreme Courts also contribute a law reform role. France does not have an independent Law Commission, but the annual reports of its Supreme Courts do make suggestions for reform. In addition, the Section du Rapport et des Etudes of the Conseil d'Etat does undertake investigations into issues of law reform and make reports. The Conseil is also responsible for pre-legislative scrutiny. Not all countries entrust this pre-enactment scrutiny to the courts. Thus in Spain, the Consejo del Estate (which is not a court) performs this role. German law reform committees tend to be set up by the ministries of justice at federation or Land level.

The diversity of national experience demonstrates that there is no necessary reason why any of the roles identified should be performed by a Supreme Court. But there is a suggestion that some formal input from a Supreme Court as a major legal institution, and not just individual members, can make a valued contribution to law reform.

6. THE SUPREME COURT AS TRAINING ESTABLISHMENT

A common feature of most Supreme Courts is that they serve to train or enhance the careers of younger judges. British readers are familiar with the referendaire system in the European Court of Justice, under which a judge or advocate general has a private office which includes younger lawyers who help in the preparation work for cases. There is a parallel in most Supreme Courts. The Tribunal Supremo and the Tribunal Constitutional in Spain have *letrados* who support the work of judges. In Sweden, assessors will often serve in a similar role in the Hogsta Domstol or in the Regeringsrätt. In Germany, judges will also serve as 'wissenschafliche Mitarbeiter' (scholarly collaborators) in the Supreme Courts or the Bundesverfassungsgericht. In France, more established judges may serve as conseillers réferendaires in the Cour de cassation. Younger judges may play a role in the administration or support services of the Cour de cassation. Young judges will serve for a time either formally as auditeurs in the Conseil d'Etat or undertaking a training placement. These younger judges do not take part in decisions. But, in most cases, they will be involved in preparing decisions and they may even write drafts of straightforward decisions. Such work obviously assists the senior judges to work more speedily and effectively. But it also helps the younger judges to engage in more difficult decisions, rather than deal with the routine decisions at first instance. As these younger colleagues return to ordinary judicial work after a number of years, they carry back experience and understanding, which helps them in decision-making and serves as an informal way of communicating values and practices within the court system as a whole. There are two features of the Supreme Court process in continental Europe which makes the involvement of younger judges as assistants effective. First, the procedure is predominantly written. The oral hearing, if there is one, will be brief, if not peremptory. Indeed, in some French Supreme Court hearings the lawyers either do not even turn up for the hearing or say nothing of substance. In such a procedure, the assistant judge can contribute very effectively to preparing the written documentation on the file. Judges are expected to find their own law (under the principle *curia novit legem*) and so the research by the assistant, followed by discussion within this judicial team, can help prepare the hearing and decision of the court. There can be preliminary or informal discussions in which the assistant can properly take part, even if he or she is absent from the formal or final deliberations. The second feature of the Supreme Courts is the collegial nature of the court. In such a setting, there is not a simple pattern of the single judge listening to lengthy submissions and taking individual responsibility for a judgment which responds to them. The court process is not concentrated on such a single moment, and the judges will work more as a team. The use of a reporter judge who prepares a draft, while others will read less of the file, generates a more collective approach to decision-making in which different people have different roles. Some will do the research, some will effectively be reviewing this work and contributing ideas. Given the number of decisions of little merit which may come to the court, judges will be engaged to varying degrees of intensity in the consideration of a case. In particular in routine cases, most judges will not be strongly involved and will welcome support.

The point is that the Supreme Court can be viewed as a judicial institution which offers opportunities for experience within the judicial career. Now, the traditional way of communicating values and expectations from the Supreme Court has been the oral argumentation between Bar and Bench. Those who were likely to be appointed to high judicial office would have appeared as QCs in arguing cases before the highest courts. Oral debate in open court has similarities to the more committee-like structures of continental Supreme Courts. Both allow senior judges to communicate their expectations. The other feature is the importance of the Inns of Court in England or the Faculty of Advocates in Scotland as a forum for interchange of ideas. In a parallel Consultation Paper, the Government seeks a pool from which the judiciary is drawn. As part of 'joined-up thinking', it could reflect on how the Supreme Court can contribute to the quality of the judicial body as a whole.

CONCLUSION

The purpose of this discussion is not to suggest that the UK should be modelling its Supreme Court on other countries. There is a diversity of practice in different countries, which reflects their own particular background, situation and traditions. On the other hand, these countries have encountered problems, which their institutions and procedures are designed to meet. This paper has tried to suggest that some of the same problems might need to be met in the UK and that the Consultation Paper really does not address them. But this does not mean that, at some future point in the operation of the Supreme Court, many of the issues will not have to be addressed.

Appointment and career of judges in continental Europe: the rise of judicial self-government

Carlo Guarnieri
University of Bologna

Traditionally, European continental judiciaries have been organised along a bureaucratic, civil service model.[1] Early recruitment was complemented by the strong hierarchical character of the judicial organisation. Therefore, in this type of judiciary guarantees of independence have been problematic because of the influence hierarchical superiors (or in some cases the government itself) had on promotions.

Since the Second World War the need for change has been increasingly felt. The main aims have been to increase external independence, especially vis-à-vis the executive, and to protect lower ranking judges from negative influence by the senior judiciary, often considered to be too responsive to governmental wishes. In addition, traditional legal education has been more insistently criticised as being unable to sustain the judge in performing the new and complex tasks contemporary societies have entrusted upon him or her.

Thus, in several countries special institutions in charge of judicial training have been instituted and collegial bodies – the higher councils of the judiciary – in charge of making all decisions affecting the status of judges have been established, an institutional innovation of deep political significance. However, not all continental countries have introduced such bodies or have entrusted them with significant powers. In Germany, for example, collegial bodies only perform an auxiliary function – and only in some Länder – and the powers of the executive – and sometimes of parliament – have been more or less left unchanged. In other countries of the European Union – Belgium, Denmark, Finland and the Netherlands – more or less strong forms of judicial self-government have been introduced only recently and any assessment is premature.[2] However, the trend toward establishing forms of judicial self-

---

1. The traits of bureaucratic judiciaries and their consequences are analysed in G Di Federico 'The Italian Judicial Profession and Its Bureaucratic Setting' (1976) 1 The Juridical Review 40; G Freddi *Tensioni e conflitto nella magistratura* (Bari: Laterza, 1978); and J H Merryman *The Civil Law Tradition* (Stanford: Stanford University Press, 2nd edn, 1985).

2. See M Fabri, P M Langbroek and H Pauliat (eds) *The Administration of Justice in Europe: Towards the Development of Quality Standards* (Bologna: Research Institute on Judicial Systems (IRSIG-CNR), 2003); and, for similar trends in Eastern Europe, E Rekosh 'Emerging Lessons from Reform Effort in Eastern Europe and Eurasia' in *Office of Democracy and Governance, Guidance for promoting Judicial Independence and Impartiality* (Washington: USAID, 2001) pp 53–71.

government has been stronger in Latin countries: France, Italy, Portugal and Spain. Together with Germany, they are the subject of our analysis.[3]

THE RECRUITMENT

Civil law judiciaries of continental Europe do not differ fundamentally from the state bureaucracy, and reflect the old division of law from politics. Judicial legitimacy rests on technical legal knowledge, and the traditional assumption that judges (like civil servants) simply apply pre-existing legal rules without interfering in the prerogatives of the political branches.[4] Traditionally, recruitment into the judiciary has been based on criteria and procedures very similar to those governing entrance into the civil service. In most civil law countries, the largest proportion of judges are still recruited directly from university through some form of public examination (normally run by the Ministry of Justice), and with no requirement of previous professional experience. Successful candidates are appointed at the bottom of the career ladder, and professional training and socialisation take place within the judiciary, with promotions usually granted on the basis of seniority and merit. Some form of either mandatory or optional training usually exists for both new recruits and senior members of the judiciary. Indeed, judicial training has become an increasingly important element in the administration of justice, and most entry-level judges are required to complete an initial period of probationary training. However, the level of training for senior members of the judiciary is far more variable and generally less structured.[5]

In most civil law countries public competition is deemed to be the most effective way of ensuring both the professional qualifications and independence of the judiciary.[6] Several specific features define this merit-based selection model. Competitions are open to young university graduates in law, usually with little or no previous professional experience. Legal education is typically multi-purpose, providing a general knowledge of all relevant branches of the law at the expense of any form of specialisation. As a consequence, selection incorporates little or no emphasis on the practical side of the work of the judiciary, and is made on the basis of written and oral exams that test the candidates' theoretical knowledge of the law. According to the underlying principle of 'functional omni-competence', recruits are supposed to be able to perform the entire range of tasks they could be assigned, from adjudicating a criminal, family or fiscal case to acting as a public prosecutor.[7] Legal training is carried out on the job and is generally supervised by senior judges. Thus, judicial socialisation takes place within, and is therefore essentially controlled by, the judiciary. All of these elements, and in particular the reluctance to

3. For a broader analysis of what follows see C Guarnieri and P Pederzoli *The Power of Judges* (Oxford: Oxford University Press, 2002).
4. G Rebuffa *La funzione giudiziaria* (Turin: Giappichelli, 1993).
5. For a recent assessment see R J Asensio (ed) *El acceso a la funciòn judicial. Estudio comparado* (Madrid: Consejo General del Poder Judicial, 2002).
6. Rebuffa, n 4 above, p 69.
7. G Freddi, n 2 above, p 62ff.

require professional legal experience outside the judiciary, encourage both the *esprit de corps* of the judiciary and the 'balkanization' of the bench and Bar, and relations between the two different sides of the legal profession can often be rather strained.[8]

However, recruitment by public competition in continental European countries has undergone some major changes. Lateral entry into the judiciary, open to experienced lawyers or civil servants on merit, has increased in an attempt to prevent corporatist tendencies. In the same way, judicial schools have been established in many European countries to provide legal education and training for new judges to fill the vacuum that exists between university education and professional practice.[9] The French have been in the forefront of both developments;[10] legal education and the training of judges and public prosecutors (who form a single professional group referred to as *magistrature*) is entrusted to the *Ecole Nationale de la Magistrature* (ENM).[11] This institution has provided a model for other countries, such as Spain and Portugal. A competition open to young law graduates (*concours étudiant*) is by far the most important recruitment channel for the ENM, but there are other ways to enter the school, and all forms of competition share a common goal: to open the judiciary to candidates from different professional environments.[12]

In Germany judges and public prosecutors, although they do not belong to the same organisation, share a common legal education and training leading to the 'qualification for judgeship' (*Befähigung zum Richteramt*). This qualification is a necessary requirement to serve in all legal professions and the higher ranks of the civil service. As a consequence, judges, public prosecutors, private attorneys, notaries, and government officials are all educated through a lengthy and highly selective route and tend to identify themselves with a larger professional group, the *Juristen*.[13] Lateral mobility among these various professions also exists, and although not widespread, their common educational experience appears to create a strong connection among the different legal professions that is characteristic of the German system.

Under German federal legislation[14] training for future judges is organised in two parts: the first, devoted to theory, takes place in a university law faculty;

8.   Merryman, n 1 above, p 102.
9.   Rebuffa, n 4 above, pp 74–77.
10. L M Dìez Picazo 'El sistema francès de acceso a la judiciatura: selecciòn y formaciòn inicial' in Asensio (ed), above n 5.
11. Established in 1970 under the Ministry of Justice, the ENM inherited the functions of the National Centre for Judicial Studies founded in 1958: A Boigeol 'Histoire d'une revendication: l'école de la magistrature 1945–1958' (Paris: Cahiers du CRIV, n 7, 1989).
12. An analysis of different recruitment methods is provided by A Mestitz *Selezione e formazione professionale dei magistrati e degli avvocati in Francia* (Padua: CEDAM, 1990); and L M Dìez-Picazo 'El sistema francès de acceso a la judiciatura: selecciòn y formaciòn inicial' in Asensio, (ed), n 5 above, pp 41–56.
13. D S Clark 'The Selection and Accountability of Judges in West Germany: Implementation of a Recthsstaat' (1988) 61 *S*Cal LR 1795; P Pederzoli *Selezione e formazione delle professioni legali in Germania* (Padua: CEDAM, 1992); and P Pederzoli 'El acceso a las profesiones legales en la Repùblica Federal de Alemania' in Asensio (ed), n 5 above, pp 57–80.
14. The *Deutsches Richtergesetz* enacted in 1961. But *Länder* also have legislative competencies in this field.

the second, made up of two years of practical training, establishes contacts with different legal environments. After completing university studies, candidates for the legal profession sit the 'first state examination'. If successful, they are granted status as temporary civil servants, allowing them to carry out their practical training and receive a small salary. During this period trainees become familiarised with the full range of legal roles they may have to perform in the near future: the judiciary (civil, criminal and administrative), Bar, civil service, and public prosecution. In the next stage, trainees can shape the curriculum to suit their individual professional aspirations. The final stage of the legal selection process is the 'second state examination', covering similar subject matter as the first but with a more practical orientation. The entire process lasts about ten years and has a remarkably low success rate.[15] It is only after completion of the second state examination that separate selections are made for judges.

Judicial recruitment in Italy still bears a close resemblance to the traditional continental model,[16] based on the set-up in France before the creation of the ENM. A national public competition is the only way to enter the judiciary,[17] which is a unitary organisation (in Italy, as in France, both judges and public prosecutors are referred to as magistrates). Law graduates usually sit the national examination immediately after completing their university studies. As a result, they have no experience in legal practice, and even if a candidate did, it would not be taken into consideration. University law faculties and various private institutions, often managed by magistrates, which focus only on preparation for the national competition, control legal education.[18] However, in 1997 provision was made for the creation of institutions managed by law faculties and devoted to the education and training of legal professionals (magistrates, attorneys, and notaries); it is presently under discussion whether in the future anyone intending to sit the examination for entry into the judiciary will be required to complete a two-year course at one of these institutions.

The entry test is made up of written and oral exams testing general knowledge in the main subjects included in law faculty curricula. The aim is to select those individuals capable of performing all possible organisational roles they may be assigned once appointed, but concern has been expressed that this system is not necessarily reliable, even for evaluating theoretical knowledge of law. Although the number of applicants has continued to increase (currently about 10,000 per year), it is sometimes hard to fill all the judicial vacancies, and there has been a growing number of successful candidates with only the minimum marks.

15. Less than the half of the initial candidates are able to pass the two exams: P Pederzoli 'El acceso a las profesiones legales en la Repùblica Federal de Alemania' in Asensio (ed), n 13 above, pp 57–80.

16. Di Federico, n 1 above.

17. A constitutional provision exists for the direct appointment of experienced lawyers and law professors to the Court of Cassation, the highest ordinary court in the country. The relevant statute was only adopted in 1998, and a few judges have recently been appointed in this way: P Pederzoli 'El sistema italiano de selecciòn de jueces. Situaciòn y perspectivas de futuro' in Asensio (ed), n 5 above, pp 81–114.

18. Currently, a bill is being discussed in Parliament to institute a school in charge of continuing education for judges and prosecutors.

Selection and subsequent training of judges and public prosecutors is the responsibility of the Higher Council of the Judiciary (*Consiglio Superiore della Magistratura*), to which we shall return. The Ministry of Justice is not involved in either the recruitment process or decisions concerning the status of judges and public prosecutors. In the absence of any judicial school, apprenticeship takes place in judicial offices under the supervision of senior magistrates, but appears less structured than in Germany. Training is divided into two phases. The first is devoted to familiarising young magistrates with different legal roles, including adjudication as well as prosecution. As in France, the second phase (lasting six months) attempts to train them in the specific functions they will have to perform once appointed (eg adjudication in civil, criminal, juvenile, and labour courts as well as public prosecution). No further weeding out of candidates occurs during this period. The reports on personal performance drafted by the Higher Council are almost invariably positive, making the initial national examination the only effective means of selection.[19]

Portugal and Spain have followed the French practice of establishing a judicial school as a central element of judicial recruitment.[20] In the Portuguese *Centro de estudos judiciarios*, trainees have to choose whether to become a judge or a public prosecutor soon after admission, since they constitute two separate professional organisations. Public competition to enter the school is similar to the French system: written and oral exams on legal subjects as well as more general social and economic issues. The separation between judges and public prosecutors is even more marked in Spain, in which the *Escuela Judicial* only selects future judges (by public competition open to law graduates) and is in charge of their education and training. However, both countries allow for lateral entry into the judiciary for experienced jurists 'of recognized competence', and they can be appointed to a small number of positions in a variety of courts.

A number of common features, therefore, define judicial recruitment in continental countries. In all cases recruitment occurs at a younger age than in the English and United States systems. The means of educating and training new judges, whether in special schools as in France or extensive on-the-job training as in Germany, partially compensate for the recruits' lack of practical legal experience. More significantly, their professional socialisation is achieved almost exclusively within the judiciary itself, which is therefore likely to become a crucial reference point for judicial attitudes. Recruitment is governed in large part by merit, and no partisan considerations openly operate in the selection process. Yet, with the exception of Italy where this process is under the full control of the judiciary itself, judicial recruitment is monitored by the Ministries of Justice, which can therefore exert some influence. However, we have to take into account that in order to partially compensate the shortcomings of early recruitment, continental judiciaries have traditionally relied on internal controls.

19. G Di Federico (ed) *Preparazione professionale degli avvocati e dei magistrati: discussione su una ipotesi di riforma* (Padua: CEDAM, 1987).
20. Ascensio (ed), n 5 above.

JUDICIAL INDEPENDENCE AND THE INSTITUTION OF HIGHER COUNCILS

In contrast to both the English and United States systems, continental European judiciaries operate within a pyramid-like organisational structure. Salary, prestige, and personal influence depend on a judge's position on the hierarchical ladder and can be improved only through promotions. These are granted on a competitive basis and according to two criteria, seniority and merit, the latter being determined through assessments by senior judges. In principle, each career step requires a specific procedure. Although the number and position of those in charge of such decisions varies from one country to another, some features are relatively constant.

Hierarchical superiors play a fundamentally important role in determining judicial status in most continental countries. Even when the final decision lies with the Minister of Justice or other institutions, promotions rely heavily on information recorded in personal reports compiled by superiors, and this highlights the critical role entrusted to the judicial elite. The 'peer review', a typical device of social control in professional organisations, is superseded here by formal and written evaluations drafted by higher-ranking judges. Thus, in civil law systems two different dimensions must coexist within the judiciary, the bureaucratic and the professional dimension. This type of model creates an almost inevitable strain between the autonomy judges must necessarily be granted to perform their judicial functions and the hierarchical control over their performance.[21]

The decision-making process for promotions in continental systems also involves others outside the judiciary: the executive (ie the Ministry of Justice) and sometimes the legislature. Traditionally, these external actors represented the most important institutional channels connecting the judiciary to the political system. However, in the second half of the twentieth century in several continental countries the prominent role traditionally played by the executive branch has been weakened substantially by the creation of new institutions, Higher Councils of the Judiciary, designed to strengthen the independence of judges. Executive – or in any case political - influence over the judiciary still seems to remain strong in Germany. Within the general framework established by federal legislation, promotions of German judges do vary at the *Land* (regional government) level, especially in regards to the number and the institutional position of the decision-makers. The power to appoint is vested in the *Land* Minister of Justice, but in eight *Länder* a committee for the selection of judges (*Richterwahlauschüsse*) has been instituted. The committee is usually made up of representatives of the executive, the legislature, the Bar, and the bench; although the proportions may vary, non-judicial members are usually in the majority. As a rule, the Minister of Justice presides over the committee when considering appointments to administrative and ordinary courts, while in the remaining cases this authority lies with standing ministers (for instance, the Minister of Labour or Finance for labour or fiscal courts). The presiding

---

21. The tension between these two dimensions and its implications for relations within the judiciary are analysed by G Freddi, n 2 above, who sees bureaucratic judiciaries as a typical example of 'heteronomous organizations'.

minister cannot vote, but does have veto power over the decision.[22] However, in all cases the procedure involves the participation of the judicial council (*Presidialrat*, a body established in each court and made up exclusively of judges, half of them directly elected by their peers), which is asked for an advisory opinion. Decisions concerning judges' promotions are based on evaluations drafted every four years by judicial superiors. These superiors have the power of 'hierarchical supervision' and can issue minor sanctions against junior colleagues for violations of professional duties. However, a right of appeal to specialised courts established at the *Land* level with jurisdiction over disciplinary matters (*Dienstgerichte*) exists, and sanctions against judges can be imposed only on their ruling.

Federal judges sitting on Germany's five Supreme Courts are appointed following the same general procedure, but with one crucial difference: the bench has no voice on the federal committee for the selection of these judges. The Committee is made up exclusively of representatives of the executive and legislative branches, namely the *Länder* ministries and an equal number of members elected by the *Bundestag*, while the presidency is held by a federal minister.[23] Promotions are made primarily on the basis of the candidates' professional qualifications, but their geographic origin also carries weight to ensure that federal courts are staffed with judges drawn from the different *Länder*. This does not mean that political patronage plays no part in the appointment process; party representation on the committee plays a role and has come under strong criticism.[24] Promotions of federal judges are decided by the federal minister without any involvement of the committee, although an advisory opinion by the judicial council is always required. At the beginning of the 1950s some judges argued in favour of concentrating all decisions affecting the status of judges, most notably promotions to higher positions, in the hands of the judiciary itself in order to remove any political influence from the process. But the main political parties and the legislature rejected this proposal. They argued that any notion of judicial 'self-government' would promote 'internal co-optation' and open up the possibility of corporatism, thus violating the fundamental principles of a parliamentary regime and especially the democratic responsibility of the judicial function.[25]

A different arrangement exists in Latin European countries where Higher Councils of the Judiciary have been created in order to preserve the independence of the judiciary. All versions of these councils share one

---

22. For further details on the committees' composition and functioning see E Teubner *Die Bestellung zum Berufsrichter in Bund und Länder* (Köln: Carl Heynemann Verlag, 1984) pp 41–91; Clark, n 13 above; and T Gas 'Les institutions de gestion et de discipline de la carrière des magistrats' in T Renoux (ed) *Les Conseils supérieurs de la magistrature en Europe* (Paris: La Documentation française, 1999) pp 119–141.

23. Ministries of Labour participate in the committee for appointments for both federal labour and social security courts, while the Ministries of Justice sit in all other cases. Designation of the presidency of the committee also follows this same criterion.

24. Clark, n 13 above, at 1822–1829; D P Kommers 'Autonomy versus Accountability: The German Judiciary' in P H Russell and D M O'Brien (eds) *Judicial Independence in the Age of Democracy* (Charlottesville: University Press of Virginia, 2001) pp 131–154 at p 141.

25. For an account of the parliamentary debate see E Teubner, n 22 above, p 30ff.

prominent feature: members of the judiciary are always granted representation, although in different proportions (Table 1 below). To understand how the relationship between courts and politics has evolved in these countries, an examination of the role of the Higher Councils is crucial, taking into account their functions, composition (above all, the ratio of judges to lay members), and the way their members are chosen. Obviously, the level of judicial independence will tend to be higher where judges hold the majority of seats and are directly elected by their peers. In the same way, guarantees of judicial independence are likely to be broader where Higher Councils are entrusted with extensive powers.

Among continental countries, Italy has undergone the most radical transformation in its judiciary and is the only country to achieve true judicial 'self-government'. The organisational characters of the Italian judiciary were established in the second half of the nineteenth century under the influence of the Napoleonic model. It retained its hierarchical structure even during the fascist regime, as the strategy then was to establish special courts to try all politically significant crimes. The bureaucratic nature of the judiciary was not questioned in the post-War Constituent Assembly, and no radical changes occurred during the transition to democracy in the 1940s and 1950s.[26] Only in the early 1960s a gradual process began to alter the traditional set-up of the judiciary, and a number of related factors contributed to this evolution. First, the Higher Council of the Judiciary (*Consiglio superiore della magistratura*), which was formally established by the Constitution of 1948, finally began to operate in 1959. The National Association of Magistrates (*Anm*), a union-like association divided into several political factions (*correnti*), became the main player in Higher Council decisions. All this led to the dismantling of the traditional promotion system, under the belief (actively supported by a large section of the judiciary) that a judicial career and its underlying hierarchy were inconsistent with the notion of judicial independence. The experience of authoritarianism and the subsequent attempt in the 1948 Constitution to shield the judiciary from all partisan influence severed nearly all the institutional connections between the judiciary and the other branches of government, especially the executive. Thus, the Higher Council makes all decisions related to the status of both judges and public prosecutors. Recruitment, appointment, promotion, transfer, and disciplinary proceedings have been removed from the Minister of Justice (who only retains the power to initiate disciplinary proceedings) and concentrated in a body that has become the main institutional bridge between the judiciary and the political system.

The extent of judicial self-government in Italy is obvious if one considers the composition of the Higher Council. After the last reform, in 2002, it consists of 16 magistrates directly elected by the whole judiciary, eight lay members elected by both chambers of Parliament from among experienced lawyers and university law professors, and three ex officio members (the President of the Republic,[27]

---

26. C Guarnieri *Giustizia e politica: I nodi della Seconda Repubblica* (Bologna: Il Mulino, 2003) pp 94–100.
27. In Italy the President of the Republic does not enjoy the same broad prerogatives as the French President. As F Gerber *Justice indépendante. Justice sur commande* (Paris: PUF, 1990) p 209 points out, these bear a closer resemblance to the French President under the IV Republic.

and the President and Prosecutor General of the Court of Cassation). In practice, the lay members are chosen to reflect the strength of the different political parties in Parliament (Table 2 below). To understand the internal operation of the Higher Council and the influence various factions of the *Anm*[28] exert, we have to take into account that inside this institution, the number of positions reserved for higher-ranking judges has been steadily reduced. Moreover, the introduction in 1975 of a proportional system of election for all members has further increased the influence of different ideological factions (Table 3 below). As it has been argued, these developments have opened the Council up to the risk of both corporatism and partisan politics.[29]

The changed composition of the Higher Council has also had major consequences for the way promotions are managed and for the general organisation of the judiciary. As a result of reforms brought in between 1963 and 1979, today a system of de facto automatic promotions operates. The eight traditional ranks on the career ladder have been reduced to three, corresponding to the main levels of jurisdiction: lower courts, appellate courts, and the Court of Cassation. The traditional promotion system, based on competitive examinations or assessments of judicial work (previously controlled by senior judges) has been abolished. In theory, promotions should be based on a combination of the two usual criteria, seniority and merit, the latter being assessed by the Higher Council by means of a 'global' evaluation. In reality, advancements depend exclusively on seniority, mainly due to the way the Higher Council has interpreted the legal rules. Professional evaluations now no longer hold any practical significance, as they are almost invariably positive or at least drafted in a way not to prevent promotion.[30] The result is a clear separation of rank from the functions judges are assigned to perform: those who meet the seniority requirements are promoted, draw their pay at the higher scale, but continue to perform the functions of their previous rank. Therefore, promotions no longer depend on the availability of vacant positions at higher levels. Automatic promotions almost invariably allow every magistrate to attain the highest rank within 28 years of service, or at least to earn the corresponding salary. Decisions still have to be made to fill judicial vacancies, but because professional evaluations are inevitably uniform, the Higher Council lacks substantive information on the applicants' qualifications, and candidates are frequently chosen solely on the basis of seniority. This in turn means that seniority becomes synonymous with professional merit. However, membership in one of the judicial factions represented on the Higher Council plays a significant part in the process, and helps explain the need for magistrates to affiliate themselves with such factions.[31]

Automatic promotions also seem to have encouraged the proliferation of both part-time and full-time extra-judicial activities. This is a phenomenon

---

28. From right to left on the ideological spectrum, the most important are: *Magistratura democratica, Movimento per la giustizia, Unità per la costituzione*, and *Magistratura Indipendente*.

29. Guarnieri, n 26 above, pp 106–114.

30. Di Federico (ed), n 19 above, pp 19–26.

31. G Di Federico "'Lottizzazioni correntizie" e "politicizzazione" del CSM: quali rimedi?' (1990) Quaderni Costituzionali at 279–297; Rebuffa, n 4 above.

that has also developed in other countries (for instance, in France and Spain), but has grown substantially in Italy because such activities do not prevent magistrates from being promoted or reassigned to their previous position.[32] By allowing magistrates to establish relations, sometimes long-term, with other institutions and also with the broader social and economic environment, these activities foster informal links between courts and politics. In the past, Italian judges looked to both the Court of Cassation and legal scholarship for their points of reference (primarily as a result of the role they played in promotions), but today reference points are increasingly found in the political environment and the media. Therefore, while severing formal institutional links with the political system and dismantling all hierarchical constraints can produce high levels of judicial independence (both internal and external), it can also help judges develop a network of less visible connections that could undermine the autonomy of the judiciary.[33]

The importance of the Italian experience lies not only in its peculiarities, but because it has become a model for Spain and Portugal in their post-authoritarian periods. However, significant differences have emerged in these countries, especially Spain. The Spanish judiciary has a similar institutional set-up to the Italian, namely a bureaucratic organisation that was not dramatically altered under the prior authoritarian regime. During the Franco period, politically sensitive cases, especially criminal cases, were removed from the ordinary courts and decided by special courts under the direct control of the regime. The transition to democracy and the Constitution of 1978 restored a unified jurisdiction, and established democratic principles such as the separation of powers and judicial independence, with the judiciary forming a separate body from public prosecutors. Within this framework, the Spanish Higher Council of the Judiciary (*Consejo general del poder judicial*) was created to ensure the independence of the judiciary from the executive.[34]

Following the Italian model, the Spanish Constitution required that the majority of the members of the Higher Council be judges, but the Council's functions were limited to determining the status of judges. The *Ley organica* of 1980 stipulated that the Higher Council be presided over by the Chief of the Supreme Tribunal and be made up of 20 members appointed by the Crown;

---

32. Institutions with magistrates as advisors or as pro-tempore staff include Parliament, the central government (especially the Ministry of Justice), the Office of the Presidency of the Republic, regional and provincial governments, as well as a range of administrative agencies. Judges also serve as arbiters in economic disputes, involving them in decisions with considerable financial consequences; F Zannotti *Le attività extragiudiziarie dei magistrati ordinari* (Padua: CEDAM, 1981).

33. For a detailed analysis of the Italian case see Guarnieri, n 26 above. The extensive use of the media by the Italian judiciary is discussed in P P Giglioli 'Political Corruption and the Media: the Tangentopoli Affair' (1996) 149 Int Social Science J 381. For a comparative assessment see V Pujas and M Rhodes 'Party Finance and Political Scandals in Italy, Spain and France' (1999) 22 West European Politics 41.

34. L M Díez-Picazo *Regimen constitucional del poder judicial* (Madrid: Civitas, 1991); P Magalhães, C Guarnieri and G Kaminis 'Democratic Consolidation, Judicial Reform and the Judicialisation of Politics in Southern Europe' in N Diamandouros, R Gunther and G Pasquino (eds) *Democratic Consolidation in Southern Europe* (Baltimore: The Johns Hopkins University Press, forthcoming).

12 were judges directly elected by their peers, and the rest were appointed by both chambers of Parliament. As in Italy, the Minister of Justice's powers were limited to funding the judicial system. The Higher Council has been in charge of appointments and promotions according to procedures that vary with the type of judicial position to be filled. In principle, advancements depend on seniority and, to a lesser extent, on merit, but appointments to the highest judicial positions also take into account the need to ensure representation of linguistic minorities. In disciplinary proceedings, senior judges share these functions with a standing committee of the Higher Council, which intervenes only in instances of gross violation of professional duties.

However, after the election of the Socialist party in 1982 the government clashed with the conservative majority on the Higher Council, and three years later this led to a reform of the *Ley organica*. The composition of the Higher Council was altered, with all judicial members elected by Parliament. The reform aimed at reinforcing the democratic character of the Higher Council,[35] and has subsequently altered the relationship between judges and other political actors, giving rise to complaints from both the judiciary and parliamentary opposition.[36] However, parliamentary selection of judicial members of the Higher Council (while fostering some collaboration between judges and political parties) seems to have reduced the role of judicial associations that the previous proportional system of election had helped to create. In 2001, following the *Pacto de la Justicia* between government and opposition, it has been established that Parliament must appoint the judicial members choosing from a list of 36 judges, prepared by the various judicial associations in proportion with their affiliation.[37]

In Portugal, after the fall of the Salazar and Caetano dictatorship, major reforms took place within the judicial system. Measures adopted immediately in 1974 included the direct election of the presidents of the Supreme Court and Courts of Appeal by their peers. Thus the most senior judicial appointments were placed in the hands of the judiciary itself with no intervention by either the executive or the Higher Council (*Conselho Superior da Magistradura*), whose composition was also reformed.[38] Following the constitutional amendments of 1982 and 1997, the 17 members of the Higher Council now

---

35. Clearly stated in the text of the *Ley organica* 6/1985 (Organización del poder judicial, 1991) pp 28–29).

36. Although it turned down a legal challenge to these reforms, the Spanish Constitutional Tribunal expressed concerns about an appointment mechanism that could produce a 'partisan logic' in the Higher Council's decision making. P Magalhães et al 'Democratic Consolidation, Judicial Reform and the Judicialisation of Politics in Southern Europe', in Diamandouros, Gunther and Pasquino (eds), n 34 above.

37. The Spanish judiciary is also divided into different groups: the *Asociación Profesional de la Magistratura*, a conservative group with the support of most judges; the *Francisco de Vitoria*, a centrist group; and *Juces para la Democracia*, on the left.

38. Under the authoritarian regime, the Higher Council (which dates back to the foundation of the Republic in 1910) was retained, although its internal structure was changed, with the executive appointing all its members. Efforts to bring the judiciary under the full control of the regime were made even clearer in a 1933 constitutional provision that established special tribunals and placed the power to appoint and promote judges in the hands of the Minister of Justice.

consist of seven judges directly elected by their peers through a proportional system, seven members elected by Parliament, and two other members appointed by the President of the Republic (one of which is usually a judge). The President of the Supreme Court, a position elected by fellow judges, chairs the Higher Council. Thus, judges now tend to hold the majority of the seats, and the Higher Council is rather representative of the whole judiciary.[39]

Differences in the structure and prerogatives of the various judicial governing bodies in Europe are even more evident when the French Higher Council (*Conseil Supérieur de la Magistrature*) is considered. In many respects the French Higher Council is at the opposite end of the spectrum to the Italian Higher Council. It has two main characteristics: a role reserved for the executive and a relatively narrow scope. There were different 'versions' of the Higher Council from 1958 to 1993, but both the President of the Republic and the Minister of Justice have always been present in the Council. However, the Council does not control judicial selection and training (functions entrusted to the ENM), and its appointing powers are comparatively limited. While a constitutional amendment in 1993 and subsequent legislation have had an impact on this set-up, the administration of judicial personnel in France is still defined by executive branch involvement.

Created in 1946 to preserve the independence of judges, the French Higher Council underwent a significant metamorphosis in the 1958 Constitution.[40] Along with the Fifth Republic's general shift in power to the executive, the President of the Republic's role within the Higher Council was expanded at the expense of the legislature. Article 65 of the Constitution changed the mechanism for selecting council members and reduced both their number and area of competence. The nine councillors sitting with the Minister of Justice and the President of the Republic were appointed by the President, although with some limitations. The Higher Council's appointment powers were also limited, confined only to the most senior appointments (about three per cent of all judicial personnel). In the remaining cases, it could only give an advisory opinion to the Minister of Justice; however, a practice gradually evolved where the Minister would not appoint judges who had been given a negative evaluation. Not surprisingly, critics of the 1958 reforms argued that 'a body established to protect the bench from possible abuses by the executive power is formed by people ... chosen by the head of that same power'.[41]

A 1993 constitutional amendment significantly changed the French Higher Council, although it did not go as far as initially envisaged. Today the Higher Council is a single body separated into two distinct panels, one with competence over judges and the other over public prosecutors. It is made up of 12 members: the President of the Republic; the Minister of Justice; a Councillor of State elected by peers; three lay members appointed respectively by the

---

39. Magalhães et al, n 34 above.
40. Under the 1946 Constitution the Higher Council consisted of 14 members: the President of the Republic and the Minister of Justice (acting as president and vice-president respectively), six lay members directly elected by the National Assembly, four judges elected by their peers, and two representatives of the legal profession appointed by the President of the Republic.
41. R Perrot *Institutions judiciaires* (Paris: Montchretiens, 5th edn, 1993) p 42.

President of the Republic, the President of the Senate, and the President of the Chamber of Deputies; and six magistrates representing a variety of ranks and elected by their peers, often the representatives of the various judicial associations.[42] The composition of this last segment of the Higher Council changes according to the type of panel: it consists of five judges and one public prosecutor when measures concerning judges are under consideration, with these proportions reversed for decisions affecting public prosecutors. The reforms also expanded the powers of the Higher Council. Disciplinary decisions made by the standing panel for the judiciary now prevail over the Minister of Justice, and the range of direct appointments by the Higher Council has also increased to include nominations to top positions of courts of first instance. In all other cases judges can now be appointed only after a favourable opinion of the Higher Council. In contrast, the functions of the public prosecution panel are more narrowly defined: this panel can only give non-compulsory advice, and such advice is not required for senior appointments, which remain under the direct responsibility of the Council of Ministers.[43]

Notwithstanding the recent reforms, the French judiciary still resembles the traditional civil law model outlined above. However, the judiciary's pyramid structure consists of two grades, while the most senior judges who sit in the Court of Cassation, the major courts of appeal, and the main tribunals are placed above (*hors hierarchie*). The position of individual judges, the functions they perform, their prestige, and salary are largely determined by advancements, and steps on the career path depend not only on seniority but above all on merit. Judges undergo very detailed work evaluations every two years, and in many cases promotion results in a transfer, although prior consent is required. French judges have higher levels of personal mobility than common law judges do, and such mobility is meant to be a device to prevent stagnation within the judiciary. Yet the procedure for promotion is rather complicated and centres on the judicial hierarchy. Evaluations of work performance are drafted by higher-ranking magistrates and recorded in personnel reports made available to everyone taking part in the decision-making process. Thus, hierarchical superiors form a key link between individual judges and appointing authorities. Each year the Commission for Advancements also drafts a list of magistrates qualified for promotion. Since any promotions must be drawn from this list, the Commission holds significant power. Its composition has recently been reformed: staffed in the past by magistrates appointed by the Minister of Justice,

---

42. As specified in the *loi organique* nn 94–100 of 5 February 1994. In France there are three judicial groups: the *Syndicat de la Magistrature*, on the left; the *Union syndicale des Magistrats*, a centrist group, the most important; and the *Association Professionnelle des Magistrats*, more conservative. In January 2000 a proposal by the Jospin government to reform the Council – and to reduce the power of the executive – broke down mainly because of the opposition of the Gaullist party.

43. Although the Jospin government (1997–2002) declared to be bound by the CSM advice also for prosecutorial appointments, the practice has not been followed by the new rightist government led by Raffarin.

today there is a more balanced composition including not only officials of the executive branch but also magistrates directly elected by their peers.[44]

Thus, in a bureaucratic judiciary political influence is filtered through the hierarchical structure and procedures for career advancements. The way promotions are organised represents the weak point of this arrangement; while recruitment by appointment or direct election tends to align justice with politics on the basis of shared values, hierarchical structures entail less visible but more diffused constraints. Desire for promotion is likely to produce a stronger incentive to comply with pressure or expectations from the Minister of Justice, judicial superiors, or even a 'self-governing' body. Italian magistrates have tended to affiliate themselves with one of the ideological factions represented on the Higher Council, and empirical research shows that 'proximity to power' is also a powerful career accelerator for judges in other countries. According to Bloch, in France the swiftest career advancements are made through stints in ministerial Cabinets or by performing other functions within the administration, especially within the Ministry of Justice.[45] At least traditionally, 'all systems tend to advantage those who have chosen to start their careers as prosecutors'.[46]

SOME CONSEQUENCES OF THE REFORMS

The creation of judicial self-governing bodies has significantly affected the relationship between judges and the political system, at least in those countries in which this institutional innovation has had the time to fully develop its effects. The Higher Councils of the Judiciary have tended to radically alter bureaucratic judiciaries by strengthening judicial independence while, at the same time, fostering new connections with the political system. The powers and composition of these self-governing bodies are critical factors; obviously the more extensive their functions, the stronger their role will be and the weaker the Minister of Justice will be. However, two additional factors are the ratio of judges to non-judicial members on Higher Councils and the way judicial representatives are chosen. Judicial independence will inevitably be stronger

44. Perrot, n 41 above, pp 354–355; T S Renoux and A Roux *L'administration de la justice en France* (Paris: PUF, 1994) pp 67–85; A Bancaud and Ph Robert 'La place de la justice en France: un avenir incertain' in Ph Robert and A Cottino (eds) *Les mutations de la justice* (Paris: L'Harmattan, 2001) pp 161–234.

45. E Bloch 'Faire carrière sous la Ve République?' (1981) 16 Pouvoirs 98 refers (at 101) to this as the 'royal path', where a figurative red carpet unrolls in front of magistrates who attempt to remove themselves 'as far as possible from courtrooms'. See also A Garapon *Le gardien des promesses* (Paris: Editions Odile Jacob, 1996) p 47; and A Boigeol *La magistrature 'hors les murs'. Analyse de la mobilité extra-professionnelle des magistrats* (Paris: IHTP-CNRS, 1998).

46. C Charle 'Etat et magistrats. Les origines d'une crise prolongée' (1993) 96-97 Acte de la Recherche en Sciences Sociales 39 at 43. In France, until the beginning of the twentieth century, three-quarters of judges on the Court of Cassation had spent most of their career as prosecutors. Today, however, it appears that the French Ministry of Justice tends to support the promotion of magistrates with experience in both the prosecution and the judiciary: J L Bodiguel *Les magistrats un corps sans âme?* (Paris: PUF, 1991) p 111.

with a higher ratio of members chosen directly by and from the judiciary. According to these criteria, the Italian judiciary seems to enjoy the highest degree of institutional independence among European civil law countries.

One of the first consequences of creating a Higher Council of the Judiciary is to increase the *external* independence of the judiciary by decreasing the traditional power played by the executive. But since no Higher Council is composed solely of judges, an important role is entrusted to the institution in charge of appointing the non-judicial members. This is usually assigned to Parliament, which allows political parties to bypass the Minister of Justice and influence the judiciary directly. The creation of a self-governing body also has consequences for the *internal* independence of the judiciary. Entrusting promotion and appointment of judges to a collegial body where normally all judicial ranks are represented contradicts the traditional hierarchical principle, whereby only higher-ranking judges are entitled to evaluate lower-ranking colleagues. In this way, the lower ranks acquire a new power, since they can participate in the process of choosing higher-ranking judges. Moreover, judicial elites have been further weakened by the loss of power of their traditional ally, the Minister of Justice. As a result, it is not surprising that challenges to the very idea of a judicial career by the lower ranks have often been successful. It is not coincidental that in the countries in which Higher Councils have been instituted the number of judicial ranks has been reduced, and the influence of senior judges' assessments of lower-ranking judges has declined. By increasingly substituting an objective parameter (such as seniority) for the subjective assessment of merit by superiors, higher-ranking judges' power has been reduced. For instance, in Italy (the most extreme case) promotions have de facto been abolished, at least from the economic point of view, and judicial salaries and rank increase simply on the basis of the number of years of service. The result has been that the erosion of traditional hierarchical controls – not balanced by reforms of initial selection aimed at bringing into the corps more experienced legal professionals – has brought about a decline of the standards of professional qualification of the judicial corps, with negative consequences for the performance of the judicial system.[47]

The erosion of hierarchical links in civil service-style judiciaries has been particularly relevant to the general expansion of judicial power. With the creation of Higher Councils, the reference group of judges has changed. Traditional members of the reference group, such as senior judges and legal academics,[48] have decreased in importance, since they no longer enjoy a monopoly of power over evaluations for judicial promotion. The very role of Supreme Courts seems to have been reduced, at least to some extent. In addition, the professional criteria of the judiciary have also begun to shift. Technical legal knowledge (or conformity to the ideology of the judicial elite) is no longer the only important element for promotion. Views of others outside the judicial system (in particular, political parties in Parliament) have gained in importance, especially if they can participate in the appointment of members of the Higher Council. Similarly, the interests of the media and the judiciary increasingly overlap, since judicial (especially prosecutors') actions provide the media with

---

47. G Di Federico 'Judicial Independence in Italy: A Critical Overview in a (Non-systematic) Perspective' in *Office of Democracy and Governance*, n 2 above, pp 83–99.
48. Merryman, n 1 above.

news. In return, the media are able to support and publicise the actions of judges and prosecutors.[49] The growing influence of these actors is partially due to broader changes in the political and social environment, but it is also encouraged by the declining significance of traditional actors brought about by the creation of Higher Councils.[50]

Inside the judiciary itself, Higher Councils tend to increase the role of judicial associations, since they organise the electoral participation of judges. In Italy, where these trends are more developed and no judicial member of the Higher Council is now elected without the backing of one of these politically oriented groups, decision-making in the Higher Council is heavily dependent on their alignments (see Table 3 below). As we have seen, magistrates interested in being promoted or transferred to another position (the vast majority) cannot fail to take into account the complex configuration of factional and party forces that play a role in the council's decision-making. In this way, political considerations have spread throughout the Italian judiciary.[51] As judicial actions gain political significance, a Higher Council may become the main institution where the judiciary's elected representatives can meet political representatives and develop a new relationship with the political system.

In common law countries, although to a different degree,[52] political considerations are inherent in the appointment process. Therefore, political influence can usually only be exerted at the moment of the recruitment because strong guarantees of independence restrict other possibilities. In civil law countries, traditionally the influence of the executive and, to a lesser extent, the legislative on the judiciary has been exerted mainly through senior judges who have been in control of judicial promotions and owe their own status to ministerial appointment. Judicial self-governing bodies have thus opened up a third channel of political influence, which can be seen as a consequence of the slow but steady attempt to limit executive power and the consequent strengthening of judicial guarantees in civil law judiciaries. Even though the extent to which the judiciary intervenes in the political process is conditioned by the evolution of the political system and by the way the judicial system is organised,[53] the connections between judges and the political system influence judges' reference groups, their conception of their judicial role, and therefore their decisions.[54]

The Italian experience suggests that the creation of judicial self-governing bodies is capable of producing a radical change in the judiciary's traditional hierarchy; this in turn can diversify the judiciary's reference group and place it, at least in part, outside the judiciary. All these processes can also support

49. D Soulez-Larivière *Du cirque médiatico-judiciaire et des moyens d'en sortir* (Paris: Editions du Seuil, 1993); Giglioli, n 33 above.

50. Garapon, n 45 above, 1996.

51. Di Federico, n 31 above; Rebuffa, n 4 above.

52. In England political influence is balanced by the role the Bar and the senior judiciary play in judicial appointments. In the United States politics plays a more overt role since judicial appointments are normally in the hands of politicians or the electorate.

53. It is obvious that in countries like France and Italy, where judges and prosecutors form a unified corps, greater potential exists for unrestrained judicial power. This possibility is stronger in Italy where guarantees of independence have been extended to prosecutors.

54. Obviously, where judges possess a high degree of independence and are free from hierarchical controls, it is extremely important to identify their reference groups and judges' conceptions of their role.

the development of forms of judicial activism. In any case, the change has produced visible divisions within the judiciary, and today continental judges tend to mobilise into formal groups according to their political orientations.[55] As a result, judges now often only present a united front when direct interests are at stake (for instance, personal interests such as promotion, and economic ones such as salary). On the other hand, in all Latin European judiciaries a Higher Council of the Judiciary is now the main (if not the only) institutional connection between the judiciary and the political system. In other words, the changes introduced in the second half of the twentieth century in Latin European countries have not so much reduced the political influence on the judiciary as they have altered the way political influence is exercised and, therefore, the relative power of political and institutional actors.

Table 1. Composition of Higher Councils of the Judiciary in Latin Europe[a]

	France	Spain	Portugal	Italy
	Conseil superieur de la magistrature	*Consejo general del poder judicial*	*Conselho superior da magistradura*	*Consiglio superiore della magistratura*
Judges	7	13	8	18
	* 5 judges and 1 prosecutor indirectly elected by magistrates[b] * 1 councillor of state elected by colleagues	* 12 judges appointed by Parliament * President of the Supreme Court ex-officio	* 7 judges directly elected by the judiciary * President of the Supreme Court ex-officio	* 16 magistrates elected directly by magistrates * President of the Court of Cassation * Attorney-General of the Court of Cassation
Lay members	5	8	9	9
	* 1 each appointed by President, President of the Senate, President of the National Assembly * President * Minister of Justice	* 8 lawyers appointed by Parliament	* 7 lawyers appointed by Parliament * 2 lawyers appointed by the President[c]	* 8 lawyers appointed by Parliament * President

a   Source: C Guarnieri and P Pederzoli *The Power of Judges* (Oxford: Oxford University Press, 2002) p 53.
b   When the French Higher Council considers issues relating to prosecutors the composition is reversed, with 5 prosecutors and 1 judge.
c   The practice is that one of the two tends to be a judge.

55. Garapon, n 15 above; Guarnieri, n 26 above.

Table 2. Party affiliation of lay members of the Italian Higher Council (1976-2002)[a]

Year	Left	Centre	Right
1976–90	3 Communists 2 Socialists	1 Centrist parties 4 Christian Democrats	–
1994	3 Progressives[b]	1 Popular[c]	2 Northern League 2 Forza Italia 2 National Alliance
1998	6 Progressives	1 Popular	1 Forza Italia 1 National Alliance 1 CCD[d]
2002	1 Ds 1 Sdi	1 Popular	2 Forza Italia 1 National Alliance 1 CCD

a   Source: C Guarnieri and P Pederzoli The Power of Judges (Oxford: Oxford University Press, 2002) p 57.
b   Alliance of leftist parties.
c   Faction of the former Christian Democrat party.
d   Faction of the former Christian Democrat party.

Table 3. Election of judges to the Italian Higher Council by *corrente* (1976–2002)[a]

Corrente (aligned from left to right on the political spectrum)

Year	*Magistratura Democratica*	*Movimento per la Giustizia*	*Unità per la Costituzione*	*Magistratura Indipendente*	*Others*
1976	755		2526	2156	506
	13%		42%	36%	9%
	2		9	8	1
1981	803		2557	2263	297
	14%		43%	38%	5%
	3		9	8	
1986	1107		2517	2078	402
	19%		41%	34%	6%
	3		9	7	1
1990	1337	714	2236	1828	
	22%	12%	36%	30%	
	4	3	8	5	
1994	1620	1133	2854	1230	
	24%	16%	42%	18%	
	5	4	8	3	
1998	1737	1105	2502	1513	
	25%	16%	37%	22%	
	5	3	8	4	
2002[b]		3177	2338	1248	128
		46%	34%	18%	2%
	5	3	6	2	

a   Source: C Guarnieri and P Pederzoli *The Power of Judges* (Oxford: Oxford University Press, 2002) p 56.
b   In 2002 the number of elective councillors has been reduced to 24, 16 of which elected by the judiciary. In this election *Magistratura Democratica* and *Movimento per la giustizia* have run together.

A Supreme Court for the United Kingdom? A view from the High Court of Australia

Tracey Stevens
Part-time Lecturer, Faculty of Law, University of New South Wales

George Williams*
Anthony Mason Professor and Director, Gilbert + Tobin Centre of Public Law, Faculty of Law, University of New South Wales; Barrister, New South Wales Bar

I INTRODUCTION

The High Court created by Australia's 1901 Constitution first sat on 6 October 1903. A century on, it is an apt time to consider how the record of the Court can contribute a different perspective to the debate over a possible Supreme Court for the United Kingdom. Of course, it cannot be assumed that common views are held of this record. Indeed, the role of the High Court and its place in the Australian political system remains hotly contested.[1] As Michael Coper has said of the successes and failures of the Court:

> 'There are no simple answers. Indeed, the questions, and the whole exercise of identifying criteria for making informed judgments about success and failure, are themselves but a gateway to the long-standing and never-ending debate about the nature of the judicial process in a final appellate court, particularly one that exercises the power of judicial review under a written constitution.'[2]

The task of assessing the record and relevance of the Australian High Court is made especially complex by the fact that, in interpreting a written constitution and in developing the common law, the Court serves a community that continues to experience considerable social, economic and political change. Hence, as Lord Porter stated in the *Bank Nationalisation Case*[3] on appeal from

---

* Parts of this paper have been developed with the assistance of T Blackshield and G Williams *Australian Constitutional Law and Theory: Commentary and Materials* (Sydney: Federation Press, 3rd edn, 2002); and R Davis and G Williams 'Reform of the Judicial Appointments Process: Gender and the Bench of the High Court of Australia' (2003) 27 Melbourne ULR 819.
1. See generally T Blackshield, M Coper and G Williams (eds) *The Oxford Companion to the High Court of Australia* (Melbourne: Oxford University Press, 2001).
2. M Coper 'The seven habits of a highly effective High Court' (2003) 28 Alternative Law Journal 59.
3. *Commonwealth v Bank of NSW* (1949) 79 CLR 497 at 639.

the High Court: 'The problem to be solved will often be not so much legal as political, social or economic. Yet it must be solved by a court of law.' This role of the High Court as part of the third branch of government has always been inherently political.[4] While the Court exercises its functions independently of the legislative and executive branches, the impact of its decisions is obvious. Moreover, decision-making by the Court often involves difficult choices of policy and judgment. While such choices arise out of essentially legal questions, the need to make them inevitably leads to debate about the capacity of the judges to make such decisions and the legitimacy of their doing so. This continues to be the case especially where the judges of the Court have the final say over a matter of law and policy by applying the Australian Constitution to strike down inconsistent legislation.[5]

Unlike most other public institutions in Australia, a central characteristic of the High Court is its independence.[6] However, even as an independent body, the Court's capacity to exercise public power depends upon perceptions of its legitimacy as a law-maker and ultimately upon public confidence in the judiciary. As Sir Gerard Brennan, Chief Justice of the High Court from 1995 to 1998, has explained:

> 'The judiciary, the least dangerous branch of government, has public confidence as its necessary but sufficient power base. It has not got, nor does it need, the power of the purse or the power of the sword to make the rule of law effective, provided the people … have confidence in the exercise of the power of judgment.'[7]

Where the High Court has enjoyed such confidence, this has provided the strongest protection against incursions into its independence.

The question of the independence of the judiciary lies at the heart of the current United Kingdom reform process. This has been expressed in particular in the idea that the United Kingdom should possess its own separate Supreme

---

4.   See, for example, M Coper *Encounters with the Australian Constitution* (Sydney: CCH Australia, 1987) ch 3; B Galligan *Politics of the High Court: A Study of the Judicial Branch of Government in Australia* (St Lucia: University of Queensland Press, 1987); G Sawer *Australian Federalism in the Courts* (Melbourne: Melbourne University Press, 1967); D Solomon *The Political High Court: How the High Court Shapes Politics* (Sydney: Allen and Unwin, 1999).

5.   Compare the famous, but cryptic, statement of Dixon J in *Melbourne Corpn v Commonwealth* (1947) 74 CLR 31 at 82: 'The Constitution is a political instrument. It deals with government and governmental powers … It is not a question whether the considerations are political, for nearly every consideration arising from the Constitution can be so described, but whether they are compelling.'

6.   This may be understood as the freedom of the Court from improper pressure from Parliament and the freedom of a judge from improper pressure to hear and decide cases in anything other than an impartial manner. See Sir Anthony Mason 'The Appointment and Removal of Judges' in H Cunningham (ed) *Fragile Bastion: Judicial Independence in the Nineties and Beyond* (Sydney: Judicial Commission of New South Wales, 1997) pp 1, 34–35. This formulation is also adopted by Kate Malleson in the United Kingdom context as 'individual' judicial independence or 'party impartiality': K Malleson *The New Judiciary: the effects of expansion and activism* (Aldershot: Ashgate/Dartmouth, 1999) ch 3.

7.   As quoted in E Campbell and HP Lee *The Australian Judiciary* (Melbourne: Cambridge University Press, 2001) pp 6–7.

Court rather than a final court of appeal located within the House of Lords. The Department for Constitutional Affairs Consultation Paper *Constitutional reform: a Supreme Court for the United Kingdom* identifies popular expectations about the independence and transparency of the judicial system as a central argument for any such reform:

> 'The considerable growth of judicial review in recent years has inevitably brought the judges more into the political eye. It is essential that our systems do all that they can to minimise the danger that judges' decisions could be perceived to be politically motivated. The Human Rights Act 1998 (UK), itself the product of a changing climate of opinion, has made people more sensitive to the issues and more aware of the anomaly of the position whereby the highest court of appeal is situated within one of the chambers of Parliament.'[8]

We approach this issue from the perspective of the High Court of Australia and examine how its contemporary role can shed light on the questions arising for a Supreme Court for the United Kingdom. After setting out the basic institutional features of the High Court, we focus on its jurisprudence, especially in the area of human rights, in order to identify the changing role of the Court and the difficulties posed by its politicisation. We then address a related issue, the process of judicial appointment, which is the subject of ongoing debate in Australia as well as in regard to a Supreme Court of the United Kingdom. From the discussion of these issues, we draw conclusions from the century of Australian experience for the United Kingdom's judicial reform process.

II JURISDICTION

In his second reading speech to the Judiciary Act 1903 (Cth), which provided the legislative basis for the new High Court, Alfred Deakin, Australia's first Attorney-General and second Prime Minister, was clear on the role the Court would play:

> 'The Constitution is to be the supreme law, but it is the High Court which is to determine how far and between what boundaries it is supreme. The Federation is constituted by distribution of powers, and it is this Court which decides the orbit and boundary of every power. Consequently, when we say that there are three fundamental conditions involved in federation, we really mean that there is one which is more essential than the others – the competent tribunal which is able to protect the Constitution, and to oversee its agencies. That body is the High Court. It is properly termed the keystone of the federal arch.'[9]

As Deakin suggested, the High Court was created as the highest court in a 'federal arch' composed of the Commonwealth and the federated States and Territories. This federal framework was established by Australia's written

---

8.   Department for Constitutional Affairs *Constitutional reform: a Supreme Court for the United Kingdom* CP11/03 (July 2003) p 11.
9.   A Deakin *Commonwealth Parliamentary Debates* 8 (1902) 10,967.

Constitution, a document drafted in Australia in the 1890s and enacted by British Parliament as the Commonwealth of Australian Constitution Act 1900 (UK) before coming into force on 1 January 2001.[10] Section 71 of the Constitution provides that the judicial power of the Commonwealth 'shall be vested in a Federal Supreme Court, to be called the High Court of Australia'. However, much is left unsaid in the Constitution and is left to the federal Parliament.

Unlike the Supreme Court of the United States, the High Court combines its distinctive federal functions with those of an ordinary Court of Appeal in matters of general law. The Court's appellate jurisdiction is outlined by s 73 of the Constitution. It embraces appeals from within the High Court itself (typically from a single Justice to a larger bench) in matters arising within the Court's original jurisdiction, appeals from any 'federal court, or court exercising federal jurisdiction' and appeals from the State Supreme Courts. This appellate jurisdiction is subject to such 'exceptions' and 'regulations' as the Parliament may prescribe. The High Court may also itself decline to hear an appeal, and Parliament has provided that in all such matters appeals may require the special leave of the Court. By s 35 of the Judiciary Act 1903 (Cth), as amended in 1984, no appeal from any State court may now be heard 'unless the High Court gives special leave to appeal'.[11] In the 2002–03 financial year, the High Court heard 325 special leave applications and granted only 65.[12]

The original jurisdiction of the High Court (that is, the range of matters in which action may be initiated in the High Court) is outlined in ss 75 and 76 of the Constitution. Section 75 lists matters in which the Court 'shall have original jurisdiction' while s 76 lists additional matters in which original High Court jurisdiction may be conferred by the Parliament. Oddly, these areas of jurisdiction left to the Parliament's discretion include matters 'arising under this Constitution, or involving its interpretation'. In those matters the Court's original jurisdiction is conferred by s 30(a) of the Judiciary Act. Section 76 also allows the High Court to be given original jurisdiction in any matters arising 'under any laws made by the Parliament'; in Admiralty and maritime matters; and in matters where 'the same subject-matter [is] claimed under the laws of different States'. Before the creation of the Federal Court of Australia in 1976, the original jurisdiction conferred on the High Court was quite extensive, but since then it has been cut back so that today, apart from constitutional cases, the only other area of jurisdiction still assigned to the High Court by s 30 of the Judiciary Act relates to '(c) trials of indictable offences against the laws of the Commonwealth'.

The original jurisdiction which the High Court 'shall have' is limited to the rather anomalous collection of matters listed in s 75 of the Constitution. Most of them involve some aspect of intergovernmental relationships with other countries; or with the Commonwealth as a government; or between States or

10. See generally J A La Nauze *The Making of the Australian Constitution* (Melbourne: Melbourne University Press, 1972).
11. The validity of this requirement was affirmed in *Smith Kline & French Laboratories (Aust) Ltd v Commonwealth* (1991) 173 CLR 194.
12. High Court of Australia *Annual Report 2002–2003*, Annexure B: Tables of Judicial Workload, pp 97–100.

residents of different States. Perhaps the most anomalous item is the jurisdiction in matters arising 'under any treaty' conferred by s 75(i).[13] In general the only jurisdiction of practical significance secured to the Court by s 75 is that conferred by s 75(v) in respect of 'all matters ... [i]n which a writ of Mandamus or prohibition or an injunction is sought against an officer of the Commonwealth'. There is no explicit reference to writs of certiorari, but the constitutionally secured jurisdiction in respect to writs of mandamus and prohibition has been held to imply the conferral of an ancillary jurisdiction to grant certiorari.[14] Because the expressions 'jurisdiction' and 'prohibition' are used in s 75 with constitutional force, and because the Crown is not an element of the judicature established by Ch III of the Constitution, Gaudron and Gummow JJ in *Re Refugee Review Tribunal, ex p Aala*[15] acceded to the view of Justice Kirby that in this context the writs should be referred to as 'constitutional writs' rather than 'prerogative writs'. The High Court's power to issue writs is further spelt out by s 33 of the Judiciary Act, but it seems clear that no such statutory provision could remove the jurisdiction which s 75 of the Constitution declares that the Court 'shall have'.[16]

Section 40 of the Judiciary Act also makes elaborate provision for removal into the High Court from any other State or federal court of '[a]ny cause or part of a cause arising under the Constitution or involving its interpretation' and (where all parties consent and the High Court 'is satisfied that it is appropriate ... having regard to ... the public interest') of any other cause or part of a cause involving federal jurisdiction. By s 42 any matter thus removed into the High Court may be remitted to the court of origin, and shall be so remitted if the High Court finds that it lacks original jurisdiction to deal with it. Other matters may be remitted to another State or federal court under s 44.

III INDEPENDENCE AND THE SEPARATION OF POWERS

The separation of the executive and legislature in Australia has not been maintained in any strict form, an outcome which reflects the intention of the framers of the Constitution to create a Westminster system of government.[17] By contrast, the High Court has enforced the separation of the judiciary from both of these branches of government. The text and structure of the Constitution, as interpreted by the High Court itself, establishes the High Court as an independent institution. Each of the key provisions relating to the judiciary are in their own self-contained Chapter of the Constitution, 'Chapter III – The Judicature', whereas the text relating to the other arms of government are set

---

13. This head of jurisdiction was apparently invoked for the first time in *Re East, ex p Nguyen* (1998) 196 CLR 354.
14. See *Pitfield v Franki* (1970) 123 CLR 448; *R v Cook, ex p Twigg* (1980) 147 CLR 15; *Re Coldham, ex p Brideson* (1989) 166 CLR 338.
15. (2000) 204 CLR 82.
16. *Plaintiff S157/2002 v Commonwealth* (2003) 195 ALR 24. See D Kerr and G Williams 'Review of Executive Action and the Rule of Law under the Australian Constitution' (2003) 14 PL Review 219.
17. This intention is also evident from the requirement in s 64 of the Constitution that ministers of State be members of the federal Parliament.

out in 'Chapter I – The Parliament' and 'Chapter II – The Executive Government'.

In *Victorian Stevedoring & General Contracting Co Pty Ltd & Meakes v Dignan*,[18] Justice Dixon suggested that, as a result of this separation of powers, the federal Parliament was restrained 'both from reposing any power essentially judicial in any other organ or body, and from reposing any other than that judicial power in such tribunals'. That dictum embodied two propositions that were accepted subsequently by the High Court[19] and on appeal in the Privy Council[20] in the *Boilermakers' Case*:

1. That the judicial power of the Commonwealth cannot be vested in any tribunal other than 'a Ch III court' (that is, the High Court and any other courts established or authorised by Ch III of the Constitution); and
2. That a Ch III court cannot be invested with anything other than judicial power (except for those ancillary powers that are strictly incidental to its functioning as a court).

The development and application of these propositions continues to provide a large part of the High Court's constitutional law case-load.[21] Such cases have enabled members of the Court to remark on the institution's independence. For example, Justice McHugh in *Kable v Director of Public Prosecutions (NSW)*[22] stated as a basic principle of the Australian Constitution 'that the judges of the federal courts must be, and must be perceived to be, independent of the legislative and the executive governments'. Similarly, in *Wilson v Minister for Aboriginal and Torres Strait Islander Affairs*,[23] Justice Gaudron discussed how the judicial power of the Commonwealth must be exercised with an impartiality that is and is seen to be 'completely independent of the legislatures and executive governments of those polities' that constitute the federation.

IV APPEALS TO THE PRIVY COUNCIL

At the time of federation, the retention of Privy Council appeals, especially in relation to constitutional cases, was a contentious issue.[24] The Australian draft

---

18. (1931) 46 CLR 73 at 98.
19. *R v Kirby, ex p Boilermakers' Society of Australia* (1956) 94 CLR 254.
20. *A-G (Commonwealth) v The Queen* [1957] AC 288.
21. See A Lynch 'The Gleeson Court in Constitutional Law: An Empirical Analysis' (2003) 26 U New South Wales LJ 32 at 46. For example, in determining the powers that can be conferred upon a non-judicial tribunal, see *Brandy v Human Rights and Equal Opportunity Commission* (1995) 183 CLR 245; *A-G (Cth) v Breckler* (1999) 197 CLR 83.
22. (1997) 189 CLR 51 at 116.
23. *Wilson v Minister for Aboriginal and Torres Strait Islander Affairs* (1997) 189 CLR 1 at 25.
24. La Nauze, n 10 above, pp 248–269. The House of Lords has also been important in the development of the common law in Australia. In *Piro v Foster* (1943) 68 CLR 313, Latham CJ stated that the High Court should defer to the House of Lords on matters of legal principle. This position changed in *Parker v The Queen* (1963) 111 CLR 610, when the High Court stated that it would follow its own decision over a conflicting decision of the House of Lords.

of the new Constitution had proposed to make the High Court of Australia the final arbiter of constitutional questions. The British government insisted that appeals to the Privy Council be retained. The eventual compromise, embodied in s 74 of the Constitution, was that in certain specified cases no appeal to the Privy Council should lie unless the High Court gave a certificate 'that the question is one which ought to be determined by Her Majesty in Council'. In other cases, the normal avenues of appeal to the Privy Council remained.

The specified cases requiring a certificate were those 'upon any question, howsoever arising, as to the limits inter se of the Constitutional powers of the Commonwealth and those of any State or States, or as to the limits inter se of the Constitutional powers of any two or more States'. As it turned out, only one such certificate was ever granted.[25] The requirement of an inter se certificate ensured that the High Court itself could control the extent to which questions affecting the federal distribution of powers might go to the Privy Council. However, this control had two qualifications. First, it was assumed that the Privy Council had power to determine any issues on which its own jurisdiction depended, and hence to determine whether or not a particular type of question did involve an inter se question. Second, the control exerted by the High Court extended only to appeals from the High Court. So long as it remained possible to appeal to the Privy Council direct from a State Supreme Court, whether by leave of that Court or by leave of the Privy Council, it was possible for an inter se matter to by-pass the High Court altogether.

Part of the compromise embodied in s 74 of the Constitution was that, apart from inter se matters, 'this Constitution shall not impair' the possibility of special leave to appeal from the High Court to the Privy Council, insofar as the granting of leave by the Privy Council itself depended on the royal prerogative. However, s 74 went on to say that '[t]he Parliament may make laws limiting the matters in which such leave may be asked'.[26] In 1968 this power to 'limit' appeals from the High Court was exercised by the Privy Council (Limitation of Appeals) Act 1968 (Cth). Thereafter, special leave to appeal from the High Court could be sought only where the High Court itself had heard an appeal from a State Supreme Court on a matter of purely State law. The power to 'limit' was further exercised by the Privy Council (Appeals from the High Court) Act 1975 (Cth), which provided that special leave could not be asked for 'unless the decision of the High Court was given in a proceeding that was commenced in a court before the date of commencement of this Act'. In short, the 1968 Act had exercised the power to 'limit' by abolishing some appeals, and the 1975 Act had further exercised the power to 'limit' by abolishing any remaining appeals apart from cases already in the pipeline.[27]

The effect of these two Acts on the doctrine of precedent was considered by the High Court in 1978 in *Viro v R*,[28] where the Court held that it was no longer

25. In *A-G (Cth) v Colonial Sugar Refining Co Ltd* [1914] AC 237.
26. See generally A R Blackshield *The Abolition of Privy Council Appeals* Adelaide Law Review Research Papers no 1 (1978).
27. The 1968 Act was held valid (by the Privy Council) in *Kitano v Commonwealth* [1976] AC 99. The 1975 Act was held valid (by the High Court) in *A-G (Cth) v T & G Mutual Life Society Ltd* (1978) 144 CLR 161.
28. (1978) 141 CLR 88.

bound by Privy Council decisions. The hierarchy of precedent follows the hierarchy of appeal and so long as it was possible to appeal from High Court to Privy Council, their Lordships' decisions had bound the High Court. With the end of the hierarchical relation that was no longer the case. The Privy Council had hitherto been, and as to appeals from the States still was, an Australian 'apex' court. However, the High Court was now also an 'apex' court, coequal with the Privy Council. It followed that the Court should treat Privy Council decisions as if they were its own, with the same degree, but no more, of precedent force.

The greater judicial 'activism' that many commentators in Australia have observed in the High Court's decisions over several years is the cumulative product of many social and individual forces. It was starting to become manifest in the 1960s, in cases like *Mutual Life & Citizens' Assurance Co Ltd v Evatt*,[29] where Barwick CJ accepted the High Court's responsibility for developing the law 'as appropriate to current times in Australia', or *Uren v John Fairfax & Sons Ltd*,[30] where the Court successfully asserted that developments of the common law in Australia and England might diverge. But the Court's declaration in *Viro v R* of its emancipation from the authority of Privy Council precedents was a final realisation of its independence.

Yet what was liberating for the High Court was a source of problems for State Supreme Courts, since the possibility of appeal from those courts direct to the Privy Council survived. What if, on the very same issue, one litigant appealed to the Privy Council and another to the High Court? If the two coequal 'apex' courts gave conflicting decisions, which one ought the State courts to follow? In *Viro v R* most judges suggested that in such a case the State courts should follow the High Court, but they gave no convincing explanation of why this should be so. In *Southern Centre of Theosophy Inc v South Australia*,[31] it was argued in the High Court that the cumulative effect of the 1968 and 1975 Acts had extinguished any surviving prerogative basis for appeals to the Privy Council, including appeals from the States, but the Court rejected this argument. These problems were finally resolved by the Australia Acts enacted in 1986 by the Australian and United Kingdom Parliaments. By abolishing the last remaining possibilities of appeal from the States, those Acts confirmed the High Court's position as the only 'apex' court with power to shape the development of Australian law.

V LEGALISM AND HUMAN RIGHTS

The Australian legal system draws from both the United States and English legal traditions.[32] In the 1890s, the framers of the Australian Constitution were

---

29. (1968) 122 CLR 556 at 563.
30. (1966) 117 CLR 118.
31. (1979) 145 CLR 246.
32. H Patapan *Judging Democracy: The New Politics of the High Court of Australia* (Victoria: Cambridge University Press, 2000) p 42. See ch 3 for discussion of the philosophical and political traditions of the framing of the Constitution and Australia's parliamentary structure.

deeply influenced by their British heritage and assumed that the Australian federation would be steeped in the Westminster tradition of responsible government. However, the Westminster tradition was an inadequate model for an Australian federal government that was to be based upon a written constitution. The drafters accordingly also looked to the United States. However, in doing so they did not adopt a United States-style Bill of Rights.

The approach taken to issues of human rights by the framers has been described by former Australian Prime Minister Sir Robert Menzies as follows: 'In short, responsible government in a democracy is regarded by us as the ultimate guarantee of justice and individual rights. Except for our inheritance of British institutions and the principles of the Common Law, we have not felt the need for formality and definition.'[33] In keeping with this sentiment, Australia's Constitution enshrines few rights. The express constitutional rights include: the requirement that Parliament acquire property only on 'just terms' (s 51(xxxi)), the requirement of trial by jury for indictable offences under Commonwealth law (s 80), freedom of religion under Commonwealth law (s 116) and freedom from discrimination based on State residence (s 117).[34] It is well established that, except for these scattered express rights, the drafters of the Constitution did not envisage that the Constitution would provide for the comprehensive protection of human rights.[35]

From this foundation, it is not surprising that human rights cases came only rarely before the High Court in its first 50 years. During this time, the Court was occupied with the development of the common law, the balance between State and federal power[36] and issues of trade and commerce within the nation.[37] Over time, the High Court also came to profess an adherence to legalism as the preferred method of judicial decision-making, especially in matters involving the interpretation of the Constitution. By legalism it was meant:

'the Constitution sets definite substantive limits on government power and that it is possible for the judiciary to determine those substantive limits simply by a process of interpretative judgment based on the letter and spirit of the constitutional text. It has involved the belief that the Court can and must draw lines to contain government power and that adherence to the strict analytical and conceptual techniques of formal legal argument provides the only sure method of approaching what is necessarily a sensitive political function.'[38]

---

33. Sir Robert Menzies *Central Power in the Australian Commonwealth* (London: Cassell, 1967) p 34.
34. See generally G Williams *Human Rights under the Constitution* (Melbourne: Oxford University Press, 1999).
35. See *Australian Capital Television Pty Ltd v Commonwealth* (1992) 177 CLR 106 at 136, per Mason CJ.
36. See the watershed decision in the *Amalgamated Society of Engineers v Adelaide Steamship Co Ltd* (*Engineers Case*) (1920) 28 CLR 129. See generally M Coper and G Williams (eds) *How Many Cheers for Engineers?* (Sydney: Federation Press, 1997).
37. For example *R v Burgess, ex p Henry* (1936) 55 CLR 608; *Australian National Airways Pty Ltd v The Commonwealth* (1945) 71 CLR 29.
38. S Gageler 'Foundations of Australian Federalism and the Role of Judicial Review' (1987) 17 Federal Law Review 162 at 176. See also G Craven 'The Crisis of Constitutional Literalism in Australia' in H P Lee and G Winterton (eds) *Australian Constitutional Perspectives* (Sydney: Law Book Co, 1992) p 1.

This approach was expressed most famously in the statement by Sir Owen Dixon at his swearing in as Chief Justice of the High Court in 1952 that: 'There is no other safe guide to judicial decisions in great conflicts than a strict and complete legalism.'[39] The context in which this statement was made is telling of the judicial method of the Court at the time. A year earlier the High Court handed down its decision in the *Communist Party Case*,[40] said to be 'probably the most important ever rendered by the [High] Court'.[41] The Court struck down the Communist Party Dissolution Act 1950 (Cth) as constitutionally invalid. It did so despite opinion polls showing that up to 80% of Australians supported the legislation.[42] The Act proclaimed the Australian Communist Party an unlawful association and vested a wide unreviewable discretion in the Governor General to declare a person to be a communist and thus unable to hold office in the Commonwealth public service or certain industries. The Court found the Act invalid because it could not be characterised as within the power of the Commonwealth, as set out in the Constitution. Further, the Court found that the recitals in the Act (which stated the government's view of communism) and the provision conferring discretion on the Governor-General attempted in themselves to set out the limits of Commonwealth power. The Court confirmed that determinations of the scope of legislative power can be undertaken only by the courts via judicial review. In doing so, the Court did not make more than passing reference to civil liberties in the decision.[43] Despite the draconian nature of the Act and its imposition on the freedom of speech and association of the Australian people, the High Court apparently did not strike down the law because it infringed any express or implied human rights.

After the retirement of Sir Owen Dixon as Chief Justice in 1965, the High Court continued to express its adherence to legalism as the orthodox method of judicial decision-making. It was espoused by the two following Chief Justices of the High Court, Chief Justice Barwick (1964–81) and Chief Justice Gibbs (1981–87).[44] At the same time, the Court continued to play little or no role in the protection or development of human rights principles. A notable exception

---

39. 'Swearing in of Sir Owen Dixon as Chief Justice' (1952) 85 CLR xi at xiv.

40. *Australian Communist Party v Commonwealth* (1951) 83 CLR 1.

41. G Winterton 'The Significance of the *Communist Party Case*' (1992) 18 Melb ULR 630 at 653. See G Williams 'Reading the Judicial Mind: Appellate Argument in the *Communist Party Case*' (1993) 15 Syd LR 3; G Williams 'The Suppression of Communism by Force of Law: Australia in the Early 1950s' (1996) 42 Australian Journal of Politics and History 220. Compare R Douglas 'A Smallish Blow for Liberty? The Significance of the *Communist Party Case*' (2001) 27 Monash ULR 253.

42. L F Crisp *Ben Chifley: a political biography* (London: Angus & Robertson, 1977) p 390.

43. *Australian Communist Party v Commonwealth* (1951) 83 CLR 1 at 187–188, per Dixon J: 'History and not only ancient history, shows that in countries where democratic institutions have been unconstitutionally superseded, it has been done not seldom by those holding the executive power. Forms of government may need protection from dangers likely to arise from within the institutions to be protected. In point of constitutional theory the power to legislate for the protection of an existing form of government ought not to be based on a conception, if otherwise adequate, adequate only to assist those holding power to resist or suppress obstruction or opposition or attempts to displace them or the form of government they defend.'

44. See S Gageler 'Legalism' in Blackshield, Coper and Williams, n 1 above, p 429.

was Justice Murphy, a member of the High Court from 1975 until his death in 1986.

Justice Murphy's judgments are the most explicitly rights-orientated decisions in the history of the High Court. The first case in which he suggested that the Constitution embodies implied freedoms was *R v Director-General of Social Welfare (Vic), ex p Henry*,[45] in which he found that: 'It would not be constitutionally permissible for the Parliament of Australia or any of the States to create or authorize slavery or serfdom.'[46] He justified this conclusion in two sentences: 'The reason lies in the nature of our Constitution. It is a Constitution for a free society.' In other cases Justice Murphy implied freedoms of movement and communication,[47] a right to be heard before being subject to an adverse order[48] and a freedom from 'cruel and unusual punishment'.[49] Justice Murphy's views on implied rights were rejected by other members of the High Court. In 1986 in *Miller v TCN Channel Nine Pty Ltd*,[50] a case dealing with s 92 of the Constitution, Justice Murphy referred to: 'guarantees of freedom of speech and other communications and freedom of movement not only between the States and the States and the Territories but in and between every part of the Commonwealth.' This drew a series of stinging rebukes, including from Justice Mason that: 'It is sufficient to say that I cannot find any basis for implying a new s 92A into the Constitution.'[51]

Justice Mason became Chief Justice of the High Court in 1987. Five years later in *Australian Capital Television Pty Ltd v Commonwealth*,[52] the Court, including its Chief Justice, held that the Constitution embodies a freedom to discuss matters relating to Australian government.[53] A distinct change in the approach of the High Court occurred under Chief Justice Mason. The Court during this period rejected reliance upon legalism to the exclusion of other relevant material and considerations and acknowledged the Court's law-making role.[54] Chief Justice Mason, for example, stated that legalism was a 'cloak for undisclosed and unidentified policy values' and called for 'policy-orientated interpretation' by judges.[55] This change in approach was one factor in a number

45. (1975) 133 CLR 369.
46. (1975) 133 CLR 369 at 388.
47. For example, *Buck v Bavone* (1976) 135 CLR 110 at 137.
48. *Taylor v Taylor* (1979) 143 CLR 1 at 20.
49. *Sillery v The Queen* (1981) 180 CLR 353 at 362.
50. (1986) 161 CLR 556 at 581–582.
51. (1986) 161 CLR 556 at 579. For further criticism, see P Bickovskii 'No Deliberate Innovators: Mr Justice Murphy and the Australian Constitution' (1977) 8 Federal Law Review 460; G Winterton 'Extra-Constitutional Notions in Australian Constitutional Law' (1986) 16 Federal Law Review 223.
52. (1992) 177 CLR 106.
53. See, on the influence or otherwise, of the decisions of Justice Murphy on the subsequent High Court, M Coper and G Williams (eds) *Justice Lionel Murphy – Influential or Merely Prescient?* (Sydney: Federation Press, 1997).
54. See, for example, C Saunders (ed) *Courts of final jurisdiction: the Mason Court in Australia* (Sydney: Federation Press, 1996).
55. Sir Anthony Mason 'The Role of a Constitutional Court in a Federation: A Comparison of the Australian and United States Experience' (1986) 16 Federal Law Review 1 at 5.

of landmark decisions that were more protective of human rights, such as *Mabo v Queensland (No 2)*,[56] the *Free Speech Cases*,[57] *Dietrich v The Queen*[58] and *Minister for Immigration and Ethnic Affairs v Teoh*.[59] This period coincided with the final abolition of appeals to the Privy Council, and marked a greater reliance by the Court on decisions of common law countries other than the United Kingdom and also on international law.[60]

The Mason Court also gave rise to fierce debate over whether it had overstepped its proper judicial bounds into a form of inappropriate judicial 'activism'. The debate over the 'activist' role of the Court is typified by Geoff Gallop's commentary in 1995, 'The High Court: usurper or guardian?', where he stated:

> 'The current High Court is characterised by two interesting features: firstly, its increasing self-consciousness as a guardian of the rights and interests of the people for whom the Constitution was established, and, secondly, its disinclination to mask its substantial role by reference to literalism and legalism. This has opened up new possibilities for litigation as a means of promoting rather than preventing social change.'[61]

Debate was also prompted by members of the Court referring to policy and fundamental values[62] and even to 'community values'[63] as appropriate and perhaps necessary factors in judicial decision-making.

When Chief Justice Mason retired in 1995 he was replaced by Chief Justice Brennan, who presided over the Court for three years. This was an important period of consolidation. In the decisions of *Lange v Australian Broadcasting Corpn*[64] and *Levy v State of Victoria*,[65] for example, the Court confirmed the implied freedom of political communication but contained this doctrine in several important respects.[66]

---

56. (1992) 75 CLR 1.

57. *Australian Capital Television Pty Ltd v Commonwealth (No 2)* (1992) 177 CLR 106; and *Nationwide News Pty Ltd v Wills* (1992) 177 CLR 1, where the Court derived an implied right to political communication from the Constitution.

58. (1992) 177 CLR 292. In this decision the Court set out the right to legal representation in a criminal trial.

59. (1995) 183 CLR 273. In this case the Court developed the concept of 'legitimate expectation' and expanded the role of international law in Australian domestic law.

60. M Dillon and J Doyle 'Mason Court' in Blackshield, Coper and Williams, n 1 above, p 462.

61. G Gallop 'The High Court; usurper or guardian?' (1995) 9(2) Legislative Studies 62.

62. See, for example, O H Lane 'The Changing Role of the High Court' (1996) 70 Australian Law Journal 246.

63. See Sir Anthony Mason, n 55 above: 'it is impossible to interpret any instrument, let alone a constitution, divorced from values. To the extent they are taken into account, they should be acknowledged and should be accepted community values rather than mere personal values.' Compare A Lynch 'The High Court – Legitimacy and Change: Review Essay' (2001) 12 Federal Law Review 1 at 5.

64. (1997) 189 CLR 520.

65. (1997) 189 CLR 579.

66. A Stone 'Freedom of Political Communication' in Blackshield, Coper and Williams, n 1 above, pp 536–537.

In 1998 Chief Justice Gleeson was appointed to the High Court, an appointment that coincided with a number of other changes in the Court. Indeed, of the seven judges who decided the *Mabo* case in 1992, only Justice McHugh still remains on the bench. The current approach of the High Court, despite some vigorous and persistent dissents from Justice Kirby,[67] has been somewhat of a return to legalism, marked by strict legal reasoning and less of an interest or engagement in rights-orientated jurisprudence. While the Court has not overruled the key decisions of the Mason Court, those decisions, in areas such as Aboriginal native title, have sometimes been severely limited in their scope by subsequent decisions.[68] There has also been the occasional explicit rejection of the approach of the Mason Court. As the most recent appointment to the High Court, Justice Heydon, stated shortly before his appointment in a speech directed largely at the Mason Court entitled 'Judicial Activism and the Death of the Rule of Law':[69]

> 'The duty of a court is not to make law, or debate the merits of particular law, but to do justice according to the law ... Thus judges swear to apply the existing laws and usages, not to unsettle them by critical debates about them and speculations about their future, and certainly not to develop new laws and usages. It is legislatures which create new laws. Judges are appointed to administer the law, not elected to change it or undermine it.'

Even today, the human rights decisions of the Mason Court are a flashpoint for debate around questions of judicial methodology and concepts such as judicial 'activism' and 'restraint'. Such debates in a nation without a Bill of Rights often do little to assist in the development of a sound and stable jurisprudence or to answer to the question posed by Chief Justice Gleeson in his 2000 Boyer Lectures: 'How then does a democracy, which functions on the basis of majority rule, institutionalise protection of legitimate minority interests?'[70] A nation without a Bill of Rights like Australia finds no easy answers to the question, nor sometimes even a satisfactory starting point. Much of the debate over human rights protection centres upon the judiciary as the only independent institution seen as capable of checking the actions of Parliament. But when the judiciary lacks the constitutional or legislative tools to perform such a role in the area of human rights, the outcome may be disagreement and discord.

VI THE HIGH COURT AND PUBLIC DEBATE

It is no coincidence that, since the Mason Court's development of a (limited) rights jurisprudence, the High Court has attracted increasing controversy and

67. See A Lynch 'The Gleeson Court in Constitutional law: An Empirical Analysis' (2003) 26 U New South Wales LJ 32 at 47.
68. See, in the context of native title, S Brennan 'Native Title in the High Court of Australia a Decade after Mabo' (2003) 14 PL Review 209.
69. D Heydon 'Judicial Activism and the Death of the Rule of Law' (2003) Quadrant 9 at 17.
70. Chief Justice Gleeson *The Rule of Law and the Constitution, Boyer Lectures 2000* (Sydney: ABC Books for the Australian Broadcasting Corporation, 2000) pp 1, 69.

its legitimacy has come under challenge, including from Australia's political leaders. For example, upon handing down the long anticipated decision in *Wik Peoples v Queensland*[71] in 1996 on native title, the Brennan Court experienced one of the most difficult periods since the Court's creation in 1903. In this case the Court found by slim majority that the grant of pastoral leases did not confer exclusive possession to the lease-holders as it did not automatically extinguish native title claims by indigenous peoples. For this, the judges were attacked as a 'pathetic ... self-appointed [group of] Kings and Queens', a group of 'basket-weavers' and even the purveyors of 'intellectual dishonesty'.[72] The decision 'induced a torrent of misinformed criticism directed not only at the High Court as an institution but also at the judges as individuals.'[73]

For much of this century, media scrutiny of the High Court has been rare.[74] Yet due to the evolution of the Court's role and the current political climate, the High Court holds a higher profile in the Australian public eye than before. Historically, the Court only received media attention when political debate became enmeshed with litigation before the Court or when a decision promised significant political ramifications. This explains the coverage given to the *Bank Nationalisation Case*[75] in 1948, the *Communist Party Case*[76] in 1951 and the *Tasmanian Dam Case*[77] in 1983. In the mainstream media, the judges responsible for such decisions have been almost completely unknown and the role of the High Court in Australian democracy has been frequently misunderstood. However, as tension between the High Court and other arms of government has increased and media attention provided to more recent cases such as *Kartinyeri v Commonwealth* (the *Hindmarsh Island Case*),[78] the *Wik* case and several matters involving refugee applications,[79] the Court is now more frequently the subject of political debate.[80]

In addition to increased political scrutiny of the Court's decisions, individual judges of the Court have become more susceptible to personal and professional scrutiny and attack. The most significant example of the latter occurred in March 2002, when Parliamentary Secretary to Cabinet, Bill Heffernan, under cover of parliamentary privilege, sought to discredit Justice Michael Kirby, the only openly gay Justice in the Court's history. Heffernan alleged that Justice Kirby had used his Commonwealth vehicle for improper purposes and was unfit to sit on a case involving child sex allegations. Documentation in support of

---

71. (1996) 187 CLR 1.
72. Quoted in Justice Michael Kirby 'Attacks on Judges - A Universal Phenomenon' (1998) 72 Australian Law Journal 599 at 601.
73. T Hands and D Davies 'Defend Thyself!' (2003) 28 Alternative Law Journal 65 at 66.
74. See G Williams 'The High Court and the Media' (1999) 1 UTS LR 136; J Waterford 'Media and the Court' in Blackshield, Coper and Williams, n 1 above, p 469.
75. *Bank of NSW v Commonwealth* (1948) 76 CLR 1.
76. *Australian Communist Party v Commonwealth* (1951) 83 CLR 1.
77. *Commonwealth v Tasmania* (1983) 158 CLR 1.
78. (1998) 195 CLR 337.
79. See, for example, *Plaintiff S157/2002 v Commonwealth of Australia* (2003) 195 ALR 24.
80. See Justice Michael McHugh 'Tensions Between the Executive and the Judiciary' (2002) 76 Australian Law Journal 567.

Heffernan's claims was later found to be fabricated and Heffernan apologised. Justice Kirby was defended by several legal professional bodies and numerous members of Parliament, and subsequently issued a statement in which he said:

> 'My family and I have suffered a wrong. But it is insignificant in comparison to the wrong done to Parliament, the High Court and the people ... I accept Senator Heffernan's apology and reach out my hand in a spirit of reconciliation. I hope that my ordeal will show the wrongs that hate of homosexuals can lead to. Out of this sorry episode, Australian should emerge with a heightened respect for the dignity of all minorities. And a determination to be more careful to uphold our national institutions – the Parliament and the Judiciary.'[81]

The incident highlighted the inadequate resources of the Court and its judges to defend themselves in such circumstances. There was no procedure or adequate avenue for the defence of the judge. The Attorney-General made a statement that the Court as an institution was not under threat and distanced himself from the incident, reiterating that it was not the role of the Attorney to speak for the courts. This was criticised, including by former Chief Justices Sir Anthony Mason and Sir Gerard Brennan.[82] The Judicial Conference of Australia issued a statement citing the failure of the government to understand the importance of upholding the independence of the judiciary and condemning the Senator's conduct as an abuse of parliamentary process. The statement included comments that the Attorney-General should reconsider his role in order better to uphold the rule of law and the independence of the judiciary.[83]

Given the evolution of the Court's role and the lack of an 'official defender' of the High Court, the current profile of the institution continues to require more effective communication with the public. The maintenance of public confidence in the Court depends on it. To date, however, the options are limited. The High Court has a website[84] and a newly appointed Public Information Officer. But, at a time when the High Court is very much in the public eye and never far from public controversy, neither may be sufficient.

VII APPOINTMENTS TO THE COURT

Section 71 of the Constitution says that the Court 'shall consist of a Chief Justice, and so many other Justices, not less than two, as the Parliament prescribes'. Other than setting a minimum number of three judges, the choice of how many judges should sit on the Court is left to Parliament. The maximum number of judges is currently set by the High Court of Australia Act 1979 (Cth), which states that the Court consists of the Chief Justice and six other Justices.

---

81. High Court of Australia 'Media Releases' (2002), available at www.hcourt.gov.au/publications_04.html as at 16 November 2003.
82. See Justice P W Young 'Current Issues' (2002) 76 Australian Law Journal 277.
83. Statement by the Judicial Conference of Australia extracted in Young, n 82 above n, at 278–281.
84. www.hcourt.gov.au.

In 1903 the Court consisted of three Justices (a Chief Justice and two other Justices). In 1906 the number of judges was increased to five, while the Court was increased to its present complement of seven judges in 1913.[85] During the Depression the number of judges was reduced to six between 1933 and 1946 to reduce cost. When in 1946 the size of the Court was returned to seven, the federal Cabinet considered increasing the number of judges to nine (in part to 'pack' the Court with more judges who might be favourable to upholding the legality of Labor Party polices). However, they were persuaded to limit the Court to seven judges by the federal Attorney-General, H V Evatt, himself a judge of the Court from 1930 to 1940.[86]

The current size of the High Court at seven judges is smaller than some other final courts. The Supreme Courts of Canada and the United states are composed of nine judges, while there arc 11 judges on the Constitutional Court of South Africa and 24 judges on the Supreme Court of India. As the Constitution specifies only a minimum number of judges, there is no upper limit on how many judges could be appointed to the Court. There are of course cost constraints and the High Court of Australia Act 1979 would need to be amended. However, at least at the time that the High Court building in Canberra was opened in 1980, it was envisaged that the size of the High Court might be increased at some time in the future. With this in mind, that building has space for nine judge's chambers.

The appointment of judges to the High Court is the responsibility of the federal executive. The only provision in the Constitution regarding the process of appointment states that appointments to the Court 'Shall be appointed by the Governor-General in Council'.[87] In practice, this means that the Governor-General formally makes the appointment acting on the advice of the federal government, which considers candidates nominated by the federal Attorney-General. The Constitution sets out that High Court judges can only be removed by the Governor-General on address from both Houses of Parliament for proved misbehaviour or incapacity.[88] Save for this removal mechanism, which has never been invoked, High Court judges are secure in office and remuneration until mandatory retirement at age 70.[89]

In regard to the criteria for appointment, the Constitution makes no mention of qualifications or background and contains no other procedural requirements. It does not even require that an appointee be qualified as a lawyer. However, the High Court of Australia Act 1979 provides more guidance. An appointee must be a judge of a federal or State court or must have been enrolled as a legal practitioner in Australia for not less than five years.[90] In regard to the process of nomination, s 6 also states that, before making an appointment, the 'Attorney-

---

85. The current practice of the Court is that all seven judges sit on cases of constitutional or other importance.

86. J Popple 'Number of Justices' in Blackshield, Coper and Williams, n 1 above, p 505.

87. Constitution, s 72(i).

88. Constitution, s 72(ii).

89. High Court judges appointed before 1977 held office for life, whereas those appointed after that, as a result of a successful referendum in that year to change s 72 the Constitution, hold office until the age of 70.

90. High Court of Australia Act 1979, s 7.

General shall ... consult with the Attorneys-General of the States'. The current convention is that the Attorney-General invites the State and Territory Attorneys-General to consult within their own jurisdictions and to appropriate candidates.[91] The Attorney-General also conducts his or her own consultations with members of the federal courts and 'others', including 'former judges, leaders of the legal profession and ministerial and other parliamentary colleagues'.[92]

Despite these procedural conventions, the extent or form of consultation is not specified and it is not clear whether this consultation process has any substantive effect on the choice of appointment made by the federal government. Further, there are no prescribed criteria for either nomination or selection. According to former federal Attorney-General, Daryl Williams (1996–2003), appointees to the High Court are chosen on 'the essential criterion' of 'merit'.[93] He has also stated: 'It is enough to say that outstanding professional skills and personal qualities, such as integrity and industry, are required, together with a proper appreciation of the role of the Court.'[94]

Despite the role of the High Court in determining the law across a full spectrum of social and political issues, it has remained a remarkably homogenous institution. Over a century, there have been 44 appointments to the Court. Of those appointments: 'Most Justices have come directly from the Bar or the judiciary. None has been a full-time academic ... [and] there has yet to be an appointment not of Anglo–Celtic background.'[95] Moreover, there has only ever been one woman appointed to the High Court (Justice Gaudron was a judge from 1987 to 2003). This can affect the capacity of the Court to maintain public confidence in the institution and its decision-making. As Sir Anthony Mason has argued:

> 'There is a risk ... that an unrepresentative judiciary may result in a loss of confidence in the system, all the more so when judges are called upon to apply community standards as part and parcel of their daily work. Once that is acknowledged, as it must be, it is important that efforts be made to ensure that the judiciary is more representative than it is at the present time and that its composition is fairly balanced.'[96]

This argument should be distinguished from the idea that the judges of the High Court should be 'representative' in the sense that they should 'represent' or specifically advocate the interests of the groups they are seen as belonging to (whether based on gender or other grounds). Courts, unlike Parliaments, are not representative bodies. A central feature of the judiciary is that it is independent of and unresponsive to political pressures. Clearly, the role of a

---

91. S Evans 'Appointment of Justices' in Blackshield, Coper and Williams, n 1 above, p 21.
92. Evans, n 91 above.
93. D Williams 'High Court Appointment' Transcript of Interview with John Mangos, *Sky News*, 17 December 2002, available at www.ag.gov.au as at 16 November 2003.
94. D Williams 'Judicial Independence and the High Court' (1998) 27 Western Australian LR 140 at 149.
95. F Dominello and E Neumann 'Background of Justices' in Blackshield, Coper and Williams, n 1 above, p 48.
96. Sir Anthony Mason, n 6 above, p 7.

judge of the High Court, as spelt out in the judicial oath, is to 'do right to all manner of people according to law without fear or favour, affection or ill-will'.[97] In any case, a seven-person body such as the High Court is ill-suited to any system of quotas based upon the idea that particular judges should represent 'constituencies'.

The lack of diversity in the membership of the High Court has prompted several inquiries into the appointment system for the High Court and judiciary in general. In 1994, the Commonwealth Senate Standing Committee on Legal and Constitutional Affairs concluded in its report *Gender Bias and the Judiciary* that Australian judges 'are overwhelmingly male, former leaders of the Bar, appointed in their early fifties, and products of the non-government education system'.[98] Nearly a decade later, some progress has been made in increasing the number of women on the bench, with women now comprising around 20% of the judiciary overall.[99] However, when the senior judiciary alone is considered, women account for approximately 14% of judges,[100] and when the bench of the highest court is considered, women are currently absent.

The current system of executive appointment to the High Court has raised many concerns, including its lack of transparency. There is no specification by the government of the day of the criteria for appointment to the High Court, other than that of 'merit'. It is often said that only the most qualified or 'best person for the job' is appointed to the Court, based on an assessment of legal ability. In fact, 'merit' in this context means more than which person has the 'best' legal skills, even if such a thing could ever be objectively judged. Governments choose one person from a range of talented (or 'meritorious') candidates, and the choice is influenced by considerations as diverse as their 'politics, state of origin, friendships, and the views of sitting Justices'.[101] These factors demonstrate why every appointment to the High Court is considered 'political', and why considerations of 'merit' cannot be confined to perceptions of a person's legal ability. For example, in part as a reaction to the perceived 'activism' of the Mason High Court in the early to mid-1990s, the then Deputy Prime Minister, Tim Fisher, publicly called for the appointment of 'capital-C conservatives' immediately prior to the federal government's appointment of Justice Ian Callinan to the Bench in February 1998.[102] The government's consideration of the political and legal views of potential appointees is, in itself, not surprising or unusual – except that, on this occasion, it was made explicit.

---

97. High Court of Australia Act 1979 (Cth), s 11 and Schedule.
98. Commonwealth Senate Standing Committee on Legal and Constitutional Affairs *Gender Bias and the Judiciary* (Canberra: The Committee, 1994) p 91.
99. Women accounted for 20.9% of the judiciary overall as at 30 May 2002: R Davis and G Williams 'A Century of Appointments but Only One Woman' (2003) 28 Alternative Law Journal 54.
100. Women accounted for 14.6% of all superior federal (High Court, Federal and Family Court) and superior State and Territory court (Supreme Court and Court of Appeal) judges as at 27 March 2003: Davis and Williams, n 99 above.
101. T Simpson 'Appointments that Might Have Been' in Blackshield, Coper and Williams, n 1 above, p 23.
102. Simpson, n 101 above, p 27.

Several members of the judiciary have commented on the possibility of inappropriate considerations or even bias affecting the current judicial appointment system. Sir Harry Gibbs, a former Chief Justice of the High Court, speaking generally of the appointment process in Australia in 1987, stated that 'most governments in Australia, whatever their political complexion, do from time to time make appointments which fall short' of the appropriate standards.[103] In 1995, Sir Garfield Barwick, a former federal Attorney-General and Chief Justice of the High Court, made similar observations in commenting that: 'Left to politicians, the appointments are not always made exclusively upon the professional standing, character and competence of the appointee.'[104] More recently, in 1999 Justice Bruce McPherson of the Supreme Court of Queensland, as Chairman of the Judicial Conference of Australia, referred to the 'absolute and uncontrolled prerogative of the executive' to make appointments, and contended that: 'There is growing evidence that the power of making judicial appointments is coming to be regarded by governments ... as a form of patronage and a source of influence that can be used to serve their short-term political interests.'[105]

There is a need for reform of the judicial appointments process in Australia.[106] There are insufficient mechanisms in place to guard against the actual or apparent appointment of candidates for partisan reasons. Australia would benefit from the creation of a judicial appointments commission and with the development of relevant criteria for judicial selection. A judicial appointment commission already has wide support in Australia. As early as 1977, Sir Garfield Barwick, then Chief Justice of the High Court, declared that 'the time had arrived' for the curtailment of the exclusive executive power of appointment through the creation of a judicial appointments commission.[107] The establishment of an appointments commission in some form has since been supported on many occasions, including by the 1994 Senate report on *Gender Bias and the Judiciary*,[108] the Australian Law Reform Commission's 1994 inquiry into gender equality in the law[109] and a 1993 study by the federal Attorney-General's Department on *Judicial Appointments – Procedure and Criteria*.[110]

---

103. Sir Harry Gibbs 'The Appointment of Judges' (1987) 61 Australian Law Journal 7 at 9.
104. Sir Garfield Barwick, quoted in M Spry 'Executive and High Court Appointments' in G Lindell and R Bennett *Parliament: The Vision in Hindsight* (Sydney: Federation Press, 2001) pp 419, 447.
105. Justice Bruce McPherson 'Response from the JCA' (July 1999) Law Institute Journal 23 at 25.
106. R Davis and G Williams 'Reform of the Judicial Appointments Process: Gender and the Bench of the High Court of Australia' (2003) 27 Melb ULR 819.
107. Sir Garfield Barwick 'The State of the Australian Judicature' (1977) 51 Australian Law Journal 480 at 494.
108. Commonwealth Senate Standing Committee on Legal and Constitutional Affairs, n 98 above.
109. Australian Law Reform Commission *Equality Before the Law: Women's Equality* Report no 69, Part II (Canberra: Australian Law Reform Commission, 1994) p 202. See also S Tongue 'The Courts as Interpreters of Community Values' (1995) 9(2) Legislative Studies 45 at 49–50.
110. Commonwealth Attorney-General's Department *Judicial Appointments – Procedure and Criteria* (1993). See also J Basten 'Judicial Accountability: A Proposal for a Judicial Commission' (1980) 52(4) Australian Quarterly 477; A Rose 'The Model Judiciary – Fitting in with Modern Government' (1994) 4 Judicial Review 323; G Winterton 'Appointment of Federal Judges in Australia' (1987) 16 Melb ULR 185 at 209–211.

The current process of executive appointment of High Court judges is inadequate. The process should be reformed to ensure that meritorious candidates from diverse backgrounds are not overlooked by government for appointment due to structural problems in the process such as the potential for patronage, and a lack of appropriate criteria. A key element of the reform process is the development of known criteria that gives meaning and substance to the inherently subjective notion of 'merit'. Without redress these issues will continue to pose a threat to the public confidence in the Court, which in turn may compromise its function as an independent judicial institution.

VIII CONCLUSIONS FOR A UNITED KINGDOM SUPREME COURT

The High Court of Australia operates within a distinctive legal framework that combines features of the Westminster and United States systems of government. This hybrid system can make it difficult to draw conclusions from the record of the High Court for a Supreme Court of the United Kingdom. In particular, the Australian system has a tendency to draw sharper lines between the judiciary and the other organs of government than does the United Kingdom system. Nevertheless, the cultural and legal similarities between Australia and the United Kingdom do make such a process worthwhile. Just as it is important for a United Kingdom Supreme Court to remain connected to the legal traditions of England, Scotland, Wales and Northern Ireland, so should it build upon the traditions of other common law nations.

The Australian experience suggests the need for a final court to be independent from Parliament as well as for mechanisms to protect the court from undue politicisation. This is particularly true in dealing with issues of human rights and other social, economic and political controversies. The Human Rights Act 1998 (UK), in incorporating into United Kingdom law the primary provisions of the European Convention on Human Rights, confirms that the highest court in the United Kingdom, unlike the High Court of Australia, has a clear mandate in the protection of human rights. To properly exercise the role cast on the courts by this Act, any Supreme Court should be separate from other arms of government and should operate with actual and apparent independence from the legislature. This could be reflected in the Act creating a new Supreme Court, which might contain a preamble setting out the nature of the Court as independent from Parliament.

Such an Act would also sever the existing connections between the judicial and legislative arms of the House of Lords, as proposed in the Consultation Paper.[111] In order to ensure consistency in approach and the independence of the judiciary as a whole, it would seem inappropriate for any holder of high judicial office to sit and vote in the House of Lords.[112] It may also be necessary to abolish the presumption that holders of high judicial office receive peerages[113] and there may not be a sufficient reason (to act inconsistently with

---

111. The Consultation Paper suggests that members of the Supreme Court should not be able to sit and vote in the House of Lords while members of the Court: Department for Constitutional Affairs, n 8 above, p 27.
112. See Question 8, Department for Constitutional Affairs, n 8 above, p 28.
113. See Question 9, Department for Constitutional Affairs, n 8 above, p 28.

the notion of independence) for retired members of the Supreme Court to be appointed to the House of Lords.[114]

The High Court of Australia not only illustrates the importance of independence in the institutional design of a Supreme Court, but also the need to recognise the potential for politicisation of the Court and its judges. Like the Australian High Court, an independent Supreme Court with a clear human rights mandate could be vulnerable to attack by members of Parliament and the media. This potential may be even greater when the United Kingdom judiciary's connection to Parliament is finally severed. A fully independent institution may be perceived as more separate and isolated from the political process and more vulnerable to attack. To reflect this concern, the Court should be given the tools to communicate its work to the public directly and through the media. This might include an effective Supreme Court website and the services of a public information (or media liaison) officer. However, the Australian experience shows that this can be insufficient to protect the Court and its judges from attack. The development of a new Supreme Court might also therefore include a focus on and the education of those outside of the Supreme Court who are in best position to explain the work of the Court and, where appropriate, to defend it in public.

The Supreme Court should also possess an appropriate judicial appointment process. The Consultation Paper sets out a number of reform possibilities, the most significant reform issue being whether appointments should continue to be made by the Prime Minister on the direct advice of the Lord Chancellor or via a judicial appointments commission. In the foreword to the Consultation Paper *Constitutional Reform: A New Way of Appointing Judges*,[115] Lord Falconer of Thoroton, the new Secretary of State for Constitutional Affairs and the Lord Chancellor (until the position is formally abolished), outlined the context of the reform proposal:

'In a modern democratic society it is no longer acceptable for judicial appointments to be entirely in the hands of a Government Minister. For example, the judiciary is often involved in adjudicating on the lawfulness of actions of the Executive. And so the appointments system must be, and must be seen to be, independent of Government. It must be transparent. It must be accountable. And it must inspire public confidence … Of course the fundamental principle in appointing judges is and must remain selection on merit. However, the Government is committed to opening up the system of appointments, to attract suitably qualified candidates both from a wider range of social backgrounds and from a wider range of legal practice.'[116]

We agree, including with the preference of the United Kingdom government as expressed in that consultation paper for a new judicial appointments commission (including for appointments to the Supreme Court[117]):

114. See Question 7, Department for Constitutional Affairs, n 8 above, p 28.
115. Department for Constitutional Affairs *Constitutional Reform: A New Way of Appointing Judges* CP 10/03 (July 2003).
116. Department for Constitutional Affairs, n 115 above, pp 3–4.
117. Department for Constitutional Affairs, n 8 above, p 30.

'The time has now come for a radical change to the judicial appointments system to enable it to meet the needs and expectations of the public in the 21st century. Any system which is introduced must, in addition to ensuring quality, also guarantee judicial independence. A Commission will provide a guarantee of judicial independence, will make the system for appointing judges more open and more transparent, and will work to make our judiciary more reflective of the society is serves.'[118]

The role of an appointments commission should be to recommend to the minister whom he or she should appoint (or should recommend that the Queen appoint) to the Supreme Court. The commission should assess potential candidates according to categories such as: legal knowledge and experience; professional qualities; personal qualities; and diversity in the judiciary.

From the perspective of two Australians, an independent Supreme Court designed to be separate from the House of Lords in both composition and function appears to be an important and worthwhile reform to the United Kingdom judicial system. In light of the Australian legal system, the current position of the United Kingdom's final court of appeal within the House of Lords does indeed seem an 'anomaly'.[119] The record of the Australian High Court demonstrates the importance of features such as independence and a separation from Parliament for a final court of appeal. This is especially the case for a court that can be expected to deal regularly with issues of human rights and other contentious matters that have the potential to politicise the court.

118. Department for Constitutional Affairs, n 115 above, p 18.
119. Department for Constitutional Affairs, n 8 above, p 11.

Appealing to history: the New Zealand Supreme Court debate

Richard Cornes*

Lecturer in Public Law, Essex University; Barrister and Solicitor of the High Court of New Zealand

A. INTRODUCTION

For a New Zealander one of the odder tourist experiences available in London – and soon to disappear – was to go to the top of Downing Street, and after a brief word with the police officer at the gates, to be ushered in to watch a hearing of the highest court of (though not actually in) New Zealand. Beginning with the arrival of British settlers the Judicial Committee of the Privy Council served as New Zealand's court of final appeal. Sitting in the very heart of London it was possible to hear lawyers with New Zealand accents argue about places and concepts quite literally a world away. Those present for the hearing of *McGuire v Hastings* on 9 May 2001 were even treated to a waita (song) performed for the bench, on which Lord Cooke, New Zealand's most prominent jurist of modern times, was sitting for the last time.[1] The Judicial Committee, led by Lord Bingham and hearing what may be one of its last significant cases from New Zealand, sang no song, swan or other, in return. It was probably their Lordships' last opportunity. On 17 October 2003, the Supreme Court Act (NZ) received Royal Assent; it was the end product of four years' debate, including within that time a General Election in which the matter was included in the (winning) Labour Party's manifesto as well as those of other parties. From 1 January 2004, a New Zealand Supreme Court consisting of the Chief Justice of New Zealand, Dame Sian Elias and four other judges, sitting in Wellington, will begin operation, replacing the Judicial Committee of the Privy Council as the court of last resort for New Zealand litigants.[2]

The debate over ending Privy Council appeals and replacing them with appeals to a New Zealand Supreme Court was lengthy and had three distinct

*   The assistance of Essex University, the AHRB and the British Academy are gratefully acknowledged. My thanks also to Meris Amos and Pat McCabe for commenting on an earlier draft. A paper based on this article was also presented at the 6th World Congress of the International Association of Constitutional Law, Santiago, Chile, in January 2004. Views expressed and any errors are mine alone.

1.   *McGuire v Hastings District Council* [2002] 2 NZLR 577, PC; the singing, and Lord Bingham's response on behalf of the Board, is reported at 585–586.
2.   The first substantive hearings may begin in July 2004, though the Court may deal with matters preliminary to substantive hearings (for example, leave applications) from 1 January 2004. See s 55. (All references to sections of an Act are to the Supreme Court Act 2003 (NZ) unless otherwise stated.)

aspects.[3] First, the 'macro-constitutional' question of whether New Zealand should stop sending cases to the Judicial Committee of the Privy Council, and if so whether Privy Council should be replaced with a domestic second level appellate court; second, a set of more detailed questions about the precise design of a new second level appellate court (for example, how many judges it should have, the nature of its leave procedure, its administrative arrangements); while the final aspect of the Supreme Court debate concerned the manner in which ending Privy Council appeals became just another aspect of the partisan political contest.[4]

This article will focus however on the first aspect of the debate – ie whether New Zealand was right to stop sending cases to the Privy Council.[5] The assumptions underlying the arguments put up by opponents to reform will be considered. It will be argued that underpinning the five sets of arguments

---

3.   For the academic literature see: Bruce Harris 'The New Supreme Court' [2003] NZLJ 15; Richard Elkins and John Ip 'Legislative confirmation and the Supreme Court' [2003] NZLJ 151; Arahia Burkhadrt Macrae 'The Declining Relevance of the Privy Council to Maori Claims' [2002] AULR 950; Noël Cox 'The abolition or retention of the Privy Council as the final court of appeal for New Zealand: conflict between national identity and legal pragmatism' [2002] NZLR 220; Megan Richardson 'The Privy Council and New Zealand' (1997) 46 ICLQ 908; Robyn Martin 'Diverging common law: Invercargill goes to the Privy Council' (1997) 60 MLR 94; Ronald Pol 'Privy Council Appeals – the principle alternatives' [1996] NZLJ 94; Sir Thomas Eichelbaum 'Brooding inhibition – or guiding hand? reflections on the Privy Council appeal' in P Joseph (ed) *Essays on the Constitution* (Wellington: Brookers, 1995); Sean Baldwin 'New Zealand's national legal identity' (1989) 4 Cant LR 173; Paul McHugh 'The appeal of "local circumstances" to the Privy Council' [1987] NZLJ 24; Philip Joseph 'Towards abolition of Privy Council appeals' (1985) 2 Cant LR 273; Peter Burns 'The Judicial Committee of the Privy Council: constitutional bulwark or colonial remnant?' (1984) 5 Otago LR 503; Robin Cooke 'Divergences – England, Australia and New Zealand' [1983] NZLJ 297; and B Cameron 'Appeals to the Privy Council – New Zealand' (1970) 2 Otago LR 172. The key policy documents are: *Appeals to the Privy Council – Report by the Solicitor-General to the Cabinet Strategy Committee on Issues of Termination and Court Structure* (Wellington: Crown Office, 1995), which lead to the Courts Structure Bill 1996 (which, if it had passed, would have ended Privy Council appeals and left New Zealand with no second level appellate court); the Hon Margaret Wilson, Attorney-General *Reshaping New Zealand's Appeal Structure – Discussion Paper* (2000), available at www.crownlaw.govt.nz; *Report of the Advisory Group: Replacing the Privy Council, A New Supreme Court* (Wellington: Office of the Attorney-General, 2002), available at www.crownlaw.govt.nz; and *Report of the Justice and Electoral Committee on the Supreme Court Bill* (the JEC Report) (2003), available at www.clerk.parliament.govt.nz.

4.   In this respect the process of constitutional reform in New Zealand is similar to that in the United Kingdom. Both countries lack any entrenched constitutional document (see also n 63 below), and so, as Foley argues (in *The Politics of the British Constitution* (Manchester: Manchester University Press, 1999)) in relation to the United Kingdom, constitutional issues easily become just another aspect of the political debate. This dynamic is exacerbated in New Zealand where the proportional electoral system has lead to a Parliament in which seven different parties are represented. The non-government parties (of which there are currently five) not only have to differentiate themselves from the government, but also each other – the Supreme Court, for reasons quite distinct from its own merits, was clearly caught up in the competition between not only the government and the opposition, but also between the opposition (or non-government) parties themselves.

against ending appeals was a denial of the contemporary nature of not only the New Zealand Constitution, but also the United Kingdom's, and of the nature of the modern relationship between the two countries: the heart of this was an attempt to resist the inevitable process of decolonisation and New Zealand's path to complete independence. The article will proceed as follows. First, I will discuss the concept of recolonisation as outlined by the New Zealand historian James Belich, explaining how it is relevant to the Supreme Court debate. I will then outline the five sets of arguments put up against ending appeals to the Privy Council. At the end of the article I will return to ask what, if any, relevance the New Zealand debate might have for the United Kingdom as it embarks on its own programme of top court reform. The conclusion will be a suggestion that the United Kingdom consider following New Zealand's example of including a purpose clause in the statute establishing its Supreme Court; such a clause would provide the opportunity to focus on the Court's role, and address concerns that the reform process itself will upset established (unwritten) understandings about the independence of the judicial branch, and the balance between it, and the legislature and executive.

B. DECOLONISATION: THE GOVERNING CONTEXT OF THE NEW ZEALAND SUPREME COURT DEBATE

James Belich characterises much of New Zealand's twentieth-century history as a period of 'recolonisation', his term for 'a renewal and reshaping of links between colony and metropolis [London]'[6] and marking a retreat from a more independent nineteenth-century New Zealand. Belich contends that the concept of recolonisation is a 'key determinant of New Zealand's modern history, without which much of that history cannot be understood'.[7] A hallmark of recolonisation was that the recolonised entity – here, New Zealand – established 'tight links with the homeland . . . [becoming] a town-supply district of London … [while] London became the cultural capital of New Zealand'.[8] Belich goes so far as to say that the recolonialist dynamic 'made New Zealand a virtual Scotland'.[9] One aspect of the colonial, and subsequently, recolonial system was the jurisdiction of the Privy Council, with its role as the 'judicial sovereign' at the heart of empire – seeing that the wisdom of the English common law took root in the colonies, amended only to the limited extent necessary to meet 'local circumstances'.

In the latter part of *Paradise Reforged* Belich goes on to outline how New Zealand was transformed between the late 1960s and the turn of the new century

---

5.   For a discussion of the provisions of the Supreme Court Act 2003 (NZ) and chronology of the reform process see Richard Cornes 'How to create a new Supreme Court: learning from New Zealand' [2004] PL 59.

6.   James Belich *Paradise Reforged: a History of the New Zealanders from the 1880s to the Year 2000* (Auckland: Penguin, 2001) p 29. See also Michael King *The Penguin History of New Zealand* (Auckland: Penguin, 2003), esp ch 30.

7.   Belich, n 6 above, p 548.

8.   Belich, n 6 above, p 30.

9.   Belich, n 6 above, p 547.

from recolonial state to largely independent South Pacific nation. Along with Joseph and Oliver I see decolonisation and the path to full independent nationhood as the 'Darwinian end point of constitutional development';[10] and ending appeals to the Privy Council and establishing a New Zealand Supreme Court is the next logical step in the evolution of the New Zealand Constitution.[11] Green Party Member of Parliament Nandor Tanzcos (who also sat on the Justice and Electoral Committee – the 'JEC' – the committee of the New Zealand Parliament which considered the Supreme Court Bill for much of 2003) captured the importance of the decolonisation process to the debate when he wrote in April 2003 that:

> 'The move to a New Zealand Supreme Court, ending the right of appeal to the Privy Council, is part of a process of decolonisation. It signifies a desire to chart our own course as a Pacific nation taking account of international, as opposed to imperial law. Whether we view it with excitement or with fear depends to some degree on where we stand on this wider issue.'[12]

I suggest that opponents failed not only sufficiently to appreciate the inevitability, and consequences, of decolonisation for New Zealand, they also failed to comprehend the nature of the contemporary United Kingdom, its attitude to its former colonies, and impact on the United Kingdom of European integration. This then is the context within which the five sets of arguments against ending appeals to the Privy Council were set; and to those I now turn.

C. THE FIVE SETS OF ARGUMENTS AGAINST ENDING APPEALS TO THE JUDICIAL COMMITTEE OF THE PRIVY COUNCIL

1. Access to the Privy Council provides New Zealand with access to judges of unsurpassed excellence

New Zealand, opponents said, should retain the Privy Council because it contains some of the best legal minds in the common law world. The National Party's minority report on the Bill (endorsed by the ACT Party) opens with the assertion that the Privy Council 'is a Court of acknowledged excellence'.[13] There are a number of responses to this collection of 'familiar clichés lauding their Lordships' Board'.[14] Perhaps the most appropriate place to begin is to ask just what the National Party understood by the term 'excellence'. The Law Lords are arguably the best judges in the English and Welsh, Scottish and Northern Irish legal systems, being qualified, and having practiced in those

10. Joseph (1985), n 3 above, at 25.
11. Leaving only the issue of New Zealand's use of the Queen as its Head of State to be addressed.
12. Nandor Tanczos 'Court bill window of opportunity' *New Zealand Herald*, 28 April 2003. See also the view of former Prime Minister and constitutional lawyer, Sir Geoffrey Palmer, who described the Privy Council as a 'colonial relic … ill-equipped to remain as New Zealand's final appellate court': reported in 'Palmer sees little use for Privy Council' *New Zealand Herald*, 19 May 2003.
13. The JEC Report, n 3 above, p 56.
14. Joseph (1985), n 3 above, at 273.

systems. The National Party's position assumes these judges, who hold no qualifications in the law of New Zealand, are nevertheless the 'best' judges New Zealand could possibly have on its final court of appeal. This position is only sustainable if one sees the law of New Zealand as still simply a sub-set of the common law of England,[15] varying only in so far as necessary to take into account 'local circumstances'; rather than a now quite separate, autochthonous legal order.[16] There remain of course many similarities between the common law in England and Wales and in New Zealand, but an understanding of the common law in England and Wales does not qualify a judge to understand the common law of what is now a quite distinct legal system – something, as we shall see below, the Privy Council has acknowledged.[17]

Furthermore, the National Party's position failed to appreciate that an 'indefinable part of a judge's qualification ... is his intimate knowledge of the society in which he resides and upon whose members and institutions he sits in judgment'.[18] As Lady Hale has argued, making the case generally for a diverse judiciary:

> 'The judiciary may or should be independent of Government and Parliament but ultimately *we are the link between them and the people.* We are the instrument by which the will of Parliament and Government is enforced upon the people. We are also the instrument which keeps the other organisms of the State, the Police and those who administer the laws, under control.'[19]

Clearly a court, the majority of whose members are selected by the British government, from British judges, can never be a link between the New Zealand government and the people of New Zealand.

Opponents to ending Privy Council appeals also failed to take into account criticisms made in the United Kingdom of the Law Lords' performance, tending to hold the Law Lords up as beyond all criticism. The Law Lords, while being judges of acknowledged excellence, are nevertheless not beyond all criticism. Consider, for example, the procedural error made by Lord Hoffmann in the first Pinochet case;[20] the long-running concerns of criminal lawyers;[21] or the current of disquiet in Scotland about their Lordships ability to deal with Scottish

---

15.   I deliberately single out England because the underlying view indicated by this argument is the now outdated one which identifies all the of the United Kingdom as 'English'; not taking into account the three distinct legal systems, or the possible divergence of the law in Wales. See eg the submission of the New Zealand Bar Association, referred to at n 34 below.

16.   See discussion of New Zealand's distinctive legal culture in Baldwin, and Cooke, both n 3 above.

17.   See discussion at p 218 below.

18.   Joseph (1985), n 3 above, at 296.

19.   Brenda Hale 'Equality and the judiciary – why should we want more women judges' [2001] PL 489 (emphasis added).

20.   See generally, Diana Woodhouse (ed) *The Pinochet Case: a Legal and Constitutional Analysis* (Oxford: Hart Publishing, 2000).

21.   See discussion by Louis Blom-Cooper and Gavin Drewry in Brice Dickson and Paul Carmichael (eds) *The House of Lords: Its Parliamentary and Judicial Roles* (Oxford: Hart Publishing, 1999).

matters;[22] or the more general critique made by Robertson based on an analysis of 407 cases between 1986 and 1995.[23] Also relevant, given the similarities between the New Zealand's Bill of Rights Act and the Human Rights Act 1998, is Barendt's critique of their Lordships' first major freedom of speech case – *R (on the application of the Prolife Alliance) v BBC*.[24] Of this case Barendt notes that not only was it the most important, but it was also, 'the most disappointing' and that 'passages in the speeches of the House of Lords are baffling, or, to be frank, obscure'.[25] Finally, Barendt ends by noting that the Law Lords had failed 'to do justice to the legal arguments'.[26]

Finally, the idea that the Law Lords are the best qualified judges to serve on New Zealand's final court, contains within it, implicitly, the idea that the New Zealand cannot provide judges of as high a quality as the United Kingdom (accepting for the moment that quality vis-à-vis New Zealand does not require any qualification in New Zealand law). A number of submitters to the JEC argued that: 'New Zealand lacks the judicial talent to maintain a full Supreme Court of quality equivalent to the current standard of the Privy Council.'[27] There are four points to make.

First, the fact that the New Zealand judges in the Court of Appeal are overturned by the Judicial Committee is not a reflection on the ability of the Court of Appeal judges. The Law Lords sitting in the House of Lords overturn each of the three first level appellate courts in the United Kingdom with roughly the same frequency, if not slightly more often, than the Judicial Committee overturns the Court of Appeal. Apart from the distinct functions of the two levels of court, the pressures on first level appellate court judges, in terms of dealing with a relatively high volume of cases, are significant. Second level appellate judges carry out their task at much greater leisure. Apart from when they have sat in the Judicial Committee, New Zealand judges have never had the opportunity to perform as second level appellate judges.

Second, until recently, presumably in anticipation of reform, judges of the Court of Appeal have been appointed Privy Councillors, thus qualifying them to sit on the Judicial Committee. There is certainly no suggestion in United Kingdom legal circles that the New Zealand judges were any less able than the British ones. There has even been the suggestion that the other Privy Council judges may be overly deferential to a single visiting New Zealand judge.[28]

Third, New Zealander's should realise that judgments of the New Zealand Court of Appeal are themselves cited in other top courts – particularly the

22. See James Chalmers 'Scottish appeals and the proposed Supreme Court' (forthcoming, 2004) ELR.
23. David Robertson *Judicial Discretion in the House of Lords* (Oxford: Oxford University Press, 1998).
24. [2003] 2 All ER 977.
25. Eric Barendt 'Free speech and abortion' [2003] PL 580 at 580–581.
26. Barendt, n 25 above, at 591.
27. The JEC report, n 3 above, p 10.
28. See discussion in Peter Spiller 'Lord Cooke of Thorndon as Lord of Apeal: The New Zealand Dimension' (2002) 10 Waikato LR 55–66. Cf the deference the non-Scottish judges show to the Scottish judges in Scottish cases: see Chalmers, n 22 above; and Roderick Munday 'Judicial Configurations – Permutations of the court and properties of judgment' [2002] CLJ 612.

Australian, the United Kingdom's and Canadian – this is a significant endorsement of the abilities of the New Zealand judges. And finally, the deference the Judicial Committee accords the Court of Appeal (discussed below) is itself an indication by the United Kingdom Court of the quality of many of the Court of Appeal's judgments.[29]

2.   Reform will swap the 'objectivity' of the Law Lords for a politically tainted, activitist New Zealand Court

The next set of arguments put up against ending New Zealand's use of the Privy Council revolved around a view that the Privy Council was a court of unimpeachable objectivity, that its judges decided matters without any hint of politics entering into their judgments, and finally that it kept an at times overly activist New Zealand Court of Appeal in check. The JEC reported that 'many submitters expressed admiration for the Privy Council's objectivity and distance from local conditions'.[30] Associated with this was a concern that the reform process itself, and the rancorous political debate into which it descended, was undermining the unwritten understandings concerning the independence and impartiality of the judicial branch. Further, that a New Zealand-based court would be composed of judges appointed for their ideological friendliness to the current Labour government, take an activist approach to the judicial role, and destabilise the existing balance between the judicial, legislative and executive branches.

The concern about judicial appointments arose because the Bill – and indeed the Act – continued the New Zealand practice of leaving the appointment of the judges entirely a matter for the executive. All High Court, Court of Appeal and Supreme Court judges are appointed by the Governor-General, acting according to constitutional convention, on the advice of the Attorney-General, or, in the case of the Chief Justice, the Prime Minister. The convention has also been that appointments are made solely on the basis of merit, with a candidate's political or ideological views being irrelevant; reform, opponents contended, would unsettle this. Finally, concern about judicial appointments was heightened by the fact the while the Chief Justice (who had been appointed by a previous National Party Prime Minister) was in post, Labour Attorney-General Margaret Wilson would get to appoint the other four (as it transpired)[31] judges who would make up the new Supreme Court's first full bench.

The concern raised by opponents to reform, concerning judicial appointments, was perhaps the best argument they made. People, unfairly, though understandably, did not trust the Attorney-General not to bring her own political agenda to bear in selecting the Supreme Court's first full bench. Although suggestions that the Bill be amended to establish either some form of appointments commission, or to include a role for Parliament in the appointment process were resisted, the government did eventually make two important concessions. First, the Attorney-General and subsequently the Prime

29. See discussion at pp 218-219 below.
30. The JEC report, n 3 above, p 13.
31. A further permanent judge may be appointed: s 17(1)(b). The Court's quorum for dealing with substantive matters is five judges: s 27(1).

Minister made clear their preference for the most senior members of the Court of Appeal to be the first judges to join the Chief Justice on the new Court. And second, the Attorney-General indicated that in relation to the first set of appointments she would follow the advice of an ad hoc advisory committee composed of the Chief Justice, the Solicitor-General, and a former Governor-General.[32] The government has also announced that it would be producing a consultation paper on judicial appointments in 2004 and it would seem likely that the days of unfettered executive discretion over judicial appointments in New Zealand are over.

In order to address the concern that the new Court would disturb the existing balance between the judges, the legislature and the executive, a sub-clause was added to the Bill's purpose clause, what became section 3 of the Act. Section 3 begins by setting out the Act's basic purpose, ie to establish a New Zealand Supreme Court, 'to recognise that New Zealand is an independent nation with its own history and traditions', 'enable important legal matters, including matters relating to the Treaty of Waitangi to be resolved with an understanding of New Zealand conditions, history and traditions', and to 'improve access to justice'. Subsection 2, inserted during the Bill's committee stage, further provides that the Act is not intended to affect 'New Zealand's continuing commitment to the rule of law and the sovereignty of Parliament'.

It is reasonably clear that the subsection was inserted to warn the Court off taking an overly activist approach in its approach to deciding cases and developing the law. While that may have been one of the reasons for the clause's insertion, the clause may have wider application. Given that there is no agreement among constitutional lawyers about the precise scope of either doctrine, the subsection may open the way for the Court to set out its own understanding of these concepts. Further, while reference to the continuing commitment of the parliamentary sovereignty may serve to encourage judicial discretion, the commitment to the rule of law also gives the Court the democratic legitimacy, it may be argued, to act as the guardian of the independence of the judicial branch, developing the common law as necessary to protect the judicial branch from any attempt by the other branches to limit its established constitutional role.[33]

3. The Law Lords keep New Zealand law 'on track'

Keeping with the implicit distrust of New Zealand judges, opponents of reform put forward a collection of arguments all of which suggested that New Zealand needed the 'trainer wheels' of the Privy Council to ensure that the common law in New Zealand law remained 'on track', or more specifically, the same (so far as possible) as that in England and Wales. The New Zealand Bar Association submitted that the Privy Council appeal was of value because it ensured 'the

---

32. And on 10 November 2003, the most senior four judges from the Court of Appeal were named as Justices of the Supreme Court. They are: Thomas Gault, Sir Kenneth Keith, Peter Blanchard and Andrew Tipping.
33. For example, by resisting attempts to restrict the courts' judicial review role via exclusion clauses.

conformity of [New Zealand] commercial law ... with English [*sic*] commercial law'.[34]

The first response to this argument is that for some time now the Law Lords have made clear that they do not see it as their role to second guess the New Zealand Court of Appeal an increasing range of cases. In *Invercargill City Council v Hamlin* the Judicial Committee was faced with an appeal in which the Court of Appeal's approach to the tort of negligence was diametrically opposed to a recent re-direction of the law of negligence in England and Wales. Speaking for the Board, which declined to overturn the Court of Appeal, Lord Lloyd of Berwick said:

> 'In the present case the Judges in the New Zealand Court of Appeal were consciously departing from English case law on the ground that conditions in New Zealand are different. Were they entitled to do so? The answer must surely be Yes. The ability of the common law to adapt itself to the differing circumstances of the countries in which it has taken root, is not a weakness, but one of its great strengths. Were it not so, the common law would not have flourished as it has, with all the common law countries learning from each other. ... [T]he New Zealand Court of Appeal should not be deflected from developing the common law of New Zealand (nor the Board from affirming their decisions) by the consideration that the House of Lords ... have not regarded an identical development as appropriate in the English setting.'[35]

Perhaps even more remarkable was the approach of the Privy Council in *Lange v Atkinson*.[36] The case concerned the question of the defences available in response to an allegation of defamation and important constitutional questions concerning the very basics of the operation of democracy in New Zealand, ie balancing freedom of expression in relation to political matters with an individual's right (via the tort of defamation) to their reputation. The New Zealand Court of Appeal's initial judgment on the nature of the defences to defamation was directly at odds, not only with Australian precedent, but also with a unanimous judgment of the same Law Lords (including, it should be noted, Lord Cooke of Thorndon) on an almost identical appeal in which they were giving judgment in the Appellate Committee of the House of Lords on the same day.[37] Rather than overturning the New Zealand Court of Appeal the Board remitted the matter back to the Court of Appeal for reconsideration, emphasising that the Court of Appeal could, if it chose, diverge from the approach taken in England and Wales. Lord Nicholls of Birkenhead, giving judgment for the Board, stated:

> 'For some years Their Lordships' Board has recognised the limitations on its role as an appellate tribunal in cases where the decision depends upon

---

34. New Zealand Bar Association *Submissions in Respect of the Supreme Court Bill* (2003) p 3.
35. *Invercargill City Council v Hamlin* [1996] 1 NZLR 513 at 519–520.
36. *Lange v Atkinson* [2000] 1 NZLR 257.
37. The United Kingdom case was *Reynolds v Times Newspapers Ltd* [1999] 3 WLR 1010.

considerations of local public policy. The present case is a prime instance of such a case. As noted by Elias J and the Court of Appeal, different countries have reached different conclusions on the issue arising on this appeal. The Courts of New Zealand are much better placed to assess the requirements of the public interest in New Zealand than Their Lordships' Board. Accordingly, on this issue the Board does not substitute its own views, if different, for those of the New Zealand Court of Appeal.'[38]

Emphasising the Judicial Committee's advisory position, and the pre-eminent role of the New Zealand Court of Appeal, Lord Nicholls went on to state:

'Their Lordships emphasise that they do not suggest that at the further hearing the New Zealand Courts are bound to adopt either the English of the Australian solutions. *Nor do they seek to influence the New Zealand courts towards either of these solutions.* If satisfied that the privilege favoured in the judgment now under appeal is right for New Zealand, although wider than has been held acceptable in either England or Australia, *the New Zealand Court of Appeal is entitled to maintain that position.*'[39]

The case returned to the Court of Appeal, and it, speaking significantly through a single judgment, re-affirmed its earlier view.[40] Certainly in this case the Court of Appeal was, as a matter of fact, the top court.[41] While these cases do indicate that the Privy Council would frequently defer to the Court of Appeal, it was still necessary for that Court to justify departing from the approach taken by the House of Lords by reference to 'local circumstances'. The *default position* was that the law in New Zealand should conform with the law in England and Wales – this was surely incompatible with the need for a state situated in the South Pacific, whose primary trading partners are in its region of the world, to develop legal principles appropriate for its own circumstances.

The next point to note is that the argument put forward by the Bar Association, that it was desirable for the commercial law of New Zealand to conform with that of England, rests on an outdated understanding of the nature of the common law in England and Wales. The Bar Association and other opponents, especially business concerns, failed to appreciate the impact on the law in England and Wales of both the European Community, and the European Convention on Human Rights via the Human Rights Act 1998. There were some rare exceptions – Jack Hodder (editor of the weekly legal newsletter *Capital Letter*), presenting what he termed a 'conservative case for reform', argued that New Zealand needed to end use of the Privy Council because the Human Rights Act was going to make the Law Lords far more rights orientated and activist.[42]

---

38. *Lange v Atkinson* [2000] 1 NZLR 257 at 262 (emphasis added).

39. *Lange v Atkinson* [2000] 1 NZLR 257 at 263.

40. [2000] 3 NZLR 385, CA.

41. Richardson goes so far as to suggest that the Privy Council's deference to the New Zealand Court of Appeal may have been fuelled by a desire to secure New Zealand's continued use of the Privy Council. See Richardson, n 3 above, at 910.

42. Jack Hodder *Submissions on the Supreme Court Bill* (2003) pt V.

Finally, opponents of reform sought to turn the argument, that ending appeals was a necessary step in New Zealand's path for full independence, around, characterising the pro-reform position as exhibiting an 'inward-looking nationalism'.[43] The National Party minority report on the Bill included the following comment: 'We consider that justice transcends nationalism.' While the ACT Party observed that the:

> 'Main reason offered by most supporters, including retired Judges and academics, was that the right of appeal was a humiliating remnant of colonialism. The case for abolition never got more penetrating than that.'

These comments err in assuming that the New Zealand legal system will necessarily be more insular as a result of ending appeals to the Privy Council. On the contrary, building on the institutional links which already exist (the Chief Justice already takes part in the Australasian Conference of Chief Justices) the new Supreme Court will be far better placed to integrate, where appropriate, legal concepts arising in the case law of other countries (including the United Kingdom) into the law of New Zealand than the Privy Council could possibly be. This is of particular importance in relation to the commercial law of Australia, given the commitments made in the Closer Economic Relations (CER) agreement to harmonise the commercial laws of both countries.[44] One might go so far as to argue that opponents of reform were themselves driven by a narrow nationalism: the narrow nationalism of a recolonial New Zealand that looked only to the United Kingdom, rather than to the wider world, and most pertinently, its CER partner, Australia. In the longer term it may well be that further evolution of the institutional links between the two country's judicial branches may be appropriate.

4.   The Law Lords are necessary for reasons relating to the Treaty of Waitangi

A.   INTRODUCTION

It would be condescending, and inaccurate, to think in terms of a single Maori position on abolition of the Privy Council appeal; certainly a significant portion of Maori society was opposed, but there were also voices in favour of reform. Maori, like New Zealand society as a whole, were split between those who wished to retain an older conception of New Zealand society, and of traditional Maori society within it, and those who wanted to push for the evolution of New Zealand society in general, and Maori society in particular. Noting the split within Maoridom, John Tamihere, Associate Minister of Maori Affairs, wrote in June, 2003 that:

---

43. Cox, n 3 above, at 233.
44. See discussion in: Michael Kirby and Philip Joseph 'Trans-Tasman Relations – Towards 2000 and Beyond'; and John Farrar 'Closer Economic Relations and Harmonisation of Law Between Australia and New Zealand', both in Joseph (ed) (1995), n 3 above.

'What is commonly held to be the opinion of 'Maori' is the opinion of an elite few, representing an iwi-based [traditional tribal based] perspective that is totally different to the opinions of the majority of Maori, who live in our cities.'[45]

Tamihere captured the nature of split well: traditionalist Maori leaders had warmed to the Privy Council after it overturned the Court of Appeal in *Treaty Tribes Coalition v Urban Maori Authorities (the Maori Fisheries case)*.[46] At the heart of that case was a contest over a two views of Maori society: a traditional one, put forward by the Treaty Tribes Coalition (representing established tribes), and a modern one put forward by the Urban Maori Authorities. The Court of Appeal had decided that the term 'iwi' ('the people of tribes') included urban Maori without tribal affiliations for the purposes of the Maori Fisheries Act 1989, under which Maori fishing quotas were being allocated. The Treaty Tribes Coalition sought to restrict the definition of 'iwi' to traditional tribes, which would have the effect of excluding urban Maori from allocation of fishing quotas. Macrae notes of the case that: 'the traditional dichotomy of Maori versus the Crown was not evident in [the] case'... [and that] while "traditional" Maori interests were upheld, this was at the expense of urban Maori.'[47]

The traditionalist Maori view, which was the more prominent, was put forward in Parliament by the main opposition party (the National Party), and the New Zealand First Party (also an opposition party).[48] The modernist view was most clearly articulated in Parliament by John Tamihere, Associate Minister of Maori Affairs.[49] To some extent National and New Zealand First were in competition with each other to attract the support of Maori opponents in order to further their parties' positions in the polls.

B. THE THREE ARGUMENTS MADE BY MAORI OPPONENTS

First, it was said, the Privy Council was necessary to protect Maori interests under the Treaty of Waitangi against encroachment from the New Zealand government. Or, as the JEC records: 'Maori have faith in the Privy Council because it is independent, and do not have a similar faith in the New Zealand

---

45. John Tamihere 'Maori verdict should back home-grown court' *New Zealand Herald*, 28 June 2003. John Tamihere is a leading advocate for urban Maori.
46. [1997] 1 NZLR 513.
47. Macrae, n 3 above, at 970. It should be noted however that while the Privy Council overturned the Court of Appeal, it did so only on the limited procedural ground that the Court of Appeal had failed to give the parties the opportunity to address it on the meaning of the term 'iwi'. It referred the substantive question concerning definition back to the New Zealand courts – acknowledging its lack of competence in Treaty issues. A New Zealand-based Supreme Court would have been able to deal with both the Court of Appeal's procedural error *and* address the substantive question.
48. It was the National Party's reliance on the New Zealand First Party (which has always been opposed to ending Privy Council appeals) to form a government after the 1996 election which lead to it abandoning the Courts Structure Bill 1996 (see n 3 above).
49. Outside Parliament see the submission of the National Urban Maori Authority to the JEC.

courts.'[50] Reviewing recent substantive cases concerning the Treaty in both the Court of Appeal and the Privy Council, Arahia Macrae comes to the conclusion that:

> 'It cannot be said that the [Court of Appeal] is not impartial or that it lacks independence from the executive. Therefore, it cannot realistically be maintained that the Privy Council is necessary as a guardian of Maori interests against the government, or the impropriety of the resident judiciary.'[51]

The reliance placed by some Maori on a handful of favourable Privy Council rulings from the late nineteenth and early twentieth centuries, in Macrae's view, denied 'one hundred years of constitutional and social development'.[52]

The second reason put forward by Maori opponents to reform was that the Privy Council was necessary to ensure the enforcement and recognition of the Treaty. The JEC recorded that one 'submitter expressed concern that if the Treaty of Waitangi was not incorporated fully into New Zealand law, the Supreme Court judiciary could relegate Maori to second class citizenship'.[53] Yet it is the modern Court of Appeal which, initially enabled by increasingly frequent references to the Treaty in statutes, has secured the constitutional status of the Treaty in modern New Zealand law.[54] Furthermore it is now clear that in relation to *substantive matters of Treaty jurisprudence* the Privy Council has considerable respect for the Court of Appeal. In the *Maori Fisheries case* while, as noted above,[55] the Privy Council overturned the Court of Appeal because, in the Privy Council's view the Court of Appeal had breached the rules of natural justice, in relation to substantive questions under the Treaty Lord Goff said:

> 'Their Lordships are very conscious of the important role played by the Courts of New Zealand, and the Court of Appeal in particular, in relation to Maori under the Treaty of Waitangi; and they fully recognise the depth of knowledge and experience of the Court of Appeal in this area.'[56]

The substantive question in that case, concerning the meaning of 'iwi' in contemporary New Zealand was not one which the Privy Council was prepared to address, preferring, as noted, to refer it back to the New Zealand courts.

The final argument put forward for retention of the Privy Council was that it represented an important direct link to the sovereign, as the decedent of the Maori's initial Treaty partner (Queen Victoria). However, Queen Elizabeth II will remain Queen in right of New Zealand, ending appeals to the Privy Council does nothing *legally* to the nature of that relationship. The JEC summed up the view of a number of Maori submitters that: 'Maori have a right of access to

---

50. The JEC report, n 3 above; and Macrae, n 3 above, at 969.
51. Macrae, n 3 above, at 971.
52. Macrae, n 3 above, at 970.
53. The JEC report, n 3 above, p 11.
54. Macrae, n 3 above, at 975, comments: 'The New Zealand Court of Appeal has been more willing in recent times to recognise and enforce Maori claims that the Privy Council.'
55. *Treaty Tribes Coalition v Urban Maori Authorities* [1997] 1 NZLR 513. See n 47 above.
56. *Treaty Tribes Coalition v Urban Maori Authorities* [1997] 1 NZLR 513 at 522.

the Sovereign through the Privy Council under Article 3 of the Treaty of Waitangi, to abolish appeals to the Privy Council would be prejudicial to Maori.'[57] This view was contradicted by the advice of the Crown Law Office, which concluded that the Bill was 'neutral in relation to the Treaty and its principles'.[58] While Macrae says of it: 'of any argument Maori could raise in opposition ... this is the least convincing.'[59]

5. The continued reliance on free appellate services, and possibly even expanding New Zealand's use of the Privy Council, is appropriate in the context of the modern relationship between New Zealand and the United Kingdom

The final, and least attractive set of arguments for retaining the Privy Council saw opponents of reform most crudely attempting to cling to the notion of a mother-England/dependent-colony relationship between the United Kingdom and New Zealand. There were two strands to this argument, neither of them terribly attractive. First, opponents said, 'the cost of the Supreme Court will fall upon the New Zealand taxpayer [while] the British taxpayer pays for the Privy Council'.[60] Second, opponents went on, if the problem was that too few cases go to the Privy Council (in its entire history it heard only eight criminal cases) then the answer is to broaden appeal rights,[61] provide more funding for litigants who want to take their case to London, expand its membership so that it includes more New Zealand judges, and even have it sit in New Zealand. The possibility that the United Kingdom could afford to send even one Law Lord to New Zealand on a regular basis (given that one or often two are already unable to sit judicially because of public inquiry work, and another one may be engaged in sitting on the Hong Kong Court of Final Appeal) is slight; and a New Zealand-based Privy Council, made up of predominantly New Zealand judges, would appear to be the very thing being resisted – a domestic Supreme Court. Finally, opponents were clearly unaware of the argument beginning to be heard in the United Kingdom that it was to time to stop burdening the United Kingdom's most senior judges with the task of hearing cases from the United Kingdom's former colonies. Sir Thomas Legg QC, a former Permanent Secretary in the Lord Chancellor's Department, said recently that he had:

> 'Never fully bought the argument that we are somehow bound to provide an elegant court and very senior judges to determine cases for the benefit of other independent and self-governing nations, just because they want us to. The historical basis is now very ancient history indeed, and the judge-power requirements of the Judicial Committee impinge seriously on those

---

57. The JEC report, n 3 above, p 11.
58. The advice of the Crown Law Office is included in the JEC report, n 3 above, p 71.
59. Macrae, n 3 above, at 973.
60. The JEC report, n 3 above, p 13.
61. National Party minority report, in the JEC report, n 3 above, p 57. See also the submission of the New Zealand Bar Association, n 34 above, para 8.

of Britain's highest court, which must be our main concern. I personally would favour a polite declaration of independence.'[62]

D. CONCLUDING REMARKS

1. Introduction

Despite all the obvious differences between the United Kingdom (a country of close to 60 million people) and New Zealand (with a population of approximately four million), the two countries do have in common one important constitutional fundamental. In each country the Parliament (unicameral in New Zealand, bicameral in the United Kingdom) is, at least in legal theory, sovereign. While there may be laws of constitutional significance, there are none that are not amenable or repealable by a simple parliamentary majority.[63] Unwritten norms and principles – principles that in other states would likely be contained within specially protected instruments – underpin their constitutional systems. This common flexibility at the heart of the New Zealand and United Kingdom constitutions means, I suggest, that there is the potential for comparative lesson learning between the United Kingdom and New Zealand. In this final section I have two points to make concerning what the United Kingdom may be able to learn from New Zealand about establishing a new Supreme Court. I make these points on a tentative basis, setting them out as suggestions for further investigation and debate as the United Kingdom reform process unfolds.

2. The arguments for and against reform in the United Kingdom will have a similar 'style' to those in New Zealand

The debate in New Zealand may be viewed as a contest between constitutional modernisers and constitutional traditionalists. The modernisers relied relatively heavily on arguments for reform based on abstract principle – reform, they argued, was necessary not because there was an obvious catastrophic failure (though there were some obvious weaknesses) in the existing system, but because the existing system was incompatible with New Zealand's status as an independent state. They were resisted by constitutional traditionalists, who sought to protect an older, established view of the constitution. Furthermore, the constitutional traditionalists relied heavily on a pragmatic defence of the status quo: the Privy Council, they said, works well, nothing of like quality could be created in New Zealand, and reform itself would be risky and carried

---

62. Sir Thomas Legg QC 'The Supreme Court', a paper presented at a conference at the Cambridge Centre for Public Law entitled 'Judicial Reform: Function, Appointment, and Structure', 4 October 2003.
63. Although s 268 of the Electoral Act 1993 (which reserves other statutory provisions, eg, concerning the holding of regular elections, stipulating that they can only be altered by either a 75% majority in Parliament, or a 50% majority at an ordinary poll of electors) can itself be amended by a 50% majority vote in Parliament.

the potential to destabilise unwritten norms concerning the operation, and role, of the final court of appeal within the constitution.

The split between the Law Lords in favour of a United Kingdom Supreme Court, and those not, has similarities to the arguments between modernisers and traditionalists seen in New Zealand. The United Kingdom modernisers (Lords Bingham, Steyn, Saville and Walker), while clearly not of the view that reform is necessary because the Appellate and Judicial Committees are in any sense failing institutions, base their case for reform on a need for the United Kingdom to adhere to a modern understanding of the need for the separation of the judicial branch from the other branches. In these Law Lords' submission the:

'Functional separation of the judiciary at all levels from the legislature and the executive ... [is] a cardinal feature of a modern, democratic state governed by the rule of law ... [and it is] important, as a matter of constitutional principle, that this functional separation should be reflected in the major constitutional institutions of the state, of which the final court of appeal is certainly one.'[64]

While the six sceptics in the House of Lords – Lords Nicholls, Hoffmann, Hope, Hutton, Millet and Rodger take the view that:

'On pragmatic grounds, the proposed change is unnecessary and will be harmful. The present arrangements work well. ... The Law Lords presence in the House is of benefit to the Law Lords, to the House, and to others including litigants. Appeals are heard in a unique, suitably prestigious, setting for this country's court of final appeal. The "House of Lords" as a judicial body is recognised by that name throughout the common law world. ... The Law Lords who do not support the proposed change consider these real advantages need not be, and should not be, put in jeopardy.'[65]

3. Reform will destabilise unwritten norms and conventions, necessitating their re-affirmation in statutory form

My final point is that one of the fears implicit in the conservatives' opposition to reform is well founded. While they may go too far in claiming that reform will be positively harmful, it is true that the very fact of reform will disturb unwritten conventions concerning the independence of the judicial branch,

---

64. *The Law Lords' response to the Government's consultation paper on Constitutional reform: a Supreme Court for the United Kingdom* (2003) para 2, p 1. Cf the lengthier arguments in favour of reform made by Lords Bingham and Steyn: Lord Bingham of Cornhill 'A New Supreme Court for the United Kingdom' 1 May 2001, University College London; and Lord Steyn 'The case for a Supreme Court' (2002) 118 LQR 382. And, against reform: Lord Cooke of Thorndon 'The Law Lords: an endangered heritage' (2003) 119 LQR 49; and the evidence of a number of former Lords of Appeal in Ordinary to the Royal Commission on Reform of the House of Lords. See generally: Charles Banner and Alexander Deane *Off with their wigs! – Judicial revolution in modern Britain* (London: Policy Exchange, 2003).

65. *The Law Lords' response to the Government's consultation paper on Constitutional reform: a Supreme Court for the United Kingdom* (2003) para 2, p 1.

the non-politicisation of the judiciary, and the constitutional balance between the three branches of the state. The solution to this is to record in statutory form constitutional principles and practices which had previously been dealt with as matters of unwritten convention. In New Zealand this has meant the beginning of a move to establish an advisory commission on judicial appointments.[66] While the Attorney-General initially resisted this, it became clear as the Bill went through Parliament that it would no longer be possible for her, especially as the minister in charge of reform, to continue to have an unfettered discretion over who to recommend to the Governor-General for appointment. Similarly in the United Kingdom, where equally, I suggest, it will not be possible as is contemplated as an option in the consultation paper on a Supreme Court, for appointments to the Supreme Court to be solely a matter for the Executive.[67]

The other concern in New Zealand was that establishing a new Supreme Court would destabilise: the existing balance between the three branches of government; the independence of the judiciary; and respect for the Treaty of Waitangi. The New Zealand solution to this was to record in the statute's purpose clause matters which had previously been governed by unwritten convention – for example, the commitment to importance of the sovereignty of Parliament, and the rule of law.[68] Reform in the United Kingdom is also likely to raise concerns about matters currently dealt with by unwritten understandings: the sovereignty of Parliament, the importance of judicial independence, and the distinctiveness of the United Kingdom's three legal systems.[69] One answer to these concerns would be, I suggest, to follow New Zealand's example and insert a purpose clause into the United Kingdom legislation establishing a Supreme Court. I end then with a possible purpose clause (modelled on the New Zealand equivalent) for the statute establishing the United Kingdom Supreme Court.

PURPOSE

(1) The purpose of this Act is:
    a. to establish the Supreme Court of the United Kingdom –
        i. to recognise the importance of the functional separation of the judicial branch from the legislative and executive branches; and

---

66. See discussion at p 217 above.
67. Department for Constitutional Affairs *Constitutional Reform: a Supreme Court for the United Kingdom* CP 11/03 (July 2003) para 39, p 29, available at www.dca.gov.uk.
68. See discussion at p 217 above.
69. Of note here is the fact that the speed with which reform is taking place in the United Kingdom will most likely make it necessary to use a Sewel motion to deal with those aspects of Supreme Court reform which touch on the Scottish legal system (justice being a devolved matter); the lack of foresight to allow for a proper debate of the issue in the Scottish Parliament is lamentable. See the evidence of Lord Hope on 2 December 2003 to the Constitutional Affairs Committee, in particular His Lordship's response to Q289 and Q300, available at www.parliament.the-stationary-office.co.uk.

      ii.   enable important legal matters, including matters arising from the devolution settlement to be dealt with by a single final court of appeal; and

    b.   to provide for the court's jurisdiction and related matters; and

    c.   to end the judicial functions of the Appellate Committee of the House of Lords and the Judicial Committee of the Privy Council in relation to the United Kingdom.

(2)   Nothing in this Act affects the United Kingdom's continuing commitment to:

    a.   the independence of the judicial branch;

    b.   the rule of law and respect for fundamental human rights;

    c.   the sovereignty of Parliament;

    d.   the distinct existence of separate legal systems within England and Wales, Scotland, and Northern Ireland; or

    e.   the enforcement of obligations arising from its membership in the European Union.

Such a clause would, as in New Zealand, provide Parliament with the opportunity to focus explicitly on the role of the Supreme Court in the United Kingdom Constitution, to reaffirm important constitutional principles which may be disturbed by the reform process, and launch the new Supreme Court with a clear direction to its judges of what is expected of them.[70]

---

70. Cf discussion in the *Judges' Council Response to the Consultation Papers on Constitutional Reform* of the need to identify in legislation the respective roles of the judiciary and the government, paras 40–43, pp 14–15. The document is available at www.dca.gov.uk/judicial/pdfs/jcresp.pdf.

Composing a judiciary: reflections on proposed reforms in the United Kingdom on how to change the voices of and the constituencies for judging

Judith Resnik*
Arthur Liman Professor of Law, Yale Law School

I. NEW DEMANDS FOR AND ON JUDICIARIES

I sit an ocean and a legal culture away. Asked to comment on reforms in England and Wales, my response is shaped by knowledge of the legal system of the United States, which shares aspirations similar with and has been much influenced by the judicial system of England and Wales, but is also very different from it.

Yet judicial systems on both sides of the Atlantic (and in many other places) have to face difficult challenges. How can governments create, select, and equip a sufficient number of individual judges to respond to the tens of thousands of complainants who come before them? What constituencies will support and fund judges, while respecting the idea and the practice that a judiciary is specially situated – authorised by and paid for the state to sit in judgment of the state? Around the world, we use the shorthand of 'judicial independence' to make the point that judges are no ordinary employees of the state because they must make decisions in individual cases that may conflict with agendas of the very governments that empower them.

To enable judges to render fair judgment in individual cases, governments have developed institutional protections for those who hold the office of the judge. Some of those protections are found in legal mandates, providing (for example) fixed terms of office and assured salaries. But much of the protection resides in customs and practices that attempt to insulate judges from the fear that, because they are employees of the state, their judgments need to be acceptable to the state.

Thus, the practice of judging is old and the idea of judicial independence is longstanding (as well as complicated[1]). But the problems of institutional designs for judiciaries have changed, as have the sources of threat to judicial

*   My thanks to Professor Derek Morgan and Robert Stevens for suggesting my participation, to Denny Curtis for wise suggestions, and to Cori Van Noy, Alison Mackenzie, and Kirby Smith for helpful research on this essay. email: judith.resnik@yale.edu. All rights reserved.
1.   See Robert Stevens *Reform in Haste and Repent at Leisure* p 1 above.

independence. During the twentieth century, different political conceptions of people, governments, and markets, as well as changing technologies, have made the prospect of adjudication plausible for whole new sets of claimants. With new demands for judging come new questions about how to organise judiciaries.

Four factors are central to the rising demand for adjudication and therefore to new challenges for judicial independence. First, the state came to be understood as itself subject to regulation, as bound by its own rules, as obliged to treat persons with dignity and respect. Individuals gained the right to use litigation to call state officials to account and to hold government to its own promises.[2] Second, in part through new information technologies, injuries experienced by large numbers of individuals, once seen as isolated and possibly idiosyncratic episodes, became visible as patterns of connected events. Third, the growth of the legal profession provided the personnel to generate regulations and responses to these many injuries, including through aggregated processes for redress.[3] A fourth factor, one that has been under-appreciated in the literature of courts, is the change in the understanding of women's rights. Women only gained juridical voice in the last century, and the radical reconception of women as rightsholders[4] – both inside and outside of their families – drove up the volume of disputes.[5]

Governments around the world have responded by multiplying both the number of judges and the venues for judging. A significant percentage of adjudication now takes place in what in the United States are called 'agencies' and in many other countries are termed 'tribunals'. With more tiers of judges and more places of judging, hierarchies of judges have been elaborated. Further, staffing and funding needs have grown. The Consultation Papers issued in July 2003 by the Labour Government are responding to these changes, and the

---

2. See generally Vicki C Jackson 'Suing the Federal Government: Sovereignty, Immunity, and Judicial Independence' (2003) 35 Geo Wash Int LR 521; James E Pfander 'Government Accountability in Europe: A Comparative Assessment' (2003) 35 Geo Wash Intl LR 611; Judith Resnik and Julie Suk 'Adding Insult to Injury: Questioning the Role of Dignity in Conceptions of Sovereignty' (2003) 55 Stan LR 1951.
3. See, eg, Richard L Abel and Phillip S C Lewis *Lawyers in Society: An Overview* (1995); Stephen C Yeazell 'Re-financing Civil Litigation' (2001) 51 De Paul LR 183.
4. See, eg, Judith Resnik 'Reconstructing Equality: Of Justice, Justicia, and the Gender of Jurisdiction' (2002) 14 Yale JL & Feminism 393; Reva B Siegel 'She the People: The Nineteenth Amendment, Sex Equality, Federalism, and the Family' (2002) 115 Harv LR 947; Rosa Ehrenreich Brooks 'Feminism and International Law: An Opportunity for Transformation' (2002) 14 Yale JL & Feminism 345; Vicki C Jackson 'Gender and Transnational Discourse' (2002) 14 Yale JL & Feminism 377.
5. One illustration from outside the United States is that the highest demand on civil legal aid funds in England has come from disputes categorised as family conflicts. See Tamara Goriely 'Making the Welfare State Work: Changing Conceptions of Legal Remedies Within the British Welfare State' in Francis Regan, Alan Paterson, Tamara Goriely and Don Fleming (eds) *The Transformation of Legal Aid: Comparative and Historical Studies* (1999) p 108. Data from inside the United States demonstrate that this arena of life also creates a higher density of disputes than do other arenas. See David M Trubek, Austin Sarat, William L F Felstiner, Herbert M Kritzer and Joel B Grossman 'The Costs of Ordinary Litigation' (1983) 31 UCLALR 72 at 87, Table I (Litigation as a Percentage of Disputes).

proposals that are made should be understood as part of a much larger story of worldwide efforts to revisit arrangements for and about adjudication. As is plain from the papers in this volume, the particular responses chosen are controversial.

How might I, a law professor from the United States, be useful? Surely not by entering an internal debate about the 'real' reasons for judicial reform or for these reforms in particular. Rather, my contribution is to offer a thicker understanding of what has transpired on my side of the Atlantic, where many of us share similar aspirations – to have judiciaries that include individuals from different strata, ethnicities, and of both sexes; and to protect all judges from incursions by self-interested participants who try to affect judiciaries through the appointments process and who then try to influence sitting judges in various ways.

As I detail below, I believe that the discussions of judicial independence in many countries have not yet taken into account how the changes of the twentieth century have produced new friends as well as new foes for the judiciary. The traditional story of judicial independence focuses on why judges ought to fear Kings, Presidents, Parliaments, and Congresses.

But today's judges have to be concerned about efforts to influence them that come from other quarters. Private sector 'repeat player' litigants (such as certain corporations, associations, and public interest groups) play a major role in generating candidates for judicial positions. Further, they provide funds for conferences and educational programmes for sitting judges. And through media campaigns, institutional litigants with resources can affect public perceptions of judicial practices and decisions. Indeed, the media itself has a major impact on judiciaries, as is made plain by the comments from the Response from the Judges' Council, urging that, upon abolition of the Office of the Lord Chancellor, the Lord Chief Justice will need a press office of its own.[6]

In addition, when judiciaries develop corporate structures to run their own affairs, they also try to influence government policies. Hard questions emerge about what kinds of questions judges ought to address in their corporate voice. The more 'the judiciary' becomes a player in government, the more others in the public and private sector will attempt to influence the policy positions adopted by 'the judiciary'.

In short, within the Consultation Papers – but not fully explored by the Consultation Papers – are major questions of how to organise a judiciary, of who speaks for the judiciary, and of whether to concentrate powers about the judiciary in one or many institutions. These issues are shared by all countries who want to provide access for many claimants to justice, who want judges to be understood as legitimate authoritative decisionmakers, and who treasure the idea that judges should be able to render judgment based on the merits of each claim. Learning more about contemporary responses in other countries such as the United States will, I hope, prove useful in evaluating what choices are better to forward these goals.

6.   *Judges' Council Response to the Consultation Papers on Constitutional Reform* (2003) pp 21–22.

II. DIVERSIFYING THE BENCH BY DIVERSIFYING THE JUDICIAL APPOINTMENTS COMMISSION

I start with those who might be described as new 'friends' of judging – new constituencies seeking to be heard by judges and to number among them. The legal profession on both sides of the Atlantic once had a membership that looked more or less the same. One of the great achievements of the twentieth century was to change the understanding of the personal dignity and rights of all human beings.[7] All persons are now able to be protected by law and are eligible to hold the power of the law, including the office of the judge.

Happily, therefore, one announced goal of the proposed new selection process for England and Wales is to help diversify a judiciary that, as the Consultation Paper *Appointing Judges* puts it, is 'overwhelmingly white, male, and from a narrow social and educational background'.[8] As currently described, however, the proposal falls short of its own goals, for it does not build diversity into the proposed Judicial Appointments Commission itself. The absence of an express commitment (and perhaps of a formula) to ensure the diversity of that Commission limits the proposal's capacity to succeed.

Many examples from the United States underscore how important the identity of those making appointments is to the diversity of those appointed. Here, I offer only two, one from the federal system and the other from the states.

Under a national Civil Justice Reform Act (CJRA) enacted in 1990, the chief judge of each of the 94 federal district courts was required to appoint a local 'CJRA' committee, a group that was charged by Congress to think about procedural reform.[9] More than 1,700 people were selected to serve nationwide, of whom some 16 percent (277) were women. Of course, disaggregated data provide more information. In some districts, no women were asked to serve. At the time of selection, women were the chief judges in five of the 94 federal districts and therefore held the power of appointment. The average number of women appointed in those five districts was 27 percent, as contrasted with the average of 16 percent across all 94 districts.[10]

Turning to the state court system, an example comes from Florida, which required three-person commissions from each area to make recommendations to the state governor on judicial appointments. Concerns about the lack of diversity on that state's courts prompted a revision of the law. Florida's legislature changed its statute to require that each nominating commission had to include at least one 'woman or minority.'

Hold aside the fact that the phrase 'woman or minority' implicitly suggests that women are white and that minorities are men, and further that it blurs all 'minorities' into one undifferentiated whole. The statutory revision 'worked'

---

7.   See Resnik and Suk, n 2 above.

8.   *Constitutional Reform: A New Way of Appointing Judges* CP 10/03 (July 2003) p 4 (hereinafter *Appointing Judges*).

9.   See 28 USC 471–482 (Supp 1992) (a provision that has since expired).

10.   These data come from the Report, *The Effects of Gender*, gathered by a Task Force commissioned by the Ninth Circuit (a federal circuit including the states of Alaska, Arizona, California, Hawaii, Idaho, Montana, Nevada, Oregon, and Washington). See *The Final Report of the Ninth Circuit Gender Bias Task Force*, republished in (1994) 67 SCal LR 727 at 787–790.

in the sense that, once the composition of the nominators changed, the composition of those nominated also changed: more women of all colours and more men of colour obtained appointments to the bench than had under the prior system. (Subsequently, a federal judge found that the statute's provision of affirmative action violated the United States Constitution as it was then interpreted.[11])

As for models from outside the United States, the Rome Statute for the International Criminal Court (ICC) aspires to create a bench of judges that includes both men and women. It calls for state parties to take into account the need for 'fair representation of female and male judges', and moreover, to have judges with expertise on 'violence against women or children'.[12] But the experience over the last few years at the International Tribunal for the Former Territories of Yugoslavia (ICTY) offers a warning. When the power to nominate is dispersed, each nominating body could assume that others would be the source of diversity. For some terms of the ICTY court, the temporary 'ad hoc' judges (serving for short periods of time) were a more significant source of women jurists than the regular full-time appointments.

In short, if judicial appointments are to come from a Commission instructed to appoint judges who represent the range of persons subject to law's protections and obligations, exploration is needed about how to structure the selection process for that Commission. It too needs to consist of a diverse group – including individuals who are committed to diversity and who have knowledge about and appreciation for the skills of a wide range of potential jurists. Otherwise, through the 'sift' and sorting of candidates, those making appointments may discount certain forms of expertise or look for particular credentials that would result in an unduly narrow 'pool' (to use terms from these debates in the United States) of 'qualified' candidates. Thus, each of the options set forth in the Consultation Papers for selection of Commission members should be evaluated in terms of whether it is more or less likely to result in the appointment of Commission members committed to the goal of diversifying the appointees. Simply put, one needs a mechanism to ensure that the Commission itself will not be 'overwhelmingly white, male, and from a narrow social and educational background'.

---

11. See *Mallory v Harkness* 895 F Supp 1556 (SD Fla, 1995), aff'd without opinion, 109 F 3d 771 (11th Cir, 1997). Whether that understanding could be revisited or other statutes upheld in light of recent Supreme Court approval of affirmative action in higher education is an open question.
After the rulings, Florida revised its statutes and instead directed the Governor, when making appointments to the Judicial Nominating Commissions, to 'ensure that, to the extent possible, the membership of the commission reflects the racial, ethnic, and gender diversity ... of the population within the territorial jurisdiction of the court for which nominations will be considered'. See Fla Stat 43.291(4) (2003). Section 26.021 directs the commissions, in turn, to consider diversity in a similar fashion.
12. See Rome Statue of the International Criminal Court, UN Doc A/Conf.183/9 at art 36(8)(a)(iii); 36(8)(b) (entered into force 1 July 2002).

III. JUDICIAL INDEPENDENCE AND AN INFRASTRUCTURE FOR JUDGES: THE EXAMPLE OF THE UNITED STATES

A second concern of both the Consultation Papers on judicial appointments[13] and on the creation of a Supreme Court[14] is judicial independence. We all aspire to have judges able to render judgments without fear of retribution and sufficiently set apart from political activities so as to have the ability to listen to claims of disputants and to assess the merits under the appropriate legal norms.

The central questions are how to organise the administrative apparatus that surrounds the judiciary and whether to centralise all powers in one entity. The Consultation Papers appropriately reflect on what array of responsibilities ought to lie with the proposed Appointments Commission.[15] Specifically, the proposal gives the Appointments Commission a narrow mandate by refusing to extend its authority to questions about the number of judgeships needed, retirement and recall, and judicial discipline.

As I will detail below, I think that distributing power related to the judiciary is a wiser route than concentrating it all in one organisation. But how judicial policy ought to be made and what role judges should play in it are more complicated problems than suggested by the Consultation Papers. Given the ambition to bring about significant reforms, many questions exist about how to deal with various policy issues (appointments, discipline, education, assignment, structure of courts), and about whether all judiciary policymaking ought to come within a single institution and, if so, what government actors (judges, Members of Parliament, Cabinet ministers) should run that entity.

The questions are many, including whether all the various judges in a dispersed judiciary, ranging from those serving within administrative tribunals to those serving on courts, should be seen as entitled to the same kind of judicial independence. If so, how shall that independence be secured? Further, given the efforts by institutionally powerful non-governmental litigants to influence the judiciary, do new protections, norms, or rules need to be developed? And, finally, does the judiciary itself, as it is increasingly organised and engaged in collective action, pose a threat to judicial independence?

Below, I explain each concern, again by providing examples from the United States. As that discussion will make plain, the description of judicial appointments in the United States that is in the Consultation Paper *Appointing Judges*,[16] and perhaps that is shared by many people outside the United States, does not reflect significant aspects of current practices. Those practices, in turn, exemplify how difficult it is to keep politics from seeping into the activities of judges.

By way of introduction, a sketch is needed of how an infrastructure for the federal court system in the United States developed. In 1915, some 120 federal judges (trial and appellate) were spread across the nation. In some states, such

---

13. *Appointing Judges*, n 8 above.
14. *Constitutional Reform: a Supreme Court for the United Kingdom* CP 11/03 (July 2003) (hereinafter *Supreme Court*).
15. See *Appointing Judges*, n 8 above, pp 43–53.
16. See *Appointing Judges*, n 8 above, pp 75–76.

as Indiana or Maryland or Massachusetts, a lone district judge served as the only federal adjudicator. These judges used different rules when deciding cases in their courts, and they had little institutional means by which to talk with each other. The Attorney General gave Congress reports on the federal courts and asked Congress for the judiciary's funds. The American Bar Association advanced the judiciary's concerns in Congress about improving judicial administration, salaries, and staffing. Further, while individual judges might contact members of Congress to gain attention about salaries, the number of judges and staff, or other issues, no means existed to do so collectively. As then-Chief Justice William Howard Taft described the situation, each federal judge had 'to paddle his own canoe'.[17]

Within a few decades, that image became obsolete. At the behest of Chief Justice Taft, in the 1920s, Congress created an official policy-making body of judges, now called the Judicial Conference of the United States. Today, that group of 27 judges obtain their positions either through seniority (for the 13 appellate judges) or by election for terms (for the representative district judges). The Chief Justice of the Supreme Court presides at the Judicial Conference, which analyses the judiciary's needs and makes policy.[18] The Judicial Conference takes positions, formally, by voting on a range of subjects, some of which relate to pending legislation.

In 1934, Congress authorised the federal judiciary to make its own rules of 'practice and procedure'.[19] Soon thereafter, the Supreme Court promulgated the Federal Rules of Civil Procedure, uniting federal practice across the nation. Those rules are a pivotal sociological fact in the forging of a collective identity of federal judges. Through the rules, judges who were thousands of miles apart shared daily practices. Over time, a federal judicial culture has developed.

In 1939, the management of the federal judiciary moved 'in house'. At the behest of life-tenured federal judges, Congress created the Administrative Office (AO) of the United States courts to collect data, submit budgets, and run the facilities for the federal court system.[20] In 1967, the Federal Judicial Center (FJC) came into being to expand the ability of the judiciary to focus on education and research.[21] Training programmes became regularised, such that new judges are now given instruction on what is expected of them as judges.

In the 1970s, under Warren Burger's tenure, the Supreme Court's chief justices began to make 'state of the judiciary' speeches.[22] In 1991, the judiciary set up an Office of Judicial Impact Assessments to file 'estimates', predicting

17. William Howard Taft 'Possible and Needed Reforms in Administration of Justice in Federal Courts' (1922) 8 ABA J 601 at 602.
18. See Act of 14 September 1922, ch 306, 2, 42 Stat 837, which created the Conference of Senior Circuit Judges, since renamed, reconfigured somewhat, and codified at 28 USC 331.
19. See The Rules Enabling Act, now codified at 28 USC 2071, 2072ff.
20. See Act of 7 August 1939, ch 501, 304(2), 53 Stat 1223, now codified as amended at 28 USC 601–612.
21. See Act of 20 December 1967, Pub L 90-219, 620, 81 Stat 664, now codified as amended at 28 USC 620–629.
22. See William Rehnquist 'The 1995 Year-End Report on the Federal Judiciary' (1996) 28 Third Branch 1 (describing the tradition of making such remarks).

how new causes of action would affect court dockets.[23] A few years thereafter, via a 'futures planning process', the Judicial Conference approved 93 recommendations to Congress as part of an official document, a first-ever *Long Range Plan*, issued in 1995.[24]

In short, over the last few decades, the federal judiciary has become an organisation with more than 1,500 judges sitting in more than 550 facilities, staffed by more than 30,000 personnel, and supported by an allocation of funds that are about one half of one percent of the federal budget.[25]

Further, and in contrast to the description of the United States federal system provided in the Consultation Paper, the federal judiciary is no longer comprised exclusively or even predominantly of judges who have life tenure. Rather, as I detail below, hundreds of non-life tenured judges work in federal courthouses across the country. Tiers of judges bring choices about which judges should have what roles, what protection, what power, and what cases. I turn therefore to how some of those questions have played out in the United States and what lessons can be drawn.

A. Judicial independence for the many judges of courts and agencies

In considering the charge for an Appointments Commission, the Consultation Paper admirably recognises that judges work in a variety of settings, from high to lower courts and in administrative tribunals. Given the multiplication of ranks of judges, the questions are (1) whether the concept of judicial independence applies to all who have the power to adjudicate and, (2) if so, whether the meaning of 'independence' varies depending on the kind of judicial officer to whom it is applied. Below, I explain the various methods by which individuals become federal judges in the United States and how the differing methods of selection affect their independence.

1. FEDERAL CONSTITUTIONAL JUDGES, FEDERAL STATUTORY JUDGES, AND FEDERAL ADMINISTRATIVE JUDGES

(a)   The life-tenured judiciary

In the United States, some of our judges are selected through a process specified by Article III of our Constitution. Their positions are created through acts of Congress, which possesses the constitutional power 'from time to time' to 'ordain and establish such lower courts' as it chooses. Such judges are nominated by the President and confirmed by the Senate. For clarity, I use the terms 'constitutional judges' or 'Article III judges' to denote this set.

23. See A Fletcher Mangum (ed), Federal Judicial Center *Conference on Assessing the Effects of Legislation on the Workload of the Courts: Papers and Proceedings 5–6* (1995).
24. See *The Judicial Conference of the United States, Long Range Plan for the Federal Courts* (December 1995), reprinted at 166 FRD 49 (1995) (hereinafter *Long Range Plan*).
25. See 'Omnibus Appropriations Bill A Mixed Bag for Judiciary' (November 1998) 30 Third Branch 1 at 1, 5 (describing 'total [fiscal year] obligations of $4.06 billion for the Judiciary', and summarising the allocations to salaries and expenses, to defender services, to juror fees, and to court security).

The controversy currently surrounding appointments of judges in the United States stems from the anomalous position held by that group. They are the only members of government who have their jobs for life, and the jobs that they have are understood as entailing a great deal of authority to shape legal norms.

Not only are these life-tenured judges an anomaly in our political system, the form that life tenure has taken in the United States is unusual when considered in light of the experiences in the states and around the world. As the United States Constitution is currently understood, our Article III judges have no mandatory retirement age and therefore have the ability to choose when to step aside and make available to a President an open slot for another life-tenured appointment. As a consequence, Article III judges can hold the power of office for many years. Further, Presidents can act strategically by selecting individuals early on in their careers to maximise the length of service.

The effects of these practices can be seen by considering the shift, over time, in the length of years that life-tenured judges have in fact served. In the early days of the American Republic, the relatively few individuals who held Article III judgeships served, on average, about 13 years on the Supreme Court and about 10–15 years in the lower courts. Today, a much larger group of lower level life-tenured judges averages about 18–22 years in office. At the Supreme Court level, the average term of those serving between 1989 and 2000 was about 26 years, and the current Chief Justice has served for more than 30 years on that court.[26]

In contrast, some of the states within the United States understand themselves as providing life tenure but also mandate retirement, for example at age 70.[27] Similarly, many nations have protections for judges, but most have mandatory retirement or fixed-term provisions. Such systems are common in Australia, Canada, France, Germany, Japan, and the new International Criminal Court.[28]

Further, Article III judges' salaries cannot be diminished during their term of service. Such judges may be removed only through impeachment, a device that is (happily) rarely used. In 1980, a major legislative reform created mechanisms for complaints to be filed (in confidential processes within the federal judiciary) and for the imposition of lesser sanctions.[29]

In short, the only moment of democratic input comes at the point of confirmation – when the choices of the President are held up to public scrutiny. Given the power of that position, my view is that inquiry by the Senate is not only constitutionally compelled (through the requirement of 'advice and consent'), it is also prudentially wise. Therefore, I have advocated that, as long as so relatively few judges have life tenure, Congress should impose upon itself a super-majority rule, requiring that confirmations occur only if 60 of the 100 senators agree.[30] As a matter of the policy of that body, the Senate should insure

---

26. These data come from an analysis of materials available on terms of service of judges. See also Albert Yoon 'Love's Labors Lost? Judicial Tenure among Federal Court Judges, 1945–2000' (2003) 91 Calif LR 1029.
27. See, eg, Mass Const Pt 2, C.3, Art 1 (2003) (a provision added in 1972 and upheld by jurists in state and federal court); Vt Const Ch II, 35 (2002).
28. See, eg, Art 37 of the Rome Statute (providing for a nine-year, non-renewable term).
29. See the Judicial Disability and Discipline Act of 1980, now codified at 28 USC 372ff.
30. See Judith Resnik 'Supermajority Rule' *New York Times*, 11 June 2003, p A31.

widespread support before approving a nominee to an Article III judgeship at the trial or appellate level. Further, I believe it wise for the Senate to take an active role in learning about prospective nominees,[31] again because of the import of the decision to confirm and the constitutional commitment to distributing the power to make that decision between the executive and legislative branches.

(b) Non-life tenured judges within the federal judiciary

The Consultation Papers focus on the life-tenured members of the federal judiciary and miss a large number of other jurists, many serving inside federal courthouses, who are federal judges. Specifically, in 1968, Congress created the position of 'magistrate' (renamed in 1990 'magistrate judge'). The number of magistrate slots is decided by the Judicial Conference of the United States (the policymaking body of the federal courts, mentioned above). The slots are filled through appointments made by each of the 94 district courts. The authorising statute[32] does specify a few requirements about both appointments and process.

For example, candidates need to have a certain number of years of lawyering experience. Further, district courts must use 'merit selection panels', to be 'composed of residents of the individual districts, to assist the courts in identifying and recommending persons best qualified to fill such positions'.[33] In 1979, Congress called for the merit selection panels to give 'due consideration to all qualified individuals, especially such groups as women, blacks, Hispanics, and other minorities'.[34] The Judicial Conference has other guidelines as well, but the ultimate decision on appointment rests with the life-tenured judges of each district court. Magistrate judges serve for eight-year, renewable terms. Although they do not have life tenure, a large percentage are reappointed, and that decision is made by the life-tenured judges with whom magistrate judges work in their particular districts.

In 1984, Congress chartered another group of judges, 'bankruptcy judges'. Unlike the number of magistrate judgeships (which are established by the federal judiciary), Congress creates each bankruptcy judgeship through specific statutes, as it does for life-tenured district and appellate judges. The 12 appellate courts that govern geographically delineated circuits have the power to appoint bankruptcy judges. These appellate courts are not obliged to use merit selection panels.[35]

The Judicial Conference has established guidelines for both appointment and reappointment of magistrate and bankruptcy judges. Some revisions were

---

31. See Judith Resnik *The Senate's Role in the Confirmation Process: Statement and Testimony in Hearings before the Subcommittee on Administrative Oversight and the Courts, Senate Committee on the Judiciary*, 107th Cong 2001, reprinted in (2002) 50 Drake LR 511.
32. See 28 USC 631ff.
33. See 28 USC 631(b).
34. See Federal Magistrates Act of 1979, Pub L No 96-82, 3(c),(e), 93 Stat 643, 644–45.
35. See 28 USC 152.

made after 2000 in light of objections (including two filed lawsuits) from bankruptcy judges who felt themselves mistreated in the reappointment process.[36] Bankruptcy judges serve for 14-year, renewable terms.

As the process has evolved over the past three decades, life-tenured judges have gained the power almost to double their own ranks. Above I referred to about 1,500 trial and appellate federal judges serving in the more than 550 federal courthouses around the United States. About half of the trial bench in the federal courthouses serve through appointment by other judges. The number of bankruptcy and magistrate judges (whom I term, for clarity, 'statutory judges') roughly equals the number of life-tenured trial court judges. In a few federal district courts, more magistrate judges serve than do life-tenured judges, and in about 16 districts, the numbers are equal. And the ranks of both sets of judges are augmented by senior or recalled judges. Appended are a few charts to provide some of the details.

The powers of magistrate and bankruptcy judges have also grown over the decades, such that they increasingly share forms of authority formerly associated exclusively with the life-tenured constitutional judges. For example, with litigants' consent, statutory judges can preside at civil trials. Moreover, they have some form of contempt power. Bankruptcy judges may also serve on appellate panels, reviewing the work of other bankruptcy judges. In short, while life-tenured judges have greater powers to issue final judgments, and a few other distinctions remain, the trend has been towards devolution of judicial authority. Thus, bankruptcy and magistrate judges represent the manufacture of more judicial person-power outside the constraints of the life-tenured, presidential nomination system.

These statutory innovations have enlarged the pool of prospective federal judges in two respects. First, Article III judges select individuals to serve as magistrate and bankruptcy judges who would not, as a political matter, have been selected by a particular senator, nominated by a President, or approved by the Senate. Second, a career ladder has developed: by first serving in the position of statutory judges, some individuals are able later to obtain an Article III judgeship. Moreover, some argue, life-tenured judges have done a better job than have the politicians in designing a selection process that is more substantive and less onerous[37] – resulting in bankruptcy and magistrate benches of special quality.[38]

---

36. See *Administrative Office of the United States Courts, The Selection and Appointment of United States Magistrate Judges* (2002); *Regulations of the Judicial Conference of the United States for the Selection, Appointment, and Reappointment of United States Bankruptcy Judges* (as amended, September 2000 and again in August 2001). These regulations structure the process while permitting some variation, district to district in the case of magistrate judges, and circuit to circuit for bankruptcy appointments.

37. For example, Judicial Conference regulations (*see* n 36 above and accompanying text) include a commitment to confidentiality of materials submitted when individuals are considered for magistrate judgeships and provide for public solicitation of nominees but not for public hearings vetting those nominated).

38. As one local legal paper has opined: 'the Bankruptcy Court now has the best bench, top to bottom, of any court in the City of Chicago.' See *in the Matter of Grabill* 967 F 2d 1152, 1160 (7th Cir, 1992) (Posner J dissenting, citing the Chicago Legal Bulletin of 13 January 1992 at 2).

But the process has also raised questions, related to the issue raised in the Consultation Paper of a 'career judiciary'. While the career ladder is not the equivalent of the European system, it has started to have some parallels. One concern is the 'bench climber'. Analysts of career judiciaries note that judges who sit at lower levels and seek promotion or reappointment have incentives to conform and to defer, and that they tend to be cautious in an atmosphere in which collegiality is a virtue and retaliation is feared.[39] Further, although life-tenured judges always had some powers of appointment (for clerks, clerical staff, and special masters), the recent years are the first in our history in which life-tenured judges play a pivotal institutional role in choosing a large number of people to serve as the initial adjudicators within the federal system. For those who believe that some form of democratic input is important in judicial selection, this system is troubling, as the statutes do not systematise methods for public input nor require deference to the views of any non-judges when appointments and reappointments are made.

Further, the more judges have power over an array of decisions, the more complex their role becomes. Economists and public choice theorists have begun to spawn a literature exploring judicial self-interest.[40] Judges may well feel that their work is under-funded, but judges as employers, as administrators, and as planners also have incentives to establish need for growth. In addition, when judges have the power of appointment, they also have the ability to bestow benefits such as salaries, staff support, courtrooms, chambers, committee assignments, and pensions. Applicants and their supporters therefore have new reasons to court judges.[41] Historically, judicial patronage has been a problem, often solved by moving powers of appointment from individual jurists or the judiciary as a whole to public officials or committees.

Yet judicial incentives also make judges likely to select able individuals to help them. In the United States, constitutional judges depend on magistrate and bankruptcy judges to shoulder a good deal of the workload burden. (Of course, a risk exists about tipping points; as the numbers of such appointments grow, the life-tenured judiciary moves more toward a group of managers.) Yet, and here more like the proposed Appointments Commission, a wiser course is

39. See, eg, Nicohlas L Georgakopoulos 'Discretion in the Career and Recognition Judiciary' (2000) 7 U Chi Law School Roundtable 205.

40. See Frederick Schauer 'Incentives, Reputation, and the Inglorious Determinants of Judicial Behavior' (2000) 68 U Cinn LR 615 (bemoaning the lack of empiricism on judicial self-interest); Jonathan R Macey 'Judicial Preferences, Public Choice, and the rules of Procedure' (1994) 23 JLS 627; Richard A Posner 'What Do Judges Maximize? (The Same Thing Everyone Else Does)' (1994) 3 Sup Ct Econ Rev 1.

41. That relationships forged in the hopes of obtaining appointments can threaten independence has been explored in the context of the history of the English judiciary. See David Lemmings 'The Independence of the Judiciary in Eighteenth Century England' ch 8 in *Proceedings of the Tenth British Legal History Conference*, Oxford, 1991 (discussing how, with parliamentary control, judges became increasingly involved in seeking 'supplementary places and honours'). By examining which individuals were actually selected in Hanoverian England, Lemmings concluded that after the Act of Settlement, more senior judges had closer ties to the governing party than had judges in earlier periods, and that through such 'policisation', a good deal of control was imposed.

to have the judiciary play a role in, but not have exclusive control over, the appointments of other judges.

Deciding how promotions and reappointments are made poses yet harder questions about judicial independence, and the problems are not limited to judges who need to get reappointed to the same position. In the United States, appellate judges (of both the intermediate and highest courts) are increasingly drawn from the ranks of lower court judges. For example, of about 1,200 judges listed in a 2001 'almanac' of federal judges, about 100 had served in a lower federal judicial position and then 'moved up'.

To the extent that we value independent judges, unafraid of encountering popular disapproval and free from needing collegial approval, the possibility of promotion may undercut the ability to feel unfettered by personal interest when rendering judgments. Further, when evaluating the records of sitting judges, what should be taken into account? Should assessment be made of their track records – for example, by soliciting information from litigants or by reviewing decisions and reversal rates? Will lower level judges respond by searching for supporters, by publishing little, and by keeping low profiles? Automatic reappointment avoids those problems but then results in a de facto tenured set of judges. A presumption of reappointment – arguably in place in the United States for our statutory federal judges – may mitigate the problems, but the bases for rebutting that presumption have yet to be clearly articulated. Moreover, some statutory judges report that they feel constrained 'to please' their superiors in order for that presumption to apply. And if reappointment comes too easily, the result becomes a de facto life-tenured judiciary, and one created with very little transparency. In short, while the Consultation Paper, *Appointing Judges*, notes the problem in terms of whether the Commission should have authority over appointments to different levels of courts,[42] the Paper does not address the effect of such decision making on judicial independence.

(c) Administrative law judges and other hearing officers

In addition to these federal judges who work in federal courthouses, yet other federal judges work in administrative agencies. Some, called Administrative Law Judges (ALJs) are chartered under a federal statute, the Administrative Procedure Act (APA), which provides for competitive civil service exams, a 'veterans' preference' that awards points to those who have been in the armed services, and job security through civil service provisions. About 2,000 ALJs are deployed in various agencies, with the heaviest concentration in the Social Security Administration, and with the availability of inter-agency transfer. An estimated 2,000 more work without the protections of the APA as line agency employees who are assigned positions as 'hearing officers' or 'administrative judges'. Controversy recently erupted when the Attorney General insisted that 'Immigration Judges' – who are not under the APA – were employees whom he had the power to transfer to other jobs within the Department of Justice. More generally, many commentators report a trend towards greater reliance on the ad hoc hearing officers who lack the special protection of the APA.

---

42. See *Appointing Judges*, n 8 above, pp 29–31.

Decisions about the hierarchy of judges and the jurisdictional authority of the various kinds of judges are inevitably political decisions. Having developed tiers and layers of judges, some working in courts and others in administrative tribunals, judgments are required about how much process, accorded by what kind of judge, should be provided. I turn next to these issues.

2. VARYING THE FORMS OF AUTHORITY AND THE DEGREES OF INDEPENDENCE OF THIS ARRAY OF JUDGES

Judges within the United States – both state and federal – have evidenced ambivalence about how to treat lower-status judges. Indeed, a question debated is whether to call them 'judges' at all. Some jurists fought to prevent others from sharing the title of 'judge' and argued that terms such as 'hearing officer' or 'magistrate' were more appropriate.[43] The desire to keep a distinctive trademark stems in part from the fear that the position of the judge is not immune from erosion; some worry about a loss of status if too many officials have that title.[44] Data on popular perceptions support the view that people do not make clear distinctions among various kinds of judges.[45] Yet such concerns have not succeeded in stopping judges and courts from multiplying – in name and in fact.

---

43. As introduced in the 1960s, the title proposed for what became the magistrate position was 'Assistant United States District Judge'. The Executive Committee of the Judicial Conference of the United States opposed that title. See Statement of Warren Olney and reports from the Judicial Conference Committee on Administration of the Criminal Law, in 'Federal Magistrates Act: Hearings on S. 995 Before the Subcomm. On Improvements in Judicial Machinery of the Senate Comm. on the Judiciary', 90th Cong, 241j–245 (1967). Thereafter, when the proposal was made to rename 'magistrates' by adding the word judge to their title, objections were raised again. Similarly, in the 1970s, Article III judges opposed using the term 'judge' in lieu of 'referee' in bankruptcy proceedings, and then in the 1980s, opposed the provision of life tenure for bankruptcy judges. See Eric A Posner 'The Political Economy of the Bankruptcy Reform Act of 1978' (1996) 96 Mich LR 47 at 71–80. Professor Posner argues that Article III district judges did so to maintain their own prestige and that they campaigned for 'trivial' markers of status, relating to modes of appointing law clerks and pensions, as well as insisting on a cumbersome appellate process to make plain that bankruptcy judges were understood as inferior in status to district court judges.
State judges have also argued against administrative hearing officers being renamed 'judges'.
44. See Walter Gellhorn 'The Administrative Procedure Act: The Beginnings' (1986) 72 Va LR 219 at 232 (describing that '"Hearing officers" [were] puffed up into "Hearing Commissioners" and ... later ... into Administrative law judges who sometimes flaunt their robes a bit too obtrusively for my taste').
45. See generally 'American Bar Association Report on Perceptions of U.S. Justice System' (1999) 62 Alb LR 1307 (describing the similarity of attitudes toward state and federal judges); David B Rottman 'Voters in Judicial Elections: Motivation, Capability, and Trust 4', paper prepared for the Summit on Improving Judicial Selection, 2000 ('Most Americans are unable to answer questions that speak to fundamental aspects of the judiciary, such as the difference between federal and state courts, the existence of an independent judicial branch of government, and even the manner in which judges are selected in their state').

In my view, the 'cultural capital' associated with higher-status judges ought to be shared purposefully with lower-status judges in a deliberate effort to mark the important role that many lower-status judges play in individuals' lives. Given caseload demands that prompt expanding judicial ranks and given our shared hopes that judges make decisions wisely, fairly, and carefully, high-status judges need to understand their deep dependence on and linked fortunes with their lower-echelon siblings. In the United States, judges within administrative agencies face special problems, and are therefore specially in need of help and attention from judges who sit in more elite settings.

A distinctive question is the degree to which all kinds of judges ought to have comparable guarantees of independence – in terms of security of salary and length of tenure, as well as protection from pressures by the government or outsiders to influence decisionmaking. A Canadian judgment is instructive in this regard. In what is called '*The Provincial Court Judges Decision*',[46] the Supreme Court of Canada required that an independent commission set salaries for provincial judges and that its decisions would be subject to judicial review.

In the United States, the federal constitutional text identified with judicial independence has been interpreted to reach only the life-tenured.[47] Rights to judicial independence for other judges emanate from the 'Due Process' Clause of the United States Constitution and (much less robustly) from American common law concepts. Moreover, the expansion of federal judicial capacity through magistrate and bankruptcy judges has been justified on the theory that, although created by the legislature, statutory judges depend on constitutional judges – not the Executive or Congress – for appointment and reappointment. But, as discussed, at least some individuals who serve as statutory judges do worry about pressures from other judges.

Yet another question is how much such judges ought to be unified or kept in separate and distinct settings. An apparently efficient approach would be to link them all together. On the other hand, by placing judges in various agencies and at different locations, a range of constituencies might be mobilised to promote the need for funding judges. One thus could have a greater number of judges and more resources for judging by scattering judges about, rather than consolidating them in a single sector that makes plain to a legislature all the funding that supports the full complement. The lack of a clear bottom line, in terms of the number of judges and the places of judging, may have utility in the political arena.

---

46. See *Reference re: Remuneration of Judges of the Provicial Court of Prince Edward Island and R v Campbell; R v Ekmecic; R v Wickman and Manitoba Provincial Judges Assn' v Manitoba* 3 SCR 3 (1997); and Robert G Richards 'Provincial Court Judges Decision – Case Comment' (1998) 61 Saskatchewan LR 575; Jacob S Ziegel 'The Supreme Court Radicalizes Judicial Compensation' (1998) 9 Forum Constitutionnel 31; Gerald T G Seniuk 'Judicial Independence and the Supreme Court of Canada' (1998) 77 La Revue du Barreau Canadian 381.

47. See Judith Resnik 'Judicial Independence and Article III: Too Little and Too Much' (1999) 72 SCal LR 657; Judith Resnik 'Inventing the District Courts of the Twentieth Century for the District of Columbia and the Nation' (2002) 90 Geo LJ 607.

B. Threats to judicial independence from repeat player litigants, using new techniques to attempt to influence process and outcome

The Consultation Papers do not explain much of the content of judicial independence. Their focus is on forms of politicisation of appointments and the risk of attempts by other government actors to influence judges. In that respect, the Papers mirror the conventional story of judicial independence, initially worried about the Crown and then, with the rise of Parliaments, focusing on two great foes – the Executive Branch (hiring and firing judges) and the legislature (seeking to control judges either through appointments, funding, or jurisdiction).

In my view, developments during the twentieth century require alteration of that narrative to include new sources of potential threats to (or supporters of) judicial independence. A first is the *repeat player litigant*, by which I mean an entity or group that appears, repeatedly, in an array of cases in a court system. Repeat players are both disputants (such as corporations, associations, or the government) and their lawyers.

To localise this discussion for a moment by (again) using the United States as an example, during the twentieth century the paradigmatic lawsuit changed, moving away from the one-on-one model to a larger scale. The term 'class actions' is symbolic of a broader phenomenon – aggregate litigation in which individual claims are viewed as sufficiently similar so as to group them (through a variety of procedural means) as a whole. Our language has tracked the shift. We no longer speak only of cases but also of 'litigations', such as the asbestos litigation or the tobacco litigation.[48] The stakes in such litigations are often high, in corporate terms and in individual terms, with outcomes ranging from bankruptcy to billions. The lawyers and litigants know it, and they work in co-ordinated groups, as do judges on some occasions. The media also plays a role, as it brings attention to certain forms of disputes. And, increasingly, coordination among participants is facilitated by the Internet.

Another shift away from the common law paradigm of private litigants disputing contracts and torts comes from the rise of human rights and public law litigation. Only in the last century has the proposition been widely established that citizens have rights against government. Further, the recognition of women as rightsholders is itself a significant and under-appreciated variable in the growth of litigation worldwide.

Such public law rights cases sometimes capture headlines, but many involve much less visible iterations, such as citizens or residents seeking benefits owed to them by government. As a result, courts and agencies have become the venues for disputes about both the overall shape of government programmes and about their applications in individual cases. Volume has risen. The kinds of claims have changed, and a great deal of adjudication is based not in courts but in administrative agencies and tribunals.

Repeat player litigants – including the government, mercantile associations, lawyers associations, major companies, and other 'interest groups' – now see judiciaries as bodies to be influenced. The repeat players have the capacity to

---

48. See Judith Resnik 'From Cases to Litigation' (1991) 54 Law & Contemporary Problems 5; Judith Resnik, Dennis E Curtis and Deborah R Hensler 'Individuals within the Aggregate: Relationships, Representation, and Fees' (1996) 71 NYULR 296.

play 'for the rules' – for the processes of adjudication. Further, the efforts at influence now operate across a large scale, with repeated efforts to gain toeholds in multi-play, multi-venue struggles. Those venues include appointments, judicial policymaking, and judicial education.

1. INFLUENCE THROUGH APPOINTMENTS

At the moment in the United States, we are watching several examples of efforts to influence the judiciary by selecting certain individuals to be judges and by targeting others for removal or for special oversight. But it would be a mistake to see this problem as exclusively based in decisions made by either the Executive Branch or Congress. Rather, repeat players from *outside* government are central figures in these conflicts.

At the federal level, the President (with the advice of the Department of Justice and some Senators) has selected some people to nominate because of their affiliation with certain private organisations that have views on the proper reading of the United States Constitution. In terms of activities in the states, two other organisations (the Chamber of Commerce and the American Trial Lawyers Association) have poured money into judicial elections in several states.[49] These battles, in turn, spark new legal issues, including the degree to which judicial elections and their financing can be regulated. A judicial candidate succeeded in persuading a bare majority of the United States Supreme Court that a state ethics regulation violated his free speech rights,[50] but subsequently, a few state court decisions have imposed other constraints on how individuals can campaign for judgeships.

I understand that, from afar, the selection processes in the United States are held up as examples of processes to avoid. But the situation in the United States ought not to be used to justify a refusal to permit democratic input into the selection of members of a judiciary. Rather, the contemporary controversies in the United States are an outgrowth of a particular and peculiar set of political contingencies – a series of narrowly divided governments, the selection of highly controversial nominees, the deteriorating interactions among members of the Senate, and the very high stakes represented by the small number of life-time appointments with no mandatory retirement provisions.

49. Judicial elections in states have become more expensive because of the entry of national participants; analysis of the 'market' in advertisements demonstrated that funders focused on particular races. See Anthony Champagne 'Interest Groups and Judicial Elections', paper prepared for the Summit on Improving Judicial Selection, 2000. As he explained: 'the continuing nationalization of state judicial elections is further shown by the U.S. Chamber of Commerce's recent efforts through the Institute for Legal Reform to support the election of pro-business judges in Alabama, Illinois, Michigan, Mississippi, and Ohio. The goal is to make both direct campaign contributions and to pay for issue advertising': p 8. See also William G Kelly 'Selection of Judges' (2000, Winter) ABA Judicial Division Record 3 (describing efforts by the Chamber of Commerce and the Trial Lawyers and 'other interest groups ... raking the candidates over the coals'.)
50. See *Republican Party of Minnesota v White* 536 US 765 (2002).

2. INFLUENCE THROUGH RULEMAKING

The attempt to influence the views of a judiciary does not stop with the act of appointment. Modern developments provide new techniques for exerting influence. For example, during the twentieth century, judges in many states and in the federal courts gained control over rules about practice and procedure. The Federal Rules of Civil Procedure, the first national set governing all civil actions, came into being in 1938.

Court rules have imbedded within them social and political values. The 1938 rules prompted relatively easy access to courts and ample rights to discover information from opponents. Time and again, over the last three decades, we have seen heated battles about changing those rules. The debates about these rules and about statutes governing procedure have increasingly become battles funded by repeat player litigants aimed at affecting judicial practices through committee meetings. The same lobbyists may appear on one day in the Congress – arguing for a particular bill – and on another at a hearing before a committee of judges about a proposed rule change. (Revisions of our class action rule provide a recent case in point.)

3. INFLUENCE THROUGH EDUCATION

Yet another method by which some repeat players are attempting to influence judges is through educational programmes. That judges should go to educational programmes was itself an idea that took hold in the twentieth century. Recently in the United States, some groups have invited and paid for judges to attend seminars, described as content-neutral and aimed at providing needed education for judges on such issues as law and economics or the complexity of environmental regulations. The programmes tend to be held at lovely resorts or at law schools.

After a few members of Congress introduced legislation to curb this practice, a heated debate developed within the federal judiciary about whether judicial attendance at such programmes should be curtailed.[51] The issue prompted bitter exchanges among judges. One group argued that such programmes are well balanced and in fact neutral or that, as judges, they can listen to anything and 'take it for what it is worth'. The other side claimed that the programmes have pernicious effects – undermining the appearance and fact of impartiality. Further, while a few human rights or civil liberties organisations provide such seminars, the more well-resourced spectrum of the private market can fund many more.

IV. INFLUENCE FROM WITHIN: A CORPORATE JUDICIARY, DEVELOPING NORMS OF JUDGING

Yet another source of risk to judicial independence comes from judges themselves promoting changes. I should note, at the outset, that most of the

---

51. See Abner J Mikva 'Judges, Junkets, and Seminars' (2002, Summer) 28 Litigation 2 (ABA Section on Litigation).

policymaking by judges is responsive to deeply felt needs for productivity and for institutional betterment. Further, I have great admiration for many of the efforts made to staff a judiciary overwhelmed by demands for decisionmaking. But through a confluence of developments (each, in its time, an appropriate accommodation, some inventive, and all politically acceptable), the United States life-tenured judiciary has transformed itself in three important respects.

First, it has supported the proliferation of kinds and sites of judging, prompting political questions about the assignment of certain kinds of cases to certain kinds of judges. Second, through its official policymaking body, the Judicial Conference of the United States, the life-tenured judiciary has taken on an active role in advising Congress about which kinds of judges ought to be assigned to which kinds of cases, and about which litigants ought to be barred from access to the federal courts. The judiciary plays a significant role in shaping statutes about federal jurisdiction. Third, judges have changed the content of the job of judging by promoting settlement of cases, management of cases, and alternative forms of resolution of cases – all as preferable to adjudication.

In short, as the twenty-first century begins, the United States judiciary has come to function in agency-like fashion and to embrace a managerial mode. The judiciary promulgates a message about what 'good judging' is by education and through rule changes, and the judiciary uses a range of techniques to forward, in a programmatic fashion, its own needs for funds and staff, as well as to impose its own particular vision of what rights citizens ought to be able to pursue in federal courts before life-tenured judges, when litigants should have access to judges located in agencies, and when litigants should be assigned to the state court system.

Because judicial independence is an artifact of culture as much as of text, the change in the norms and practices of judges serve to undermine forms of independence of judges. The repeat player litigants that I mentioned above know well that they can try to influence judicial policymaking, and they regularly present their views to judges at rulemaking hearings, in educational fora, and in legal arguments. I know that federal judges aspire to keep themselves above that fray, but nonetheless, they have helped to turn the judiciary into an arena in which repeat players want to be.

Moreover, having a smorgasbord of judges means having to make choices about which judges get which kinds of cases. As it promotes one form of judgeship over another and as it prefers certain litigants over others, the judiciary appears partisan. By playing roles in creating tiers of judging and controlling traffic to the various courts, the judiciary has shifted from being responsive to whatever cases come its way. Instead the policy makers in the judiciary have come to see themselves as entitled to structure the rights of access of litigants to various courts.

In my view, judges ought to be agnostic about which cases come before them. Yet, when I along with a hundred other law professors recently wrote a brief to the Supreme Court urging that it uphold a congressional statute vesting

---

52. The Civil Rights Remedy of the Violence Against Women Act, 42 USC section 13981.

jurisdiction over a new civil rights claim in the federal courts,[52] I knew that I wrote to a bench in which one member had repeatedly raised questions about the propriety of the legislation[53] and further that the Judicial Conference had opposed an earlier draft of the statute when it was first proposed in the early 1990s.[54] The judiciary, under the leadership of our current Chief Justice, had taken up the role of policymaker and, in that role, had pressed hard about why a particular new civil right should not be created.

Let me draw a clear distinction between individual judges and this structural role. In the United States, individual judges have long played a role in commenting on particular issues and in advising governments,[55] and the historical pattern continued in the United States in the twentieth century. If an individual judge believes that he or she need to opine about the wisdom of a government policy or proposed jurisdictional grant, it may be unwise and it may provide grounds for recusal. Judges are citizens, and they have to decide individually how to discharge that task consistent with ethical requirements of judging.[56]

But in the United States, what has developed is very different – what I term the creation of a 'programmatic judiciary'.[57] As a corporate entity, the federal judiciary educates, plans, lobbies, and opines about the shape, nature, and future of judging. In terms of the positions taken in the last few years in the federal judiciary's corporate voice, I have mentioned a few but let me here offer a summary. The federal judiciary has argued for limited growth in the number of life-tenured judges and in some instances for retrenchment,[58] for better salaries and courthouses,[59] for

53. See William H Rehnquist 'Chief Justice's 1991 Year-End Report on the Federal Judiciary' (January 1991) 23 Third Branch 1 at 3; William H Rehnquist 'Chief Justices Issues 1992 Year-End Report' (January 1993) 25 Third Branch 1; William H Rehnquist *Remarks at the American Law Institute*, 75th Annual Meeting, 1998, pp 13, 17–18.

54. See Judicial Conference of the United States, Ad Hoc Committee on Gender-Based Violence (September 1991). Subsequently, in 1993, after redrafting to take some of those criticisms into account, the Judicial Conference took no position on the question of whether the civil rights provision should be in the statute. In 2000, the Supreme Court ruled, in a decision by the Chief Justice for a five-person majority, that Congress had exceeded its constitutional authority when creating such a provision. See *United States v Morrison* 529 US 598 (2000).

55. See Stewart Jay 'Servants of Monarchs and Lords: The Advisory Role of Early English Judges' (1994) 38 AmJLH 118.

56. These issues are explored in greater detail in Judith Resnik 'Trial as Error, Jurisdiction as Injury' (2000) 113 Harv LR 924.

57. Judith Resnik 'The Programmatic Judiciary: Lobbying, Judging, and Invalidating the Violence Against Women Act' (2000) 74 SCal LR 269.

58. See *Long Range Plan*, n 24 above, p 98 (Recommendation 15) ('The growth of the Article III judiciary should be carefully controlled so that the creation of new judgeships, while not subject to a numerical ceiling, is limited to that number necessary to exercise federal court jurisdiction').

59. In addition, and relying on a long tradition of private interest-based associations, federal judges have organised another group, the National Federal Judges Association, focused most intensely on judicial salaries and benefits.

expansion of the statutory federal judiciary,[60] for less federal jurisdiction,[61] and for a presumption against creation of federal rights if enforced in federal court.[62] Illustrative positions include views by the Judicial Conference that Congress should not create federal jurisdiction in a range of cases, from health care rights to the feared computer failures during the Y2k year.

Threats to the independence and coherence of the judiciary, in this account, come not only from high-profile politicised battles targeting particular judges but also from low-level administrative decisions and from doctrinal reinterpretations – from a series of small decisions, all of which may be sensible in the individual moment but which, when viewed with the luxury of a century's hindsight, raise serious problems for judicial independence. The life-tenured judiciary is itself a central actor in this tale, as it has promoted the blurring of judicial roles between Article III judges and non-Article III judges, between adjudication and dispute resolution, between public and private dispute resolution, and between the judiciary as a distinctive branch and other federal agencies. I am less sanguine than some that, a hundred years from now, values of independence of judgment and of procedural regularity will still apply to actors named 'judges'.

V. REFORMIST AGENDAS

This commentary has, I hope, helped to raise many questions about the problems implicit in but unresolved by the current packet of proposals for reform. The problems of enhancing or preserving judicial independence are complex, and the current set of Consultation Papers has yet to develop fully how the organisation of decisionmaking about the administration of justice and the need to equip judges with staff, education, and authority affect both the law and practice of judicial independence.

To press for more elaboration is, implicitly, to raise questions about the aspirations of the current movement for reforms in England and Wales. Is the problem one of equipage: that the current composition and shape of the

---

60. The *Long Range Plan*, n 24 above, p 94 (Recommendation 10) ('Where constitutionally permissible, Congress should be encouraged to assign to administrative agencies or Article I courts the initial responsibility for adjudicating those categories of federal benefits or regulatory cases that typically involve intense fact-finding'); p 161 (Recommendation 65) ('Magistrate judges should perform judicial duties to the extent constitutionally permissible and consistent with sound judicial policy', and in commentary calling for consideration of expanding the role of magistrates).
61. The *Long Range Plan*, n 24 above, p 83 (Recommendation 1) ('Congress should be encouraged to conserve the federal courts as a distinctive judicial forum of limited jurisdiction in our system of federalism. Civil and criminal jurisdiction should be assigned to the federal courts only to further clearly defined and justified national interests, leaving to the state courts the responsibility for adjudicating all other matters'); pp 84–88 (Recommendations 2–5, criminal jurisdiction); pp 88–94 (Recommendations 6–10, civil jurisdiction).
62. The *Long Range Plan*, n 24 above, p 88 (Recommendation 6) ('Congress should be encouraged to exercise restraint in the enactment of new statutes that assign civil jurisdiction to the federal courts and should do so only to further clearly defined and justified federal interests').

judiciary is insufficient to make good on the promise of providing responses to a myriad of claimants? Is the challenge one of legitimacy: that the current judiciary comes from too narrow a slice of society and lacks a mandate sufficient to enable it to render judgment on the widening array of claims brought in part through engagement with the European Union and the rest of the world? Is the task to help link judges in the various levels and places of adjudication who may lack sufficient connection to each other? Is the current dispersal of policymaking about judges (with the criminal and civil systems under different ministries) dysfunctional or a wise decision to avoid centralisation? Is the concern that judges are genuinely at risk of losing an understanding of themselves as independent adjudicators? Or that some parts of the government may have less loyalty to the concept and custom of judicial independence than is desirable? Or that the pressure on judicial independence will grow as the judiciary works more on human rights and other legal issues of a nation more deeply enmeshed in a federation and in a worldwide network of adjudicators?

Yet even this long list of questions is insufficient, for a focus on justice systems ought not imply an autonomy that does not exist. Judicial reforms of the past century in the United States have never been 'only' about judicial processes or procedure. Some of the changes stemmed from interest and concerns coming from a professionalised judiciary, as well as of academic and practicing lawyers, and of court users. But of equal import have been the many pressures for change that came from larger social movements – some aimed at reframing an understanding of the American constitutional project, others hoping to create a powerful national government, while yet others wanted to limit the national government and regulation more generally. Courts are institutions very much expressive of the social orders in which they sit, and efforts to change courts need to be understood as attempts to reorient the polities that authorise judges to sit in judgment of them.

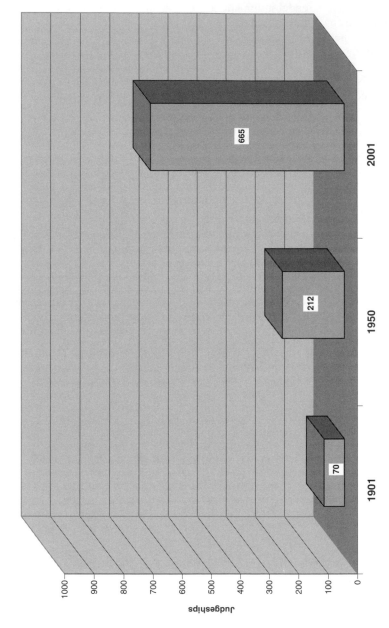

Authorized Article III Federal District Court Judgeships,
Nationwide: Comparing 1901, 1950, and 2001

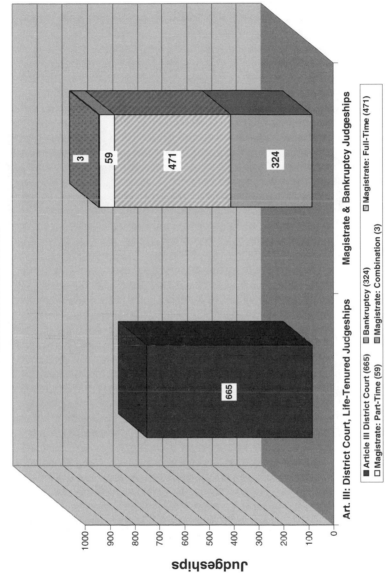

Authorized Trial Level Federal Judgeships in Article III Courts, Nationwide: 2001

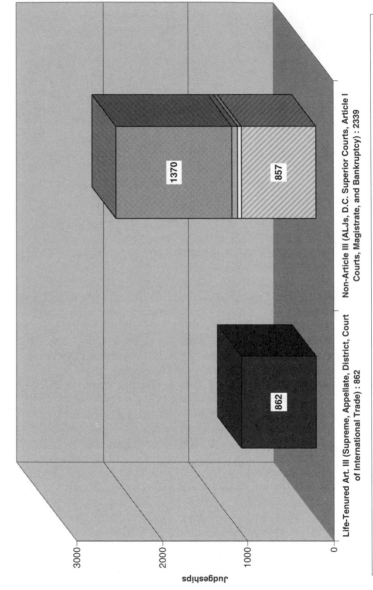

Authorized Federal Judgeships, Including Article I Courts and Administrative Law Judges,
Nationwide: Fall 2001

Judicial authority in a changing South Africa

Hugh Corder
University of Cape Town

'Our legal system cannot be outclassed ... There are attacks, incriminations and accusations that our judgments in law are not objective and independent ... To say our courts are just and impartial is not saying much. The truth is that there are no courts anywhere in the world whose judges' ... integrity is higher than ours.'

H J Coetsee, Minister of Justice, 1986[1]

'The South African Constitution is different [from those which formalise an historical consensus of values]: it retains from the past only what is defensible and represents a decisive break from, and a ringing rejection of, that part of the past which is disgracefully racist, authoritarian, insular, and repressive, and a vigorous identification of and commitment to a democratic, universalistic, caring and aspirationally egalitarian ethos expressly articulated in the Constitution.'

Justice Mahomed, Constitutional Court, 1995[2]

Debates about the proper role and limits of judicial authority in the state are unusually heated, enduring and inconclusive. Talk about judicial review, the democratic deficit, the counter-majoritarian difficulty and the separation of powers matters, because what is at stake is the formal identification of the ultimate forum for political decision-making in a constitutional democracy. Few countries have enjoyed the luxury of a gradual evolution of their governmental systems, informed by rational public debate, such as has been the experience of the established democracies of the developed world. Occasionally, however, it seems to me that the need urgently to design institutions of governance to facilitate democratic transformation in a revolutionary climate provides a clear and necessary resolution to the intractability of such debates about judicial power in the state.

I would argue that South Africa is a case in point, at least in so far as the formal structures of judicial appointment, tenure and jurisdiction are concerned, as well as the manner in which judicial authority has been exercised over the past decade, as I hope to demonstrate in what follows. While acutely sensitive to the dangers inherent in 'transplanting' systems to foreign soil, it may be

---

1. *Cape Times*, 11 January 1986.
2. *S v Makwanyane* 1995 (3) SA 391 (CC) at para 262.

that the common ground which exists historically between the judicial process in the United Kingdom and South Africa provides at least some basis for useful comparison. More than this, it would be a particular satisfaction if, especially after the horrors of apartheid, developments in the former colony were able to assist progress in the imperial power.

A. STRUCTURAL AND SUBSTANTIVE BACKGROUND

In order to understand the current judicial function and court system in South Africa, it is important briefly to note its origins and past record. Although the Dutch settlers who arrived from 1652 brought the Roman-Dutch authorities with them, the administration of justice was rudimentary until the British introduced a Charter of Justice for the Cape Colony in 1827.[3] The formation of the Union of South Africa in 1910[4] brought with it the unification of the highest courts of the constituent colonies (the Cape and Natal) and former Boer republics (Orange Free State and Transvaal) and the establishment of a single appellate court for the whole country in Bloemfontein, the judicial capital. This 'Appellate Division of the Supreme Court of South Africa' had national jurisdiction as the highest judicial authority in the state, within geographical borders which have not changed since, but had no original jurisdiction.[5] Appeal to the Privy Council in London was a possibility seldom exercised, and abolished in 1950.[6] Apart from changes to the regionalisation of jurisdiction consequent on the creation of the 'homeland' system under apartheid, this foundational structure of the superior court system remained in place essentially unaltered until 1994.

The administration of justice was largely British in origin and nature, as was the substantive content of the law applied by the judges, with the exception of most of private law and the criminal law.[7] The judges were appointed by the executive (the Head of State on the advice of the Prime Minister): any 'fit and proper person' could have been appointed to an office with security of tenure, dismissal following only after an address by both Houses of Parliament, an event which has not occurred to this day.[8] Once on the Bench, judges were guided by the English rules of the law of evidence and procedure, as well as by the doctrine of parliamentary sovereignty as developed at Westminster. This

---

3.   The classic treatment of the origins of the South African legal system is to be found in H R Hahlo and Ellison Kahn *South Africa: The Development of its Laws and Constitution* (Cape Town: Juta, 1960) chapters 5 and 6.

4.   By virtue of the South Africa Act 1909 of the Parliament at Westminster (7 Edw VII, c 9).

5.   For a summary account of the development of the courts in the nineteenth and twentieth centuries, see Hugh Corder 'The Judicial Branch of Government: An Historical Overview' in D P Visser (ed) *Essays on the History of Law* (Cape Town: Juta, 1989) pp 60–78.

6.   By the Privy Council Appeals Act, 16 of 1950.

7.   To describe the legal system, as so often happens, as 'Roman Dutch' is at best partially accurate; indeed, even before the post-apartheid period, South African private law had begun to borrow heavily from European sources more broadly.

8.   See the Supreme Court Act, 59 of 1959.

meant that there was no constitutional authority for judicial review of legislative action, except in the most limited circumstances as will be seen, although judicial review of administrative action has, until recently, been the guiding source of the development of administrative law.[9]

How did this system express itself in practice? As regards the composition of the judiciary, all but one of the judges appointed up to 1990 were white and male, with a broad 'balance' being maintained between the two major political and language groupings of the period.[10] Clear political manipulation of the judicial appointments process occurred only in the decade or so which followed the electoral success of the National Party, with its apartheid policy, in 1948.[11] In the application and development of the law, this judiciary generally supported the status quo determined by the white minority, with some notable exceptions in individual cases. Many studies of judicial attitudes,[12] mainly focused on appellate courts, reached remarkably similar conclusions, of which the following[13] is a useful summary:

'... the overall picture [of judicial attitudes] which emerges is one of a group of men who saw their dominant roles as the protectors of a stability [in the society]. This conception of their task was, doubtless, influenced by their racial and class backgrounds, education and training. The judges expressed it in terms of a positivistic acceptance of ... legislative sovereignty, despite a patently racist political structure, and a desire to preserve the existing order of legal relations, notwithstanding its basis in manifest social inequalities ... There can be little argument that the picture of the appellate judiciary, as a body of fearless fighters for the ... unrepresented majority, is a myth.'

How had such a myth ever taken hold in the public imagination, at least of the white minority, as well as in legal and judicial circles in many other parts of the world? The answer must be traced to the early 1950s, when the Appellate Division used its limited power of judicial review of legislative action (in regard to the non-racial franchise in the Cape Province) to declare as unconstitutional and invalid two Acts of Parliament which sought to place 'coloured' male voters

9.   See L G Baxter *Administrative Law* (Cape Town: Juta, 1984) for the most authoritative statement of administrative law in its 'common law' guise.

10.   Two leading sources for a critical review of the South African judiciary generally are Albie Sachs *Justice in South Africa* (London: Chatto Heinemann, 1973); and John Dugard *Human Rights and the South African Legal Order* (Princeton: Princeton University Press, 1978).

11.   See Dugard, n 10 above, pp 10–11, and Christopher Forsyth *In Danger for their Talents* (Cape Town: Juta, 1985) chapter 1, a detailed study of the record of the Appellate Division from 1950 to 1980.

12.   Apart from Sachs and Dugard, both n 10 above, and Forsyth, n 11 above, see A S Mathews *Law, Order and Liberty in South Africa* (Cape Town: Juta, 1971); and Hugh Corder *Judges at Work* (Cape Town: Juta, 1984). A more philosophical approach was taken by David Dyzenhaus *Hard Cases in Wicked Legal Systems* (Oxford: Clarendon Press, 1991).

13.   See Corder, n 12 above, pp 237 and 240.

on a separate electoral roll.[14] At the same time, several acts of the public administration and the executive in the implementation of early apartheid measures were set aside through judicial review of administrative action.[15] It is well known, however, that by the mid-1960s at the latest, this judicial resistance to the undermining of the rule of law had been defeated, both by legislative intransigence as well as judicial acquiescence, and that the ensuing decades witnessed ever more abject abandonment by the courts of the basic tenets of justice in the face of legislated injustice and executive tyranny.[16] The notion of the 'judiciary as saviour' proved remarkably tenacious in the midst of this slide into state lawlessness,[17] but by the time of the successive states of emergency of the late 1980s the idea had effectively been abandoned, even by the most optimistic.

Yet amidst all the bleakness and sense of impending doom, debates continued to rage in the literature, in university lecture rooms, and among liberal and progressive lawyers within South Africa and the ranks of the liberation movements and exiles abroad, about the role of the courts as a means of struggle against apartheid, and about the potential for law and the courts to transform post-apartheid South Africa from a racist oligarchy to a constitutional democracy.[18] Furthermore, questions were raised about the capacity of the law through the courts to assist socio-economic development in a country with such radically unequal distribution of wealth.[19] Even the apartheid regime was moved to enter the lists, with an instruction to the South African Law Commission to investigate and report on the protection of 'group and human rights' through the law,[20] while the rising tide of constitutionalism in central and eastern Europe facilitated the revival of 'rights discourse' within the constitutional planning of the African National Congress leadership.[21]

Thus, by the time that Nelson Mandela walked free from prison in early 1990, a remarkable confluence of thinking on constitutional democratic matters had occurred at the level of general principle among most of those who would

---

14. See *Harris v Minister of the Interior* 1952 (2) SA 428 (AD), and the useful summary of these events in Dugard, n 10 above, pp 28–34.

15. See, for example, *R v Ngwevela* 1954 (1) SA 123 (AD); *R v Abdurahman* 1950 (3) SA 136 (AD); and *R v Lusu* 1953 (2) SA 484 (AD).

16. For a graphic account of the final effects of apartheid on the Appellate Division, see Stephen Ellmann *In a Time of Trouble* (Oxford: Clarendon Press, 1992).

17. See the apologia for the judiciary by Adrienne van Blerk *Judge and be Judged* (Cape Town: Juta, 1988).

18. All of the works cited in nn 10–12, 16 and 17 above contain such discussions. See further Hugh Corder and Dennis Davis 'Law and Social Practice: An Introduction' in Hugh Corder (ed) *Essays on Law and Social Practice* (Cape Town: Juta, 1988) chapter 1, and all the chapters in Part Two of that book.

19. See the articles by Dennis Davis 'The Case against the Inclusion of Socio-Economic Demands in a Bill of Rights except as Directive Principles'; by N Haysom 'Constitutionalism, Majoritarianism, Democracy and Socio-Economic Rights'; and E Mureinik 'Beyond a Charter of Luxuries; Economic Rights in the Constitution', all of which appeared in (1992) 8 SAJHR at 475, 451 and 464 respectively.

20. See *Project 58: Group and Human Rights*, which ran from 1986 to 1994, producing several reports which influenced government thinking and the general debate about rights protection.

21. See the Constitutional Guidelines published in August 1988.

engage in negotiation and drafting the constitution of a liberated South Africa over the following six years. This sense of common purpose had been assisted by ever more frequent meetings between lawyers from South Africa and those in exile in 1988 and 1989. This did not mean that there was nothing to debate and fight over in the ensuing talks, but it did imply that many of the fundamental questions about the role of judicial review in a democracy had been considered in some depth, smoothing the passage of a Bill of Rights and a constitutional court as keystones of the future Constitution.[22]

B. NEGOTIATING A COMPROMISE: PRAGMATISM AND LEGITIMACY

'To distrust the judiciary marks the beginning of the end of society. Smash the present patterns of the institution, rebuild it on a different basis ... but don't stop believing in it.'

Honoré Balzac[23]

'It is to be noted how lapses in the administration of justice make an especially disastrous impression on the public; the hegemonic apparatus is more sensitive in this sector ...'

Antonio Gramsci[24]

I first juxtaposed these quotations in print almost 20 years ago,[25] in the depths of a state of emergency, in an attempt to depict what seemed to me to be the two major challenges facing the body politic in South Africa as it turned its attention to the structure and role of the judicial branch in a future South Africa. On the one hand were those who argued for the protective force of the rule of law as enforced through an impartial and independent judiciary with a considerable degree of authority to review and check the exercise of power by the legislature and executive in a constitutional democracy. By the very nature of the racial composition of the legal profession, including the Bench, and because of the grudging acknowledgement of the objective fact that some space had been preserved for some level of political activity by the opponents of apartheid within South Africa by isolated but principled judgments of the Supreme Court and by the adherence to a fair degree of legalism ('rule by law') by Parliament until the mid-1980s, it was recognised that the existing judiciary would in all likelihood have to play some role in a democratic South Africa.

---

22. Those seeking further detail on the process of constitutional change are referred to Hassen Ebrahim *The Soul of a Nation* (Cape Town: Oxford University Press, 1998); and Richard Spitz with Matthew Chaskalson *The Politics of Transition* (Johannesburg: Witwatersrand University Press, 2000). A brief summary can be found in Hugh Corder 'Towards a South African Constitution' (1994) 57 MLR 491.
23. *Splendeurs et miseres des courtisanes* (Paris: Garnier-Flammarion, 1968) p 367.
24. *Selections from the Prison Notebooks* (London: Lawrence and Wishart, 1971) p 246.
25. See Hugh Corder 'The Supreme Court: Arena of Struggle?' in W G James (ed) *The State of Apartheid* (Boulder, Colorado: Lynne Rienner, 1987) pp 93–115.

On the other hand, the overwhelmingly negative record of the superior court judiciary in matters where individual rights clashed with state power combined with the mockery that was the administration of 'justice' in the magistrates court and the tribunals which maintained the 'pass laws' (which prevented Africans from residence in most urban areas) to produce in the vast majority of the population a weary cynicism at best or a crisis of legitimacy at worst in regard to law and the courts. This last point of view was graphically reinforced through the many forlorn challenges to all aspects of emergency rule from 1985.[26] This led in turn to great suspicion among many activists about the sudden espousal by those associated with the minority regime of limited government, a Bill of Rights and a supreme Constitution with a final court acting as interpretive guardian – some went so far as even to form an 'anti-bill of rights committee'.[27] Such was the forbidding context in which negotiations about the future structure of the courts took place.

Much has been written about the series of informal and formal discussions which took place from 1990 to 1994 in the production of the legislated formula which enabled the transition of political power to the electoral majority to occur *relatively* peacefully.[28] I will focus here only on the negotiations which dealt with the role, jurisdiction and structure of the courts, and the appointment and conditions of service of the judiciary, including those already in office.

The blueprint for the future constitution was extracted from the proceedings and points of agreement reached in the 'Convention for a Democratic South Africa' (CODESA), which existed formally from December 1991 to May 1992.[29] In between the plenary public gatherings of political leaders which initiated and then inconclusively closed this critical episode in South Africa's constitution-making process, 'working groups' bargained hard in closed session to reach points of agreement which would act as the guidelines for the eventual constitution. Many of these points found expression in the list of 'Constitutional Principles' contained in a schedule to the 1993 (interim) Constitution,[30] which in turn provided the framework of standards against which the validity of the 1996 (final) Constitution[31] was to be assessed. (I assume that it is well known that the formal key to political transition was the two-stage nature of constitutional negotiations: the first the production of a constitution of limited life, agreed to by political groupings *prior to* the holding of the first free elections based on universal franchise; the second, modelled on and constrained by the first, negotiated by that first freely elected Parliament, within two years of its first sitting and having to be 'certified' by the Constitutional Court for compliance with the Constitutional Principles contained in the first Constitution, before taking effect.)

---

26. See Ellmann, n 16 above, passim.
27. A 'Black Law Students Anti-Bill of Rights Committee' was established in Pretoria in 1988.
28. See, for example, the works cited at n 22 above.
29. For a contemporary account of the proceedings at CODESA, see Steven Friedman (ed) *The Long Journey* (Johannesburg: Ravan Press, 1993).
30. Act 200 of 1993, a statute of the tri-cameral 'apartheid' Parliament set up in 1983, the Principles being contained in Schedule 4.
31. Act 108 of 1996, the 'Constitution of the Republic of South Africa'.

Among these Constitutional Principles are the following, relevant for present purposes:

'Everyone shall enjoy all universally accepted fundamental rights, freedoms and civil liberties, which shall be provided for and protected by entrenched and justiciable provisions in the Constitution ...'[32]

'The Constitution shall be the supreme law of the land ...'[33]

'The legal system shall ensure the equality of all before the law and an equitable legal process ...'[34]

'There shall be a separation of powers between the legislature, executive and judiciary, with appropriate checks and balances to ensure accountability, responsiveness and openness.'[35]

'The judiciary shall be appropriately qualified, independent and impartial and shall have the power and jurisdiction to safeguard and enforce the Constitution and all fundamental rights.'[36]

Such was the recipe for the drafting of the final Constitution, but the principles were also the effective backbone of the interim Constitution, the terms of which were agreed to through the achievement of 'sufficient consensus' among the participants in the Multiparty Negotiating Process held from April to November, 1993. The hallmark of this Constitution was the extensive use of bilateral bargaining between the two major groups of players (the apartheid regime and the African National Congress), such that the product reads much like a contract of compromises, a feature also present in regard to the judiciary.[37]

A number of proposals for the enforcement mechanisms of the Bill of Rights was made by four of the parties, but there was broad agreement on the following elements: an expanded concept of standing to sue for the protection of rights; a crucial role for some form of constitutional court as the final arbiter of rights protection; and the necessity for subsidiary investigative and mediating bodies such as a human rights commission and an ombudsman.[38] All of these elements found their way into the interim Constitution, but it is necessary in the present context only to deal with the second issue.

The 'technical committees' which assisted the negotiators by proposing draft constitutional provisions received only one submission on the structure of the highest court. This came from the then government, and recommended (along

---

32. 1993 Constitution, n 30 above, Schedule 4, Principle II.
33. 1993 Constitution, n 30 above, Principle IV.
34. 1993 Constitution, n 30 above, Principle V.
35. 1993 Constitution, n 30 above, Principle VI.
36. 1993 Constitution, n 30 above, Principle VII.
37. In addition to the works listed at n 22 above, see Steven Friedman and Doreen Atkinson (eds) *The Small Miracle* (Johannesburg: Ravan Press, 1994).
38. For further detail see Lourens du Plessis and Hugh Corder *Understanding South Africa's Transitional Bill of Rights* (Cape Town: Juta, 1994), chapter 6; and Spitz n 22 above, chapter 11.

German lines) a second (Constitutional) Chamber for the Appellate Division in Bloemfontein as the final court on constitutional issues, presided over by the Chief Justice. This proposal ignored the highly contested nature of the part which the Appellate Division had played in the maintenance of the injustice of apartheid and emergency rule, particularly in the immediately preceding decade.[39]

After a fair degree of controversy and brinkmanship, especially over the manner in which its members should be appointed, the interim Constitution stipulated that a new Constitutional Court (CC) should be established, separate from the Supreme Court, with ultimate jurisdiction in constitutional matters. The provincial divisions of the then Supreme Court (which would continue to exist) would enjoy limited constitutional jurisdiction, but this would not extend to the Appellate Division, an effective sanction for its track record in the protection of fundamental rights. The Appellate Division would, however, retain its role as the highest court in non-constitutional matters, although the CC would determine what qualified as such matter.[40]

The appointment of judges would involve the establishment and participation of a Judicial Service Commission (JSC) with both lawyer and 'lay' membership, while the final and formal authority would rest with the President, as Head of State. An attempt by the then government and the ANC to allocate the power to appoint all members of the CC to the executive (the President in consultation with the Cabinet) was foiled by the spirited intervention of the small but articulate Democratic Party, a strong proponent of liberal democracy. The JSC would play a pivotal role in the appointment, removal from office, and conditions of judicial service and the administration of justice in general.[41] As these provisions in the interim Constitution have remained essentially unaltered in the final Constitution, I will defer detailed treatment of the composition and role of the JSC to the next section.

One important element in the judicial puzzle remains to be dealt with, however, and that is the fate of those judges then holding office. The options were clear: retain them all; dismiss them all; reappoint them all, subject to a formal process; or dismiss them all, requiring those who wished to serve the future state to apply for reappointment according to the new method for selecting judges. In the end, several factors combined to produce the following resolution of the problem: all serving judges who swore an oath of allegiance to the new Constitution would be entitled to continue in office,[42] and all subsequently did. Among the arguments which pointed to this compromise were the following: the pragmatic realisation that the day-to-day running of civil and criminal trials could not be suspended for the time it would take to set up the JSC and then reappoint old or appoint new judges; the fact that the pool of lawyers eligible for appointment as judges would be very small if all 'old' judges were to be excluded; the strong urge for legal continuity, which even conspired to ensure that the interim Constitution was one of the last Acts passed by the last apartheid Parliament; and the overwhelming emphasis on

39. See Du Plessis and Corder, n 38 above, pp 196–197.
40. See Spitz, n 22 above, pp 191–197.
41. For further details, see the 1993 Constitution, n 30 above, Chapter 7.
42. 1993 Constitution, n 30 above, s 241 (2), read with Schedule 3.

reconciliation which was beginning to take hold of the process, and was epitomised in the conduct of Nelson Mandela. Pragmatism seems to have had the edge, although the urgent need to establish legitimacy remained on the agenda.

C. THE PRINCIPAL FEATURES OF THE JUDICIAL BRANCH OF GOVERNMENT UNDER THE 1996 CONSTITUTION

A number of innovations in the judicial process accompanied liberation in 1994, all of which were consolidated and even strengthened in the process of debating and drafting the final Constitution of 1996. Among such changes were:

- a radically extended capacity for standing to sue, such that group or class actions, and actions in the public interest, are now possible;[43]
- related to standing, the Constitutional Court has on occasion entertained 'amicus briefs' from groups which are not directly parties to a dispute but whose work and expertise would assist the court in its deliberations,[44]
- the provision at state expense of considerable research assistance to the judges of the Constitutional Court, with some further but limited such assistance being provided to other courts; and
- the renaming of the provincial divisions of the former Supreme Court as High Courts, while the Appellate Division is now known as the Supreme Court of Appeal (SCA).[45]

These changes occurred, of course, in the context of the incorporation of a Bill of Rights in a supreme Constitution,[46] enforced and interpreted by the superior judiciary, all divisions of which have had constitutional jurisdiction[47] since early 1997. A wide range of rights is protected in the Bill, which is modelled loosely on the Canadian Charter of Rights and Freedoms of 1982, the rights being granted in an open-ended fashion (for example, 'everyone has the right to freedom of association'[48]) but each is limitable in terms of a general limitations clause[49] (which provides essentially that such limitation must be 'reasonable and justifiable in an open and democratic society based on human dignity, equality and freedom' and must be proportional in its impact to the objective sought to be achieved by the limitation).

Against this background, it is clear that the CC plays a pivotal role in determining the success of the enterprise, which in turn highlights its composition and the manner of the appointment and conditions of service of its members. The CC now consists of the Chief Justice, the Deputy Chief Justice

---

43. 1996 Constitution, n 31 above, s 38.
44. Provided for in the Rules of the Constitutional Court.
45. 1996 Constitution, n 31 above, s 166 (b) and (c).
46. 1996 Constitution, n 31 above, Chapter 2.
47. 1996 Constitution, n 31 above, s 172.
48. 1996 Constitution, n 31 above, s 18.
49. 1996 Constitution, n 31 above, s 36.

and nine other judges, all of whom must be South African citizens[50]. It generally sits en banc, but at least eight judges constitute the quorum.[51] At all times, at least four members of the CC must be persons who were judges (of a High Court or the SCA) at the time of appointment.[52] A judge of the CC, unlike other superior court judges, holds office for a non-renewable term of 12 years or until he or she reaches the age of 70, except where an Act of Parliament extends such term.[53] Currently, the law provides[54] that a CC judge must perform 'active service' beyond the expiry of their 12-year term or their seventieth birthday until they have completed a period of 15 years service as judges or have reached the age of 75. All judges enjoy a substantial security of tenure during their term of office, removal from such office being possible only on the grounds of suffering from an incapacity, being grossly incompetent or guilty of gross misconduct. Removal by the President can only occur after a finding by the JSC that such grounds exist and after a two-thirds majority vote of the National Assembly (the directly elected lower house of Parliament).[55]

Judicial appointments since 1994 have continued to be made formally through the President as Head of State, the major change being the involvement of the JSC. This follows a pattern widely observed in other countries, and imposed on all former British colonies in Africa which gained their independence in the 1960s, as part of the model constitution generated in Whitehall.[56] The South African variant has many more members than is typical elsewhere, in an attempt to be as inclusive of as many interest groups as possible. The JSC consists of the following:[57]

- the Chief Justice as Chair;
- the President of the SCA;
- one Judge President (of a High Court) designated by all Judges President;
- two practising advocates (barristers), two practising attorneys (solicitors) and one teacher of law, in each case nominated by their constituency;
- the Minister of Justice (a member of the Cabinet);
- six members of the National Assembly, of whom three must be from opposition parties;
- four delegates to the National Council of Provinces (the indirectly elected 'upper' house of Parliament) designated by the Council with the support of two-thirds of the nine provinces; and
- four persons designated by the President (as Head of Government) after consultation with the leaders of all the parties in the National Assembly.

---

50. 1996 Constitution, n 31 above, s 167 (1).
51. 1996 Constitution, n 31 above, s 167 (2).
52. 1996 Constitution, n 31 above, s 174 (5).
53. 1996 Constitution, n 31 above, s 176 (1).
54. Judges' Remuneration and Conditions of Employment Act, 47 of 2001, s 4.
55. 1996 Constitution, n 31 above, s 177 (1) and (2).
56. See Hugh Corder 'The Appointment of Judges: Some Comparative Ideas' (1992) 3 Stellenbosch LR 207.
57. 1996 Constitution, n 31 above, s 178.

Thus it will be seen that the JSC has 23 permanent members, of whom eight are drawn from different parts of the legal profession, one is a member of the executive, ten are members of the national legislature and four can be drawn from any constituency. In fact, the proportion of lawyers (either practising or lapsed) is greater than it appears, as the members of the legislature and those appointed by the President tend also to have qualifications in law (there are currently at least six lawyers among this number). The number of members of the JSC increases by two when vacancies at High Court level are being filled, the Judge President of that court and the Premier of the relevant province being added to its ranks ad hoc.

The JSC's role as regards appointments to the High Court and 'promotion' to the SCA, as well as to the office of Judge President, is determinative, as the President 'must appoint ... on the advice of ...' the JSC, which in practice means that the JSC recommends a single person for such appointments.[58] Appointment to the offices of Chief Justice of the CC and his or her Deputy, and to President of the SCA and his or her Deputy, are the prerogative of the President as head of the national executive, although he is bound to consult the JSC in regard to all such offices, as well as the leaders of all parties represented in the National Assembly in the case of the Chief Justice and Deputy.[59]

The appointment process for judges of the CC is more complex, reflecting the heightened political role of that court. The JSC must provide the President with a 'list of nominees with three names more than the number' of vacancies which exist. The President has the power of appointment as head of government after consulting with the Chief Justice and the leaders of the parties represented in the National Assembly. If the President finds an insufficient number of 'acceptable' nominees on the list, he must advise the JSC of the reasons for this view, and the JSC must supplement the list, from which the President must make the appointments necessary.[60]

Thus far the formal provisions in the Constitution: how has the JSC operated in practice? The pattern was set in late 1994 by the first high-profile meetings held to determine the list of nominees for filling the balance of the positions on the first CC (six in number, the Chief Justice and the four members appointed from the ranks of serving judges having already been determined by the President in terms of the interim Constitution). The Commission called publicly for nominations and applications for these positions, then short listed over 20 persons for interview in public – no radio microphone or television camera was admitted, but reporters for the print media were present, as well as interested members of the public. The Chief Justice and the members of the JSC agreed in advance on a series of issues which would need to be canvassed in the interviews as well as areas which it would be unwise to cover. Thus the candidates' activities during apartheid, membership of secret organisations and views generally on judicial review and the protection of human rights were probed, while their stances on contentious matters likely to come before them if appointed to the CC (such as the death penalty and abortion) were out of

58. 1996 Constitution, n 31 above, s 174 (6).
59. 1996 Constitution, n 31 above, s 174 (3).
60. 1996 Constitution, n 31 above, s 174 (4)

bounds. Once the interviews were complete, the JSC went into closed session to evaluate the applicants and reach their recommendations.

With one exception in the meeting which followed immediately, the JSC has settled into this manner of functioning since. It typically meets twice a year, for a few days at a time, having advertised some time in advance the vacancies for which it will be conducting interviews. The Constitution provides[61] that 'any appropriately qualified woman or man who is a fit and proper person' may be appointed as a judge, although 'the need for the judiciary to reflect broadly the racial and gender composition [nationally] must be considered' when recommending candidates for appointment.[62] In the latter respect, there has been a substantial shift in the demography of the judiciary over the past nine years: from the situation in early 1994 of one black and two white female judges out of 164, the current breakdown by race and gender is (out of a total of 214 judges): 128 white men (60%), 14 white women, 42 African men, eight African women, eight 'coloured' men, two 'coloured' women, and 11 'Asiatic' men and two Asiatic women. The proportion of 'black' judges has thus risen to about one-third, while the number of female judges (at 25) is still quite low (about 12%). As regards seniority, seven of the 11 Courts are now headed by black judges.[63]

The work of the JSC has been applauded by most observers[64] in the legal profession, although there have been a few isolated appointments which have been criticised. While calls for a speedier racial and gender transformation of the Bench continue to be made in political circles, within the profession there is concern that the initial pool of potential black or female judges has been exhausted, and that it will take a little longer for substantial numbers of such lawyers who are suitable for appointment to come through the system. Judicial ranks have been diversified further through the appointment of attorneys and academics as judges, including to the ranks of the CC and SCA. One of the ways in which the number of potential judges has been broadened has been through a series of educational seminars for 'aspirant judges' arranged nationally with donor support over the past five years or so.

In addition, extensive use has been made of the appointment for short periods (one to three months) of 'acting judges'[65] to allow potential judges to experience what it is like to serve on the Bench and also to assess their suitability for a permanent appointment. Indeed, the JSC is now very reluctant to consider anyone for appointment unless he or she has served as an acting judge.[66] This is a controversial step as acting judgeships are essentially in the gift of the

61. 1996 Constitution, n 31 above, s 174 (1).

62. 1996 Constitution, n 31 above, s 174 (2).

63. See Penuell Maduna (Minister of Justice and Constitutional Development) 'Address at the Banquet of the Judicial Officers' Symposium'; and M T Moerane 'The Meaning of Transformation of the Judiciary in the New South African Context' (2003) 120 SALJ 663 and 708 respectively, at 665 and 713. It is noteworthy that 128 judges (60%) have been appointed over the past nine years: see Maduna, above.

64. For a perceptive early review, see K Malleson 'Assessing the performance of the Judicial Service Commission' (1999) 116 SALJ 36.

65. As contemplated in the 1996 Constitution, n 31 above, s 175.

66. See Moerane, n 63 above, p 713.

executive, acting in 'concurrence' with the administrative head of the court (Chief Justice or Judge President) in which she or he will serve. On the other hand, a spell as an acting judge (a practice in place for many decades in South Africa) may well afford a lawyer who is considering judicial office the opportunity to gauge the desirability of taking such a step, and acting judges have helped frequently to reduce the heavy workload resting on the permanent judiciary.

The restructuring of the South African courts and the diversification of the judiciary is thus well in hand, which has gone some way to addressing the issue of the deficit in legitimacy of the administration of justice caused by centuries of racist oppression, exacerbated by the inhumanity of apartheid. In what remains of this piece, I will survey aspects of the judicial record, particularly that of the CC, since 1994.

D. GENERATING PUBLIC CONFIDENCE WHILE SHOWING RESPECT FOR THE LEGISLATURE AND EXECUTIVE

Any review of the early jurisprudence of the South African CC must needs take account of the balance struck between establishing its legitimacy in the eyes of the majority and earning support from Parliament and the Cabinet.[67] While this sort of balance is integral to much of the debate about the proper role of judicial review in a constitutional democracy, the weight of responsibility resting on this first CC as guardian of the 'foundational values' of the Constitution[68] has been particularly onerous. I would say that the substantial majority of opinion would acknowledge the positive impact which the judgments of the CC have had on the general growth of respect for human rights and government limited by law notwithstanding some critical commentary.[69] Before considering some landmark cases which have contributed to this view, we should note several factors which have aided and detracted from the Court's task in trying to achieve this self-conscious objective.[70]

---

67. This may seem an odd tension, in that the legislature at least ought not to be out of step with the 'majority' in a democracy. In reality, however, and especially in the current socio-political circumstances of South Africa, I would argue that the urgent needs of the majority in the socio-economic sphere may well run counter to the medium-term policies of the legislature and executive, leaving it to the Courts to resolve the tension, guided by a reading of the Constitution.

68. As are to be found in the 1996 Constitution, n 31 above, s 1.

69. Much has been written on the work of the CC so far. Within South Africa, the leading journals in this respect are the SA Law Journal and the SA Journal on Human Rights. The latter has devoted specific attention on an annual basis to an analysis of the previous year's activities of the CC: see (1996) 12 part 1; (1997) 13 part 2; (1998) 14 part 2: (1999) 15 part 2; (2000) 16 from 283 to 371; and (2001) 17 from 210 to 287 – each part contains statistics detailing judicial activity in the previous year's cases.

70. There is no doubt that the CC judges have set themselves, and the Court, this task. This kind of statement recurs in many of the early judgments handed down, as well as in extra-curial pronouncements by the judges: see, for example, Arthur Chaskalson 'The Third Bram Fischer Lecture' (2000) 16 SAJHR 193.

On the positive side, the members of the Court are, almost without exception, men and women with a deep knowledge of the political and socio-economic reality of South Africa. Several of them were directly involved in political activity,[71] outside their careers as lawyers, while the practising lawyers all were involved in or at least familiar with attempts to use the law in the struggle against injustice.[72] The court has been ably led, so that no obvious factions or groupings have developed, which is no mean feat considering the strength of many of the personalities on that Bench. As has been mentioned, the judges have been assisted by young researchers of great calibre and the Court boasts of an increasingly significant library, leading to judgments which refer, again as a matter of policy, to an extraordinarily wide range of foreign comparative law. This feature has in turn rapidly propelled the CC into international prominence, engendering respect for its work throughout the world.

Perhaps the single most significant source of support for the Court came from the uncomplicated, warm and frequently expressed respect for its work accorded to it by ex-President Mandela. That he chose to do so on several occasions immediately in reaction to judgments which had found legislative or executive conduct unconstitutional[73] made such a stance all the more significant. President Mbeki has been far less forthcoming in this respect, and some Cabinet ministers have made critical comments on occasion, but usually in circumstances in which public opinion is strikingly in support of the Court's judgments.[74] The Court has also benefited from a relatively light case-load, as well as the arguments of a highly competent group of counsel who have carved out for themselves enviable reputations as constitutional experts in a relatively short period.

On the other hand, the CC has for most of its existence had a majority of white members[75] who have written many of the most significant judgments.[76] Despite permitting television cameras into the court room and the issuing of a

71. Albie Sachs, a prominent member of the African National Congress for over 30 years and the victim of a bomb attack by an agent of the apartheid regime, is the most obvious example.

72. The Chief Justice, Arthur Chaskalson, a member of the defence team in a number of prominent political trials and the founder of the major public-interest law firm, the Legal Resources Centre, is the leading example. The late Justices Didcott and Mahomed were in the same mould, the former as a member of the judiciary.

73. For example, *Executive Council, Western Cape Legislature v President of the Republic of South Africa* 1995 (4) SA 877 (CC).

74. Such as in the *TAC* case (*Minister of Health v TAC (No 1)* 2002 (5) SA 703 (CC); *In re certain Amicus Curiae Applications: Minister of Health v TAC* 2002 (5) SA 713 (CC); and *Minister of Health v TAC (No 2)* 2002 (5) SA 721 (CC), see n 116 and accompanying text below), in which the court ordered greater provision by the state of anti-retroviral treatment for those infected by HIV/AIDS – the Minister of Health initially made dismissive remarks about the Court's stance.

75. Until the end of 2002, this majority consisted of: Chaskalson CJ, and Ackermann, Goldstone, Kriegler, O'Regan and Sachs JJ, to which must be added Didcott J until his death in 1998. I must hasten to add that these judges have very varied backgrounds – South African society remains, however, very conscious of race.

76. This is in no way to minimise the judgments handed down by the other members of the Court, especially those of Mahomed J (until his move to head the SCA in early 1998) and Langa DCJ.

press release summarising the issues and main findings in each case, the reporting of judgments in the public media has been extremely uninformed and often inaccurate. This has been particularly damaging in highly controversial cases – indeed, it was the poverty of the coverage of the first case, involving the constitutionality of the death penalty,[77] which persuaded the Court to begin to issue media releases. Failure by the legislature speedily enough to remedy findings of unconstitutionality by the CC have not assisted the development of respect by the public administration, and the lack till now of a permanent and imposing court building as well as the public row about the tenure of office of the CC judges[78] have affected its image negatively in the eyes of many.

The true test of its worth, however, must be based in its judgments, and I seek to substantiate my positive assessment of the role of the CC by focusing on four important cases. Each illustrates one or more important aspects of its function and image in the government of the post-apartheid South Africa. I make no attempt fully to describe and analyse the judgments; my aim is rather to use the cases to demonstrate the CC's responses to the challenges faced by the judiciary, in upholding the values of the Constitution and the quest for a constitutional democracy.

The CC deliberately chose one of the most vexed moral, political and ethical questions, the constitutionality of the death penalty, as the first case to be heard.[79] Although it was the second case in which judgment was given,[80] *S v Makwanyane*[81] was a tour de force, there being a leading judgment[82] concurred in unanimously and declaring the death penalty to be unconstitutional, as well as ten further separate concurring opinions, giving each Justice the opportunity to put her or his view on record.[83] The primary ground for holding capital punishment to be unlawful was the (interim) Constitution's prohibition of cruel, inhuman or degrading treatment or punishment,[84] although this view was strengthened by the rights guaranteeing equality, life and human dignity.[85]

Makwanyane set the standard and the tone for the future judgments of the Court. In judgments replete with references to comparative legal experience and lofty declarations of the significance of the move to constitutionalism in South Africa, it signalled the adoption of a 'generous and purposive' approach to constitutional interpretation; of a willingness to accept the relevance of legislative history without becoming a slave to the 'original intent' of the

---

77. *S v Makwanyane* 1995 (3) SA 391 (CC).
78. See F Du Bois 'Tenure on the Constitutional Court' (2002) 119 SALJ 1.
79. On 17 February 1995.
80. *S v Zuma* 1995 (2) SA 642 (CC) was the first, fully two months before *S v Makwanyane* 1995 (3) SA 391 (CC).
81. *S v Makwanyane* 1995 (3) SA 391 (CC).
82. By Chaskalson P (as he then was styled).
83. For contemporary reviews of the judgments, see (1996) 12 SAJHR 61 at 61–78 and 138–141.
84. 1993 Constitution, n 30 above, s 11 (2).
85. 1993 Constitution, n 30 above, ss 8, 9 and 10 respectively. The right to equality was particularly important, there being substantial suspicion, if not direct evidence, that the death penalty was imposed unduly frequently on black South Africans.

founders of the Constitution; of the courage to accept the duty imposed on it by the Constitution, in the light of the drafting context, to resolve the issue,[86] despite the weight of public opinion appearing to be to the contrary – in effect, to lead a reluctant public in a direction determined by moral and ethical considerations; and yet too of an appreciation that public support for the decision could be triggered by references to traditional African concepts of human solidarity[87] ('ubuntu' – a person is a person through other people) and to the strong desire to break decisively from the ghastliness of the immediate past, with which the widespread and frequent use of capital punishment was implicitly associated.[88]

One commentator[89] speaks of: '... the Court's commitment to creating a new culture of human rights ... and to upholding the supremacy of the Constitution, as well as [its] cautious and often hesitating recognition of the complexity of its relationships to the framers of the Constitution, public opinion and the newly democratised representative institutions ...' In making this commitment in as charged a context as the death penalty,[90] and in taking such a strong and united stand at the outset of its life, the Court was indicating both to the public at large and their elected representatives that it intended playing a leading yet sensitive role in the development of constitutional politics in South Africa.

This emphatic start was followed by any number of significant yet less dramatic decisions, many of which set aside apartheid-era statutory provisions,[91] some of which addressed ambiguities in the new constitutional arrangements,[92] while yet others began to explore the limits of freedom[93] and the concept of equality.[94] Perhaps the next most revealing case, however, was *AZAPO v President of the Republic of South Africa*,[95] in which the Court's commitment to the compromise essential to an understanding of the Constitution was severely tested. The issue at stake was whether those who had committed gross violations of human rights under apartheid would, after receiving 'amnesty' from the Truth and Reconciliation Commission (TRC), be absolved not only

---

86. All indications during the negotiations were that the political parties preferred this issue to be resolved by the Court.

87. Referred to by no fewer than six of the judges as support for their view.

88. In the 1980s South Africa had the highest annual rate of capital punishment of any country; several high-profile campaigns to save the lives of those sentenced to death for politically inspired acts of violence contributed to a moratorium on the carrying out of such sentences in 1989.

89. H Klug 'Striking Down Death' (1996) 12 SAJHR 61 at 70.

90. About 400 convicted prisoners languished on death row.

91. For example, *S v Bhulwana; S v Gwadiso* 1996 (1) SA 388 (CC); and *S v Williams* 1995 (3) SA 632 (CC).

92. *Executive Council, Western Cape Legislature v President of the Republic of South Africa* 1995 (4) SA 877 (CC); and *Premier of KwaZulu – Natal v President of the Republic of South Africa* (1995) 12 BCLR 1561 (CC).

93. For example, *Case v Minister of Safety and Security; Curtis v Minister of Safety and Security* 1996 (3) SA 617 (CC), which dealt with the possession of pornography and the right to privacy.

94. For example, *Brink v Kitshoff NO* 1996 (4) SA 197 (CC); *Larbi-Odam v MEC for Education, North-West Province* 1998 (1) SA 745 (CC); and *National Coalition for Gay and Lesbian Equality v Minister of Justice* 1999 (1) SA 6 (CC).

95. 1996 (4) SA 671 (CC).

from future criminal prosecution but also civil liability, in the form of claims against them from the surviving relatives of the deceased. The challenge was thus to the constitutional validity of the Act of Parliament[96] which authorised and established the TRC, and the claimants were the Azanian People's Organisation (the successor to the 'black consciousness' movement pioneered by Steve Biko and colleagues in the 1970s), Biko's widow and the family of Griffiths and Victoria Mxenge, lawyers and anti-apartheid activists, both of whom were murdered by the apartheid regime. The appellants relied on their rights to life, dignity, not to be subject to torture and access to court, as well as on the tenets of international law, both customary and treaty-based, in arguing that the Act pushed the concept of 'amnesty' too far.

Significantly, the leading judgment for a unanimous CC was delivered by Mahomed DP, the most senior black judge in South Africa, with a separate concurrence by Didcott J, the most vocal opponent of apartheid who served on the Bench before 1990. With typical verbal flourishes masking obvious anxiety, if not distress, Justice Mahomed dismissed the challenges both domestic and international, relying ultimately on the simple reality that, without the compromise on amnesty contained in the 'postscript' to the interim Constitution there would have been no transition of political power, and the CC itself would not have existed. As he put it:[97]

> 'Even more crucially, but for a mechanism providing for amnesty, the "historic bridge" itself [between the past and the future] might never have been erected. For a successfully negotiated transition, the terms of the transition required not only the agreement of those victimized by abuse but also those threatened by the transition to a "democratic society" ... If the Constitution kept alive the prospect of continuous retaliation and revenge, the agreement of those threatened ... might never have been forthcoming, and ... the bridge itself would have remained wobbly and insecure ...: It was for this reason that those who negotiated the Constitution made a deliberate choice, preferring understanding over vengeance, reparation over retaliation, ubuntu over victimization.'

A further justification[98] for the stance of the Court was that the offer of complete impunity for the perpetrators was the basis for the 'long and necessary process of healing the wounds of the past, transforming anger into a mature understanding and creating the emotional and structural climate essential for "reconciliation" and "reconstruction"'.

While the Court no doubt read the political climate of the country correctly and while the subsequent work of the TRC, although imperfect and often contradictory, provided an extraordinary forum for expressing grief, anger and guilt which assisted the achievement of a degree of reconciliation and truth, the judgment was something of a gamble at the time, and was subject to a fair

---

96. Promotion of National Unity and Reconciliation Act, 34 of 1995, s 20 (7).
97. *AZAPO v President of the Republic of South Africa* 1996 (4) SA 671 (CC) at para 19.
98. To be found in *AZAPO v President of the Republic of South Africa* 1996 (4) SA 671 (CC) at para 17.

degree of criticism.[99] Nevertheless, this case marks an early milestone in the CC's role as an astute player in the South African body politic, content if uncomfortably to adopt a cautious pragmatism, the better to achieve the long-term goal of a firm foundation for the constitutional democracy of which it is a key element.

The third case which I have chosen to discuss briefly is one of a series of challenges[100] to the exercise of executive power, in this instance the appointment of a commission of inquiry by the President, as Head of State. One of the interesting developments since 1994 has been in administrative law,[101] as the common law origins of judicial review of administrative action seek to reinvent themselves as an expression of the right to administrative justice guaranteed in the Bill of Rights.[102] An aspect of this part of the law concerns the distinction between 'executive' as opposed to 'administrative' action,[103] on the former of which the shadow of the royal prerogative powers under Westminster still falls.[104] The *SARFU III* case[105] concluded that the appointment by the President of a commission of inquiry did not fall into the category of 'administrative action', but was nevertheless able to be reviewed for constitutionality against the requirements of the provision in the Constitution which authorised such an act,[106] as well as the 'principle of legality'.

Of greater interest for present purposes was *SARFU II*, in which the recusal of five members of the CC, including Justice Chaskalson, was sought by respondent, on the basis of a 'reasonable apprehension' of bias, in that the justices concerned had a longstanding connection with President Mandela personally or the African National Congress.[107] In order to emphasise the unanimity and solidarity of the ten justices who heard the case, the substantial judgment[108] was delivered in the name of 'the Court'. It took a refreshingly candid view of the reality of the situation in a society such as South Africa, and of the justices' own relationship to that process of transition. At the same time, there can be no doubting the annoyance and anger felt by all the members of the Court at this attempt to impugn their impartiality.

---

99. See, for example, John Dugard 'Memory and the Spectre of International Justice: A Comment on *AZAPO*' (1997) 13 SAJHR 269; and D Moellendorf 'Amnesty, Truth and Justice: AZAPO' (1997) 13 SAJHR 283.

100. The case to be discussed is the second of three involving the same parties as follows: *President of the Republic of South Africa v SARFU* 1999 (2) SA 14 (CC) (SARFU I); *President of the RSA v SARFU* 1999 (4) SA 147 (CC) (SARFU II); and *President of the RSA v SARFU* 2000 (1) SA 1 (CC) (SARFU III).

101. For a good summary of the developments see Cora Hoexter *The New Constitutional and Administrative Law (Volume Two – Administrative Law)* (Cape Town: Juta, 2002) chapter 1.

102. 1993 Constitution, n 30 above, s 24; 1996 Constitution, n 31 above, s 33.

103. 'Administrative action' is the key to unlocking the rights to administrative justice, both in the Constitution, and the Promotion of Administrative Justice Act, 3 of 2000, s 1.

104. A relatively early judgment of the CC ruled that the prerogatives no longer existed after 1994, unless and to the extent that they were incorporated in the Constitution: see *President of the RSA v Hugo* 1997 (4) SA 1 (CC).

105. See n 100 above.

106. 1996 Constitution, n 31 above, s 84 (2) (f).

107. See n 100 above.

108. It runs to 44 pages in the law reports.

The judgment is noteworthy for all sorts of reasons, among others for the test for 'bias' which it adopts,[109] but its chief significance lies in the numerous comments about the role of the judge in a supreme court with the power of judicial review. In a discussion rich in comparative references,[110] the Court's view was that 'absolute neutrality of a judicial officer can hardly if ever be achieved'[111] and that, in a 'multicultural, multi-lingual and multiracial country such as South Africa, it cannot reasonably be expected that judicial officers should share all the views and even the prejudices of those ... who appear before them'.[112] Judges in the highest courts were likely to be strong-minded people with 'propensities', which may have been articulated publicly prior to appointment to the Court.[113]

Furthermore, the fact that a constitutional judge may have engaged in political activity prior to appointment was not uncommon, and it had never been seriously suggested that judges did not have views on law and society: indeed, a judge so remote from the world that she or he had no such views would hardly have been qualified to sit as a judge.[114] In South Africa, so soon after the transition to democracy, it would have been surprising if many candidates for the Bench had not been active in or sympathetic towards the liberation struggle.[115]

The judgment contains much more of interest to students of the judicial process but for present purposes sufficient indication of its importance has been given. It provides a frank and often intimately detailed account of the judges and how they see themselves as both formally removed from but nonetheless interacting with the rough-and-tumble of political life. The final case to be reviewed thrust the Court starkly into highly contested political terrain, and forced the judges to confront the extent to which it was proper to defer to the executive authority in the socio-economic sphere.

The Treatment Action Campaign (TAC), a non-governmental organisation agitating for widespread, state-sponsored treatment for the millions of South Africans suffering from HIV/AIDS, clashed with the Minister of Health in the CC on three occasions in April and May 2002.[116] At stake was the adequacy of the government's grudging and selective policy of test sites for the administration of an anti-retroviral drug to pregnant women to try to arrest mother-to-child transmission of HIV/AIDS, weighed against the socio-economic rights to have access to health care services, and the right of every child to 'basic health care services'.[117] In addition, the appellant minister was

---

109. *President of the RSA v SARFU* 1999 (4) SA 147 (CC) at paras 36, 38, 41 and 48.
110. See particularly *President of the RSA v SARFU* 1999 (4) SA 147 (CC) paras 40, 42 and 45.
111. *President of the RSA v SARFU* 1999 (4) SA 147 (CC) at para 42.
112. *President of the RSA v SARFU* 1999 (4) SA 147 (CC) at para 43
113. *President of the RSA v SARFU* 1999 (4) SA 147 (CC) at para 44, adopting the view of Rehnquist J in *Laird et al v Tatum et al* 409 US 824 (1972) at 836.
114. *President of the RSA v SARFU* 1999 (4) SA 147 (CC) at para 70.
115. *President of the RSA v SARFU* 1999 (4) SA 147 (CC) at para 75.
116. See *Minister of Health v TAC (No 1)* 2002 (5) SA 703 (CC); *In re certain Amicus Curiae Applications: Minister of Health v TAC* 2002 (5) SA 713 (CC); and *Minister of Health v TAC (No 2)* 2002 (5) SA 721 (CC).
117. 1996 Constitution, n 31 above, at s 27 (1) (a) and 28 (1) (c), respectively.

questioning whether government was constitutionally obliged (and could be ordered by a court) 'to plan and implement an effective, comprehensive and progressive programme' such as that argued for by the TAC.[118]

In the face of such a 'polycentric' decision and an executive which had adopted the most extraordinarily obstructive and irrational stance on the issues, supported by the President,[119] the Court closed ranks once more, its unanimous decision being conveyed in a judgment of 'the Court'. The CC had on two previous occasions been faced with demands for the implementation of socio-economic rights – first, for access to health care by an individual,[120] and then for access to basic shelter by a community of 900 adults and children.[121] The Court had refused the first claim, but granted the latter. The TAC application, on the other hand, was highly controversial and had a far wider potential impact, both financially and in respect of the numbers of people affected.

After distilling the essence of the factual and other disputes between the parties,[122] the Court set out its views on the enforcement of socio-economic rights. It proceeded on the basis that such rights were 'clearly' justiciable, which meant that the question before the Court was whether 'the measures adopted by the government to provide access to health care for HIV-positive mothers and their newborn babies fall short of its obligations under the Constitution'.[123] After an extensive and detailed review of the evidence and arguments put before it,[124] the Court concluded that government policy was unreasonably inflexible, and that it would have to be substantially reviewed.[125]

Having reached this conclusion, the Court had to define the limits of its powers to require compliance with its orders by the executive. Earlier in the judgment, it had held as follows:[126]

'It should be borne in mind that ... the Courts are not institutionally equipped to make the wide-ranging factual and political inquiries necessary for determining what the minimum-core standards ... should be, nor for deciding how public revenues should most effectively be spent ... Courts are ill-suited to adjudicate upon issues where Court orders could have multiple social and economic consequences ... The Constitution contemplates rather a restrained and focused role for the Courts, namely, to require the State to take measures to meet its constitutional obligations and to subject the reasonableness of these measures to evaluation [which may have budgetary implications]. In this way the judicial, legislative and executive functions achieve constitutional balance.'

118. See *Minister of Health v TAC (No 2)* 2002 (5) SA 721 (CC) at para 5.
119. President Mbeki's views on HIV/AIDS are widely known, and have been greeted with much scepticism, if not derision.
120. *Soobramoney v Minister of Health, KwaZulu – Natal* 1998 (1) SA 765 (CC).
121. *Government of the Republic of South Africa v Grootboom* 2001 (1) SA 46 (CC).
122. *Minister of Health, v TAC (No 2)* 2002 (5) SA 721 (CC) at paras 10–22.
123. 2002 (5) SA 721 (CC) at para 25.
124. 2002 (5) SA 721 (CC) at paras 40–79.
125. 2002 (5) SA 721 (CC) at paras 80 and 93–95, respectively.
126. 2002 (5) SA 721 (CC) at paras 37 and 38.

In the face of argument from the government counsel[127] that it was only competent for the Court to issue a declaration of rights and that the doctrine of the separation of powers requires that the Court make no order which would have the effect of requiring the executive to pursue a particular policy, the Court acknowledged[128] that 'there are certain matters that are pre-eminently within the domain of one or other of the arms of government', and that all branches of government 'should be sensitive to and respect this separation. This does not mean, however, that Courts cannot or should not make orders that have an impact on policy'. The Court was under a duty to grant effective relief in all cases, and this could include the issuing of a mandamus and the exercise of supervisory jurisdiction, for which the Court cited comparative authority from the US, India, Germany, Canada and the UK.[129] The Court tailored the relief ordered accordingly.[130]

The TAC case illustrates yet another aspect of the jurisdiction and operations of the CC, and is likely to be of great significance in the future, as the quest for the 'progressive realisation' of socio-economic rights gathers momentum. It may well mark a shift in the type of issue to be brought to that Court, the first decade of its existence having been dominated by ensuring the completion of the Constitution-making process,[131] the declaration as unconstitutional of many of the most egregious legislative relics of apartheid and first forays into defining key notions such as dignity, equality and freedom. The immediate future is likely to see much more of the last type of dispute before the Court, as well as the enforcement of socio-economic obligations. In all such matters, the Court will have to balance deference (as respect) to the legislature and executive with its duties to the people as a whole, through the Constitution. It has shown that it is acutely conscious of this role, and has proved adept at playing its part till now.

E. TAKING STOCK: FORM AND SUBSTANCE

I hope that the picture sketched above has provided a reasonable glimpse of the nature and extent of the formal changes brought about in the judicial process in South Africa since the advent of constitutional democracy in 1994. While much at this level has changed, a sense of continuity has also been preserved, and the challenge must be to harness what is good from the past to the changed authority of the new dispensation to ensure ever-increasing implementation of the substantial objectives set in the Constitution. It is a not inconsiderable undertaking.

---

127. 2002 (5) SA 721 (CC) at paras 96 and 97.
128. 2002 (5) SA 721 (CC) at para 98.
129. 2002 (5) SA 721 (CC) at paras 106–111.
130. 2002 (5) SA 721 (CC) at paras 124–133.
131. Through the 'certification' of the 1996 Constitution: see *Ex parte Chairperson of the Constitutional Assembly: In re Certification of the Constitution of the Republic of South Africa, 1996* 1996 (4) SA 744 (CC); and *Certification of the Amended Text* 1997 (2) SA 97 (CC).

Constitutional change in South Africa over the past 15 years owes a massive debt to foreign influences, whether direct or indirect, material or intellectual, offered or requested. The 'borrowed' nature of many of the provisions and processes of the Constitution and the extensive but selective use of comparative judicial precedent in so much of the constitutional jurisprudence outlined above are but two beneficial manifestations of such foreign contributions. In an increasingly unified world, there are lessons here that all countries should heed.

Judges and politics: an essay from Canada

Allan C Hutchinson*

Osgoode Hall Law School, York University, Toronto

> 'We are here as on a darkling plain
> Swept with confused alarms of struggle and flight,
> Where ignorant armies clash by night.'

Matthew Arnold[1]

It is said of statistics that what they reveal is interesting, but what they hide is crucial. Much the same can be said of the present British debate over constitutional change and the courts. The various constitutional reforms proposed seem to be obvious and long overdue – abolishing the post of Lord Chancellor; setting up a Supreme Court separate from the House of Lords; and establishing a judicial appointments committee. However, at least as presented and dealt with by the government and the judges, while these innovations are interesting and generally positive, what they fail to mention or address is much more crucial and revealing. The government papers and the judiciary's response resolutely refuse to tackle the central issue of what it is that judges do and whether it is done in a suitably legitimate and proper way. For all the sound and fury of constitutional engagement, the main antagonists share a deep and disturbing assumption that judicial power has and will continue to be exercised in a non-political, objective and neutral manner. In this paper, by reference to the Canadian experience, I will challenge that assumption: it is not that judges are unprofessional or corrupt, but that adjudication is inescapably political and non-objective. Instead, I will offer a very different account of the adjudicative performance and propose a more complementary set of institutional reforms.

I.

What should a Supreme Court do to ensure that the government is meeting its constitutional responsibilities? Are there limits beyond which judges should not go in supervising government activities? If so, how are those limits to be determined? These important issues were confronted by the Canadian courts in the Fall of 2003 in *Doucet*.[2] While the Canadian courts had over 20 years of

---

*   I am grateful to Derek Morgan, Luke Woolford and Michael Abdelkerim for their critical comments and helpful suggestions.
1.   M Arnold 'Dover Beach' in *Dover beach and other poems* (New York: Dover Publications, 1994).
2.   *Doucet-Boudreau v Nova Scotia (Minister of Education)* [2003] SCC 62.

experience under their collective belt in tackling the Charter of Rights and Freedoms, they had not staked out any comprehensive position on the precise role of courts in remedying Charter wrongs. *Doucet* obliged them to reveal their hand a little more fully. A trial judge had decided that it was incumbent on the Nova Scotia government to provide French-language secondary schooling in certain areas. While the government did not deny the parents' rights under s 23 of the Charter to have such schooling for their children, it had decided not to prioritise those rights and had delayed fulfilling its obligations. However, not only did the trial judge order the Province to use its 'best efforts' to provide school facilities and programmes by specified dates, he also retained jurisdiction to hear reports on the status of those efforts. The Province contended that this continuing judicial supervision inappropriately trespassed onto the government's political discretion. The Nova Scotia Court of Appeal agreed and held that, while courts have broad-ranging powers under s 24(1) of the Charter to fashion remedies, the Charter does not extend a court's jurisdiction to meddle in the details of a Province's administrative management: there were limits to the courts' authority to interfere with what were matters of political judgment. A majority of the Supreme Court of Canada had no such qualms.

By the narrowest of 5-4 margins, the Supreme Court decided that the Constitution and legal tradition demanded that the trial judge should remain seized of the issue. Speaking for their colleagues, Iacobucci and Arbour JJ recognised that the courts should be cautious in involving themselves in such matters. However, the courts must complement their purposive interpretation of Charter rights with a purposive approach to remedies in order to ensure that Charter rights are given full and meaningful protection. While the court must also be sensitive to the limits of its role as judicial arbiter and not interfere unduly with the roles of the other branches of governance, the judicial crafting of remedies will vary according to the right at issue and the context of each case: the advancement of democratic ends should not be accomplished by undemocratic means. Although the remedy was admittedly creative and novel, it did balance the parents' rights against the Province's privilege to decide upon the details of educational planning. Accordingly, the majority held that, in the particular circumstances of the Nova Scotia schools and mindful that delay might defeat the parents' rights, a supervisory remedy 'took into account, and did not depart unduly or unnecessarily from, the role of the courts in our constitutional democracy'.[3]

The dissenters took a much more restrained line and were strongly critical of the majority's position. Drawing heavily on the common law doctrine of functus officio, the minority were not at all convinced that the trial judge's order was clear and maintained that, once a court had issued its decision, it ought to rely upon the government to act with reasonable diligence and in good faith: it was not the role of courts to act as direct overseers or superintendents of the executive function. Moreover, on behalf the minority, LeBel and Deschamps JJ insisted that it was vitally important that the courts respect the appropriate constitutional boundaries and balance between the different branches of government power: democracy demanded that the

---

3.   [2003] SCC 62 at 28, per Iacobucci and Arbour JJ, as joined by McLachlin CJ, Gonthier, and Bastarache JJ.

judicial role be limited and modest. Although it was imperative that citizens' Charter rights be properly and fully enforced, the minority took the definite view that this did not permit the courts to interfere in the legitimate exercise of executive discretion. Indeed, chastising the majority for its rather cavalier approach to such delicate constitutional considerations, the minority considered that invasive remedies, such as the trial judge's in this case, were illegitimate and amounted to a virtual micro-management of administrative management which 'led to the improper politicisation of the relationship between the judiciary and the executive'.[4]

Not surprisingly, the Supreme Court's decision was greeted with a deluge of public and academic commentary. 'Activism' was the word on most people's lips. It sounds as if it is something positive – healthy, vital and purposeful. But, when it is used in connection with courts, many hear it only as having disturbing negative resonances – uppity, illegitimate and uncontrolled. At the heart of these responses was the concern that the courts might have gone beyond the bounds of what it is that unelected judges should be doing in a constitutional democracy; they might have vacated the realm of legal decision-making and trespassed into the arena of political discretion. The advent of the Charter of Rights and Freedoms in 1982 pushed the courts more into the spotlight and asked them to resolve more controversial disputes. With a higher public profile, the courts' work has come under closer and more critical scrutiny. Indeed, as the public and academic commentators tend to be the same people, the only difference between the public and academic debate is one of greater length and occasional subtlety of contribution. After over 20 years of debate about the legitimacy and reach of Charter review by courts over government action, the main thrusts of the response were predictable and well-rehearsed.

On one side were those who viewed the majority decision as further evidence that the judges had overstepped the bounds of their authority and competence: it was blatant and unwelcome 'judicial activism'. By interfering in the fiscal administration of public programmes, an unelected, unrepresentative, and unchecked judiciary had violated the separation of powers and imperilled 'established traditions of responsible government'. Some went so far as to see the decision as a 'gratuitous and arrogant' power-grab which bordered on the 'monarchical'. However, on the other side, there was applause for a bold court which had overcome the pusillanimity of some its members to provide meaningful and effective protection to people's constitutional rights. If the Rule of Law was to be truly respected, it was thought essential that constitutional entitlements be effective remedies; it was not only desirable, but necessary that governments not be allowed to evade, complicate, or ignore court orders. Far from imperilling responsible government, the *Doucet* decision had contributed to the legitimacy of Canada's democratic commitments by giving the Charter 'muscles' and 'teeth'.[5] While both sides have something

---

4.   [2003] SCC 62 at 45, per LeBel and Deschamps, as joined by Major and Binnie JJ.
5.   For a sampling of the responses, see Gunter 'Judicial Arrogance Borders on Monarchial' *National Post*, 20 November 2003, p A18; Makin 'Top Court Pursuing Activism' *The Globe and Mail*, 13 November 2003, p A16; 'Judicial Rule' Editorial *National Post*, 8 November 2003, p A19; Young 'Court Gives Our Toothless Charter Sharp Fangs' *The Toronto Star* 23 November 2003, p F07; and Roach 'Do We Want Judges with More Muscle?' *The Globe and Mail*, 13 November 2003, p A27.

important to contribute, I am not convinced that either has taken a defensible or convincing stance: the Charter debate is much broader and deeper than both sides contemplate or accept. Consequently, it is important to examine the courts' and the commentators' arguments at greater length and to explore an alternative viewpoint which contends that, whether activist or restrained, the judges are involved in an inevitably and thoroughly political endeavour: all efforts to separate law from politics are doomed to failure. Nevertheless, while my critique is decidedly radical, it is not deliberately negative. An acceptance that adjudication is thoroughly political does not strike the death-knell for democracy.

II.

The more traditional position is that taken by the minority and championed by a cadre of conservative academic critics. Accelerated by Charter adjudication, but not restricted to it, the Canadian judicial system is considered to have lost its way and to be hastily on its way to political hell in an activist handcart. The courts, especially the Supreme Court of Canada, are condemned as having become highly politicised and highly interventionist in their decisions and judgments. Effectively abandoning established legal principles and modes of legal reasoning, the judiciary has unwisely and indulgently shifted its focus to an analysis based on 'values'. Moreover, unlike the traditional understanding of judicial decision-making, this resort to values has more to do with a judge's own subjective political commitments than an objective assessment of a case's legal merits. Critics charge that, when recent judicial pronouncements are looked at as a body of work, they have not only become blatantly political, but reflect and instantiate a particular and partisan set of liberal-feminist commitments. In effect, these critics charge that 'judicial activism' is not a careless aberration by an overworked judiciary, but a concerted dereliction of official duty by a politically motivated judiciary. As such, there is an indignant call to return to the passive and neutral virtues of judicial restraint so that the promise of Canadian democracy can be redeemed. Of course, judicial activism has no part to play in such a restorative vision of law.[6]

While this nostalgic call for 'judicial restraint' is expressed in the most passionate and least restrained terms, it has garnered considerable support. However, while this traditional critique is long on the details of the judiciary's current political fall from constitutional grace, its adherents are very light on how a purely legal mode of principled adjudication can be performed. While these exhortations to 'stick to the law' are seductive, they offer little suggestion of how such a seemingly prosaic practice can be achieved. At a theoretical level, three initial observations come to mind. First, the ascertainment of legal principles is itself fraught with political contamination and content. 'Established' is simply a way of saying that certain controversial moral or

---

6.   See, for example, F Morton and R Knopff *The charter revolution and the court party* (Peterborough: Broadview Press, 2000); and R Martin *The most dangerous branch: how the Supreme Court of Canada has undermined our law and our democracy* (Montreal: McGill University Press, 2003).

political commitments are now accepted by the legal community as settled; this is less an endorsement of the principles' apolitical nature and more an acknowledgement that general acceptance is a form of political validation. Secondly, the range of established principles is extremely broad and often encompasses competing maxims; there is no neutral or non-political way to select between contradictory principles. Thirdly, even if it is possible to isolate a relevant and exclusive legal principle, it is far from obvious how that general principle can be applied to particular facts in an entirely objective or impartial manner.[7] In short, despite the critic's yearning for a simpler and more professional age, there is no purely technical and non-political way to engage in a principled mode of adjudication. This is especially true of the Charter. Not only is what amounts to 'freedom' or 'equality' the stuff of fierce ideological debate (and how one relates to the other), but how such values are to be enforced within s 1's 'such reasonable limits as can be demonstrably justified in a free and democratic society' merely invites judges to wade even deeper into the political waters. Adjudication necessarily involves political choice.

The fact is that the dissatisfaction with 'judicial activism' is itself a political campaign. Behind the traditional rhetoric of principled adjudication, there is a very definite and partial political agenda. While it is understandable why such critics would prefer to occupy the neutral territory of formal constitutional technique rather than contested turf of substantive political alignment, the effort to portray and promote a non-political mode of constitutional adjudication as being possible and desirable is a neat but deceptive manoeuvre. When a closer look is taken at those occasions on which the critics raise the spectre of activism and those on which they do not, it will be seen that the difference is a blunt ideological one. Those decisions that do not fit their political agenda are condemned as activist and those that do fit are defended as appropriate. The constitutional line is one of their own political making. In general, those decisions which promote greater equality (for example, gay rights, aboriginal land claims, etc) are dismissed as activist and illegitimate, whereas those which defend greater liberty (for example, election spending, male property rights, etc) are show-cased as valid exercises of judicial authority. Yet, in terms of their fit with the opaque constitutional text and the courts' activist tendencies, there is nothing to choose between them. It is only that some substantive values are preferred over others. Accordingly, the claim of 'activism' is simply a veiled criticism that the courts are being too progressive and making decisions that do not reflect desirable conservative values: any court that stands by and lets constitutional values be ignored or belittled is at fault. But there is no technical or purely legal way to decide what those values are – law is politics by other means. The Charter is a contested site for political debate, not a definitive or neutral contribution to that debate.

Indeed, the *Doucet*[8] decision itself is a good example of the disingenuity of those who reject 'judicial activism' in the name of traditional judicial virtues. As the judgments of the minority reveal, theirs is less a rejection of political decision-making and more a championing of a particular and partial view of

---

7.   See A Hutchinson *Work-in-progress: evolution and the common law* (Toronto: University of Toronto Press, 2004).
8.   *Doucet Boudreau v Nova Scotia (Minister of Education)* [2003] SCC 62.

constitutional politics. Despite repeated incantations about 'the separation of powers' and that 'the legislature and the executive are ... the principal loci of democratic will', the minority makes no real effort to demonstrate that this is somehow an accepted legal principle as opposed to a contested political commitment. It is not at all that the majority reject these general principles, it is that they have a different view of what those commitments demand in the particular circumstances. Moreover, it is unconvincing for the minority to maintain that the judiciary 'should avoid turning themselves into managers of the public service'. The entire history of administrative law confounds such trite observations about the need to 'avoid interfering in the management of public administration'. Furthermore, while it is important to recognise that there are constitutional boundaries to judicial action, those boundaries are not independently given, but are developed and negotiated by the courts themselves. While judges must respect that the executive and legislative branches are 'the principal loci of democratic will',[9] that is not the point. In light of the fact that the judges, including members of the *Doucet* minority, regularly and rightly interfere with executive and legislative authority when they breach the Charter, the real point is when and how they should so interfere as a matter of constitutional requirement, not whether they ever should. Accordingly, the difference between the majority and minority judgments is not between legitimate and illegitimate modes of adjudication, but between competing visions of an appropriate constitutional and democratic order. Each has to be defended in political terms: there is simply no method by which to declare that one is more intrinsically legal and, therefore, non-contestable than another. It hardly advances the democratic cause to deploy subterfuge and to pass off political commitments as constitutional mandates. Decisions should be celebrated or condemned for the substantive values that they uphold, not for their vague failure to respect some spurious formal distinction between making and applying law.

III.

The Charter crystallised the long-standing dilemma of the courts in trying to reconcile their new role as active guardians of fundamental values with the democratic values and traditions of Canadian society. They had to develop a way to act decisively as well as legitimately. In the Charter's early years, judges relied upon the old standby of 'liberal legalism' – a sharp public/private distinction, neutral interpretation, and objective balancing – as a method for legitimising their decisions and reconciling the courts' role with democracy. However, it soon became clear that this jurisprudential modus operandi was failing to placate either liberal or more radical critics who complained that judicial review was not fulfilling its functions as effectively or as democratically as it might. Not only were the courts' efforts at preserving a sharp distinction between legal analysis and political judgment becoming more transparent and unconvincing, but the substantive political values which animated their decisions were being revealed as increasingly outdated and

9.   [2003] SCC 62 at 37, 41, 33, 37 and 41, per LeBel and Deschamps JJ.

unresponsive to contemporary Canadian sensibilities. Indeed, 'liberal legalism' was unable to command a sustained consensus even amongst judges. In response, the Supreme Court began to nurture a less legalistic and more pragmatic approach to its constitutional duties. Ironically, these very efforts to bolster their democratic legitimacy by relying upon an apparently more overt mode of democratic justification revealed even more starkly how undemocratic the judges' involvement judicial review under the Charter.[10]

In recent years, there has been a turn to 'dialogue theory' as an alternative justification for judicial review. Judges and jurists have begun to accept that a strictly legalistic mode of constitutional adjudication is not available or viable and that some reliance upon contested political commitments is not only inevitable, but also desirable. The primary concern is less with politicisation itself and more with 'the degree to which judges are free to read their own preferences into law'.[11] As such, activism is less about whether judges rely on political preferences at all and more about the sources of such values and the extent to which they rely on them. Cautioning that judges are not free to go wherever their personal political preferences take them, the dialogic approach does not abandon the idea or practice of maintaining a barrier between legitimate legal analysis and illegitimate political decision-making. Instead, in contrast to the anti-activists, it is argued that the distinction is much fuzzier, that the domain of law is much more expansive, and that the boundary between law and politics is much less breached. However, like the anti-activists, they do concede that there is a point at which the judges can be said to be no longer doing law; they will have wandered off into other parts of the constitutional and political domain. In some important sense, law is to exist separately from its judicial spokesperson such that law places some non-trivial constraints on what judges can do and say. While legal principles are more open and sensitive to political context, law is not only reduced to the contingent political preferences of the judiciary.

Consequently, the general thrust of the dialogue theory is that, because the legislature possesses the final word on Charter matters by virtue of the s 33 override power, the courts can proceed to engage in a more overt balancing of political values under the s 1 'reasonable limits' provision. The claim and hope is that the courts and the legislature will engage in an institutional conversation about the Charter and its requirements on particular and pressing issues of the day: the courts and the legislators have complementary roles that enable legislation to be carefully tailored to meet the government's political agenda and respect Charter values. The most prominent judicial advocate of a dialogic approach has been Justice Iacobucci who insists that 'judicial review on Charter grounds brings a certain measure of vitality to the democratic process, in that it fosters both dynamic interaction and accountability amongst the various

10. For a full and unimpeachable account of these developments, see A Petter *Twenty years of charter justification: from liberal legalism to dubious dialogue* (forthcoming, 2004).
11. K Roach *The Supreme Court on trial: judicial activism or democratic dialogue* (Toronto: Irwin Law, 2001) p 106. See also Hogg and Bushell 'The *Charter* Dialogue Between Courts and Legislatures (Or Perhaps the *Charter* of Rights Isn't Such a Bad Thing After All)' (1997) 35 Os HLJ 75 (1997).

branches'. In establishing a 'dialogic balance' and 'retaining a forum for dialogue' between the different branches of government, the courts must tread a thin, but vital line between deferential subservience and robust activism.[12] The courts and legislatures are to be dialogic partners in an institutional conversation to advance shared democratic goals.

While this resort to 'democratic dialogue' does at least concede the normative nature of Charter decision-making and represent an effort to get beyond a discredited liberal legalism, it seems to have let the political cat out of the judicial bag without any plan for getting it back in or keeping it suitably leashed. The majority judgments in *Doucet* again offer compelling evidence of this claim. Indeed, suspiciously bereft of any reference to 'dialogic theory', the judgment of Iacobucci and Arbour JJ spends much of its time, directly and indirectly, trying to repel the debilitating spectre of judicial activism. Although the majority emphasise time and again that 'courts must ensure that government behaviour conforms with constitutional norms but in doing so must also be sensitive to the separation of function among the legislative, judicial and executive branches', they are relatively quiet on how that separation is to be achieved. Eschewing the notion that there is some 'bright line' in existence, their only serious suggestion is that judges must be thoroughly pragmatic and contextual in their assessments: 'determining the boundaries of the courts' proper role, however, cannot be reduced to a simple test or formula; it will vary according to the right at issue and the context of each case.' The conclusion that 'the judicial approach to remedies must remain flexible and responsive to the needs of a given case' is unlikely to give comfort to those critics who look for some discipline in or direction to the courts' future performance.[13] Indeed, an uncommitted observer might be forgiven for thinking that, on the question of whether 'law is politics', the court has given up the ghost rather exorcised the wraith of judicial activism.

Accordingly, with its apparent rejection of judicial objectivity, lack of normative content and vague invocations of democracy, the most recent juristic approaches to judicial review actually serve to undermine fatally the project of justifying Charter adjudication's democratic legitimacy. Although dialogic theory is intended to calm fears that the courts are undisciplined and unlimited in their powers, it manages to reinforce the perception that courts are not only at the centre of the crucial process through which political discourse and values are shaped and sustained, but also that courts get to determine the role and contribution of the other branches of government. The 'degree to which judges are free to read their own preferences into law' seems to be reducible to the rather oxymoronic conclusion that they will be as 'free to read their own preferences into the law' as 'their own preferences' allow. There is a huge gap between the rhetoric of democratic dialogue and the reality of judicial performance. Presenting judicial review as part and parcel of a democratic dialogue merely underlines the extent to which democracy has become a

---

12. *Bell Express Vu Limited Partnership v R* [2002] 2 SCR 559 at paras 65–66. See also *Vriend v Alberta* [1998] 1 SCR 493; and *Corbiere v Canada (Minister of Indian and Northern Affairs)* [1999] 2 SCR 203.

13. *Doucet-Boudreau v Nova Scotia (Minister of Education)* [2003] SCC 62 at 19, 20 and 25, per Iacobucci and Arbour JJ.

pathetic caricature of itself. An elite and stilted conversation between the judicial and executive branches of government is an entirely impoverished performance of democracy; it is an empty echo of what should be a more resounding hubbub.

IV.

It is understandable why most judges and jurists wish to ground an objective practice of judicial interpretation that obviates judicial value-choices and that does not tread on the democratic toes of legislative or executive decision-making. However, it is a misplaced ambition and doomed to failure. As judicial review involves unelected judges invalidating the actions of elected legislators or executives, all judicial review is anti-majoritarian and, therefore, presumptively undemocratic; no theory can reconcile judicial review with majority rule. The *Doucet* minority are surely correct to emphasise that 'the legislature and the executive are ... the principal loci of democratic will'.[14] Because there is no way to bring such a project to a satisfactory conclusion, continuing attempts to do so merely exacerbate the problem of democratic legitimacy and erode the very confidence that the legal establishment is trying to maintain. A better response would be to acknowledge that adjudication in a society of diverse and conflicting politics is an inevitably ideological undertaking. Once this is done, courts will not necessarily become otiose or surplus to democratic requirements. Instead, it might be accepted that both courts and legislatures are involved in the same game, namely delivering substantive answers to concrete problems. In doing so, neither courts nor legislatures have a lock on political judgment about what is the best thing to do. Having abandoned the crude Bickelian counter-majoritarian challenge to the courts' democratic legitimacy,[15] the Supreme Court should follow through on the political logic of its own analysis; it must have the institutional courage of its own jurisprudential convictions about democracy being more a formal and majoritarian ideal.

Once liberated from the confining strictures of traditional thinking, the question of how and whether courts act with democratic legitimacy is of a very different order and character. The Bickelian difficulty has little to say about what values are important to democracy other than an unthinking regard for majoritarian processes. Once the principle of democracy is accepted to have a substantive as well as formal dimension, the justification for judicial action must also be viewed in substantive as well as formal terms. The work of courts need not be judged by their capacity to be objective and impartial nor by their willingness to be consistent with, and not interfere with, majority politics.

---

14. *Doucet-Boudreau v Nova Scotia (Minister of Education)* [2003] SCC 62 at 41, per LeBel and Deschamps JJ.
15. See A Bickel *The least dangerous branch: the Supreme Court at the bar of politics* (New Haven: Yale University Press, 2nd edn, 1986) pp 14–18. For a more sophisticated approach, see E Chemerinsky *Interpreting the Constitution* (New York: Praeger Publishers, 1988) pp 11–12; and Chemerinsky 'Foreword: The Vanishing Constitution' (1989) 103 Harv LR 43.

Instead, they can be evaluated in terms of the value choices that they make and the contribution that their decisions make to advancing substantive democracy in the here-and-now. If the traditional presumptions – that legislatures are unprincipled and political and that courts are principled and reasoned – are dropped, it is possible to arrive at a very different understanding and account of the relation between courts and legislatures. For instance, the conclusion is possible that legislatures and courts are both principled and unprincipled to greater and lesser extents at different times and that each can further (as well as inhibit) the cause of democratic justice on a particular issue as much as the other. Moreover, as *Doucet* suggests, reliance on 'principles' is no less political and no more legal in any essential sense. The more pressing conundrum, therefore, is that, if democratic procedures do not guarantee democratic outcomes and democratic outcomes need not result from democratic procedures, how can we best organise constitutional arrangements so that democracy as a whole is more than less likely to prevail?

Accordingly, the appropriate inquiry in a constitutional democracy is not to ask whether the courts have acted politically and, therefore, improperly, but whether the political choices that they have made serve democracy. Because this democratic assessment is substantive and political undertaking, not formal and analytical, it will always be a contested and contestable issue. Nevertheless, what counts as a democratic decision is not entirely reducible to a political and, therefore, open-ended debate about what is most appropriately democratic at the time and under the circumstances. The formal dimension of democracy insists that some account is taken of the general institutional location and position of relative governmental agencies. The fact that legislators are elected and judges are unelected has some political salience. However, as *Doucet* evidences, while judges must respect that distinction, such an allocational decision will itself be political and context-specific. In determining the courts' role in a functioning democracy, there is no authoritative and organising meta-principle to which the courts' can resort that is not itself political and controversial. The scope of the courts' role and power is itself part of the continuing debate about democracy which is a task of the most enduring and political kind. Of course, the concern that courts are interfering too much in the political process is also a valid one. There is a keen need to be vigilant about what courts are (and are not) doing. Any court that tramples too often on the policy-making prerogative of Parliament and legislatures is asking for trouble: judges need to recognise that they are part of democracy's supporting cast, not its star-performers. But, as the anti-activists fail to acknowledge, that democratic watch should itself be open and honest. It is what the courts are being active about which is the key. It is no more or less political to maintain the status quo than it is to subvert it; conservatism is as ideological as progressivism.

Despite the denials and resistance of traditional judges and jurists, the common law is awash in the roiling and mucky waters of political power. While judges and lawyers claim to keep relatively clean and dry by wearing their institutional wet-suits of abstract neutrality and disinterested fairness, they are up to their necks in ideological muck. And this is no bad thing. Because it is only when judges come clean, as it were, and admit that they have political dirt on their hands that they will appreciate that adjudication generally and constitutional adjudication particularly amount to an organic and messy process that has a similarly organic and messy connection to those social needs which it claims both to reflect and shape. So enlightened, judges might begin to accept that they are involved in a political enterprise whose success and legitimacy are best evaluated not by the courts' formal dexterity and technical competence, but by their substantive contribution to the local advancement of social justice. Abandoning the persistent attachment to a false distinction between a relatively unsoiled practice of principled adjudication and a contaminated involvement in crude politics would be an excellent place to begin such a commitment. As long as its practitioners and their juristic apologists present the constitutional law as an insulated and insular process, courts will run the considerable risk of being unresponsive to and unreflective of the needs they are supposed to address. On the other hand, if judges and jurists are more willing to concede that the worlds of law and politics are intimately related, it might become possible to give society's needs the kind of direct and substantive attention that they merit. It is difficult enough for judges to fulfil their daunting roles without them also pretending at the same time that they are engaged in an entirely different enterprise. Efforts at local substantive justice are not enhanced by a mistaken belief that universal or formal coherence is at stake. Legitimacy is best attained by candour and frankness, not by denial and dissemblance.

V.

What has all this got to do with the present constitutional upheavals in the United Kingdom? In particular, what has this Canadian contretemps got to do with whether the House Lords should be replaced by a Supreme Court? My answer is 'absolutely everything'. The most important issues confronting the courts in the United Kingdom today are exactly those which underlie the *Doucet*[16] decision and which animate public and academic debate in Canada today. This is the problem of 'judicial activism' – how can and should the judiciary fulfil its legitimate responsibilities in a way which vigorously enforces contested constitutional dictates as a matter of law against the legislative and/or executive branches of government, but which, at the same time, accepts that it is a body of unelected and unrepresentative bureaucrats which has no direct democratic mandate to make political decisions? Yet the main adversaries in the present constitutional ferment in the United Kingdom seem intent on refusing to acknowledge, let alone deal with, that central conundrum. Indeed, while they disagree about much, they join forces in their uncritical acknowledgement that the judicial task has and will continue to be satisfactorily accomplished. If the threat or fear of judicial activism is seen to be a problem at all, it is something for other courts and other jurisdictions to worry about. While the government is at pains to reassure that the need for reform 'does not imply any dissatisfaction with the performance of the House of Lords as our highest Court of Law ... [because] its judges have conducted themselves with the utmost integrity and independence ... [and] are widely and rightly admired, nationally and internationally', the judiciary congratulates

16. *Doucet-Boudreau v Nova Scotia (Minister of Education)* [2003] SCC 62.

itself on 'the calibre of our existing judiciary, which has resulted in our judiciary being admired around the world'.[17] This is arrogance, complacency and denial on a grand scale.

As in Canada over 20 years ago, the introduction of a Bill of Rights in the United Kingdom has not so much heralded in a new kind of adjudicative performance as highlighted the essentially political dimension of judicial responsibilities. What was once assumed has now become contested. Or, at least, it has been challenged in academic quarters and in the more critical circles of the legal profession.[18] The sad fact is that the judiciary itself almost wilfully refuses to concede that there might be such an issue, let alone that it might be confronted. The most that the government is prepared to concede is that there might be a perceptual problem in regard to the judicial branch of government: 'the considerable growth of judicial review in recent years has inevitably brought the judges more into the political eye ... [and it] is essential that our systems do all that they can to minimise the danger that judges' decisions could be perceived to be politically motivated.'[19] The judiciary are loathe to even make such a concession. Consequently, the present debate is really a faux-debate. Whereas the most crucial challenge to judicial performance is relegated to a vague and distant phantasm of largely foreign concern, the contending forces exhaust themselves (and the peripheral public) in a much less important wrangle over institutional arrangements. While it is clearly a positive contribution to the democratic project not to have the legal system's senior officials being judges, legislators and, in the case of the senior Law Lord, executives, there will be little genuine progress made in democratic terms unless and until the political dimension of adjudication is acknowledged and addressed. Simply to ignore that possibility, let alone its reality, is an insult to democracy and its citizens.

A glance at the decisions by the House of Lords under the Bill of Rights give the lie to the claim that adjudication can proceed without any concerns or qualms about the judges' neutrality and political orientation. Reading decisions like *R v DPP, ex p Kebeline* and *Wallbank* might not persuade critics that the judgments were ideological in any overtly bias fashion, but it is difficult to resist the minimal conclusion that political values played an important and integral role in the judges' opinions.[20] This is not to suggest that the judges acted inappropriately or undemocratically. My charge is much less crude and

---

17. See Department for Constitutional Affairs *Constitutional reform: a Supreme Court for the United Kingdom* CP 11/03 (2003) p 5; and Judges' Council *Response to the Consultation Papers on Constitutional Reform* (2003) p 26.

18. For a solid survey of the extensive literature and its present 'dialogic' turn, see Poole 'Review Article: Dogmatic Liberalism? T R S Allan and The Common Law Constitution' (2002) 65 MLR 463; and Clayton 'Judicial Deference and "Democratic Dialogue": The Legitimacy of Judicial Intervention under the Human Rights Act' [2004] PL.

19. Department for Constitutional Affairs, n 17 above, p 12.

20. *R v DPP, ex p Kebeline* [2002] 2 AC 326 and *Parochial Church Council of the Parish of Aston Cantlow v Wallbank* [2003] UKHL 37, [2003] 3 All ER 1213 on the 'freedom' of the courts to adopt a more expansive interpretative role in order to avoid declaration of incompatibility under the HRS. There is a good discussion of this in T Campbell 'Incorporation through Interpretation in T Campbell, K D Ewing and A Tomkins (eds) Sceptical Essays on Human Rights (Oxford: Oxford University Press, 2001) p 79.

much more nuanced. As I have been at pains to point out in my discussion of *Doucet* and its aftermath, it is not that the judges act unprofessionally when they act politically, it is that the professional performance of adjudication cannot be done without resort to contested political values. My account does not in any way report that adjudication is arbitrary or whimsical. Notwithstanding the occasional fall from judicial grace, there is no suggestion that judges do anything other than make a rigorous and responsible fist of their judicial duties. However, this does not refute my claim that law is inevitably and inescapably political in operation and outcome. A realistic understanding of the judicial function leads to the appreciation that adjudication is a subtle combination of freedom (ie judges can cobble together the broad range of available doctrinal materials into the artefacts of their choosing) and constraint (ie judges are historical creatures whose imagination and craft are bounded by their communal affiliations, interpretive prowess, and personal commitments).[21] As a profoundly and pervasively political undertaking, adjudication behoves its participants and observers to acknowledge that questions about whether decisions are 'politically motivated' are pertinent and pressing. To ignore flatly and completely such a debate about law and politics is to offend *any* account and practice of democracy.

For both the government and the judges, the most contentious item of constitutional business is the need to protect and ensure 'the independence of the judiciary'. This is an important mission. However, the clash between government and judiciary occupies only a small corner of the overall terrain on judicial independence; it is what is not debated and disagreed about that is more significant. Both parties seek to ensure that there is 'sufficient transparency of independence from the executive and the legislature to give people the assurance to which they are entitled about the independence of the Judiciary' and that the perception continues that 'the Law Lords, like the judiciary as a whole, are independent of the executive and are not susceptible to political pressure from any direction'.[22] While it is important that such shields are in place, it is by no means obvious that 'judicial independence' is tantamount to the judiciary being left entirely to its own devices and desires. If judicial independence is seen only to be about preserving an almost unaccountable and self-regulated body of constitutional actors, it will not necessarily serve the broader democratic interests of the polity. Indeed, as played out between the government and judiciary, there is no sense in which it might be the politics of the judiciary that is and ought to be in contention. Again, the shared assumption is that, as long as the executive and legislative branches of government keep their noses out, all will be well and non-political because the judiciary can be entrusted to act in a suitably professional and technical manner. As I have insisted, this by no means follows. It is axiomatic that the judiciary be free from government interference whether from the executive or legislative arm of government. However, even if this is secured, it does not

---

21. See A Hutchinson *It's all in the game: a non-foundationalist account of law and adjudication* (London: Duke University Press, 2000); and D Kennedy *A critique of adjudication: fin de siecle* (Cambridge, Mass: Harvard University Press, 1997).
22. Department for Constitutional Affairs, n 17 above, p 12; and Judges' Council, n 17 above, p 48.

mean that all allegations of 'politics' have been resolved. There is much more to politics than whether the judiciary is making decisions which are favourable to the government of the day. For example, decisions which go against the government are not by that fact free from politics. Presumably, decisions which go against the government can be as equally politically motivated as those that do not go against the government. Judicial independence, therefore, is about much more than institutional independence: it is also about political leanings.[23]

VI.

The true colours of the judiciary and, to a lesser extent, the government (which, of course, is itself staffed by lawyers on these matters) are revealed in the details of proposed changes to the judicial appointments process. After all, the 'who' of adjudication is as or more important than the 'what'. As regards the new Supreme Court, the government's preference is for a 15-member Commission (comprising five judges, five lawyers, and five non-lawyers) to recommend a limited number of names to the Prime Minister who would then make the appointment. Again, the concern is primarily perceptual: 'whether or not the system really is biased, the perception has an impact which is real enough.' However, the government concedes that the appointments must be based on 'merit' because 'the public must have confidence that judges are independent, impartial and of complete integrity, as well as possessing the intellectual skills and personal qualities of the highest calibre which are required for the discharge of their duties'. Not surprisingly, the judiciary resoundingly echo these sentiments. While 'increasing the diversity of our judiciary ... will help to generate public confidence in the justice system', the judiciary maintain that it is imperative that 'best qualified candidate is appointed irrespective of his or her background' and that the Commission avoid 'becoming so anxious to achieve diversity that sight is lost of the primacy of merit'.[24] Nevertheless, notwithstanding these reservations, Lord Falconer, the Lord Chancellor, recently told the Commons' Constitutional Affairs Committee that the new appointments body must select women and ethnic minority judges. While it would be up to the Commission to decide on the actual criteria, Falconer did hint at the fact that 'targets' might need to be set to ensure that a representative diversity is achieved.[25]

As viewed by both sides, there is a shared assumption that 'merit' and 'diversity' are somehow independent and unrelated categories: an increase in diversity will threaten to undermine merit and a reliance on merit will preclude diversity. This is entirely wrong-headed. First of all, 'merit' is an entirely relative notion. Whether a person has the necessary capacities and talents to be successful at a given role or activity will depend upon an evaluation of the nature and that role. As I hope will now be obvious, what qualities and

23. See J A G Griffiths *The politics of the judiciary* (London: Fontana Press, 5th edn, 1997).
24. Department for Constitutional Affairs *Constitutional Reform: A New Way of Appointing Judges* CP 10/03 (2003) p 20; and Judges' Council, n 17 above, pp 4, 28 and 31.
25. 'No Further Delay on Judicial System Reforms' *Press Association News*, 6 January 2004.

characteristics best comprise the 'good judge' will itself be a political and contestable debate. If, as the British judiciary seem to maintain, the holding of judicial office is purely about the intellectual and formal attributes of professional judgment, then there is little point in bothering too much about diversity. However, if that were the case, there is no reason to expect that the judiciary would be a starkly un-diverse body as it presently is. Indeed, one could be forgiven for thinking that greater diversity would indeed be an improvement in merit because, with no visible minorities on any superior court and with the first women appointed to the House of Lords only very recently, there has been a consistent willingness to translate 'background' into 'best qualified'. But if, as I have argued, adjudication involves an inescapable political element, it will be important to ensure that the judiciary represents a broader cross-section of society than it presently does. This is not to argue that diversity and merit are one and the same thing or that diversity will always be preferable to merit. On the contrary, it is to argue that diversity and merit are interconnected. While there is a need for meritorious candidates, it is nonsensical to believe that only white males possess the necessary meritorious qualities; this is the very essence of racism.

Recognising that adjudication requires and expects judges to make choices among competing political values and that there is no neutral way to make those choices, it will be wise to work towards a process of appointment which embraces this operating assumption rather than one which goes to enormous lengths to hide and reject it. By appointing more women and visible minorities to the courts, the merit of the bench will be enhanced in that citizens might be reassured that more than one set of political values and experiences will be in play when judicial decisions are made. In making this plea for increased diversity, I am not claiming that identity is a reliable proxy for set values: people of similar backgrounds and identities do not possess the same politics merely by virtue of that fact. However, as a pragmatic consideration rather than an ontological assertion, it can be safely suggested that background and identity matter. It is a conceit of established groups (white, male, heterosexual etc) to maintain that professional objectivity is the only valid touchstone of legal knowledge. Too often that objectivity has turned out to be little more than those group's own partial and establishment interests in intellectual garb. If British society were rid of discrimination and had achieved a genuine state of equality, the appointment of women (visible minorities, gays etc) to elite institutions (white, male etc), like the proposed Supreme Court, might not be so urgent or desirable. However, the fact is, of course, that society is still very much marked by discrimination and inequality. Accordingly, to be a woman (visible minority, gay etc) is still to be the object of persecution because of, and not in spite of, one's identity. Unfortunately, the courts are no less culpable

26. As appointments to the Supreme Court of Canada show, the performance of its women judges has been varied and far from uniform in their political commitments. See, for example, *Morgentaler v The Queen* [1988] 1 SCR 30 at 161–184, per Wilson J; *Lavallee* [1990] 1 SCR 852 at 856–897, per Wilson; *Symes* [1993] 4 SCR 695 at 776–832, per L'Heureux-Dube; *R v Seaboyer* [1991] 2 SCR 577 at 597–642, per MacLachlin and at 643–713, per L'Heureux-Dube; and *R v Carosella* [1997] 1 SCR 88 at 114–155, per L'Heureux-Dube.

than any other institutions in this history. Consequently, the experience of being a woman (visible minority, gay etc) remains critical to a full understanding of what it is to be a woman (visible minority, gay etc) and why women (visible minority, gay etc) judges are required in today's society.[26]

Judicial independence must also be balanced against judicial accountability. One of the better ways to achieve that is by way of diverse appointments through a democratic process. Indeed, the proposal to have the appointing Commission dominated by lawyers and judges in terms of numerical supremacy and controlling influence is simply unacceptable. There is an inevitable politics to judicial appointments; there always has been and always will be, even if it masquerades under the dubious label of 'merit'. The choice is not between a political and a non-political process of judicial appointments. Rather, it is a straightforward choice about whether the politics of the judiciary or the politics of the public at large, as expressed by its elected representatives, should prevail. While many will consider this a weak or even dangerous reform, it is necessitated by the nature and performance of the judicial function in a twenty-first century constitutional democracy. Such a politically informed and politically charged process will not contribute to a greater politicisation of the judiciary because judges are already and inevitably a thoroughly political group. It will instead bring those politics into public view and render them more available for public scrutiny: the politics of the public has more democratic legitimacy than that of the judges. Hence, the need to ensure judicial independence is not resolved by abandoning all efforts at accountability. There needs to be a democratic trade-off between independence and accountability. If judicial independence is to mean that judges are left almost unregulated in their activities and behaviour, it is vital that the process by which they are appointed be as democratic as possible. This most certainly does not mean that the legislative branches have no role to play as the present debate seems to suggest. Indeed, it is only with the involvement of these branches of government that the courts can be entrusted to fulfil their adjudicative responsibilities in a meaningful, if strained democratic manner.

Mindful of the adage that 'politics is the art of the possible', it is worthwhile offering some alternative proposals to the tepid proposals for reform put forward by the government. While there are more radical measures which might be taken, there are several less extreme steps that could be adopted which would better incorporate the understanding that law is politics and that judicial decision-making requires judges to make contested and controversial political choices.[27] The most important innovation would be to create a more democratic appointments process. This could be achieved by establishing an independent commission. Any such body would need to be as diverse and as representative as possible. Accordingly, it might consist of about 15 members of whom five would be appointed from the House of Commons, five would be judges, and

---

27. Of course, there is no compelling reason why courts should remain at the centre of constitutional politics. For instance, Mark Tushnet has been developing a rich and provocative body of work on how best to develop non-judicial forums for constitutional decision-making. See, for example, *Taking the constitution away from the courts* (Princeton: Princeton University Press, 1999) and 'Non-Judicial Review' (2003) 40 Harv J on Legis 453. . See Ewing 'A Theory of Democratic Adjudication: Towards a Representative, Accountable and Independent Judiciary' (2000) 38 Alta LR 208.

five would be citizens; tenure on the committee would be limited to three years and the chair of the Commission would be one of the lay members. Confident that no particular constituency (ie judicial, political or lay) had a lock on the Commission's work or decisions, the Commission's task would be to establish appropriate criteria for appointment which took seriously the need for a diverse and talented judiciary. Candidates could be identified either by application, nomination or search: interviews would be held and candidates would be subject to an intensive vetting. There could be rules to ensure both geographical representation (ie two supreme court judges for Scotland and one for Northern Ireland) and diversity in terms of women and visible minorities. Also, threshold rules for eligibility in regard to professional experience and qualification might be relaxed to ensure that otherwise meritorious candidates are not excluded. Contrary to the government's view that 'it is at lower levels of the Judiciary that the criteria might need to be re-examined',[28] such innovations are best made at the highest level in order to confirm the sincerity and importance of the commitment to diversity and change. In all its activities, the Commission would ensure that diversity was not a secondary consideration, but a primary component of 'merit'.

The recommendations of the Commission would be final and direct. The diverse composition and democratic operation of the Commission would obviate the need for approval by the Prime Minister or confirmation hearings in Parliament. This is not because such procedures are 'inconsistent with the move to take the Supreme Court out of the potential political arena', but because the Commission itself will perform such a role more effectively and will be less likely to turn the appointments process into a media circus as in the United States. Furthermore, there should be a complement of nine Supreme Court judges who, except on leave applications and conflicts, should always sit as a full court: this would not only reduce the opportunities for inconsistent decisions, but would also avoid any suggestions of manipulation in panel-selection. It cannot simply be concluded that, whereas 'in the United States, appointments to the Supreme Court are more political, and therefore there is a stronger possibility that the composition of the court might affect the outcome, ... this is not the case in the United Kingdom'.[29] Also, there should be a public register of 'judicial interests' and a tougher set of conflicts rules under a comprehensive Code of Judicial Conduct which could be administered by the Appointments Commission. Judges should also have a fixed tenure of appointment of no more than 12 years. While the Commission would have the power to receive complaints and discipline judges, it would not be able to dismiss judges without formal approval by Parliament. Finally, to put the performance of the Supreme Court judges on a more secure and less amateurish footing, there should be a better administrative infrastructure and support staff: better communication on the court's activities could be developed and executive 'headnotes' of decisions might be provided. While this package of reform proposals will not guarantee both the democratic accountability and institutional independence of the judiciary, it will better deal with the realities of judicial authority and power in a constitutional democracy.

---

28. Department for Constitutional Affairs, n 17 above, p 33.
29. Department for Constitutional Affairs, n 17 above, pp 34 and 38.

VII.

Much of the immediate Canadian response to *Doucet*[30] has been framed by the concern over whether the judiciary had trespassed on forbidden political ground. However, there seems a broader and more troubling dynamic underlying the litigated issue – that democratic choice should not be only between rule by a judicial elite or a governmental elite, but through a political process that is more responsive to broader constitutional and democratic concerns. To conceive that the *Doucet* decision resurrects only the dilemma of whether courts can or should invade the political domain misses the main point: courts cannot exercise their powers and responsibilities without reference to contested values and principles of governance. The real and neglected issue is not the politicisation of the judiciary, but the democratic failure of the executive and legislative in fulfilling their constitutional responsibilities and mandate. If governments and legislatures were truly representative and were doing more of what they were supposed to being doing in a constitutional democracy, the question of what judges do would be less pressing and more incidental. If there is a crisis in Canadian democracy, it is to be found in the fact that politicians and legislators are simply not 'democrats' in the full sense of the term. 'Democracy' is used more as a rhetorical cloak for elitist practice than a measure and guide for popular politics. After all, a drop in voter turn-out in federal elections from 76% in 1979 to 61% in 2000 is hardly reassuring.

Ironically, the Canadian Charter of Rights and Freedoms is viewed favourably and increasingly so by large majorities in all regions, with the highest rate of approval of 91% in Quebec, and the lowest of 86% in the West. Moreover, 71% say that the Court and not Parliament should have the final say when the Supreme Court declares a law unconstitutional because it conflicts with the Charter. Indeed, 66% say they trust judges to do the right thing either all the time or most of the time. Furthermore, 'the Charter is seen as important to Canadian identity by more people than is the national anthem or the flag'.[31] Nevertheless, the fact that public opinion polls show considerable support for the Supreme Court is less an accolade for judges and more a slap in the face for politicians, particularly those leaders who preside in and over Cabinet. Judges can only ever do a second-best job at making up the democratic deficit in the present performance of Canadian politics. The Supreme Court decision in *Doucet* is indicative of that. While the judiciary has some defined and important function in Canadian politics, it must be limited and partial. Being neither elected by nor representative of Canadians, judges can never be entirely or rightly sanguine about the force and solidity of their democratic legitimacy. On the other hand, while the executive can lay claim to greater democratic legitimacy, its practical exercise of power offends its democratic pedigree. Too often, political leaders seem to dance to their own tune rather than that of the people they represent. Increased 'rule by Cabinet' is hardly that much better than extended 'rule by the Supreme Court'. While the statistics reveal interesting support for the courts, they express profound dissatisfaction with

30. *Doucet-Boudreau v Nova Scotia (Minister of Education)* [2003] SCC 62.
31. Centre for Research and Information on Canada *The Charter: Dividing or uniting Canadians?* (2003) p 6.

the political leaders: only 22% of Canadians trust their leaders to do the right thing at all.

To revamp the legislative and executive process in line with greater popular participation and political accountability will require a monumental effort. Any changes – proportional representation, recall legislation, accountability audits, genuine ministerial responsibility, referenda etc – must themselves be products of the very democratic process that is to be enhanced. There are no easy solutions to the present undemocratic trends. However, the debate around judicial activism is something of a distraction. Improvement in Canada's democratic status will not come from increased interventions by judges in the micro-management of governmental policies. Indeed, judicial supervision is a short-term crutch that actually harms a limping polity in the medium- and long-term. The replacement of one elite rule (executive) by another (judicial) can only be considered positive under the most warped sense of democracy. So, if there is a desire to reign in the judges, there must also be a commitment to ensuring that elected politicians and officials are living up to their own and demanding constitutional and democratic responsibilities. At present, they are palpably not. But simply construing the democratic challenge as being one about whether the judges stay out of or stray onto the political terrain is to misrepresent the problem and, therefore, to hamper any genuine solutions.

Despite the regular rounds of self-congratulation about Canada's ranking as one of the best societies to live in, there is a serious erosion of basic democratic precepts.[32] The twin foundations of democracy – popular participation and political accountability – are going the way of the polar ice-caps. There seems to be an implicit Faustian bargain between elite and rank-and-file that the price of socio-economic advancement (which is still questionable when looked at in other than mean or median terms) is at the cost of democratic involvement. The Charter and its judicial enforcement are part of that arrangement. Whatever else it means, democracy demands that there be more power to the people and less to the elites. Aristocratic rule is no less palatable because judges and political leaders are the new dukes and barons. And, it is certainly no more acceptable when such elites wrap themselves in the trappings of democracy. While there has never been a golden age for Canadian democracy, what now passes for 'democracy' is an exclusive, sporadic and sketchy conversation between the judicial and executive branches of government over what is best for the country. In this exchange, the voices of ordinary Canadians play no real or substantive role. Of course, a robust judiciary has a definite role in a vital democracy, but judges can only ever do a second-best job at making up the democratic deficit in the present performance of Canadian politics; they are neither positioned nor skilled to handle such a task. Nevertheless, it is a sign of a healthy democracy that Canadians are at least arguing about and grappling with 'judicial activism' and its implications for a constitutional polity. If the present debate about establishing a new Supreme Court is anything to go by, the British are still in denial and have not even begun to take the problems seriously – 'ignorant armies', 'confused alarms', and 'a darkling plain' indeed.

---

32. See, for example, Human Development Report *Deepening democracy in a fragmented world* (2002).